Empowering Women in Real Estate

A collection of stories from 10 years of Empowering Women in Real Estate®

KAREN W. COOPER

Copyright © 2024 Karen W. Cooper

All rights reserved.

ISBN: 9798340139221

DEDICATION

This book is dedicated to my nephew, Chase Steven Wenner;
January 30, 2009 – August 21, 2023.

Your life matters. It always has, and it always will.
Find Your Rhythm

CONTENTS

Acknowledgments	i
Where It All Began	1
2014	Pg 6
2015	Pg 19
2016	Pg 40
2017	Pg 77
2018	Pg 114
2019	Pg 182
2020	Pg 238
2021	Pg 267
2022	Pg 294
2023	Pg 352
2024	Pg 294
What's Next	Pg 420

ACKNOWLEDGMENTS

A book? What?! 9 years ago, my friend and Platinum Group Real Estate OG and "team mom", Jodi Hooper put it on my goal list at our retreat. It's a powerful thing when someone else believes in you. The thought of writing a book had been circling around in my mind but hearing someone else suggest it out loud was just the push I needed. It just took a while to make it happen.

Speaking of the power of people that believe in you, there have been two that have influenced me in a million ways seen and unseen. To my business partner, Vicky Noufal, life and business are much more fun with you by my side. How a girl from Lovettsville, Virginia got paired up with a girl from Beirut, Lebanon, I'll never know. Actually, I do know, and it was very clearly divinely ordered. Jackie Fields-Gleadall has been my mentor (and my lender!) since my very first day in real estate more than 22 years ago. She is wise and fun and a force to be reckoned with. The two of you push me and believe in me when I don't, won't, can't. You are two of the greatest blessings of my life, and the best friends I have ever known.

Literally everything you will read here is made possible because of my husband, Joshua Cooper. He has truly seen me, loved me and valued me, the real me, from the very beginning. His unconditional love and support have given me the confidence to dream big, to put myself out there (no matter how uncomfortable it is) and he has taught me that it is okay to share vulnerably and authentically. He has given me the ultimate safe place, which I have wanted to create for you, and I will forever be grateful.

To my boys, Ben, Ryan and Tyler, thank you for your patience. It's not fun when you want to talk to Mom and she's on the phone (usually with Ms. Vicky) or in a meeting. Thank you for showing me what it means to try new things, to have courage, and to speak up for yourself. Being your Mom will always be my most favorite job of all.

WHERE IT ALL BEGAN

I like to say that I started in real estate by accident, but really, when I look back over my career (and my life) it has most certainly all been part of a bigger plan. It was early 2002 and my then-fiancé (now husband) and I just happened to be buying a home for sale by owner. We knew the owners, and they approached us knowing that we were getting married in a few months. This led to me also selling my home for sale by owner, and throughout the process of both I was the one who was explaining the contracts to everyone, filling everything out, and doing my best to find comps by pouring over the newspapers and checking what limited resources existed online.

Fast forward a few months and I found out that later that summer I was going to be laid off from my project management position in the pharmaceutical industry. This was my second layoff, and I could relocate for another position in the industry or stay in my tiny hometown of Lovettsville, Virginia ... where I have lived my entire life, and where our entire family is ... and do something else. I chose something else. That something else was real estate.

After several interviews I landed a coveted spot on a highly successful, nationally ranked rainmaker team working for Sherry Wilson, a pioneer for teams in real estate, at RE/MAX Leaders, the franchise she owned. In the beginning, I did everything to make my business work. I was part-time receptionist at the office on the weekends to bring in some income, plus consulting a few hours per day to finish out a project for my old company, and otherwise totally immersing myself in the wonderful world of real estate, 24/7. Back then, before every listing was on the internet, "walk ins" were a common occurrence. I went into the office every single day so I could pick up any "overflow" leads, and duty shifts that the more experienced and busy agents didn't want. I took any and every opportunity, sometimes driving 90 minutes one way to show a single house. Rental leads, open houses, listings and buyers no one else wanted. You name it, I took it. And it paid off.

I went on like this for months, only taking a break that fall for my wedding and honeymoon, then picked right back up when I returned. There were times I wanted to quit. It was hard work, people are not always kind, but I knew that if I was going to be successful long term, time was of the essence. I started in mid-July and sold 8 houses that first year.

My "why real estate" has changed over the years depending on my season of life. In the beginning, it was simply to replace my former income. Then when I fully understood that this was a business, my business, it was about building that to be long-term and sustainable. Now it is more about leading, teaching and inspiring other women in the industry to build successful businesses on their terms. It has always been about supporting my family, my community, and financial freedom. Whatever the why, wherever I've been in my career, real estate has been the vehicle to so much more.

Not quite 2 years after starting my career my first son, Ben, was born. The market was strong, and I closed well over a handful of transactions the month he was born. It was a challenging pregnancy, with periods of bedrest and being induced 3 weeks early due to my blood pressure. At 34 weeks pregnant and nesting to the extreme, I suddenly HAD to move, and we quickly went under contract. My 36-week appointment was right after settlement, and that was when we found out they needed to do some testing and planned to induce me soon after. We ended up moving into our new home 1 week before Ben was born.

Two days later, and with horribly swollen ankles and feet, I was sent home and my baby had to stay. Already a huge emotional roller coaster when he was diagnosed with situs inversus and later Kartagener's Syndrome ... the week he spent in the Special Care Nursery was one of the hardest of my life. My business carried on thanks to my team, and I honestly don't recall being worried about it during that time ... I suppose because I had plenty of other things to worry about! Within a few weeks I went back to work, and truly counted my blessings that my parents lived close by and would care for my son while I worked.

Two years later in 2006, almost to the day, my second son, Ryan, was born completely healthy with a rather uneventful pregnancy and birth. Our market was shifting then. Homes were harder to sell, loans were more difficult to obtain, and prices were starting to adjust. A month or so before he was born, I stepped into the Office Manager role at my office to fill an unexpected vacancy in addition to selling. This additional income was helpful as the market was changing, which as a still relatively new ... and definitely very naïve agent I was totally unprepared for. I thought the land of milk and honey, which had been our market up until then, would return quickly. I could not have been more wrong.

I remember sitting at my kitchen table not long after Ryan was born working on my laptop, pumping breast milk, and talking to an agent from our team on the phone all at the same time. She was confused by the noise in the background ... she thought the breast pump was a dot matrix printer! Laughing through the tears was about all you could do. With my parents caring for my now toddler and newborn, it was full time back to work again in a few weeks.

Having two young children, a busy career and so many responsibilities was daunting to say the least. I learned a few things very quickly during this time. First, any of my children's "firsts" didn't count until I saw them. I remember my mom calling me while I was at work to say that someone rolled over or took a step or said a new word. To combat the guilt and sadness of missing it, I decided it didn't "count". Eventually she stopped reporting these things to me until I could see them on my own. Second, I really learned the value of implementing a routine or system that worked for me. Trying to get myself and a toddler and then a toddler and an infant ready and out the door in the morning was exhausting. I realized that it was a lot easier to throw on gym clothes, drop them off, and then go to the gym near my office and get ready there. To be clear, the routine was less about working out ... I usually only walked on the treadmill and stretched for a bit ... and more about being able to shower and put my make up on alone! No matter the motivation, this worked for a season and was just what I needed at the time.

Fast forward to 2008, which was one of the most difficult in my life. I miscarried my third baby at 10 weeks. Any woman who has gone through that knows that the pain and emotional toll carries on for a very long time after. The real estate market was in shambles, and I went from closing consistently 50+ transactions per year to barely able to eek out 10-12. That may not sound too bad, but on a rainmaker team with a very (very) low split we couldn't make ends meet. My husband had a very successful career in the fire service, but living in an expensive area, my income was vital to our existence. We defaulted on credit cards (which we were using to get by on, thinking the market was going to turn around any minute), and nearly lost our home.

Early the following year I had had enough and was ready to take control of my life and business. I found out I was pregnant with what would be our third son and left the comfort and "security" of my team to go out on my own as an individual agent. It was one of the best decisions I have made in my career.

My former team allowed me a phenomenal start. The learning experience and foundation that I was able to build was truly invaluable to my business, and I will be forever grateful to my former team leader, but the time had come that I had outgrown that model. I was terrified to make the change, but two months behind on my mortgage it was make or break time. From the day I started on my own I immediately felt empowered and at peace. By the time my third son, Tyler, was born in September of that year I had earned enough to stop foreclosure on our home, bring my mortgage current, and save enough for a proper maternity leave.

The next couple years were still incredibly stressful. Tyler was diagnosed with the same syndrome as my first son Ben, and my parents were no longer able to care for my children full time. For the first 9 months of my youngest's life I worked with him by my side with only occasional help. Looking back, it was time that I treasure. It was also a time to rebuild my career and finances, but not without lots of setbacks, trials and tribulations.

The lessons I learned during this time both as a mother and as a businesswoman were invaluable. While I certainly could have gone without the stress, I learned that no matter the situation, I could handle it. With my husband's support, we could work through hard things and come out the other side. As a mother, I understood the value of memory making. Sometimes I was just going through the motions and "checking off my list" the memories I wanted to make with my kids and the photos I wanted to take, but now I have those memories, and they are sweet.

I learned to prioritize time with my family over business. No matter how busy or how many clients "need" me, my children need me more. The key is to set boundaries. It is okay to turn off your phone when you are on vacation. It is okay to take Sundays off with your family. It is okay to prioritize your children's games and school plays and dinner together. Set expectations with your clients, everything is an appointment and should be treated as such. I've operated my business this way for over two decades and honestly cannot think of a time that I have lost business as a result. Be clear on your value and what you bring to the table, but I'll tell you what your value isn't. Your availability. You bring and offer so much more than your ability to drop everything and run out the door.

Now, 22 years in, life is good ... because I worked hard and invested both time and money for over two decades to make it so. I've been willing to take risks, make shifts, anticipate changes in the market and the industry, and to be the bad guy when necessary. I've been on a rainmaker team, been an individual agent and even served time as a managing broker after a period of burn out. As owner of the Platinum Group Real Estate Team since 2015, along with my business partner and fellow powerful mom in real estate Vicky Noufal, I love pouring into the women (56 as of this writing) on our team and teaching them how to grow and flourish as women, mothers and business owners. Don't get me wrong. There are still struggles, both plentiful and big, but I understand now that I am not alone, and these seasons come and go.

Ten years ago, I founded what began as just an online community, Empowering Women in Real Estate® ... now with over 38,000 members all across the country (and beyond!). As women in real estate, I've heard over and over again about the struggles of trying to "do it all", balancing life as a partner, mom, business owner and more. Women feel isolated and struggle with direction in their real estate business. On an almost daily basis we are inundated with the shiny new objects designed to make our business easier and better, but the reality is we all already have what we need. Right now, within each of us is the drive, confidence, wherewithal and ability to make it happen ... we just need to call on it. And take action. The taking action part is the key.

Just about 5 years ago I stepped out of my own personal production in favor of serving our real estate team, and at the same time began to grow the business side of Empowering Women in Real Estate®. I still prospect for new business every day (I teach my exact system in the Inner Circle), and consistently generate $15M+ in sales volume each year, served by my team members and referral partners. Having the ability ... and the courage ... to evolve my real estate business with my seasons of life and the direction of the market and industry has been an incredible blessing.

Time is fleeting. Today my children are 20, 18 and 15. My mother, father, mother-in-law and youngest nephew have passed. At 51 I've had my own share of health struggles with 10 breast surgeries over the years including two mastectomies and 30 radiation treatments. Take the trip. Read the extra bedtime story. Enjoy the dinner. Go to the game. You, your family, and even your business, will be better for it.

2014

<u>Milestones:</u>
7-29-2014 – First Post in the Facebook Group is Published!
12-15-2014 – Hosted the first EWRE® Happy Hour at Stonewalls Tavern at Lansdowne Resort in Lansdowne, Virginia

> **Karen Wenner Cooper**
> July 29, 2014
>
> Empowering Women In Real Estate was founded by a realtor/broker who was craving a safe place to share ideas and challenges. A place for inspiration and motivation. A place to help one another work towards a balance between personal and business life. A place to grown and learn, as consistent education is the path to growth and continued success. Most of all, this is a place to empower women in the real estate industry ... empowering you to set and reach your goals, to dream big, to help others, to be your best self. To help ordinary women to do extraordinary things!
>
> This is a safe, no judgement, space to ...
> -Air frustrations in dealing with the day to day balance.
> -Share tips and tricks that have worked for you ... in working with clients or in leading a balanced life.
> -Pass along info on that great pair of shoes that you found that allows you to look professional, feel good, and walk around showing 25 three-level townhouses without hurting your feet.
> -Request advice on a challenge you are dealing with, either personally or professionally.
> -Share your go to recipe that your family will actually eat, and you (or your spouse!) can prepare quickly after a long day of showing property and attending home inspections and settlements.
> -Talk about the great exercise class that you discovered that actually feels a little like fun, and not like one more thing you have to check off your list for the day.
> -Mention the local (Northern Virginia) "hot spots" where you can go with your laptop and grab some free wifi and maybe a bite to eat or cup of coffee and feel comfortable, or to take clients to when you are far from your office and need a spot to talk over paperwork, properties you've shown them, or just to get to know each other better.
>
> This is not a space for ...
> -Selling services.
> -Announcing open houses, broker's opens and new listings (Loudoun Realtor Forum is great for this!).
> -Bashing (by name) other realtors, brokerages, lenders, title companies, etc.
> -Drama.
>
> This is the space for Empowering Women In Real Estate! Please feel free to invite all the women you know working in this industry who can benefit from this type of network!

August 4, 2014

I have always believed that you need to surround yourself with the "right" people, that we will become like those that we most often associate with. That is part of my inspiration for forming this network. I've seen it happen in my own life ... spend a lot of time with people who are always negative and finding fault everywhere, and suddenly that is mirroring back in my own life. Now I make a conscious effort to affiliate with people who are on the same path that I am, some further ahead, and some a little bit behind, but together we help to encourage and motivate each other, and learn from each other.

August 6, 2014

Do you know your why? Why you are willing (maybe even eager) to work hard and sacrifice? I do think our "why" changes depending on your season in life. For me, my why consists of these 4 people ... my husband and my 3 sons. I work hard to show them the value of hard work in your life, to provide opportunities and experiences for them, to show them what it means to be passionate about something you believe in. What is your why?

August 9, 2014

When I was a new agent back in 2002, I received a lot of advice from colleagues. Some of that advice proved to be incredibly useful (and accurate) and I have used it and shared it again and again in my career. Things like, preview to get to know the market to increase your knowledge and confidence, everything (personal or work related) is an "appointment" (your clients don't need to know which is which), and the importance of setting expectations with your clients from the very beginning. In a few weeks my fall new agent training class will be starting again. During one of the first couple sessions I teach a class called, "You Have Your License, Now What", where I share this advice, as well as other tips, tricks and best practices that I have learned along the way. I know that we have a lot of new/newer women to the real estate industry who are a part of this group, so tell us ... what is the best advice you received when entering the real estate industry?

August 14, 2014

I'm a big fan of education. Not in the "all book smart, no common sense" sort of way, but more along the lines of I think that we can (and should) always be learning and growing. Whether it is learning focused on your line of work, mindset work (my current favorite) or learning a new skill or hobby, when I am learning I feel most alive. Aside from the required continuing education that is required in our line of work, do you make it a regular practice to take classes and learn new things?

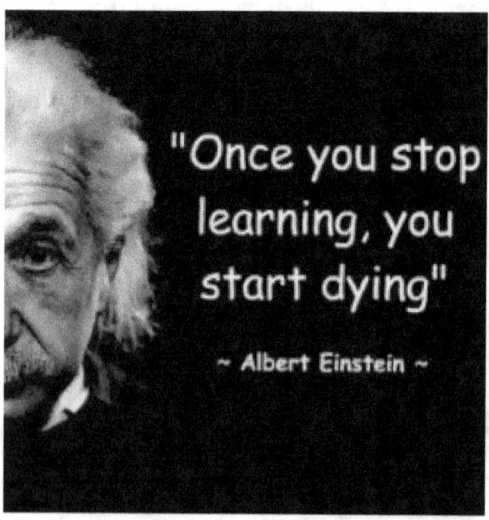

August 26, 2014

Do you have an intentional morning routine that helps to prepare you for the day? Everyone has a morning routine ... from the regular time you get up to the order in which you get ready, eat breakfast, etc. What I'm talking about today is intentional time in the morning to help prepare yourself mentally/physically/spiritually for the day. I certainly don't consider myself a morning person, but over the past year I have really come to value - come to NEED - some quiet time in the morning. With school starting next week it is going to look a bit different than it did over the summer. I'll have "my" time for coffee, some reading and some writing (to you!) on the front porch, then big kids (they are 10 and 12) up at 6:30 and on the bus between 6:50-6:55, get myself ready for the day, then get my preschooler up by 8, and dropped at school by 8:30, at which time I will head into the office. I've always checked email first thing in the morning, but I am trying to make a conscious effort NOT to do that until I get to the office. If something is urgent, my agents call or text me in the morning and that works well. I've found that once I start down the rabbit hole of email, the path of my day usually changes. How about you, what is your morning routine?

September 3, 2014

Do you feel like you are rushing all the time? I certainly have/still do a lot of days. I move fast, talk fast, walk fast. Rarely am I ever doing one thing at a time. Truly, I LIKE to be really busy and juggling lots of things. I've started to notice though that life moves incredibly fast, time goes fast, kids grow fast, and the faster I move within it, the more it all feels like a blur. I've been really trying to focus on simplifying my life (fewer things, fewer things to do, grace not perfection) and finding a little bit of (somewhat) quiet time being still each day. I find that it helps me to be calm, and actually more productive than when I am flying around getting things done. Am I the only one who feels this way?

September 9, 2014

"They" (whoever that is) say that "attitude is everything". In this case, I would tend to agree with them. I've seen it in action in my own life, and I see it now with agents I work with. If you don't believe that open houses work, or that your buyers will never get off that fence, or that you won't get that listing from the interview that you went on, then absolutely that is exactly what will happen. The problem I have always found though, is that it is HARD somedays (at least for me) to keep my attitude in check, especially on days (like yesterday) that I am feeling tired and/or disappointed with myself for a particular reason. To help me snap out of it, I usually find that a coffee break with a friend, a talk with my husband, or a few quiet minutes outside will usually help. As much as I dreaded it, yesterday I had a session with my trainer (thanks to a lot of great advice here, I have started scheduling sessions twice a week, making that appointment really works for me!) after work. I was telling myself all sorts of negative bs before I went, but after the first few minutes felt better, and actually "refreshed" (go figure) afterwards. How about you? Do you ever find yourself in a funk or bad attitude? When you do, what do you do to get yourself out of it?

September 11, 2014

Yesterday I met with one of my agents who was very upset with how things are going with one of her buyers. Despite working very hard for the client and getting them the home that they want, the buyer keeps questioning her integrity, and conveniently "forgetting" conversations and things that were explained to them. Of course there are always 2 sides to the understanding of things, but I know this agent well, and I firmly believe that the "problem" lies somewhere within the buyer, who is refusing to allow their agent to communicate with their lender or title company. If they weren't under contract, I would suggest parting ways with the client. My advice was to keep everything strictly professional, and all communications to email. I also offered to have a conversation with the buyer, and even suggested assigning a different designated agent if that would help. My guess is that we have all been here at some point (I know I have) with the client who will not be pleased with what you do no matter what and questions all of your intentions. How would you handle this type of situation?

September 22, 2014

It's a fresh new week! For me, I have always found that establishing daily habits and routines help me to be more organized and successful. This week, I'm working to start a new habit. It's a simple one, just laying out my outfit the night before. Except for my 20 minutes of "me" time for coffee (and writing to you!) in the morning, the rest of the time is a blur, and I am racing against the clock to get kids on the bus and the youngest delivered to preschool and myself to the office. I'm hoping that this habit will help me to feel less stressed in the morning.

I can think of quite a few daily habits that can help to boost your success. Real estate is not a passive business. In addition to working with active clients and transactions, you also need to be taking action on a daily/weekly basis to help to avoid the up and down nature of the business. How about creating a daily habit to write 1 personal note a day? Maybe calling to follow up with 1 past client per day? Preview 5 properties per week to boost your market knowledge. Spend 30 minutes per day prospecting. What daily or weekly habit can you start today that will help to grow your business?

September 26, 2014

How many times do we spend our time, effort and money on something that seems like a waste of time? The marketing idea that promised lots of buyers, the open house that no one came to, the meeting with a buyer that is years away from buying. I strongly believe that nothing is ever a waste of time. Whether that action results in a success or failure, either way the end result is growth. One idea leads to another. We need action to grow. Don't be afraid to put yourself out there, no matter the result, it will put you one step closer to your goal!

October 1, 2014

It is great to see so many people in our industry talking about safety and how to stay safe. It is a shame that it took such a horrible tragedy (the death of realtor Beverly Carter) to put this at the front of our minds, and I only hope that it stays there, and we continue working diligently to change the "instant gratification" mindset of so many consumers (and agents) in our profession. As mentioned yesterday in a thread, Beverly Carter told her husband where she would be, and many of us use that as our safety net, but obviously it is not enough. Sadly, I think that so often as women we are taught to "be nice", to not offend anyone, to not speak up when we are uncomfortable. I want to see that change not just for us but for the generations of women after us. We need to trust our gut and our instincts, and teach our daughters to do the same, and teach our sons to respect the time and space of people around them and to not take "offense" when someone wishes to handle something differently than they want. We've all had that experience of that sign call or internet call who is in the area and has to see the house "right now". We worry about upsetting our broker or team leader if we don't comply and lose the lead. We worry about offending the lead and potentially losing that sale for our seller or the buyer transaction. I'm here to say that it IS worth all of those things. We are professionals. We provide an incredible amount of value to our clients and in what we do. There is no amount of internet or technology anything that can or will replace that. We need to treat ourselves that way every time, and eventually the consumer will catch on. It's not worth the risk.

October 6, 2014

"Go the extra mile, it's never crowded." - Never have I felt this to be more true than in the real estate industry. Sadly, sometimes it's not even about going the extra mile, it's doing the basics. Early on Friday afternoon I had to call a broker for a time sensitive issue with one of my agents. I called the office, called his cell phone twice, and left a somewhat detailed message. It is now Monday morning, and that person has still not returned my call. It never ceases to amaze me how many times over the past nearly 2 years as a managing broker I've experienced this. When I was selling, I would experience it with other real estate "professionals" as well ... calls would go un-returned, emails not answered. The "basics" of the job weren't even done, much less the extra mile. Part of my objective with this group is to change that. Let's vow together to raise the bar, to go the extra mile, to not only do the "basics" exceptionally well, but to really go above and beyond with the service and level of expertise that we provide. Not only is this good for us (what a great feeling to know that you have really done your best for someone), but it is good for our clients, and we are setting a good example for our colleagues. Some of whom, really, really need it. Happy Monday let's make it a great week!

October 7, 2014

Confidence is key in so many things that we do. Presenting yourself as a confident professional helps your clients to feel at ease, and to feel more comfortable in choosing to work with you and to trust your advice. I have never been the person who felt comfortable in striking up the random conversation with the person next to me in line at the grocery store, or just bringing up what I do for a living and then handing out my business card. When I was selling, to help combat my "shyness" I would often wear my name tag while I ran errands between appointments and people would strike up a conversation with me (sounds cheesy, I know, but it worked!) ... but then, what to say to them! Is it just me or does nearly every time you are talking to someone, and they find out what you do they ask "so, how's the market?". To help build my confidence, I would memorize a statistic or two about our local market (DOM, inventory levels year over year, etc.), and ensure that I did plenty of previewing (if I wasn't out showing) so I would have lots of properties to talk about. This really worked like a charm for me.

Anytime someone asked, "how's the market", I could fire back with a stat that made me sound really smart, and/or start talking about a beautiful new house that I had just seen. I felt comfortable and confident knowing that I would have something to say when the topic of real estate came up, and (I think) I sounded very together to be able to mention real life statistics and properties in our local market. What are your favorite tips and tricks to help you to increase your confidence?

October 8, 2014

Have you ever heard of Parkinson's Law? It says that work expands to fill the time available. I've heard this often, but never really "got it", then suddenly a week or so ago it finally resonated with me, and I see how this is working in my own time management and productivity quest. I only wish that I had figured this out when I was in the field! When I was selling it seemed that the work never ended, but I see now that is also because my workday, my workweek, never ended. It was easy/tempting to take a break midafternoon to run some errands or play around online when I was tired or frustrated, because I would plan to work later in the day after dinner or once the kids were in bed, or the next day, or catch up on emails on Sunday morning, and on and on. Now that I have more specific "office hours", I find that I am getting so much more done each day, and I finally realized that it is because I am focused on getting it done during those hours. I know that I want to leave the office by a certain time and that I don't want to have to catch up in the evening, so I am working more focused and diligently during those office hours to ensure that I get the work done, and I do! There are still the issues that come up and the calls or emails that I have to attend to "after hours", but those are the only things I am attending to during that time. I see now how this could have worked for me when I was in the field. Scheduling specific "hours" for myself each day and doing those weekly client update emails and market research during those hours. Making the client calls pro-actively during those times would likely have cut down a bit on them reaching out to me later on. Of course, there is and will always be an element of needing to take appointments and show property on the evenings and weekends, and managing time sensitive details during those times, but I think that if you schedule yourself specific work hours to get the miscellaneous stuff done then hopefully that stuff will be finished then and not bleed into every other available time. Do you schedule specific work "hours" for yourself, or do things as they come?

October 9, 2014

I have another time management tip for you today! Recently I discovered the benefit of using a timer to stop from "watching" the clock. I'm sure you've been there too ... you know that you need to leave for that appointment in 45 minutes but trying to finish up some things before you go (maybe even some things that you need for that appointment). It seems like every few minutes you are breaking your focus to check the time to make sure you won't be late, which slows down your ability to get anything finished, and you usually wind up late anyway! I've started setting the timer app on my phone for a couple minutes before I need to walk out the door. Now I can actually focus on what I am doing and be productive since I am not constantly watching the clock. Sounds simple, but this has really been working well for me. How about you, what is your best time management tip?

October 15, 2014

I heard a great quote late night from Elizabeth Gilbert (author of, among other things, "Eat, Pray, Love"). She said that whatever your goal, destiny, personal legend (according to Paulo Coehlo, author of "The Alchemist"), long term plan, etc. is, that we are always either moving toward it or moving away from it. This really resonated with me. While goals, plans, etc. can look, feel, seem a long way off, they really aren't ... as we are constantly moving towards it, or away from it. This can really help with day-to-day decision making ... if your goal is to close 5 more transactions by the end of the year, is sitting an open house this weekend going to move you closer or further away from that goal? If your goal is to lose 20 pounds, is having that candy bar during your afternoon crash going to move you closer or further away from that? I really like this way of thinking, how about you?

October 22, 2014

Have you ever had one of "those" days? You know the one ... where no matter what you do it doesn't seem to turn out right. No matter who you try to help, they don't seem to see it as help. No matter what your good intentions, they aren't understood. You work, and work and work to help others, only to find that while they smile nice to your face, when you turn around, they are complaining and being negative and tearing apart all of the good things that you are trying to do. We've all been there, but I am here to say don't let that stop you from continuing to put your good out there in the world! The sad reality is that many people would rather jump on the bandwagon of negativity and tearing others down, rather than building them up. I want to change that. Keep putting out good. Be helpful. Be kind. Work hard. It is making a difference. It is helping others. There will be days and times where you see it happening, and others that you don't. Think about the people who have helped you along the way. The person who encouraged you, whose words resonated with you at just the right time. I've had so many of these people in my life, and I'm sure that they have no idea of the help, the boost, the positive impact that they have provided. My long-winded point here is keep going, keep helping, keep encouraging. You will make a difference, you ARE making a difference, day by day, bit by bit, moment by moment.

October 23, 2024

Is it just me, or does it feel like the fall season is almost a "starting over" time? After the more carefree, easy times of summer, moving into the fall/winter season seems to be a fresh start. Are there certain rituals/things that you do going into this season? For me, I usually like to attend some sort of educational conference, and spend a lot of time focusing on business planning for myself and with my agents ... reviewing what they did this year, how did it match up with their goals that were set, what worked and what didn't, where did their business come from, etc. Then we put together a plan for the following year. This feels like a great way to "cap off" the year and get ready for the new one. How about you?

November 3, 2014

What are you allowing that you do not want to continue? Is it the seller that won't adjust their price for the current market/won't keep their home in proper showing condition/won't allow showings, but yet blames you for the lack of an offer? Is it the buyer who runs you ragged across 3 counties looking at multiple types of homes in many different price ranges? Is it a lack of leads or enough business? Take an action step today towards the direction that you want to go. Practice (and then use) some new dialogues with that challenging seller and be prepared to let them go if they refuse to "get it". Schedule a meeting with that unfocused buyer reviewing everything that they have looked at and help them to focus on what they really want so you can move forward with purpose. Leads and business rarely falls in your lap (without having previously sown some seeds), update your database then use it to make some calls, send out some mailers or newsletters, do some pop bys. Stop allowing what you don't want in your life and start taking some steps towards what you do.

November 6, 2014

Do you do too much? I've certainly been guilty of this, and I think as a mom, in some ways it is hard to avoid. Too many irons in too many fires, and as a result nothing is really getting any focused attention. Are you trying to advertise/market yourself and your business in multiple different ways and different places, so many that none of them are being done with any focus or consistency? Focus is key. Identify the most important areas in your life right now ... business growth and stability, personal relationships, children and family, personal health (those are mine, by the way) ... and then identify the one or 2 things in those areas that are most important for you to focus on right now, and let the rest go. Trust me, this is easier said than done, and as much a reminder for me as anything else, but so worth it when you really apply your focus in a few areas. That is when you will see the most impact and growth.

November 7, 2014

I once watched an interview of Maya Angelou where she told a story about a dinner party guest in her home who told a very negative, rude joke. She immediately grabbed that person's coat and escorted them to the door saying, "not in my house". She went on to talk about the power of words, and how negative words are a poison. I really believe that is true. If you are constantly speaking lack, not enough, anger, pain, sorrow, negativity over your life, your life (and the life of those around you) will be poisoned by it and that is all you will ever know. The same is true when you are exposed to other people who do this. You can be having a great day, then "that" person who has the constant negative view comes in spewing their poison, and it's like the life, the joy, is sucked right out of the room. Before you know it, others in their presence start doing the same. No one's life is ever perfect or devoid of worries or troubles, but there is truly a difference in how you approach it. Everyone needs to vent or complain a little bit, but when it is constant complaining without offering or considering a solution ... well, that's just whining. Don't bring negative to my door, if you do, I may just go find your coat.

November 13, 2014

Are you a worrier? I come from a looong line of worriers. My natural inclination always is to worry about the littlest of details, the ones I can't change, things that won't happen for years, things that really don't matter. When I find myself slipping into this old habit, I try to get outside, do/focus on something I can control, pray, take action on something, or think about things I am grateful for. What do you do when you are feeling worried?

November 17, 2014

Ahh, Mondays. I think most people have a strong reaction to them one way or the other. For folks with "regular" jobs, it signals the start of the work week, and they may not be super happy about it. For those of us in real estate, it may actually represent a slower day or a bit of a break after a busy weekend. Early in my career, after months of working every day, I started working with a coach who wanted me to schedule a day "off" (mostly just no appointments and not going into the office), and I chose Mondays. After working all weekend, and with my clients back at work it seemed like a natural fit. Now, while it is a little rough getting up on Monday morning, I generally start the day with excitement to get into the office. How about you? How do you approach Mondays?

November 20, 2014

For me, this is one of my busiest times of year. I am working on 2015 business planning sessions with my 120+ agents, which basically means back-to-back appointments most days. I actually really love these sessions. I love to dream and plan and set actionable steps for achieving those dreams and plans. I've been talking to several of the agents I've been meeting with this week about scheduling regular previewing time into their schedules every week. I think previewing is especially powerful for newer agents, although I believe there is benefit for everyone. Previewing gives you an opportunity to get to know the market firsthand, to have a strong grasp of a variety of neighborhoods and price points, and just to get yourself "out there" in the market. One of the agents I met with indicated that she was recently at an association training/orientation for new agents and the topic of previewing came up and some new agents were talking about their difficulties in previewing as some listing agents/sellers really discouraged them from previewing and felt "put out" for having to prepare their home for "just a preview". Seriously?! I couldn't even believe it. No, it is definitely not always convenient to leave your home and to have it prepared for viewing, but that is part of the process. If you want to sell it, you need to let agents see it! I do recommend to my agents to be up front with the seller that it is an appointment to preview, to be timely with their appointment, and to let the seller know that they can stay if need be. I would think that listing agents would warmly welcome previewing to get another professional opinion about how their home shows and compares. I always set the expectation up front with my sellers that agents would be coming in to preview, and that it was a good thing. For me, I know that when I had seen a listing once (either for showing or previewing) that I was so much more likely to go back and show it again to a buyer or to talk about it when I was reviewing listings with my clients as I was familiar with it, and it was top of mind. How about you? Do you preview on a regular basis? How do you feel about other agents previewing your listings?

November 24, 2014

A couple weeks ago several friends/colleagues and I were talking about this on our way back from a business retreat ... every generation has a family member or two (usually an entrepreneur) who is a little different from the rest. One who thinks differently, acts differently, takes risks differently. Looking back, it is usually that one who advances the family forward. It is amazing when you look back through your family line and think of how your life has been enabled, made better, of how the opportunities that you have are as a result of all those who came before you. In my family it has been the women of the past few generations who have had the biggest influence. They were hard workers, doing what they had to do to take care of their family. My grandmother was certainly one of my biggest influences. She left school in the 7th grade and had my mother when she was 16. She never really worked outside of the home, never had a driver's license, but she was very focused and diligent about the work that she did in her home. She followed routines each day, was incredibly productive, and her home always shined (I didn't quite get that part from her). She was strong, had the mouth of a sailor (that part I got), and didn't take crap from anyone, but always presented herself in public as a very proper lady. I'm very lucky, and proud to be like her, and extremely grateful for all of the ancestors that came before me, that provided me the option to be the "different" one. Who in your family tree has been your biggest influence?

December 17, 2014

Did you watch the sunrise this morning? I did. It was absolutely beautiful. The colors change in a moment, muted yellow one minute, then tinged with red, then red reflecting all through the sky and clouds. It was changing constantly, moment by moment ... only I couldn't necessarily see all of the changes until I looked away and then looked back again. Life is like that too. A series of constantly changing moments, so much so that while you are in it, looking at it, you may not really notice the changes until you step back, reflect and look again. This time of year, is a great time for reflecting on the year that has passed, and the year that is ahead. A great time for planning and implementing changes in our lives and businesses. Have you already taken the step back to look over the year and to plan for the one ahead? What observations have you made about 2014, and how you want to grow from that and (possibly even) change in 2015?

2015

Milestones:
5-14-2015 – First Book Club, "The Four Agreements"

11-11-2015 – First In-Person Meet Up, discussion on doing business by sphere of influence at my Leesburg, Virginia office.

March 2, 2015

I've had this article saved for a while now but haven't taken the time to read it until just now, and it really spoke to me. When is the last time that life excited you? Day to day life, the work, the chores, the super long to do lists (and I even love to do lists) can be incredibly draining and really suck all of the fun out of it. We work in a business that never shuts off. Just when you think you have a moment of peace to relax, or you get your rhythm and you are cranking through your to dos, the phone rings (or your kids need something, it's like they can sense the second I am feeling relaxed or productive). It can be easy to lose your excitement. We often don't take time for "fun" things, or the things that will re-energize us. We say we don't have time, but really, we must make time. Taking the time for yourself, to do something different, to learn something new, can give you a new perspective, a spark, and that then makes everything else flow just a bit more easily. That is definitely how I felt last week after attending the Century 21 Global Conference. Taking just a little time out of the routine and attending learning sessions was just what I needed, and I came back refreshed and ready to kick butt (theoretically speaking, of course). The article attached is long, but I think it is worth it.

The following excerpt is my favorite part:
"But just because you are an adult does not mean you must live a life void of excitement, passion, and joy. Just because you are no longer a beginner does not mean you can't have Beginner's Eyes like a child. You can. Simply go off the beaten path:
Take a different route
Accept a challenge
Learn something new
Say yes to invitations that go outside your comfort zone
Surround yourself with Livers of Life
Stop expecting and be open to the unexpected"

I love that! What can you do today to go off the beaten path, even just a little bit?
https://www.handsfreemama.com/2015/02/23/whens-the-last-time-life-excited-you/

June 11, 2015

Have you ever experienced "divine redirection"? I love to follow Fabienne Frederickson of ClientAttraction.com. Just yesterday morning I watched a video where she talked about this, and then experienced it first-hand a few hours later when I was with a family member about to go into surgery (literally, minutes from going in) and something unusual popped up and it was cancelled on the spot. This has happened in my business too. When I first got into real estate 13 years ago it was because I was getting laid off (again) from my job in the pharmaceutical industry. My choices were to take a position more in the "hub" of this industry in Princeton, NJ, or do something else. I chose the "something else", which was real estate, and it was the best divine redirection or "course correction" I can ever imagine. When this happens, I think you can either "fight" to stay on the original path or go with the (new) flow and see where it takes you.

June 19, 2015

With the "official" first day of summer this weekend, this seems like a good time to kick off our summer challenges series. Today's topic is how to handle vacations and keep your business going at the same time.

We all need a vacation, am I right? It can be so hard in this industry to truly unplug. We worry that we will lose opportunities. We worry that clients we are working with will start working with someone else. We want to take excellent care of our clients at all times and worry that they won't be well taken care of if we are away.

My first summer in business I had a pre-planned vacation shortly after I started that was scheduled with extended family even before I knew I would be going into real estate. I was brand new and working hard for every opportunity I could find. There was a buyer I had just started working with before I left. I was panicked that I would lose them. I spent hours while on our vacation on the phone, sending listings, addressing concerns. We left for our vacation 2 days late so I could show him more houses, and then after being gone only 3 or 4 days, came home early so I could show them more. Not fair to me, my husband or my family that we were vacationing with. I'm sure you can figure out the punch line ... they NEVER bought a house. Ever. Not from me, not from anyone. Of course, there was a lesson in pre-qualifying there that I didn't understand yet as a new agent which is a great story for another day. Bottom line is I vowed not to do that to my family again.

I am a firm believer that you can (and must) take a little time away for yourself and your family and that your business and clients will not suffer. In my business I have always had a trusted colleague and/or assistant cover for me while I am away. I set the expectation with my clients who will be taking care of them while I am gone, I make it clear that they can expect the same attention from that person while I am away (showings for buyers, handling contracts, showing feedback for sellers, etc.). My voicemail and email out of office auto reply refers any "new" business to the person covering for me.

Typically, depending on what is going on, I may check in once a day or so with the person covering for me. This has always worked beautifully for me and (knock on wood) without issue during vacations and even 3 maternity leaves. Once while on a 2-week vacation, Stacy Mallonee ratified 4 contracts for me while I was away. Best. Vacation. Ever.

July 1, 2015

During my years as a managing broker, one of my observations in working so closely with so many agents was how many didn't look at the big picture in their real estate business. Yesterday I was reminded of one of those examples. I remember having a conversation with an agent once about how their listing had gone under contract so quickly that the post sign never made it up, and so they were happy to be calling to cancel the install and looked at me like I had two heads when I said they should still have it installed. The same thing just happened to me ... a listing went under contract before the sign was installed. Instead of calling to cancel the install, I called my installer and asked them to put up the "under contract" rider along with the sign. A couple days after it was installed, a neighbor called me from my sign and wants to list their home and buy another one. Well over $1M in volume from a $50 sign install. That is a pretty incredible return on investment. This business requires that you invest in it, both time and money, consistently over the long term. It doesn't matter if your goal is to be a super, mega, ultra producer (or whatever term is used to describe people who do a lot of transactions these days) or if it is to help a handful of folks every year. The tasks are the same (just on a different scale). You've worked hard to have that listing or buyer that you are working with, and you are working hard to do a great job for them. Why not invest in yourself too so that transaction can lead to your next one?

July 8, 2015

Many, many years ago a friend introduced me to the teachings of Abraham by Esther Hicks. It's pretty far out, new age-y kind of stuff (much of it based in the Law of Attraction), but the messages are so good. I found Esther's voice to be so soothing as she shared the messages, I often listened to her CDs in the car between appointments. One message that I seemed to hear again and again was about "upstream" thoughts vs "downstream" thoughts. How many times does it feel that we are fighting, pushing to accomplish our goal or whatever it is in that moment, and it is just extra hard ... it's like trying to paddle up stream against the current. You may make tiny, slow progress but it is difficult, exceedingly difficult and you really won't get too far, if anywhere. Achieving our goals and dreams aren't easy, hard work is involved. Sometimes though, you just need to stop fighting to go upstream (you aren't supposed to be going that way) and just relax and allow yourself to be carried downstream.

I've felt that so many times for myself, in particular this year. I'm still working hard, but it feels infinitely easier, it feels right ... and that feels really good.

July 14, 2015

The last couple days have been one (or two or three) of "those" days. You know the days ... nothing seems to go right. I have way too much to do and not enough time to do it in. I'm leaving for vacation on Saturday, have 2 new listings going on the market this week, 1 the week I get back, and several other active clients requiring attention. All "quality problems" as they say. Every time I would start to gain a little momentum knocking one of the many things off my to do list, I would get interrupted, stopped in my tracks, or completely derailed. Silly things, like trying to hang up some of my wet laundry to dry but we are out of hangers in the laundry room and so I am on a wild goose chase throughout the house trying to find more. Like trying to do a "mind map" for a class I am taking that utilizes an app, only I can't download the app because I hadn't yet downloaded the new iOS for my iPad. So, I download the iOS, go do something else while it is loading, and then COMPLETELY forgot why I was doing it in the first place. Please tell me I'm not the only one. It's been 2 days full of this kind of stuff. For me, I usually find that when this is happening it is my sign to take a step back, take a deep breath, refocus and start again. I'm being told to slow down. How about you? How do you cope when you are having one of "those" days?

July 29, 2015

Today is a big day ... it is the 1-year anniversary of Empowering Women in Real Estate!

In just 1 year we have grown to well over 1200 women in the real estate industry ... realtors, lenders, stagers, title company executives and more.

When the idea for this group first came to me one morning in the shower (is that where you get your ideas too?), I was really feeling the need for a supportive group to share ideas and to support one another (remember - no selling here, there are a lot of other great groups for that). This group has been so successful in meeting that need thanks to your participation and willingness to engage, support and empower one another. Our challenges in this industry are unique, and I truly believe that by being there for each other and by helping others to grow and be better, that we will all grow and become better and stronger ourselves.

August 3, 2015

Whether you are a fan of Barbara Corcoran or not, you have to love this message. I find it to be so true. It's hard when you have been in business for a long time and successful at what you do ... the tendency is to do what you know and not deviate, not stretch. I've found (and I have a wonderful friend who is a beautiful example of this -- I'm looking at you Jackie Fields-Gleadall!) that when you step outside of your comfort zone, when you stretch, even just a little, that is when the magic happens. Magic to me meaning most reward, most growth, most impact on myself and those around me. For me at least, growing, stretching and learning has to be a lifelong pursuit. Barbara Corcoran shared this via social media today as her "Monday Motivation", I hope you will find it to be the same for you!

August 6, 2015

I love this quote from Maya Angelou. It applies in so many areas of our lives, and in our business. I've often said one of the hardest things about being new in this business is that you don't even know what you don't know. Think back to your beginning weeks/months in real estate. Certainly, we all made mistakes. Did things a certain way until we realized that there was a better way.

As silly as this sounds, for me in the very beginning (first few months probably) it was understanding that it was up to me to make things happen not to just "facilitate" them, if that makes sense. I remember struggling a bit and then the light bulb came on as I was leaving my office one evening. My clients were looking to me for recommendations and advice, not to just open doors and fill out contracts. Not busy? Need leads? Don't just wait for them to fall in your lap, proactively prospect for them, make connections. It was a mindset shift that made all the difference in the world for me.

August 17, 2015

Do you have a regular "schedule" for following up with your active (active listings, those under contract) clients?

On Friday I was talking to a friend about this. She participated in a Brian Buffini Peak Producers class that I led a couple years ago and remembered a lesson from Brian that a call out (that you make) takes 30 seconds, but a call in (from your client) takes 15 minutes or more (or something like that). I had completely forgotten about this, but it makes total sense. When you are on the defensive and the client is calling you first, it does tend to be a longer, and harder, conversation.

My challenge for you today is for you to be the first to call (or email or text depending on your client) with that check in or update. It is so hard I know ... hard to find the time, hard to know what to say, especially if it is a listing that has been sitting for a while. So, whether you do it today, or set aside the time that you will do it later this week (I do my updates on Wednesdays), taking that time to be proactive will feel so good ... to you and your clients!

August 20, 2015

Have you ever had that experience when your computer or your phone or some other device isn't working properly, seems stuck, is moving slow? Then you unplug it or power it off for a few minutes, turn it back on and then magically it is working perfectly again?

We are like that too.

I've had a crazy week, lots to do, cramming even more than usual into a shorter period of time in preparation to take a couple days for end of summer fun with my husband and kids. After appointments in the morning yesterday, I had an entire afternoon to catch up on emails, follow up with clients, work on my database, etc. Except, I was spinning my wheels. I'd start on this one thing, then remember something else, move over to do that, then the phone would ring, then I would remember that first thing I didn't finish, and on and on and on. I spent several hours going nowhere fast and didn't seem to be accomplishing anything except seeing how long my list was of things that had to get done that day and the clock rapidly ticking down until time for my nanny to go home and for me to finish up for the day.

Then I stopped. I went outside and slowly walked down my long driveway to bring up the trash can. Then I walked down again to get the recycling container. Then I walked down again to get the mail. Then I fixed a cup of tea. All the while my phone was taking a break too, inside, on my desk. The whole thing took less than 10 minutes, but after that break? I accomplished more in the following 2 hours, despite a couple unexpected phone calls and dealing with a "situation" (Have you ever had movers pack the radon canisters for a test in progress? Me either.). Having that little break was just what I needed to clear my head and focus again.

So, next time you are feeling frustrated or having trouble getting done what you need to do, take a break. I bet it will be just what you need to "re-boot" and start working at full capacity again. Do you work regular little breaks into your day?

September 3, 2015

While I was on vacation in July, I noticed that the stone in my engagement ring was loose. I took it off and set it aside, and finally took it to the jewelers to be tightened. The nice folks there also cleaned it for me ... cleaned the stone and polished the platinum band and setting. When I picked it up yesterday between appointments I was amazed when the clerk took it out for me. I've always loved my ring, and while I knew it had dulled over time, I didn't realize just how much until I saw it all polished up and cleaned. As the clerk handed it to me, she said, "Now you can fall in love with it all over again!"

Her comment reminded me of a conversation with an agent friend a couple weeks ago who commented that after a couple of particularly difficult transactions, that she had "fallen out of love" with real estate. That happens to us all from time to time, doesn't it?

In the beginning, everything is new and exciting. Every call and appointment is viewed as an opportunity to learn and grow and expand your business. Over time, the luster starts to wear off. Those tough transactions, losses and long hours can really wear you down, without even realizing how much, and your excitement for your business can dull.

For me, I've learned that the best way to keep that shine and excitement, and even just the energy to keep going through the rough days is to spend time with like-minded people ... this group is a big part of that! Working closely with people I know and trust keeps me motivated and energized. While I may be having a bad day today, someone else's energy can help to bring me up and vice versa.

Do you ever have those days/times when you feel like you need to fall back in love with real estate all over again?

September 11, 2015

I think this is the perfect message for today. None of us know what life holds for us or the people we love from moment to moment. Things can change in an instant. Enjoy those moments, and wherever you are, be all there, in that moment.

Isn't that the hardest thing to do? I am so guilty of doing many things at one time, not being truly present in the moment. If you are with your clients, focused on your business, then be all there ... not taking other calls, thinking about what's next. When you are with your family, partner, children, friends, be fully present with them.

I'll be working on putting this into practice myself today. My littlest boy is 6 today! I'll be focusing on work and clients for the next 2 hours, then it will be all about him this afternoon as we have a birthday lunch of his choosing and then a visit to Toys R Us and Target so he can spend his birthday money. If anyone needs me this afternoon, I'll be in the Lego aisle.

September 13, 2015
For real estate agents, Sundays rarely equal a day of rest and is often more like our Friday. Chances are though, for the others in our families the hustle and bustle of a new week starts tomorrow.

About a month or so ago I started a quick Sunday routine in my house which has really helped me to be more prepared for the week. It only takes about an hour, and the kids help. We do a lot of those little silly things that are a major annoyance at 6:15 on a Tuesday morning when I am desperate for a cup of coffee before I get the first round of kids up for school, or at 8:30 on a Wednesday night when we've just gotten home from baseball and need to eat dinner fast, get everyone cleaned up and off to bed. Things like ... filling the napkin holder on the kitchen table, filling the baskets/containers on the kitchen counter for coffee, tea and sugar, emptying all the trash cans in the bedrooms and bathrooms, making sure all the bathrooms have toilet paper, tidying up and running the vacuum, watering the plants. These are quick, silly things (and the house being "tidy" lasts about 15 minutes, but still), but it really helps to eliminate some of that rushed craziness during the week.

I've also started sitting down with my planner and mapping out my schedule for the week. Setting aside some time blocking for working on my business, making notes of any important things that need to get done, time sensitive tasks, etc.

So for today, with my husband working a 24 hour shift and my showing assistant handling a showing for me, I'm going to finish another cup of coffee and enjoy the wonderful cool breeze from the front porch, do my weekly prep and catch up on some paperwork and emails, pick up the grocery order and lunch for my boys, then we will cheer on our Redskins to another loss, I mean hopefully a win, this afternoon.

September 21, 2015

I have a friend who used to work in car sales. She used to say that there is a saying in that business that "there's an ass for every seat". It's one of my favorite sayings, I use it all the time. It applies to buyers and listings, and it applies to agents and clients. My interpretation of this saying is that for everything (car, house, agent) there is the right "person" (driver, buyer, client) for them. We've all had those listings that were unique and hard to sell. Those clients who were so difficult. Not because we aren't good at what we do or that they didn't respect us (okay, maybe sometimes) but that we just weren't a good fit for one another. I've had clients that I have struggled with, but other agents that I work with have had no problem with whatsoever.

This saying is the first thing I thought of when I saw the thread here over the weekend about professional dress. There's an ass for every seat. (See, it works for everything!) Will there be clients and colleagues who don't feel that a strapless dress or wearing jeans or a shirt with holes in it or cutoff shorts is professional and tasteful? Yep. Will there be clients and colleagues who know you and love you who don't care if you meet them wearing a potato sack? Absolutely. There are a lot of things that women do that tear each other down. I don't think that asking the question or expressing differing opinions falls in that category. The BEST THING is that we can ask those questions and have those different opinions and still respect each other as professionals.

For me personally, there is a distinction in my "work" wardrobe and my casual wardrobe, and it boils down to 2 things: 1) What is the first impression that I want to put out there, and 2) What makes me feel comfortable and professional. We talk about first impression all the time with our listings and even the contracts we submit on behalf of our buyers, and the impact that has on how our listing is viewed and our offer is received. Like it or not, right or wrong, I think that applies to how we present ourselves in business as well. I feel pretty confident that if I show up to a 1st time meeting with a potential seller for a listing appointment wearing a t-shirt and jeans, I'm going to have more ground to make up during the course of that appointment demonstrating my experience and professionalism because their first impression may not have been as favorable or as reflective of that.

I read an article recently about dressing for the day you want to have, which really made a lot of sense to me. Even if I am planning to work from home and catch up on emails or phone calls and not leave the house, I am simply not as productive if I stay in my comfy clothes or jammies all day, as I am if I get dressed and put on real shoes (not sure what the shoe connection is for me, but it makes a huge difference).

Bottom line in whatever you do ... the way you dress, the way you conduct your business, etc. ... do it for you and OWN IT. If wearing a crop top and cut off shorts helps you to feel confident and to do your job effectively (I actually attended a walk thru once with an agent who was wearing that exact outfit), then do it, own it and don't give a crap what anyone else thinks. If wearing a suit, hose and heels makes you feel good in the way you present yourself in your work, then by all means do that too. Just know that however it is that you choose to present yourself there are some who won't like it and some who won't care. Their "reaction" to you has EVERYTHING to do about them, and pretty much nothing to do about you. As they say, there's an ass for every seat.

October 5, 2015

In my family, we avoid change like the plague. It's like it has been imprinted in my DNA. Avoid change! Avoid something new! Change is bad! Change is foreign! On and on.

But here's the thing ... change is absolutely inevitable. It is a part of life. We, those around us, the entire world around us is literally changing every single moment. Fighting that change is not only fruitless, but frustrating, maddening, depressing, fear inducing, on and on.

For me, even though my first gut instinct with every change or new experience in my life is to resist, I've found that the faster I embrace it and pour my focus into that change and moving forward, the better. I love this quote attributed to Socrates, "the secret of change is to focus all of your energy, not on fighting the old, but on building the new".

Now, even though it's still scary, when I am faced with a change I dive in fully and completely and don't look back. What I've learned through this is that all of my fear and angst surrounding a change or new experience is purely anticipatory ... What if this happens? What if that happens? What will I do? What if it's bad? ... BUT ... What if it's good? What if it's fun? What if it's the best thing that ever happened to me? I've found that by focusing on the latter, by focusing on building the new, on creating the new routine (which soothes my anxiety) every change, every bit of newness, has opened a new door, a new window, a new way of thinking and doing for me, which has always been good ... even if the change wasn't my choice in the beginning.

How do you cope with change in your life?

October 14, 2015

On Sunday my husband was watching a football show on ESPN, and it caught my attention when they did an interview piece on Julio Jones, a wide receiver for the Atlanta Falcons (football fans - I am pretty well certain to mess up some of these details!). This player is in his 3rd or 4th year in the NFL and had been a relatively "quiet" player up until this season, where he is now one of very best in what he does (rushing yards, passing yards ... not sure). The reporter was asking him why was it that he thought that his performance had been so explosive this year over years passed, especially since he has had that potential the whole time. Julio said that the key for him this year was his offseason. In years past he had been injured or not fully healthy and therefore couldn't truly be as active during his off season. For this year, his coach challenged him to have a really focused offseason, and the results of that is showing in his performance today.

I thought that was really powerful and got me thinking about our "offseason" in real estate. We are almost there. fall market classically starts to quiet in November, and usually stays that way for a little bit into January. The steps you take, the things you do during this offseason will help to propel you forward into your best ever 1st quarter, and even 2nd quarter and beyond.

For my offseason, I've always participated in some sort of business/goal planning to look at where my business came from in the current year, what marketing and steps I took and whether or not they were successful, and then to set my goal for the new year, along with the steps I will take to get there. I usually also participate in one or two bigger picture training/seminar events (this year it is the Virginia Women's Business Conference in November, one of my favorite events), a holiday mailing to my entire database, and pop bys to my buyers from that year.

This year I'm kicking it up a notch with a client event with my team in December (Breakfast with Santa!), as well as a 90 Homes in 90 Days Challenge. Every listing, contract and lease counts toward the 90. This challenge has us thinking in different ways about our database, how to engage, and how to make things happen. Even if we don't hit our goal at the end of the 90 days, the steps that we are taking towards that goal is instilling new habits, which will put us that much further ahead in the new year.

The offseason isn't meant to be all work. I'm looking forward to lots of fun with my family, a couple nights in Williamsburg, and being "off" as much as possible in the days between Christmas and New Years. This way, I will be excited and ready to go on the first workday of 2016.

October 16, 2015

We all want different things, experiences, happenings in our life. Maybe it's -- I want to be a better agent. I want to be a better friend. I want to be healthier. I want to lose 10 pounds. I want to be more engaged with my children. I want to connect more with my database. I want financial freedom. I want to sell 25 homes this year. I want to take a walk every day.

We all have these wants, but ...
"I want" doesn't make it happen. "I want" isn't enough.
Ouch. That stung a little when I first heard it on a podcast, but it's so true.

You can't "want" your way to success, a different life, a stronger relationship, a healthier body. Wanting is the start ... the setting of the goal, the forming of the intention, but plain and simple work, effort, new habits, different priorities are what will get you there.

So, figure out what you want. Identify what will get you there, what you need to do to make it happen, and then do it. Make it a priority in your life. Even when it's hard. Do it over and over again and eventually, it will become easy.

What do you want, and what can you do today to start making it happen?

October 21, 2015

A couple weeks ago I attended a real estate finance class taught by a successful Florida realtor with an amazing story.

The class was excellent and all about how to handle your finances in the real estate industry, but the moment I was struck by most was when we were talking about LLCs vs C Corps, etc. and a manager asked him how best she should answer that question when asked by her agents. The speaker told her to gently hold the sides of their face, look into their eyes and say, "Until you are consistently closing 1 transaction a month for a year, it doesn't matter."

Let that sink in for a moment.

The message is that we get so distracted on the "tool" or device or whatever is going to "get us there" in our business, that we often lose sight of what really works ... YOU! More specifically, you, working. Working on the basics. Engaging with the real estate market and your database. Until and unless you are consistently producing in your business, then none of that other "stuff" matters.

But if only I had the right website, I'd be more successful. If only I had the best follow up tools I'd be able to do more business. When I find the right search app for my clients I'll close more deals."

If only and when ... the most dangerous and deceptive words of all.

Yes, there are tools and technologies and resources and websites that can help us to work our businesses better and more efficiently, but the bottom line is that they only work as well and as hard as you do. Having the tool available to you is great, but if you don't actually use it, invest time in learning how and entering your clients in or whatever it is, then it won't work.

So many of us are getting ready to get ready. "I'm getting ready to take my business to a new level. I'm getting ready to promote my brand in a big way. I'm getting ready to engage with my database."

Stop getting ready already, and just do it. Do anything. Take action.

You are always, and always will be, your best tool. Your best asset. Your best opportunity for success. If you don't work, nothing else will.

October 30, 2015

I love fall, Halloween, the month of October. I love Thanksgiving and Christmas, and fully acknowledge and accept my ornament addiction.

But what I really love, is goal planning season.

I know, I know, but I can't help it. This is the time of year when I love to sit down and review where I've been both personally and professionally through the year, set my goals for the new year, and most importantly, set the intention, steps and plan for HOW I am going to achieve those goals. I've done this my entire career. In the beginning years with my team leader, then with my team, and for the last 2 years when I was a managing broker it felt like I did 2 or more of these sessions a day with my agents for pretty much the entire month of November and first two weeks of December.

Exhausting, but fun at the same time. My boys and my husband and I even sit down on New Year's Day and make our "goal" list of things we want to do as a family in the coming year.

Yesterday I put the finishing touches on the business planning worksheets for my new team and can't wait to sit down with them in a couple weeks to work through it all. It feels so good to be doing this for myself again! I like to look very specifically at WHERE my business and leads have come from during the previous year. From the very beginning I've been obsessive about tracking my leads. By knowing where the leads are coming from, and then where the transactions are coming from, I'm able to know which of my marketing efforts are working, and which ones aren't. It's fascinating to me to see how my leads have gone up and down over the years, directly proportionate to my level of engagement in my business. This then makes it much easier to establish the marketing plan for the new year knowing what has and hasn't worked.

Do you do this sort of review and goal setting for your business each year?

November 16, 2015

Did anyone else watch Super Soul Sunday on OWN yesterday? Oprah was interviewing Shonda Rhimes, a mother of 3, and the creator/writer/producer of Greys Anatomy, Scandal and other popular shows. The topic of conversation was her new book called, "Year of Yes".

Shonda spoke about how she has been so focused on her work and her "things to do" that she always and immediately said "no" to new things ... no to party invitations, no to speaking engagements, even no to playing with her kids. She was all work, and no fun. She talked about the reason she said no to so many things, which for her was completely fear based. Boy, can I relate to that.

After a particular "wake up call" experience, she decided that for a year, she would say yes ... and the result was that she completely changed her life. She stretched and grew as she did new things, her relationships with her children changed as she said yes to playing with them, she lost over 100 pounds by saying yes to eating only what she "craved" and nothing else.

This is something that I feel that I constantly need to work on. When I look back and think about the times I said yes in my life, even though I was afraid, those experiences, adventures, invitations turned out to be completely life changing for me in a very good way. Even if it turned out to be not "just right", saying yes eventually led to what was not only just right, but absolutely amazing. A reminder I need more of and need to say yes more often.

When faced with a new adventure, new opportunity, invitation, etc., what is your first gut reaction? Yes, or no?

November 17, 2015

Yesterday we talked about saying yes ... yes to life ... yes to things we say no to mostly because we are afraid.

Today, let's talk about saying no. Recently a group member mentioned that she feels like she has swung in the opposite direction from saying yes to everything to saying no to everything. There should be a healthy balance, and how do you figure that out? Know your priorities, know your why.
We can't do and accomplish all the things and be everything to all people (repeating this in the mirror to myself right now).

Every time we say yes to something ...
-Running out the door for the disrespectful client who always wants to see houses with 1 hour notice on a Sunday morning
-Answering the phone at 11 pm at night or 6:30 am in the morning for the local client who wants to chat about what color they should paint the kitchen
-Leading the PTA committee for the fall fundraiser
-Watching a friend's kids on a weekday that school is closed because she has to work (you do too!)

Means saying no to something else ...
-Church services/Sunday morning breakfast with your family
-Restful sleep/morning quiet time to help you recharge and get ready for your day
-Extra time to spend prospecting, taking a client to lunch, visiting your child at school for lunch/spending an hour in their classroom
-Spending the day doing something fun with your children or spending a focused day of work in your business

So, when faced with the "can you", "will you", "you're invited", "can you help", take a moment and think first before you automatically respond. Is this something you would love to do but are afraid/not sure you're good enough/talented enough, "ready"? Then you should probably say yes.

In saying yes, what will you have to say no to, and which of those is more important? What are things in your life right now that you are saying "yes" to when you should really be saying "no"?

December 2, 2015

I've found over the years that there is no faster path to pissing me off than to tell me I can't do something. I'm not talking about parents parenting young children, but adults telling other adults they can't do things. They won't be successful. Without me/us/this/our guidance, you won't do as well.

Why do we do that to each other? I believe that there is plenty of success, abundance, goodness, happiness, money, transactions whatever it is you are looking for to go around. Just because one person is successful in something, does not mean that there will then not be "enough" left for you to be successful.

In my experience, when someone is telling me I can't, it is usually based in their own fear. Fear for me to do something or try something new because they are afraid for me, but also because they would be afraid to do it themselves. For others, I've found that it is their subtle (or sometimes not so subtle) way (consciously or unconsciously) to keep the other person "down" by making them unsure of themselves. This usually comes from the "you can't do this without me", somehow implying that you aren't good enough on your own, because your plans for success for yourself doesn't fit into their plans of success for themselves (and the role they see for you in it).

My point here is to remind you (and me) that the next time someone tells you that you can't, just remember that actually, you CAN. And you will. Then go do it and be great at it.

December 9, 2015

Do you struggle to accomplish things, and sometimes don't complete them because they aren't perfect? I love this quote attributed to Voltaire, "Perfect is the enemy of the good".

A colleague and I were talking about this a few days ago. She had a list of about 100 pop bys that she wanted to do this month. The last 2 years she has done a similar amount, and partly as a result her business has really taken off. So much so, that this year, she really does not have time to deliver them herself, and so she is paying someone to deliver them on her behalf. She was worried that she was going to miss the "point" of these by not getting that eye to eye contact herself by delivering them personally. Is the "perfect" way to deliver them personally, and see each client one on one? Sure is. But, if that isn't possible, do you not do them at all? Definitely not. Having someone deliver them for you is still going to achieve wonderful results and is much better than not doing it at all.

This past weekend my team and I had our very first client appreciation celebration, which almost didn't happen. We were set on the simple theme of Breakfast with Santa and picked a date. And then we pretty much talked ourselves out of it. In our effort to have a "perfect" event (one that included more activities for the kids, one that would appeal to more than just our clients with children, one that would be less expensive so we could invite more clients), at one point we ended up changing the plan and then scrapped the event all together. Then, we got our wits about us, went with our original plan, and it actually turned out to be the most wonderful event. We wouldn't have changed a thing. Would it have been more ideal to have an event that also appealed to our clients without children? Yes, but we can do that with our mid-year event. Did the children need more activities? Nope. Breakfast, plus a visit with and photo with Santa and some holiday coloring pages were just enough.

Sometimes, we allow our pursuit of perfection to stop us. Perfect is an illusion. Do we still strive to do great things? Yes, definitely, but don't hold yourself back from taking action because something isn't perfect. Taking action will always be better than doing nothing.

December 18, 2015
"Begin with the end in mind." That's an old-school Stephen Covey quote. You've probably heard it a ton of times, but do you understand it? Think about it? Practice it?

Time moves FAST. Life changes QUICKLY. What are you doing right this minute? Drinking coffee? Getting ready for a busy day? How do you feel? Relaxed? Stressed? Agitated?

Now fast forward 1 year. December 18th, 2016 at 6:50-ish in the morning. What are you doing? How are you feeling? Will you want to be doing and feeling the same things on that morning as you are on this morning? If yes, your path is probably clear, but if not (and I'm guessing there is a not, at least in some area of your life) then what are you going to do now, tomorrow, next week, next month so that December 18th, 2016 is different, FEELS different than it does today?

Begin with the end in mind.

Many, many, many years ago I was meeting with an HR representative at the pharmaceutical company I was working for talking about their college tuition reimbursement program. I had my associate's degree in business but had not gone on to pursue my bachelor's degree. Partly due to finances. Partly due to other circumstances. Their tuition reimbursement program was an amazing program (which ultimately allowed me to finish my bachelor's degree debt free), but I was hesitant, voicing my concern about how long it would take (3-ish years) to finish up my degree while still working full time. The woman told me, very wisely, that the time was going to pass anyway, at the end of that 3-ish years would I rather have my degree, or not. So smart, and so true.

Where do you want to be 1 year from now? How do you want your business to look, your life to look, your health to look? If you feel like you have a long way to go to reach your goal, and maybe 1 year isn't enough, it is probably pretty daunting, maybe even enough so that you don't even try. But the time will pass anyway. One year from now you can be where you want to be, or you can be that much closer to it, or you can be stuck. In the same place. Again. Still wishing and wanting.

Begin with the end in mind. Figure out where you want to go, what you want to be, how you want to feel. Then what are the steps that you need to take, the actions that you need to complete to get there. Get started on those steps and those actions right now. A little at a time. A day at a time. For your business, this should all be part of your personal business plan. For your life, your health, your finances, call it your personal life plan, you need one of those too.

The time will pass anyway. Take some steps, baby steps if you must, one day at a time, so that when December 18th, 2016 is here you can look back and say I am exactly where I want to be.

December 23, 2015
It's the most wonderful time of the year! We hear that so much around this time, don't we? For many, this is the most wonderful time. The shopping. The presents. The trees. The lights. Parties. Time with friends and family. Celebrating the birth of baby Jesus.

For many though, this is one of the hardest times of the year. For those who have lost loved ones, struggling with personal and health issues, who don't have strong family ties, this can be so hard. I've seen the posts floating around Facebook about this, and I certainly do feel this acutely this year, but that's not my point here.

The peace, love and joy and general merriment that we tend to share and experience this time of year, why do we limit it to once a year? So many of us go crazy this time of year trying to get it all done, to meet a certain standard, for what? A day or two of get togethers and celebrations? My husband was at the mall yesterday getting a few last-minute things and was struck by just how mean and miserable everyone seemed to be. What's up with that? I thought this was the most wonderful time of the year.

What if, instead, we take that desire to help others, to be present with family, to celebrate a power greater than us, and apply that principal all year round? There are so many wonderful charity events this time of year, the toy drives and coat drives, the food pantries receiving a higher-than-normal amount of donations. But aren't there still children in need, people who are cold and hungry other times of year? What if instead of cramming it all into a few days, weeks, a month, we make this a part of our very way of being and doing? How would that change your life, your children, your family, your community?

Last night a dear friend and I were talking about this. We are so BUSY. Busy, busy, busy. I've come to hate that word. We piss away our days doing what? Rushing from one task to another, from point a to point b. Grumpy because we're tired, there are too many things to do, we've set an impossible standard for ourselves.

My thought today ... challenge yourself to find something good, to intentionally have a little joy, to connect with your people (family, friends, clients), to give to others not just once a year, but every single day. See something that you know a loved one would enjoy? Don't wait until Christmas or their birthday. Buy it, wrap it beautifully (or don't), and give it to them. Don't wait until once a year to prepare a special meal for family and friends. When the mood strikes, do it. Develop a relationship with your local support services and do what you can to help others throughout the year.

Another day, another month, another Christmas ... it isn't promised to any of us. Find a way to enjoy each day, each moment. The joy is there, you just need to look for it.

December 29, 2015

In just a couple of days the new year will be upon us. 2015 was a year that brought me incredibly low lows with health and family, but also some wonderful and amazing highs that I didn't even know were possible. I've seen changes and turns of events that didn't make sense, but as time goes on became clear that it was all on purpose for another purpose. What I thought was coming together to "save" me, turns out was actually piecing together to support and lift up someone I love ... or maybe it was both. If I could summarize 2015 in a word it would be "unexpected".

There are some people I follow who choose a word for each year to help set their intention and keep their focus for the new year. Maybe even to meditate on. It's an interesting concept I'd like to explore. So, for 2016, my word is "faith". My intention is that my year will be centered around faith in my business, my team, myself, that everything will be okay, in a power greater than myself. Now it's your turn. Looking back on 2015, what is one word that would describe your year? What word do you want to focus on for 2016?

2016

Milestones:
7-29-2016 – My very first time sharing a video in the group for our 2-year anniversary!

February 2, 2016

When is the last time you shook your life? Did you do it on purpose or was it done for you?

My life was majorly shaken up last year following the passing of my mother. I was very comfortable ... yet I was also uncomfortable, and didn't really realize it. Numb may be a better word. Suddenly, everything was different, and what was "comfortable" was obviously no longer so.

So, as described in the quote below, I held onto (or tried to hold onto) the clearly very best parts ... the gold ... and let the rest go in favor of new experiences, some freshness, a new chapter. The part that was let go wasn't bad, it had just served its purpose, run its course. What has emerged has been more wonderful than I could ever imagine. Harder, yes. Sometimes uncomfortable, definitely. Yet incredibly fulfilling, like all of the pieces of a puzzle have finally started to come together.

Next time an opportunity is staring you in the face, or when you find that you are too comfortable, or when an unwelcomed earthquake is wreaking havoc in your life ... Stop. Grab onto the gold. Say thank you, and let the rest go.

> I AM A FIRM BELIEVER THAT EVERY FEW YEARS ONE NEEDS TO *SHAKE* ONE'S LIFE THROUGH A SIEVE, LIKE A MINER IN THE YUKON. THE GOLD NUGGETS REMAIN, THE REST FALLS THROUGH LIKE THE SOFT EARTH IT IS.
>
> AMY POEHLER

February 23, 2016

What motivates you, propels you forward toward your accomplishments? A lot of people may say, "my family", "having a goal", "winning", even "making money", but stop and really think about it for a moment. When you are making a change in your life, when you are growing and accomplishing things, being propelled forward, is it because a problem is pushing you in that direction, pushing you to take action, or are you being led there by your dreams?

Really think about it. When I look back, think back over my experiences and the times that I grew the most, I was more often being pushed by my problems. A problem/situation/issue in my life had become so uncomfortable that there was no choice but to act, to move, to take a step in another direction. As a result, these experiences were painful, lengthy, long and drawn out, and not usually welcomed ... until I got to the other side of course and realized what it was all about.

Then when I think about the times that my dream, my goal, led me to act, progress seemed ... easier. Not that there still wasn't hard work involved with the change, but it didn't seem to be as painful. It was joyful even.

I suppose there is no right way. Both approaches will eventually get you in the direction you are supposed to go, but I do think that when your dreams are leading that you will go farther, faster.

Can you see how this principle has been at work in your life? Do you tend to be pushed or led? Are you experiencing something right now that feels like pushing? Instead, why not stop a moment. Think about the direction you are moving in, change your internal dialogue about that experience and visualize, dream, about how it could be different. Then instead of being pushed by the "problem" that "started" it all, let that dream lead you. I have a feeling that may make all the difference.

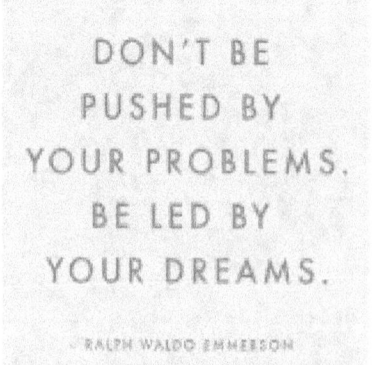

DON'T BE PUSHED BY YOUR PROBLEMS. BE LED BY YOUR DREAMS.

RALPH WALDO EMMERSON

February 25, 2016

Yesterday I was having a bit of an "off" day. You know those days ... just not feeling it, had been working too many days in a row without a sufficient break, my morning hadn't gone as I had thought, and the weather here was horrible with the gray skies and chilly rain.

I decided to run an errand before starting work when my husband called. His meeting had finished early (it was actually supposed to be his day off) and he was near me, so we decided to meet for lunch before I headed to the office. As I approached a spot in the road near the restaurant where I was to yield, I noticed that I slid a little as I stopped to wait for traffic to pass. Then, the car behind me SLAMMED into me. Well. Boy did the four-letter words fly. My mood went from bad to worse. I sat there for a minute stunned, ticked off, aggravated now that I was going to have to deal with insurance and a car repair. One more thing to have to do.

As I got out of my car (a large SUV) the driver of the (medium sized) car who hit me approached me SOBBING. It hit me (no pun intended) that she was having a far worse day than I. Her car was really messed up, one headlight totally broken out, hood pushed up a good 6 inches or more, there was broken pieces all over the ground. She was crying, saying "Are you okay?", "Is your car okay", "I'm late for court" (we were near the courthouse), and she was a bit disheveled. I could see in that moment that she needed some grace. So, I gave her a big hug (or two), told her it was going to be okay, and sent her on her way.

The damage to my car wasn't a big deal, some scratches here, a little dent and cut in the metal there, my husband was able to "pull" out the big, dented part at the bottom and push down the bumper "step" (I don't know anything about cars). Even if it had been more, I don't think I would have handled it differently. I could literally feel her struggle, and me standing there yelling at her the four-letter words I had been expressing the minute before, or gathering her info to put in a claim on her insurance was going to do more harm than good. So, I gave her grace instead.

When have you needed a moment of grace in your life or your business? What about those around you? We've all had those encounters with the bitter agent, the one angry with life it seems, who then puts that on you. The one who feels that fighting with the cooperating agent is the best way to represent their clients (it's not). In times of change and volatility or stress the worst parts of us tend to show up. Look for opportunities in your life to give grace to someone when they need it. It may just change your life.

March 7, 2016

How often to you put things off until "someday"?
Someday, when I have more time, I'll fully execute my marketing plan.
Someday, when I'm less busy, I'll work prospecting into my weekly schedule.
Someday, when my children are older, I'll take the time to exercise each day.
Someday, when I get the process just right, I'll implement follow up systems into my business.

Does any of this sound familiar to you? It certainly does for me. We put things off until some future time, until "someday", until we are less busy, we wait to do things until we can get them just exactly right, perfect.

Life is busy. You have to make the time for what is important to you. The time will not just magically appear. Nothing is perfect. If you are waiting for perfection or to get something just right before implementing it in your life or business, it will never get done.

Someday is not a day of the week. Don't wait. Life will not wait for you. Time will not make itself available for you. You must go after it with intention.

March 11, 2016

Yesterday while I was taking a walk, I was listening to a podcast of a sermon by Bishop TD Jakes and there were a few points that really struck me.

He said, "are you so focused on being the teacher that you have forgotten how to be the student"?

Wow, right?! I had to go back and listen to that part a couple times. He also spoke about how when we are really good at one thing/area in our life, we tend to allow that to let us think that we are good in every area, but we are not. We need help. We need guidance. We need to learn. This was the third "time" this week that a need to learn/to be the student has showed up for me, and so I know it's time to pay attention and figure out what that is.

Do you spend time regularly learning in your life and your business? It doesn't matter how many years or how many transactions, I believe strongly that there is always something new, something more to learn. How about in your life in general? Do you take the time to learn new hobbies, to try new activities? It's hard to take the time for classes or training. It is humbling to put yourself out there as not knowing everything (which is silly, no one knows it all), but it's worth it.

March 28, 2016

Yesterday I watched an interview with Pastor Joel Osteen, talking about his book, "I Am". He says that whatever follows the words "I am" will show up in your life. When you say, "I am tired", "I am not ready", "I am struggling in my business", "I am worried", "I am stressed", it's like you are inviting it into your life.

I believe this. Many books and speakers, Tony Robbins, Zig Ziglar, talk about the power of our words, the power of positive affirmations. You can use those words to speak positively of yourself, or you can use them negatively. There really is a difference.

Try it today and see how it feels. Pay attention to the words you say to yourself and turn them around. Try these instead ... "I am full of energy", "I am a successful businesswoman", "I am an engaged partner", "I am a joyful mother", "I am ready to move forward", "I am advancing in my career", "I am grateful". Happy Monday!

April 5, 2016

At the Buffini Success Tour in Richmond last week Brian talked about time management and the importance of scheduling the important things. He also talked about building in "fire breaks" in your day. Specific blocks of time with no appointments once or twice a day (could be 30 minutes to an hour) to address the extra "stuff" that comes up or the fires that need to be put out. I really love that idea. When you have a day jam packed with appointments and things that need to be done, having something unforeseen come up (like the jammed lockbox on my listing yesterday that we couldn't open for the walk through) can throw your entire day off track.

I really love that idea and want to be more intentional about scheduling time like that into my day. After the two days at the Success Tour last week my husband drove down with our 3 sons to pick me up and we drove over Great Wolf Lodge in Williamsburg and stayed there for 2 nights. All told, the time at the resort only amounted to about a day and a half, and I came back just in time for a listing appointment, but the time was just enough and well spent.

Usually, I tend to think that I need to schedule huge chunks of time (several days or a week) for a "break" like this, but this was a great lesson to me that just a little break can be just right. I came back feeling refreshed, and my whole family enjoyed the little trip. When is the last time you took a break?

April 8, 2016

It's hard to believe that we are already a week into the month of April, time goes so fast! How was your first quarter? Have you taken time to review your goals and your business to make sure you are on the right path?

One mistake I see many people make (I've often made it myself) is they set goals and establish their business plan each year, then don't look at it again until the end of the year. You need to tend to it regularly. This doesn't need to be a "beat yourself up" session. In fact, it can be quite the opposite. This is a way to be gentle with yourself, touch base, check in, see where you are.

I would encourage you to set aside some time, schedule it with yourself, even better do it with some friends, colleagues, accountability partners to do a first quarter review. What worked and didn't work? Are you tracking towards your goal? Do you need to adjust your goal? How about the marketing plans and budget that you set for the year ... are you on track or do you need to make some adjustments? Have you been implementing the things you said you would do? This step is important to growing a purposeful business, and an intentional life. Make the time for it, you're worth it!

April 11, 2016

My husband has this theory about restaurants, that the more varied their menu is in different types of cuisine and dishes, the less likely it is to be good. As much as I hate to admit it, I think he's right. When I think about my favorite restaurants, the ones that have consistently really great food they focus on one type of food or serve a very limited menu.

This applies to our businesses as well. There are so many distractions. So many different things to try. When I was at the Success Tour in Richmond a couple weeks ago Brian Buffini talked about the shiny object and how many phone calls we as agents get from those trying to sell us the next best new product or technology or service that will boost our business. Do you ever get these calls? Have you ever attended a real estate convention and walked around all of the vendor tables with the latest and greatest new technologies and toys? What makes the one in booth 15 better than the one in booth 62?

It's you.

YOU are the common denominator. Without you and your focus none of it will work. So, the question then is what do you focus on? When you try to do too many things, when you are burning your candle at both ends and in the middle, nothing is getting your full attention, and that will show in your results.

My hope for you today is that you do less, with more focus. There is so much to do in our daily lives, both personally and professionally. The thinner you spread yourself, the harder it will be. Focus on the most important people and tasks that will lead you to the good life and a great business. Beware of the shiny object. Spend some time each day taking care of yourself. Even if it's just 10-15 minutes doing something that you enjoy, or just doing nothing at all.

Take some time today to make a list of what is absolutely most important to you, most critical to your life, your family, your happiness, your business. Place your focus there. When something new pops up and you are tempted by the distraction, reference back to that list. Does it fit there? When you are saying yes to something, that means you are saying no to something else, there are only so many hours in a day. Make sure that what you are saying yes to isn't going to detract from your priority list.

Focus on the most important parts of your business, the relationships. Focus on the people who really mean something in your life, and let the rest go. You don't need it anyway.

April 14, 2016

Yesterday I spent the first part of my day with the incredible women on my team talking through our first quarter review. What worked for us. What didn't. What we wanted to/needed to change moving forward. The value of relationships. The fear of success. There was no talk of specific numbers, a successful first quarter for one may have been 2 transactions, for another 10. That wasn't the point of the gathering. Both were right.

Balance and success aren't opposites. That was our "theme" if you will. Everyone in that room (and all of us here) are balancing real life with business. Real life is messy. Families are messy. Children. Spouses. Ailing parents. Siblings that need help. Death. Divorce. Illness. Finances. Depression. Self-confidence. The list is endless. Somewhere in the midst of all of that we still have to take care of ourselves, and oh, hey, that business that we love too. The business that pays the bills. The business that our family (may or may not) rely on for primary income. The business that (hopefully) we love … and if not, stop. Stop it right now. Life is too precious and too short to waste a second where and with who we aren't supposed to be.

Life requires a lot from us, mentally, physically, emotionally.
Our business requires a lot from us, mentally, physically, emotionally.
We are in this business to serve others. We help them through one of the most stressful times of their lives, and what for many will be their largest

financial investment. It can be draining. They can be needy. So how do you balance that? Balance your own stressful, draining, needy life, while simultaneously helping others with their own stressful, draining, needy stuff?

Find the joy. Every moment with everyone will not be magic and rainbows, but there is a distinct difference between working with people who respect you and appreciate you and those who do not see your value. Just say no. Even if they are your only client or the closest thing you can see in your pipeline to a payday. The mental and emotional toll that it takes on you will make you unavailable to new business and new opportunities. It will set you back. Let them go.

Set boundaries. Unless it is vitally urgent, there really isn't much that can and should be accomplished at 9 o'clock at night. Even 8 o'clock at night. Turn off your phone. Don't respond to emails. When you send or respond to emails late at night you are not being valuable by being super available. You are sacrificing yourself and teaching others that they can expect you to be responsive late at night. You email. They respond or feel obligated to respond. Then you feel obligated to respond again. It becomes a vicious cycle.

Be productive. Busy and productive are two very different things. You can be a crazy woman running all over creation with a huge pipeline that individually nets you pennies on the dollar, or you can productively serve a few and net not only more money, but more TIME that you can then invest back into your business, yourself, your family, which will then turn around and produce more in the big picture.

Spend time with those who lift you up. And lift others up too. Life is hard. We all have bad days. When you bring that bad day to the table the energy for everyone around you plummets. Everyone feels it, whether they know you well or not. Your clients feel it. Your partner feels it. Your children feel it. Take a walk. Breathe in the fresh air. Vent it out to a friend. Do something nice for someone else. There is no better way to lift your own spirits, to get out of your own way, than by spending time doing something nice and unexpected to help someone else.

Being successful does not have to come at the expense of your family, yourself, your emotional well-being. Being successful is defined differently by everyone. Don't let anyone make you feel badly about how you define that success ... be it with big numbers, flashy things, wonderful vacations and life experiences, or large chunks of time being fully present and available for those you love, taking care of someone you love. Can you do that while still seeing the beauty and joy in each day and cultivating meaningful relationships (both personally and in business)? THAT is the true measure of success.

April 18, 2016

When you are faced with challenges in your real estate business (or in life), do you focus on the limitations?
-This buyer is a waste of time, the property they are looking for doesn't exist.
-I can't _____ because I'm ... too afraid, haven't done it before, might make a mistake, don't know how, comfortable.

What if instead, you look for solutions?
-That property may not exist in my marketplace, but what about an hour south of here, or in the neighboring state that is only 30 minutes away?
-I could _____ if I ... find a mentor, ask someone who has done it before, make a phone call, google it, put on my big girl pants.

What if instead, you look for opportunities?
-I know a great agent in the next town over where the buyer can find everything on their wish list. I'll set up a referral and an introduction. They will find the home they really want; I'll earn a referral fee and have more time to serve someone else.
-I can _____ because ... she did it before and look how well it turned out, the greatest reward comes from pushing through the fear, even if I make a "mistake" I will grow and learn something new.

Check your dialogue next time you are facing a challenge or an objection. Resist the urge to jump straight to the limitations, and instead focus on the solution or opportunity. I promise you, in every situation, they exist!

April 19, 2016

It was a gorgeous day here in Northern Virginia yesterday, perfect for having a meeting outside with two business partners/friends/teammates over some Rita's Italian ice. We had a great discussion about how to ask for referrals. When do you ask, how do you ask, what do you say. How often to follow up, pop by, send notes. There were a lot of "Buffini-says" moments in the conversation.

One thing we kept coming back to was being afraid of asking for the referral. On the surface, it may not look like that, but when you break it down, it is.

I'm afraid they will say no.
I'm afraid it will be awkward.
I'm afraid they will think I'm super sales-y.
I'm afraid they will think that is the only thing I care about.

The reality is, if this is someone you know or have done business with before (and liked) they aren't going to be rude or say no to your face. Yes, it may feel awkward (to you) at first, but if you find something to say that works for you, it won't come across overly sales-y or not genuine.

Many, many (10?) years ago I started saying that I did business by referral. Now at the time, I actually did very little business by referral (I was on a rainmaker-style team), but it felt comfortable to me to introduce the idea of referrals by saying that. And before you knew it, I was doing a significant amount of business by referral, and for the past 7 years, the highest percentage of my business comes from repeat clients and referrals.

I'm not always the best at asking for the order myself. Haven't we all had those moments at the settlement table when you see the opening for you to ask for the referral, but you can't get the words out of your mouth? I know I've been there. I'm also a big believer in "teaching" people how to refer me. When I look back over my business, when someone refers me once, they are much more likely to do it again and again. You need to reward the behavior. Even if the "referral" is simply the friend/past client saying they gave someone my name, I immediately follow up with a handwritten note thanking them for their trust in me, reminding them that referrals are the heart of my business and including a little something. How (and when) do you ask for referrals in your business?

April 20, 2016

Are you afraid of success? That sounds really silly, right?! Who's afraid of success? Isn't success (personally, professionally) what we are striving for? That's what I thought too, until I read one of my favorite books, "Make It Happen" by Lara Casey.

Last week during our quarterly review I read a passage about the fear of success. I won't quote the entire section here, but here is an excerpt ...

"When we look a level deeper, our greatest fear may actually be the very thing we are chasing: success. Why? If we finally realize our potential, we might be thrust into a life of responsibility that we can't handle.
-I am afraid of trying because I might actually succeed.
-I am afraid of success because I might have to step out of my comfort zone.
-I am afraid of success because it might not be what I expect, and then I'll have to start over.
-I'm afraid of success because I believe I'll have to keep doing whatever I did to become successful nonstop forever, and I'll be trapped!
-I am afraid my success will be selfish.

We fear success because it may invite a bigger opportunity for failure, it might take us away from our loved ones, or it might put us under the microscope of others.

So, we decide that success is for everyone else, not us. We don't take risks because we think we are small. We don't do anything great because we think we weren't made that way." (end excerpt)

Wow, right? Do you recognize any of that? I know I do. Especially the part about stepping out of my comfort zone and being selfish. Part of me definitely fears success, always has. I was having this conversation with two friends last week about what changed for me, why am I more able to handle that particular fear now, to charge forward (mostly) confidently. For me, it is the people in my life, my business partners, my mentors, my team. In the first "phase" of my career I got a wonderful start on a rainmaker team. The splits were low, but everything was provided, and I learned so much. More than I know I could have on my own. As years went by though, and past clients started calling me back directly, and my sphere of influence started contacting me, and I started receiving referrals, it became pretty clear that it was time to go off on my own, but I was afraid. I was comfortable, yet uncomfortable at the same time. I was settled yet unsettled at the same time.

Then, I met Vicky Noufal, Carmelle Shea, Jodi Hooper, Stacy Mallonee and Jackie Fields-Gleadall. We had known each other and had been working together already for quite a while, but as our relationships deepened, I saw how much they believed in me, believed in themselves, and that gave me confidence. It still gives me confidence. It allows me to see the fear, recognize it, and push forward confidently anyway. They (among many others) lifted me (still lift me) up.

Do you fear success? My best advice to you is to align yourself with those who will lift you up. Spend time with those who will help you to push forward, who see you as the special, capable woman that you are. I promise you, it will change your life, it did mine.

May 2, 2016

"Don't dig up in doubt what you have planted in faith." Have you ever done this? Established your business plan, set your goals, prepared your pop bys all with faith in yourself and what you can accomplish ... then doubted yourself to the point that you stop, fall short, don't follow through? I've seen it happen over and over again with wonderful people in our industry. I see it happen with me.

It's one of the reasons I try NOT to be seen when dropping off my pop bys. I'm sure if someone is watching when I do these, it must be hysterical. A couple weeks ago I dropped off a couple pop bys to two past clients, both of whom I haven't seen in person in several years, and who live in the same neighborhood as another client I was visiting for lunch. I was prepared, excited, ready to do my pop bys. Then it was actually time to do them.
As I slowly drive down their street and begin to approach the house, the doubt hits. What if they're home? What if they don't remember me? What if they are annoyed that I stopped by? Maybe I shouldn't stop, is that a car in their driveway?

Then (after sometimes driving by twice) it's now or never ... I pull up (always with the driver's side towards the house), usually double parked, and in an instant, flashers on, open my door (leave it open for a quick exit) and sprint to the door. It is surely the fastest and quietest I ever move in my entire life. Hang the bag on the doorknob, run back to the car, careful not to look around so as to not make eye contact with anyone. Once back in my car and safely up the street I send them a message letting them know I was in the neighborhood and dropped something off at their door.

Does this sound familiar to you at all? It's kind of crazy when you think about it ... has someone ever dropped off a little gift at your house or place or business that had you annoyed? That you didn't appreciate or remember them? So then why do we doubt ourselves? When you set a goal for yourself, do you start to back track on it as you doubt your ability to achieve it? When it comes time to implement that business plan that you carefully and thoughtfully put together, do you begin to slowly pick it apart until you are back to the "safe" version that is just "okay" and will keep you in the same spot in your business year after year?

The next time the doubt shows up, whether in the form of an actual person or the voice in your head, look the other way. Take an action step toward what you are afraid of, no matter how small. Call or message a friend or colleague who will help boost you up and keep those roots firmly planted. Take a time out, go for a walk, preview a property, remember again why what you are striving to achieve is important to you, your business, your family. Stay in faith, it's the best place to be.

May 9, 2016

I love this quote by Lily Tomlin, "I always wondered why somebody doesn't do something about that. Then I realized I was somebody." Haven't we all said or thought some version of "why doesn't somebody do something about that" from time to time?

In our business, it's the agents sharing lockbox keys, or who don't even have keys and have their clients view properties via the listing agent. It's the buyer who is regularly 20-30 minutes late to each appointment, then wants to add on one or two more houses on the spot. It's the agents who feel that the best way to represent their client is to fight with the agent on the other side every step of the way.

Frustrating, isn't it? You wonder why, and perhaps have even said to your colleague or turned to your broker and asked why someone doesn't do something. Guess what? You are someone, and you can do something.

Agents sharing lockbox keys, or not showing up to remove their lockbox days after settlement? My association has a list of very specific fine-able offenses. Take action. Report it. Move on, instead of continuing to complain.

Are your sellers exasperated because agents don't extend the courtesy of leaving a business card after showing their home, thereby signifying that they were there? Are you banging your head against the wall because agents won't provide you with feedback after showing your listing, no matter how many times you call, email, send surveys? We all miss things from time to time, but I have found that the agent who is consistently unprofessional in one area, is or will be unprofessional in others.

Raise the bar yourself. Model the behavior you want to see. Conduct business the way it should be done. Your colleagues will notice and will want to work with you when you present offers on their listings or when you have a listing that their buyer is considering. The consumer will notice that you do things differently, handle yourself differently. Sometimes that means speaking up when they are consistently late for the appointment and explaining why it is difficult (or not possible) to add on additional properties on the spot. Sometimes it just means saying no and moving on to those you can help who respect what your do and your time too. No matter how big or small, there is always something that you can do, often just by improving your own actions.

May 11, 2016

I really like this quote ... "hustle beats talent when talent doesn't hustle." Isn't it so true? Especially in our industry. I'm on my 14th year in real estate. I work hard, happily. I no longer have that worry if I'm going to "make it" in this business. I'm fortunate to have a very loyal customer and referral base. Since coming back to the field last June I feel a "calmness" about my business that I've never felt before, which is so refreshing.

All of these things are great, but they can also lead to complacency. You can get too comfortable. Stop learning. Stop growing. It can feel like you have everything figured out, but the truth is our business, our market, the way we communicate and reach those clients and prospects is constantly changing, constantly evolving. If we don't keep learning ourselves, making adjustments in our business, eventually, it will affect our business.

I get it, how are you going to keep learning and trying new things when you are already so busy? You have to make time. Schedule an appointment with yourself or others. This doesn't need to be an overwhelming task. Take a class at your brokerage or association level. Have a "mastermind" session with other agents. This can be a great way to learn new ideas and get to know each other.

We are getting close to 2000 women in the real estate industry from all over the country in this group! Start here, find a few women in your area and schedule a casual lunch or coffee for next week, or a even just a call. Use the power of your network to learn and grow.

May 13, 2016

Why do so many of us look outside ourselves for safety, security, validation? Have you ever done this? I certainly have, particularly when I was much younger, in my teens and early twenties. It shows up in unhealthy relationships. It shows up in bullying too. The mean girls who find their validation and success in trying to push down or detract from others.

It can also show up in our business, in the lies we tell ourselves. That we can't be successful without "x" (a person, place or thing to hang onto). Or in the stories that others tell us to try to keep us where they want us (you can't do it without me). The bottom line is that you can. Really, you probably already have, you just don't recognize it.

I've learned this twice over for myself in my career. Hearing I'd never make it or do as well without _____. Only both times, I did. And both times came out so much better, so much stronger on the other side than if I had stayed stuck where I was.

In her new book, "Find Your Extraordinary" by Jessica Herrin (a great read!), the author talks about how in business we know what to do, we just need the motivation and inspiration to actually do it. Isn't that so true? We know that we need to preview listings. We know that we need to call our clients to check in. We know that we need to ask for referrals. We know all of these things and more, but yet we struggle with the motivation, the push to actually get it done. This is our career, and so many of us treat it as our hobby.

The mind is a powerful tool. YOUR mind is your most powerful asset. Make the decision to live the life you want, to make things happen for yourself, to do the things you already know to do. To build the type of business you want on your terms. You can, and when you fully understand that you will.

May 23, 2016

It's Monday! What does your day look like today? If you had appointments all weekend, then maybe today is a day "off" or day of rest for you. Early in my career I had the opportunity to work with a coach and after months and months of working 7 days per week one of the first things she taught me was that I truly needed a day off each week in order to be my most productive. Ideally two days, but we started with one. No appointments, a periodic check in with email and voicemail, and then the day to myself. That was my Monday for quite a long time.

Now my day(s) off more often fall on the weekend, and so Monday is the start of the work week for me. For today, I'm starting my morning spending some time planning out my week, a listing appointment midday, signing a new listing early afternoon, then doing a staging "walk through" for a friend/colleague for their own personal home before it goes on the market.

My plan is to wrap up the day by 5 so we can have an early dinner together as a family before my husband goes to a little league baseball meeting tonight. As much as I love to have my day free flowing, I know that I am my most efficient and effective when I have a schedule identified for my day. Time for email, time for follow ups, time for appointments. I know that when I plan my work intentionally, then I can also plan my "play" time intentionally.

June 8, 2016

Have you ever experienced a "summer slump" in your business?
I've certainly witnessed it (and participated in it) before but didn't really have a "name" for it until I saw a Tom Ferry video a week or so ago. Summer is here, the weather is beautiful, kids are out of school or are about to be out, and vacation season is about to be in full swing. If you have children at home, it can be logistically harder to work during the summer, and hey, you might want to actually enjoy it too, right?

So how do you balance REALLY ENJOYING your summer and not completely shutting your business down for the rest of the year? (which is what will effectively happen if you check out for the summer)

We discussed some ideas for how to do this during our team meeting yesterday. Here are a few of my favorites:

-Timeblock (surprise!) both work and play time. Pull out a calendar, maybe print a blank monthly view from online, and start filling in all the things ... kids' camps, vacations, barbecues, scheduled events. Now fill in the fun time you want to have. Want to spend two days a week at the pool? Block off those days and build in your work time. Maybe you work from 9-12 those days, and spend the rest of the day poolside, maybe you plan longer hours working the other days of the week. It is possible to have fun and still have a productive business this time of year.

-Partner up with a "vacation" buddy. Plan to cover for each other's vacations so you can truly relax and enjoy your family time. Maybe even plan with them to trade off some "fun day" coverage too ... is it your afternoon at the pool? Maybe they could be your back up to help with business or last-minute showing requests, and you do the same for them when they are spending the day on the golf course, etc.

-Set a summer goal. This could be number of transactions but will probably be more impactful for your future business to base it on activities. A certain number of pop bys. A certain number of hours per week working ON your business, following up, previewing, etc. Involve your partner, spouse, children in the goal too! Plan a reward, maybe a fun family trip, that is dependent on you delivering 30 pop bys this summer. I'd be willing to bet that suddenly you will have lots of little accountability partners and people around you wanting to help you prep and deliver them!

-Establish an easy summer marketing plan. Maybe it is a regular post with a focus on fun local community events. Maybe it is a summer client party. Maybe it is a list of summer "helpers" (pet sitters, lawn care services, pool cleaners, etc.) that you mail.

The work that we do today we will be paid for in about 3 months. The quality of your fall business is dependent on the activities you do this summer. Do them intentionally, and also play and have fun intentionally, you can do both.

June 10, 2016

One of our discussions this week at our team meeting was about how to protect yourself from toxic people and toxic transactions. Have you ever had one of those? Unfortunately, if you've had the opportunity to interact with at least a few clients then you've likely come across some of these people or been in a transaction with them. People who are rude, disrespectful of you, your time, your knowledge, your experience. I truly believe that some of them just don't know any better or understand how our industry works. Others are just mean people who will do and say whatever to get what they want. They will drain you of your drive, your energy, and your ability to serve your other clients.

So, when you find yourself in one of these situations, what do you do? How do you get out of it? First, as painful as it may be, I think you must have an open conversation. Separate the facts about the situation/behavior from what you are guessing (I think they call me with one hour's notice to see homes because they don't respect me or my time) and ask questions. If the conversation doesn't go well, or you just know that this is not someone you want to work with, I have two scripts to share with you. One for the client that may just be a bad personality mix for you and would do well with someone else, the other that you wouldn't give to your worst enemy.

For the client/prospect who is referable ...
"Jim, I have so enjoyed working with you. I'd like to connect you with my colleague Suzy moving forward. Based on your needs and style of doing business, I know that she can provide the very best service to you. She will be giving you a call within the hour."

For the client/prospect who is not referable ...
"Joe, I would really like to be able to help you, but at this point what you require from your agent and the market is more than I can give. I wish you the very best."

The key to being able to avoid these types of clients in the first place is working by referral and regular prospecting and engagement with your database. When you have choices ... meaning a strong pipeline of good people to work with ... it is easier to say no to the ones that are bad than if they are the only prospects you have. You don't have to settle for that.

June 22, 2016

What are some of the challenges that you are experiencing in your business? Not enough business? Difficult/disrespectful clients? Need more consistent transactions?

The answer to everything that ails your business is prospecting. (I just heard the collective groan)

Think about it ... Not enough business? Prospecting will enlarge your database and bring more business. Working with difficult/disrespectful clients? Prospecting will bring more leads to your business which in turn gives you more choice and will allow you to more confidently address and weed out the bad ones. Need more consistency? Prospecting consistently will bring more leads and more opportunities on a consistent basis which will lead to a more balanced and consistent business.

Now look, I even groan a little when I talk about prospecting, but I think that is because we need to change our language, our definition of prospecting. Yes, prospecting can mean cold calling and door knocking, but those are just two forms. There are so many different ways that you can prospect. Cold calling and door knocking aren't me. I've never done them, and never plan to start. I know agents who do, and they are extremely successful, and that's great. They have found what works for them, and they do it consistently. So, what works for you?

Prospecting is also lunch with past clients, coffee with your favorite vendors, delivering pop bys, sending a client appreciation mailing/email each month, sitting an open house, engaging with social media (not just sharing funny cat videos, I love those too, but that isn't prospecting), writing a real estate blog or feature in your local paper or HOA newsletter.

Prospecting is any proactive ACTION that you take to engage with others in a way that could potentially grow your business. The key word there is action. The second key word not in that sentence, but possibly more important is consistency. You must find time to prospect consistently, make it part of your daily routine. If that seems overwhelming at first, then start with a 1-hour appointment with yourself each week to focus on taking deliberate prospecting action in your business. Then next month increase that to 2 hours per week, and so on. My guess though is that once you start to see the results and benefits of regular prospecting you will get hooked on it and make it part of your regular routine. That is when you will make the shift from a purely transactional real estate agent to a business owner.

June 23, 2016

Today will be one of my most productive days all year! The reason? I am on vacation starting tomorrow! Are you like that also? Super focused and productive right before you leave for a trip or vacation. It is amazing the things you can get done in a short period of time when the goal is right in front of you and the motivation is there.

Taking vacations can feel difficult in this business. I've known many agents over the years who never tell their clients that they will be away for fear of losing something. I've known agents who basically work through their whole vacation. That isn't a vacation, it's just working in a different location. Getting away can be hard, but is worth it and necessary, and your business does not need to stop in order for you to have that break.

Today I will notify all of my current clients who have active or under contract listings, buyers who are under contract or actively looking, agents I am involved in transactions with currently, as well as potential clients that I am talking with but who have not signed yet that I will be away. I will introduce them (via email) to my business partner who is covering for me and I make the point to tell them that my partner can do everything for them that I can ... show property, write contracts, negotiate offers on their listing with them, get a new listing started, etc. I think it is important to specifically say the words of what they can do so there is no confusion or fear to reach out to them.
I also send a summary email of what and who I have pending or is likely to pop up while I am away to my partner that is covering for me, and tonight or tomorrow morning I will change my voicemail to indicate that I am out of the office and set my email out of office auto reply including coverage details.

With so many people texting these days, I also set up a keyboard shortcut (on the iPhone, it is under settings, general, keyboard, text replacement) that says that I am out of the office, until when, and to please contact my partner and provide her number. This way if I get a text, I only have to type in a few letters to get this message to pop up and send vs typing it all out each time and looking up my partners phone number.

While I am away, I don't communicate about work with anyone but the person covering me and only if necessary. I do check my email, usually in the morning before the rest of my family is up and sometimes in the afternoon. The only time I respond is if it is a new client/referral reaching out to me for the first time, in which case I reply and connect them with my partner and assure them that they can help until I return. Anything else that may come through that is time sensitive I will forward to my partner in case they didn't get the message. I've been doing vacations like this 2-3 times a year throughout my career for as far back as I can remember and as far as I am aware it has never cost me any business.

My very first year in business, maybe 6 weeks into my career, we had an extended family vacation scheduled that had been scheduled for months. I had a buyer that I was working with who wasn't very respectful of my time, and I was too new and unsure and didn't have enough other prospects to manage that confidently. Not only did I start my vacation late by a day or two to accommodate him, but we came back early after only 3-4 days there. I effectively ruined not only my vacation, but my soon to be husbands as well, and impacted that of the family we were vacationing alongside. That buyer never bought anything. Ever. Not from me, or anyone else (I checked the tax records). I vowed after that experience never to let that happen again.

July 15, 2016

Do you spend dedicated time each day or week prospecting for new business? Prospecting can be such a dirty word. We had a great discussion about this at our team mid-year "state of the union" earlier this week. What does the word "prospecting" mean to you? The first thought is usually door knocking and cold calls. Activities that for many of us (including me) are not part of our business plan. However, prospecting for new business is vital to our businesses. We just need to reframe it, change how we think of it.

Prospecting is not just cold calling. It is also going to lunch or coffee with a past client or vendor. It's sitting an open house, delivering pop bys, hosting a client event, engaging on social media. These are all specific activities, taking action, which actively allows you to connect with others in a way that can (and will) grow your business. We handed out a sheet of 25 ways to prospect at our meeting ... and cold calling and door knocking didn't make the list!

We don't need to fear prospecting and the perceived rejection that can come along with it. Take a moment and step outside of the traditional "prospecting" box and think of things that you are already doing or can implement in your business that allows you to actively engage with others in a way that can grow your business.

July 20, 2016

Recently I was listening to a podcast and the realtor being interviewed talked about the concept of resting instead of quitting. This resonated with me so deeply. In 2012 I was having one of my very best years ever in business, but thought I had to do it all myself. I didn't understand how to delegate, how to ask for help, and definitely not how to rest. With three young children at home (my boys were 8, 6 and 2 at the time), and personally closing well over 50 transactions that year I was TIRED.

Even with taking a vacation where I mostly unplugged, and taking Sundays each week with no appointments, I didn't really understand how to turn it off or take a break. I would squander my time during the day if I wasn't on appointments by running some errands, or if I was working at my computer, I would spend hours endlessly researching something, anything that would help me to feel better, to be more productive. Then it would be time for my nanny to go home, I'd spend time with my family, then after they were in bed I would stay up into the wee hours of the night "catching up". Does this sound familiar to anyone?

Instead of learning to rest, learning how to properly manage my time, my energy and my business, I quit. After 10 years in business, I quit to become a managing broker. It seemed like the perfect answer, only it wasn't. I truly enjoyed the work, and loved so many of the people, but in time I came to see that it wasn't a good fit. That it wasn't the right fit for me. Unfortunately, it took the loss of my mother and the subsequent life changes for me to see that, but that is a story for another day.

Now, a little older, a little wiser, I've been back in the business of real estate sales, starting my business over, for 13 months now. This year I am on track to come very close to matching that last crazy busy year in production, with already having closed 28 transactions year to date. The difference this time, is I don't feel as tired.

I'm a wife, I'm a mom of 3 boys, I have a house, dogs, cats, and an aging parent to take care of, all on top of a busy, wonderful career that I love that includes a team of 12 incredible women to look after, help, manage and care for along with my business partner. I'm tired, I should be tired. You should be too. The difference now is that I am learning to rest. Learning to delegate, to ask for help, whether it is at work or at home. Now, with the right infrastructure in place for my business, strong systems and good energy and people, I've been able to get outside of my own head (because inside I have to do it all, just so, inside is hard), see more, understand more, do more ... and rest more.

Are you tired? When is the last time you rested in response to feeling tired? I'm not talking about just how many hours of sleep you get a night, but actually taking time off, time unplugged, taking a break for you. Whether it is 2 hours on a Tuesday afternoon to turn off your phone and read a book, or 20 minutes today to take a nap or a walk outside before lunch, when you feel tired, rest.

July 26, 2016
In order to help my youngest son get ready for full day school in the fall, we've been meeting with a counselor to work on some behaviors that can help

him to be more successful (last year was a little bumpy). To help him (and us) he has a point chart for the things that he is working on, and he can save up his points and cash them in on things like extra video game time, a toy at Target, etc. Needless to say, he is a fan of the chart and very motivated when something he wants or is interested in is on the line. As a result, during our first couple weeks of doing this, he immediately started working the system. For example, one of the behaviors is saying excuse me. He is the youngest of 3 boys, and when other people/his brothers are talking he would constantly interrupt and talk over them to get the attention of the person he wanted, even though he didn't really have anything to say. So, we've been working on saying excuse me, acknowledging that he has something to say ("just a moment"), and he waits patiently until it's his turn. Except when he wants to earn points for something, he wasn't quite doing it that way. He would walk up to anyone in our family, even when no one was talking and say, "excuse me", then of course pointing out to me what a great job he did.

I mentioned this to the counselor at our next session, and she said something that really stuck with me. She said that by practicing the behavior like this when it didn't really matter (or even really apply) would help to make it that much easier when the situation is harder, and it really counts. Think about that for a moment. We think about and promote practicing for things like sports, or playing an instrument, for performances, being in a play or dance number, but really, this applies so much to real life and our businesses. When is the last time you practiced your listing presentation, or have you ever? How about words to say or questions to ask when qualifying a new buyer or helping them to decide which home is right for them? My guess is probably not often, or even at all.

Brian Buffini talks about how in real estate our on-the-job training isn't really training at all but happens in real life scenarios in front of clients when it counts most. Many real estate coaches are big advocates of practicing your "scripts" with others and role playing. I certainly did my fair share of that in the beginning of my career and now looking back find that it was invaluable, even though I didn't like it. There is huge benefit to that, but there is also benefit in taking each real estate opportunity seriously and applying your full effort, even when it seems like a waste of time, if for nothing more than to make you better and to practice. Personally, I need to re-read that last sentence every day. I HATE wasting time, but like most things in life, it's all about your attitude and how your approach it. It's not wasting time; it's helping you to build your skills and grow your business.

So, the next time you have the opportunity to show a house to a new buyer that you are pretty sure is a waste of time, take an hour and do it anyway. That is a terrific chance to practice presenting the buyer agency agreement and asking questions and communicating with a potential buyer. When the dreaded internet lead comes in and doesn't answer the phone or respond to your first email, practice your follow up skills and tenacity. When you get a call for a listing appointment that is a major long shot (their best friend is a realtor too, they aren't planning to move for another year), go anyway and give your very best presentation. When you have the client who runs all over you and is disrespectful of your time, practice saying no and taking control of the scheduling, so when it really counts (an appointment conflicting with an important event with your spouse or child) it will be easier to do what you need to do.

Practice doesn't just make perfect (there's no such thing), but practice does make it easier to do the right thing, respond at your best, and grow your business when it really counts.

August 15, 2016

It's a sunny, beautiful late summer Monday morning here in Northern Virginia. My kids are still asleep, even my dogs slept in this morning (which means I slept in this morning). On a day like today, or on any day really, what motivates you to get going, to get to the office, to get your work done?

We all know what we need to do to work on our business. Make our calls, follow up with current clients and leads, make appointments, preview properties, not to mention all the work in our business to ensure that the details of our transactions are going smoothly, and our listings are being properly marketed. We know what to do, but sometimes it is hard to actually do it, to take action. It is easier to fall down the rabbit hole of the internet looking for a great new tool to help stay organized or to make those follow ups easier, when really there is no substitute for just doing it. It is easier to be busy, than it is to be truly productive.

Les Brown has a quote that I love, "If you do what is easy, your life will be hard. If you do what is hard, your life will be easy." We all need some motivation now and then, so what motivates you? Is it fun contests or challenges with your team or colleagues? Is it staying focused on your big why? Is it money? Is it your goal? Is it accountability to a person or coach? On a beautiful day like today when it would be so easy to do something else, what motivates you to stay on track, to take action?

August 22, 2016

What do you have faith in? Yourself? God, a power greater than you? The universe? Your spouse, partner, family? Your business, clients?

My word of the year for 2016 is faith. At the beginning of the year, I intentionally bought cute little signs with my word on it as a reminder and put them in places I would see them most often. The counter in my bathroom, my family room, by my desk at home, on the wall in my office.

Faith for me this year has looked like many different things. Learning more about my spiritual faith. Having faith that everything will work out with respect to some specific challenges. Being faithful in my belief that there is a plan for me, my family, my team, my business. Mostly, having faith has meant trusting. Trusting that no matter how much I want to control everything, that someone/something else is in control, and that plan is so much bigger than anything I could ever dream up for myself.

This quote stopped me when I saw it in my Facebook feed. "Faith doesn't make things easier; it makes them possible." Because I have faith in God, myself, my husband, my family, my business partner, my team, my friends, my business, anything is possible. Because I have faith in what I am doing, in the plan designed for me, anything is possible. That is a powerful truth worth trusting.

August 24, 2016

During my team meeting yesterday, we had a great conversation about prospecting. It's been our theme for the 2nd half of 2016, and something that we have been spending a lot of time talking about, thinking about, and taking action on. Yesterday we were talking about farming ... not the kind that my family did raising cattle, vegetables and grain a couple decades ago in my hometown, but the kind we do in real estate. Most often you hear agents talk about their geographic farm, the area that they focus on and market to, which could mean a specific neighborhood, town or even an entire zip code.

You can farm other things too. Your database (that one should be a given), a special interest group or community. Think about where you spend your time. Do you volunteer with a local dog rescue? Spend time at your child's school or with the PTO? Are you part of a local running club, youth sports group, church, civic organization? All of those can be your farm.

The key, I think, with farming, and really anything else we do in our business, is consistency. There isn't anything I can think of in this business that will provide you with an immediate result where you do it once, and you have a lead that closes ... I mean, we would all be "real" top producers if that was the case. The closest thing to that is probably an open house, but that varies too. How many do you sit where no one comes, or all the visitors have agents already, and then you walk away from another one with several great new buyers to work with? Our job requires consistency (so does most everything in life, by the way), and the tendency can be to stop when you don't receive the desired result quickly. You can send a mailer 3 times, call an internet lead back twice, sit 1 open house, email 5 newsletters and get no results ... until you send the 4th one, call a 3rd time, sit the 2nd open, and email for the 6th month in a row. It's about tenacity. It's our job. If you think it won't work, then it won't. But if you see the possibilities and focus on the activities, it absolutely will.

August 29, 2016

Today marks the first day of school for my children here in Northern Virginia. I've always loved the first day of school! It's a chance for a fresh start, a new beginning. Almost like a new year starting over. This year, for the first time ever, all 3 of my boys will be in school all day, with my youngest starting 1st grade, my middle starting 5th grade, and my oldest starting 7th grade. This is a bittersweet feeling, an end to the "little kid" season of my life. I tossed and turned for a long-time last night, remembering how first grade is such a year of transition. At the beginning of the year, they are still so young, and by the end they are more mature, more responsible. The days of them wanting to hold my hand are numbered, and the times that my youngest wants to curl up on my lap or snuggle next to me will likely end before I realize the time that was the last time.

It is the end of one season, and the beginning of another. More than anything, I love watching them grow and helping them to be independent. I love listening to them as they learn to voice their own opinions. It's frightening too. They are so pure and innocent, how do I make sure I am not making them afraid of new experiences and different places? How do I make sure they aren't afraid to take chances, to try new things, that they feel empowered and confident to be who they are?

Today, like most days, I am so grateful for this career and this business. All of my children were born after I started in real estate. Having the flexibility to be there for them, to volunteer in their classrooms, to be present is truly a gift. I tried to trade that in once for more security, and learned very quickly that the price was high, too high for me. This is where I belong.

September 8, 2016

On Tuesday my team and I went to a terrific class called the "Zone of Genius" led by Matt James and sponsored by a local title company. One of the exercises we were asked to do was to list out all of the tasks and activities that we did for our business over the course of the past week. My list had things like listing appointments, team/retreat planning, 2017 marketing planning, ratifying contracts, responding to emails, signing listings, payroll, mentoring meetings, agent interviews, scheduling appointments, appointment prep, and so on.

Then he had us plot these tasks on a matrix. There were four quadrants with boxes for incompetencies, competencies, excellence and zone of genius. The idea was that the boxes above the line were things that bring you joy, raise your energy level, make money, move your business forward, and that you are good at, and below the line you dread, have a negative (or a neutral) effect on your energy, you aren't good at, could be done by someone else, may or may not make you money, etc.

Plotting this out was so eye opening to me! First, I felt so grateful that my tasks were pretty equally split above and below the line. Most interesting though was what was in my zone of genius. For me, one of those is going on listing appointments/presentations. When I'm there, I LOVE it. Absolute joy. I love learning about the house, presenting my strategies, answering questions, reviewing pricing, all of it. When I leave, I feel pumped up, excited, confident. But, I dread these appointments. Dread them. That makes no sense. How can something that I enjoy so much and do so well at be something that I don't necessarily look forward to?

I realized through the exercise that because of all of the other things on my to do list, namely those below the line, that the appointments feel like a distraction from getting all the things done. Only really, I need to shift my mindset. It is the other things that are the distraction, and the priority is the appointment. Since the class I haven't had time to do much with this information yet, but I did go into my appointments yesterday with more excitement. My thought is to plot out all of my responsibilities and tasks on the matrix (including personal ones) to help me to better identify where I need to be focusing and where I need to let go, delegate, or maybe even drop all together. What would be in your "zone of genius"?

September 11, 2016

September 11, 2001, is one of those days in history where people who were adults (or even older children) remember where they were (route 340) and what they were doing (driving to work) when they heard of the attacks. They likely remember what they were doing before (hanging up laundry on my clothesline and thinking what a perfectly beautiful day it was), and in the days after (on standby at the firehouse). Accounts of witnesses and survivors are chilling, horrifying, often inspiring. When the absolute worst of humanity shows itself, the absolute best rises above and to the top every.single.time.

Heroes, both those for whom it is a job, a calling, and regular folks step in and step up and we remember them and their actions with gratitude.

September 11, 2009, in the wee hours of the morning was the definition of bittersweet. Only with pain and anguish combined with the sweetness and excitement of a first-born baby when my friend gave birth very, very early to her precious, and still, baby girl, then went home empty handed.

Later that morning in the same hospital, I checked in preparing to give birth to my third born son, when my nurse comes in to turn down the volume on my fetal monitor. The mom in the next room just had a loss and could hear my baby's strong heartbeat where hers was gone. A couple more hours pass, and my sweet boy is born. September 11th will forever be a day that I am overwhelmed with gratitude for God's goodness.

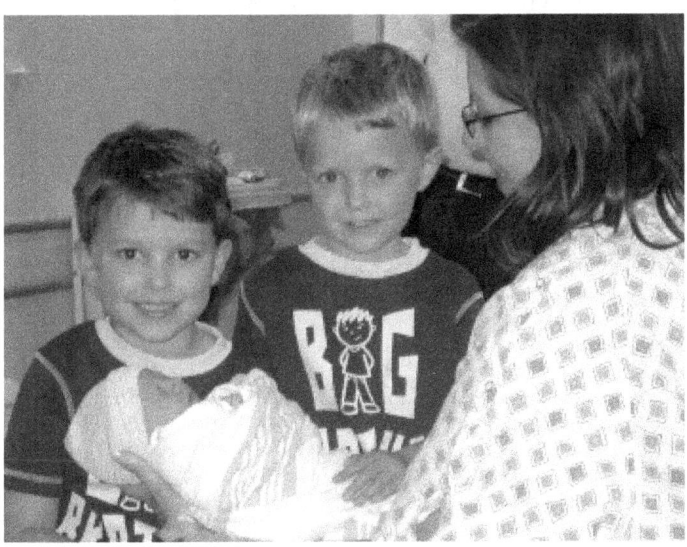

September 15, 2016

"The grass is greener where you water it." I can't remember where I first heard this, or who it originated from, but it really struck a chord with me. It is so easy in our jam-packed lives and especially in our industry to fall into this trap. So many parts of our business are hard. Long and often unpredictable hours. Constant ups and downs in market fluctuations, leads and business. When things feel hard, it is so easy to focus on that and look longingly elsewhere. The biggest example of this for me was 4 years ago. My business was booming, I was severely underutilizing my part time assistant and running myself into the ground. I was exhausted. I remember many days sitting at my computer in tears and fantasizing what it would be like to have a

9 to 5 job again. To just show up somewhere at start time, do my work, and come home at my end time. It seemed like such a dream, not to mention the steady paycheck.

Then a couple months later I was approached out of the blue by the owner of my then brokerage who had been acting in the managing broker role saying it was time for them to hire someone for the position. He was sure I wouldn't be interested but wanted to talk to me first. The grass seemed SO green on that side! I jumped relatively quickly and without a lot of hesitation.

It was great for a while, only I quickly realized I was still working long hours and had given up my independence. Gone was the creativity in my business, and the flexibility to plan my schedule around my family. I was the executor, performing and delivering on the tasks and plan that was set forth and given to me, no matter how I felt about it. The grass isn't always greener on the other side. It is greener where you water it.

I've been back in the field now for a little over a year. The hard parts of this business are still here, but my attitude, mindset, focus has changed. I understand more than ever that it is truly what you make of it. If you think that postcard mailer won't work, if you say that call nights aren't your thing, if you think that internet leads are a waste of time then guess what? You're right. Your action and your focus will follow your mindset and your words, and you will struggle in your business over and over and over again.

Try watering your business where you stand. Put a positive focus on it. Apply a concentrated effort. Focus on the parts that are good, and soon the parts that aren't will become less and less of an issue for you.

September 26, 2016

We all know this person, probably have even been this person a time or two ... the person who through their actions or inactions, willingly or blindly create problems or drama in their life, and then get upset by it.

I'm doing it right now. I've been up since 4 am on flooded basement watch. 11 years ago, when we had our pool put in, they crushed the gravity drain coming out of our basement. Not necessarily a huge deal, except when we receive large volumes of heavy, heavy rain (like today). We only discovered the issue 8 or 9 years ago when our basement flooded after several days of heavy rain. It hasn't flooded since, but we worry on days like this, and water has started backing up in our basement stairwell, so we have to put in a little submersible pump and turn it on every hour or so to make sure it doesn't flood the basement. Of course, the days when this happens always seems to also be on days that my husband is at work and my schedule is especially full. Like today.

Now, the root cause issue (crushed drain) isn't my fault, and certainly I can't control the rain, but what I can control is a repair and it hasn't been a priority. Between frustrating and lackadaisical contractors, and just so many other things that are more in our face and demanding immediate attention, this hasn't been on the list. Except on days like today. When it's too late of course. My inaction is making this much harder right now than it needs to be.

We do this in our business too. The complaints, frustrations, even whining about not having enough business or good leads or upset about the leads that we do end up working with because there aren't enough options. Yet, we don't take action. We don't take the time or money to invest in our business, to focus on our database or lead generation. If you don't do the activities, you can't expect to get the results, simple as that.

Nothing is promised, and little is just given, and generally that which is "easy" will tend to come with the highest price. You need to be invested in your life, your business, yourself. Staying down in the hole of the frustration and the "why me" and "it's not fair" isn't going to get you anywhere. Take action, do the work, so when it rains, you'll be ready, and maybe even able to dance in it.

September 28, 2016

Yesterday during a business lunch meeting with a friend, the topic of opportunities came up. He said that opportunities are like the sunrise, they come and go, and if we don't catch them when they appear, that particular one is gone, never to be repeated.

I thought that was a great analogy. We were talking about it within the framework of business readiness ... laying the groundwork, the foundation, having the systems in place in your business so that you are ready when the opportunity presents itself, but it can be applied in lots of different ways.

How about when you receive a new lead or inquiry, or a phone call from a referral? If it takes you several hours to get back to that person, the opportunity is likely missed completely, or the relationship starts off on a less than professional tone (this happened to me just yesterday).

If you are a broker or team leader, this happens when growing. Agents don't classically move around a lot. When I have made changes, it was usually after 6-7 years, and most agents I know are about the same. If you miss an opportunity to connect with an agent who will be a great fit for your team or brokerage, that opportunity is gone, as they aren't likely to make another move anytime soon.

Keep your eyes open for the sunrises, for the opportunities in your life and your business. Take time to plan and prepare for them so you are ready when they come along. That is the true mark of a business owner. Be purposeful, intentional about your business and your life. Then, when the sunrise appears, you are ready to soak it all in.

October 5, 2016
Fear is a liar. Think about that for a moment.

Sometimes fear is that person, well intentioned or not, words spoken out loud or how they make you feel, who tells you that you can't do it. You can't do it without them. You can't do it because no one in your family has ever done it before. You can't do it because it may not be safe, you don't know how. You aren't good enough, worthy enough, capable.

I've worked intentionally for many, many years (and sometimes over and over again) to remove those people from my life. Instead, now the voice of fear tends to be in my own head. I can't do that. Who am I to think that I could do that. No one cares what I have to say. That isn't safe, I'm safer at home. I can't do that because I don't know how, no one I know has ever done that before. I'm not good enough, worthy enough, capable.

It's all a lie. Every word of it.

You can. You can do it on your own, without them, him, her, anyone. You can be the first in your family, first amongst the people that you know, to accomplish that. You know whether something is really safe (physically or emotionally) or not and can distinguish the difference. You can figure out how. There are people who care what you say, who care about learning from others, collaborating.

Don't let your fear or the fear that others have and try to place on you keep you small, in a dark corner, quiet. You are capable, I am capable. Expose fear for the liar it is. For me that usually means taking action, doing something that is uncomfortable, even if it is just a baby step. Embrace the truth of who you are and what you can do. You can, and that is the truth.

October 12, 2016

I'm currently on vacation with my family at Walt Disney World. We love to come here, no matter how many times we come there are still so many different things to see and experience, the environment is "controlled" enough to appeal to my fearful side, yet open enough that I feel like we are exploring each time.

One of the things we love are riding roller coasters. As a little girl I remember my dad taking us to theme parks every summer teaching us to ride them all with our hands up in the air. I do the same with my boys, and they love them too, although my middle son is sometimes a little apprehensive at first, usually once he rides once he loves it and wants to do it again.

My husband is different though, he has always feared the rides. Every time we go, he tends to try something new that he hasn't done before and loves it every time. On Monday we talked him into riding Space Mountain for the first time ... it's a roller coaster that takes place in a building, in the dark, fast, going in circles, up, down, super fun! He has always worried that it would make him sick. We were talking about it, and I suggested that he just get on and not think, it's the thinking that causes the problems and talks us out of things. Sure enough ... he rode, loved it, and now wishes he had tried it before thinking of all of the other trips that he sat out, missing the fun.

How many times do we do this in our lives and our businesses? We over think. We read the warnings, over and over again. We listen to others who are afraid themselves and take on their fear and worry. What if instead we just stopped thinking, let go, and just do it, take action, make the change? I know in my own life whenever I've done this my only regret has been not doing it sooner. Even if you don't like it, it's a "failure", you are uncomfortable, at least you know. You can stop thinking about it and move on to taking action on something else.

Trust me, I know how hard it is to stop the overthinking. I come from a long line of female role models in the overthinking and worrying department. I learned that it would be better to stay home, inside and safe than to risk being out, exposed, uncomfortable. The problem is, how much are you really living then? Stop being a spectator, be an active participant in your life. Get out there, stop overthinking, let go, take risks and have fun. Who knows where it will take you!

October 26, 2016

I love words. I love to read them, listen to them, speak them. Beautifully strung together words to make a point or inspire are like music to my ears.

Whenever I hear or read things that I love, quotes, little snippets, words that motivate or inspire me, I quickly jot them down in the notes app in my iPhone. Anytime I need a quick boost, I'll read through it. When I am prepping for the "quote of the week" for our team meeting I read through it. Oftentimes when looking for inspiration to post here I'll read through it.

One that I have heard, written down, and used this week was by Tom Ferry. I've heard him say it probably hundreds of times in his videos and podcasts ... "what got you here will not get you there." That resonates with me so much. In every area of our business and life, when you are growing, learning, striving, the things that you did to get you to where you are now will not get you to that next "level", whatever that is for you. Whether it is growing your business, expanding your database, improving your health, growing in your role as a mother or partner, in order to level up you have to grow too.

Try new things. Step outside of your comfort zone. Sometimes changing your surroundings in terms of physical space, and even in terms of people. The plateaus will come. Maybe you have landed at a good spot, maybe you're comfortable. I have found that with your business eventually it will start to slip as others around you grow and stretch and do new things. The times when I have grown the most in my business, made the biggest strides was when I learned something new, tried something new, stretched beyond what was comfortable, and set my ego aside. My ego thought I knew enough. I was doing well. I don't need to learn anything. What I'm doing works. The working and doing well part may have been true enough, but eventually I got stuck ... it was only when I started focusing on learning, realizing all of the wonderful different ways there are out there to run and grow my business (my way wasn't the only good way), that the magic really started to happen.

So, take a few minutes today and think about what got you to where you are today, and where you want to go. Then figure out what that next new step will be and act on it. Don't be afraid to learn, to try, to do, to act, it will make all the difference.

October 28, 2016

Yesterday I finished the book, "Loving My Actual Life", by Alexandra Kuykendall. It's a great little read. The author essentially takes on a bit of a happiness project in her own life by identifying one area that she would focus on each month for 9 months. For example, one month she focused on exercise, one month quiet time, one month building relationships, then meal planning, then finances, etc. The book is written sort of journal style ... after explaining what area she is working on and why, there would be journal entries covering how it went (or sometimes didn't). She would wrap each month up by reviewing her progress, and what, if any, strategies she adopted that month that she would continue moving forward.

I thought this was a great way to stay present and grateful in your life, while at the same time making strides in areas that are important to you. I'm thinking about trying something similar for myself in 2017. If you were to pick areas of your life to focus on, what would they be?

November 2, 2016

I love this quote by Emerson, "do not follow where the path may lead, go instead where there is no path and leave a trail". Someone always has to be the first. Throughout history there are many people, leaders for things big and small, who were the first. Those in front forging the path. People standing up for women's rights, civil rights, entrepreneurs and businesspeople creating products and services we never knew we needed or could even exist. Susan B. Anthony, Martin Luther King, even Bill Gates and Mark Zuckerberg.

You have to imagine that for people like this, people we know today, maybe even you ... that when you start to lead the way, do something new, try something new, and especially once you start to achieve success or progress with the movement, the naysayers come out. Those who don't believe in the same things shout from the rooftops why you are wrong. Businesses who are in the same industry or maybe even compete with you start the fear mongering ... "that model isn't sustainable", "they will fail", "it won't work". Likely those who are saying it can't be done, were likely once the ones that others were saying that about too. They are just further along the path.

The next time you hear someone else spewing that kind of negativity, or maybe you find that you are thinking it yourself, stop and think of those who have blazed a trail in other areas. Realize what is possible. Focus on what is possible. Don't be afraid to abandon the well-worn path for the new trail. Whether you are leading the way, or supporting those who are, know and acknowledge that there always will be new and different ways of doing things, building a business, supporting and standing up for the rights of others. Those "old" ways were once the "new" ways that everyone was afraid of or talked badly about. You can forge ahead into the future of what is possible, or be left on the old, worn, tired path doing the same old, same old. The choice is yours, which path will you take?

November 4, 2016

My husband is a firefighter and is currently on shift work. Since he works every other weekend, his days off fall during the standard work week. While the kids are in school, we love to take a long walk on those days on the dirt road by our house. While we were walking yesterday, I noticed that I had to keep reminding myself to look up. I tend to focus on the grayish-brown dirt and gravel road as we go. I just keep my head down, focused on the task at hand and push forward.

It suddenly dawned on me how often I do that, and how many times I have said that to someone else, I did just a couple days ago. I like to just keep my head down and work. I like it that way. I detest drama. I can't stand gossip, trivialness, negativity, and all that other "stuff" that seems to go on when groups gather. So, I keep my head down and work. With my head down I go faster. I like to do everything fast. Walk fast, talk fast, eat fast, finish things fast. With my head down I'm focused, my work gets done, I'm efficient. With my head down I can keep up with my (6' 2") husband. I can avoid the rocks and the ruts in the road as I see them coming.

But ... I also miss all of the beauty. When I look up, and not just eyes straight ahead on the big picture in front and what is to come, but up above me, it's incredible! I saw the red and orange- and yellow-colored leaves. The tree branches swaying in the breeze. As I looked up, I felt grateful, and couldn't help but have a smile on my face. While looking up I didn't seem to think or feel anything else. As I looked up, I was moving so. much. slower ... but the reward was worth it.

Oh, my goodness how much do I do this in my business and life! Do you? I'm so busy keeping my head down, avoiding all of the BS, focused on my work, that I am sometimes missing all of the beautiful things too. So, I'm going to focus on looking up, going slower (that's painful for me, even just to type!). I'm still going to avoid the drama and "bad" stuff that I don't care to be a part of, but I am not going to allow that, or my drive to be efficient, or my hyper-focus on the task at hand to allow me to miss the good stuff too. Look up friends, it's a big, beautiful world out there.

December 7, 2016

Last week at the Virginia Women's Business Conference one of the speakers I listened to was talking about "practice". She said that you will get really good at what you practice. That makes sense, right? I'm forever telling my 12-year-old son to practice his instrument (baritone), his teacher recommends that they practice 15 minutes per day. During baseball season my two oldest boys practice hitting baseballs in the front yard every day. My youngest son is learning to read, and so we practice by reading a book a day. Professional athletes practice for hours and hours. Want to run a marathon, you have to practice. We all know this.

But did you know that it can go the other way too? What do you say about yourself, your business? You aren't good enough, there isn't enough business, your clients don't really want to hear from you that often, online leads are crap, you need someone else to provide leads for you, you can't do it on your own. How many times have you said or thought those things or something similar? The words roll off your tongue effortlessly, without a second thought, or even a thought at all. That only comes from one thing ... practice.

Instead, practice something new. Don't call it a mantra if that seems too out there for you, it's just practice. Practice reminding yourself that you are capable, that you are a good wife-mom-friend-business woman. Remind yourself that you are good at what you do, that your clients are delighted to hear from you, that you offer valuable information and experience to the world, and that needs to be shared. The more you practice these words, thoughts and feelings, the better you will become at them.

December 27, 2016

I'm knee deep into winter break right now, and really enjoying it. Other than a home inspection for a friend and a settlement, I'm doing a lot of nothing this week and it's fantastic. My husband and I started taking off this week between Christmas and New Years a couple years ago and it has fast become one of our very favorite weeks of the year. Yesterday we played games, ate leftovers, put together Lego sets and watched Monday Night Football. Today will likely look very similar.

One of the things I like to "work" on this week is my personal goal setting. This is my second year using the PowerSheets goal planner from Lara Casey and I really enjoy them. My business goals were largely set last month, so the focus for this is on myself and my family. There are quite a few prep pages that go through a series of questions for looking at what did and didn't work, identifying your true goals and priorities, etc. It takes a good bit of thought and consideration, so I like to take my time going through it.

I've learned that I busy myself to hold off the worry and anxiety. That means a lot gets done, but many times it isn't what is most important or productive for the bigger picture. So, for 2017 I've decided to keep it completely simple and am only setting 3 personal goals for myself related to my health, our finances, and my relationships with my husband and sons. I still plan to make a list of "projects" and tasks that I want to finish (cleaning out a closet, finishing my 2015 family scrapbook (that was a rough year), etc.), but overall, my focus will be on just a very few things.

They say that the days are long, and the years are short. If you have children, this especially rings true. But still, so much can happen in a year. The time will fly by, it is so easy to get caught up in the stuff and the day to day grind that, for me anyway, if I don't spend at least a little time intentionally planning and working on certain things that I want to do or accomplish before you know it the time is gone, and you can't get it back.

2017

Milestones:
2-23-2017 – First Monthly Meet Ups launched in 9 cities across the US
5-24-2017 – First Coffee Chat (via Facebook Live), featuring Kara Macdonald
5-29-2017 – "How to Avoid the Summer Slump" course launched
5-31-2017 – First mention of the Daily Business Builders™
9-29-2017 – Hit 5000 members!
11-21-2017 – "Goal Setting & Business Planning" packages available for sale

January 3, 2017
It's the first day back to work for me after enjoying winter break home with my boys. I'm a little sad to see it come to an end, but excited to get back to work too. We have a lot of great things happening this year, and I can't wait to get started. Last night I was reading "The Best Yes" by Lysa Terkeurst. This is a book that I started ages (maybe even a year or more) ago, but put down after a couple chapters, and now I know why. While I really liked what I was reading back then, it wasn't really speaking to me. When I picked it up again yesterday it's like I can feel every word, meant just for me.

In one of the chapters I was reading last night she talks about how we "steer where we stare". I was immediately transformed to my 15–16-year-old self, sitting in my driver's education classroom. One of the (few?) things I've always remembered and thought about from that class was my teacher talking about the importance of looking straight ahead and keeping oncoming cars and the lines at the side of the road in our peripheral vision because what we look at is the direction we will move the car towards.

Are you looking ahead? Or are you trying to look back, go back (you can't)? Are you looking at the cars passing you on the highway, going places you want to go or think you should go? Or are you staring at the shoulder, the ditch on the side of the road, the roadblocks, difficulties, things you are afraid of? Where you stare, you will steer. Keep your eyes forward, staring down your path. Yes, be aware of what is going on around you, but don't let it distract you. Look in the direction that you are going, the direction of the goals and plans you have established for yourself and your business. Keep moving in that direction. That focus, that movement, is the only thing that will get you there.

January 5, 2017

I've often had a tendency to be an over thinker, and when I overthink, I talk myself out of good things, out of taking action, out of doing the things I know I should be doing. The things I NEED to do. It really does begin and end in your mind. If you focus on what could go wrong or on what isn't exactly right (giving myself a pep talk here), then you will never step forward, you will never have the opportunity to even see what could happen or come from something. Tweak as you go. Improve future versions, but don't not do it because it isn't perfect.

About 2 months ago my business partner Vicky Noufal created a new mailer that she is sending out to parts of an area that she farms. I loved her idea, and we discussed that I needed to do the same. I planned to do it, only I haven't done it yet. Why? Because it isn't exactly the way I would like it. Some of the words aren't just as I would say them. There has been a lot going on with the holidays, etc. and it felt overwhelming to think about, re-write, re-do, and so what have I done? Nothing. What has Vicky done? She is on her 3rd round of her mailer, even though we've discussed some edits that SHE wants to make. She has done it, sent it, even though for her the words aren't just right either, and what has happened as a result? She signed a listing yesterday from someone who received her mailer.

Now here's the thing ... what is my concern with the words being just right? That it won't work? That someone won't respond to it? Obviously as Vicky experienced that didn't matter, and besides who am I to judge exactly what someone else will and won't respond to? You won't know until you do it. What I do know for absolute certain is that by NOT doing it, nothing will happen. Nothing. No result. No calls. No appointments. No listings. No new buyers. It is better to get started, to send it as is and at least give myself the opportunity that something will happen vs. guarantee that nothing will by not doing it. What do you need to stop overthinking, obsessing, trying to perfect that you need to just do already?

January 17, 2017

Do you tend to operate from a place of an open or fixed mindset?

When you have an open mindset, you can see potential in yourself. That anything is possible. That where you are now, isn't where you always need to or will to be. An open mindset doesn't avoid or fear change and tends to focus on the possibilities.

A fixed mindset can't see growth, or anything different than the right now (good or bad). It is intimated by anything and anyone different and is afraid of change.

When I think back to when I was a little girl, I definitely had an open mindset (maybe most children do). I thought anything was possible, that I could do or achieve anything. Then somewhere along the way someone (probably well intentioned) or just life in general shifted my mindset. Convinced me that I shouldn't, I wouldn't be able to, and I shouldn't even want to. When I think back to many of my challenges as an adult, those that were most difficult or stressful on me, occurred when I was coming from a fixed mindset. Those times that I have been focused on an open mindset (most especially the past few years), there have certainly still been challenges, but I feel like I have been more able to roll with the punches and handle them more gracefully.

February 1, 2017

Yesterday I attended a workshop on time management and organization ... two of my favorite topics! The first presenter mentioned a concept that we have talked about here before ... you teach what you allow. We do this in our personal lives and in our businesses. Most certainly not on purpose, but it affects us none the less.

How many times have you answered a client call at 9 pm at night (not related to a time sensitive contract negotiation), and then before you know it they are calling you late in the evening somewhat regularly? You've taught them that it is acceptable.

How often do you respond to a quick email from a client at 10:30-11 pm at night thinking you are being helpful and providing good service, and now they are emailing you every night expecting responses? You've taught them that you are working and responsive at that hour and it is okay.

It is also okay to teach what is acceptable and reasonable for you. When you get that late call, respond instead with a quick text, "I saw that I just missed your call. I'm getting ready for bed/getting my children to bed, may I call you in the morning?". You've responded professionally, established a boundary, and I guarantee they won't call that late again for something that is not urgent or time critical. Do you have some habits in your business that you are allowing others to run your day? How could you "teach" something different?

February 6, 2017

Did you watch the Super Bowl last night? Whether your team won or lost, you have to stop and admire, be in awe even, of the incredible amount of time, effort and practice that led up to the game and production for everyone involved. From the players who undoubtedly have spent hours and hours over the course of many years practicing, working out and studying plays to the grounds and production crews who have down to a science how to set up and break down basically a mini concert at half time seamlessly within minutes. Can you imagine the amount of rehearsing that went into that? Speaking of halftime, whether you are a Lady Gaga fan or not, the amount of endurance and conditioning it takes to dance and sing like that must be the result of many long hours of rehearsals. Last week I heard a snippet of NBA star LeBron James saying that his career and success was made at 4 am. He said that in order to do what others cannot do, you must be willing to do what others won't. For him that meant being in the gym practicing at 4 am.

How often do we look at those who are successful or are further along the path than we are and forget what went into getting them there. There is no overnight success in our business or any other. Success, significance, mastery, takes years and years of practice. Failures. Being told no. Losing the listing or the buyer. Being hung up on, yelled at, unappreciated. Sacrifice, investment of time and money, being willing to do what others don't and won't .... this and more has been repeated over and over (and over) by those who now make it look effortless. Are you willing to do what others won't to get yourself there?

February 15, 2017

Over the weekend one of my team members was responding to a lead that came in on one of my listings. Our first red flag should have been that he was calling after 6 pm on a Saturday evening requesting to see properties the next day. As she was going through the standard questions that we ask ... things like, are you working with an agent, how did you come across this listing, what caught your eye about it, have you been pre-approved by a lender ... he became so angry. The lender question set him off and he told her so rudely that of course he had talked to a lender, that he wouldn't be calling otherwise, and that "it was all we realtors care about" and never to call or contact him again.

Now. This is a mindset I can't understand. Is it really reasonable to think that you as a complete stranger to me can call up and expect to have a homeowner and their family leave their home so you can walk through it at your whim without being asked a few questions? Doesn't our listing agreement (I know this varies by state) say that we will show the property to qualified buyers? How do I know if I don't ask the question?

I think that part of the seller's responsibility when their home is on the market is to be flexible with showings and to make sure their home is ready to show. The buyer's responsibility is to take a few steps to ensure that they are shopping in their comfortable price range so as to be respectful of everyone's time. Sadly, over my 15 years in this business I've had my fair share of rude people. They call me wanting something (information, a showing) and become incorrigible at the slightest question from my end. In my experience, there is typically a reason behind the rudeness that often stems from not being prepared, ready or qualified, or simply just not wanting to be questioned. That or they already have an agent and we are just the vehicle to open a door at their convenience, or they view us as simply a shady salesperson and don't want to "engage".

Whatever the "reason", rudeness is never okay in my book. We are all just people trying to do a job, trying to help someone else. Why not engage in a conversation to understand the point of view instead of just yelling and being rude? Has this ever happened to you? How did you handle it? What sorts of questions do you ask when you get a buyer call requesting to see your listing?

February 20, 2017
I loved this the moment I read it ... "you are allowed to be both a masterpiece and a work in progress simultaneously." Boy, isn't that the truth. How often do we put off something because we don't feel ready enough?

-I'll start daily prospecting once I get my system down.
-I'll do my client mailers once I've cleaned up my database.
-I'm not going to have anyone over until I replace my carpet.
-I'll wait to plan that beach trip once I lose 10 pounds.

And on and on and on. Does any of this sound familiar to you? It does to me.

Here's what I will tell you ... you are enough, just right, just as you are. Are we all a work in progress? Absolutely. Learning, changing, evolving never stops. Are there things in your life, your home, your business, about yourself that you don't feel prepared enough/ready enough to share? Yep. My list is long.

Yet, life moves past us at lightning speed. Waiting one month to perfect your database before starting your mailer can quickly turn into 2 then 4, then 6. Waiting until you lose weight to go on a trip can take weeks and months to get to where you feel you "need" to be and then suddenly vacation season is over and you are waiting another year.

-Your clients who receive your mailer will be happy to "see" you. Maybe you don't hit everyone this month, or send to a few that have moved on, but next month you look a little closer, and then the next and then the next. Each mailing will get better.
-Your daily prospecting will help to develop the system. Some of the best systems are those that are created as you go out of real-world needs and scenarios.
-Your house guests will be too busy enjoying your company to notice or even care about your carpet.
-The warm sun and sound of the ocean waves will replenish your spirit, not judge you for carrying a little extra weight here and there.

Do the things. Live your life. Take action. Enjoy as you go. We are all just right, right now.

February 24, 2017

It's going on 3 years ago now since I founded this group, and when I did it was with the belief that many women in our industry crave a connection with other like-minded industry professionals to share ideas, stories, and to learn from one another. My experience yesterday with our first Monthly Meet Up only confirmed that.

Yesterday we had Meet Ups in 9 different cities. Some groups were small, just 2 or 3, some had 10 or 11, others were larger. The groups were comprised of women from all experience levels. At my Meet Up the "newest" agent had only been licensed a few months, the most experienced industry professional had 25+ years. All age groups, different ethnicities and backgrounds, and many different brokerages. We had agents, brokers, lenders, designers and title executives. Many full-time career agents, and some dual career.

The most refreshing aspect that I felt is how willing everyone was to share their questions, their concerns and their ideas. Even though we were from different companies and that we technically "compete" with each other on a daily basis in our local market, there was such a feeling of respect between the women at the table.

From everyone I talked to afterwards, we all left refreshed and energized and eager for next month's Meet Up. Sharing ideas and supporting others will never "lessen" your own opportunities, if anything it will help you to grow and expand. Celebrating another's success doesn't somehow mean you failed. Success isn't this pie where there is a limited number of slices and just because someone else got some that it somehow means that there won't be enough for you. There is room for us all, I truly believe that deep in my heart. Don't be afraid to connect with those around you, to share and to teach. In my experience it will only serve to enrich your own life, business and experience.

February 27, 2017

Last week's edition of "The Brian Buffini Show" podcast was an interview with NFL star Justin Forsett. The message behind the interview was how Justin persevered despite many obstacles in his life going back to childhood, throughout college and in his NFL career. One of the things that struck me was how through each "stage" of his life he would talk about how he would "excel at the things he could control". There was a lot he couldn't control. For example, one of the issues he continuously dealt with was his size. For a professional football player, he is small in stature, and so he was often overlooked. However, he said that one thing he could control was how hard he worked at practices, how well he knew the playbook, how he supported his teammates. He knew that by excelling at those things that he could control it would open him up to more opportunities, and it did.

There are many things we can't control in our businesses (and life too). I've heard agents say it's harder for them to succeed because they aren't from where they currently live and don't have a strong sphere. It's hard for them to compete because they are newer or have less experience than others in their office or market. We can't control market fluctuations, final sales prices and whether or not that buyer is going to write on the 50th home we've shown them.

What we can control is how well we know the market. Can you spit out market stats without looking? Do you have a rough idea of the selling prices for typical homes in your area or neighborhood? We can control how well we know and can present our marketing plans and listing presentations. We can control how many people we meet or talk to on a weekly basis by how much we put ourselves out there. We can control how well we know and can explain our contracts. Excelling at these things that we can control will propel us far further in our business than anything else. Don't focus on the obstacles, the unknowns, the what ifs. Focus on what you can do, what you can control and do that extraordinarily well. I promise, it will be worth it.

March 1, 2017

Viola Davis. I heard a few snippets of an interview with her earlier this week after she won an Oscar. She talked about "imposter syndrome", and how despite her tremendous success in her career she was still waiting for someone to "find her out". To figure out that she wasn't that good/didn't belong.

Have you ever felt that way? I know I sure have. I've been in this business for 15 years. I've personally helped well more than 600 families to buy, sell or rent homes and still there are many days when that little voice on the inside is saying "who do you think you are", "you aren't that good", "someone's going to figure you out", "just stay small over here to the side, big things are for someone else".

The older I get, the more I understand me, the more I try the hard things, the easier it becomes to tell that voice to take a hike. I've learned that the voice isn't "me". It isn't my gut or my intuition trying to protect me, it's fear trying to hold me back. I know this because the times I ignored it and did the big thing anyway, put myself out there, the rewards have been great.

March 3, 2017

Have you ever had a great idea or been excited to go a new direction in your life only to have those nearest and dearest to you ... friends, colleagues, family members ... try to discourage you, tell you it can't be done, hold you back?

Looking back, I can honestly say that I am pretty sure that it has happened to me with just about every big change or big step in my life. Yesterday I attended a businesswomen's luncheon, and the guest speaker was telling the story of how it happened in her life as she learned and grew and moved to explore a new part of herself. She remarked that she couldn't understand it, she was still the same woman that they had always known and loved, why the resistance?

When this happens, I've often thought that the naysayers, the doubters who were driven by fear ... fear for me that things wouldn't work out, fear for themselves that our relationship may somehow change as a result of the growth, or just simply their fear of something new. When I read this quote, it took my breath away for a moment ... "The doubters are just dreamers with broken hearts."

That puts a little different perspective on it doesn't it? My mother was always the biggest doubter in my life. I know she loved me so much (she's been gone 2 years this month), and was so proud of my accomplishments, but her first reaction always to any big change (or even sometimes the small ones) was to doubt, to question, to discourage me. I know she was afraid for me. She was afraid something would go wrong, she was afraid for what she didn't know, she was afraid for the change. I've also come to know that she was a doubter because of her own broken heart, and she wanted to try to protect me from that too.

My hope always, what I strive for as a mom, is to encourage my boys to try anything, that they can do anything. I don't want them to feel afraid to try or to feel afraid to fail. It is all just a little bit more experience that will help you to grow and move to the next great experience in your life.

Can we do that for each other too? If I'm growing and moving and doing something different that doesn't somehow mean that you are less than because you aren't. If you see a colleague trying a new marketing technique that seems silly to you, don't criticize ... bravo to them for trying something new. I hope it works great, and maybe someday I'll be trying it too.

Online forums like this are wonderful ways to connect with others, but our point can also be easily miscommunicated, and sometimes we can just feel way more brave typing it out from behind a computer screen than we ever would saying it in person. The responsibility to treat others with respect goes both ways. If you feel wronged or hurt by another's comments, message them, have a phone conversation, go out for coffee. My guess is that when you do that conversation will go completely differently.

No matter what though, I know for sure that this is true ... the person who is doubting your dreams, the naysayer, the person who is rude, snarky, petty, and just plain mean ... none of anything that you are experiencing from them has anything to do with you. It is most assuredly a result of their feelings, their hurt, their pain, their "not good enough", their fear that is being projected outward. Because after all, the doubter is just a dreamer with a broken heart.

March 15, 2017

Most days I feel like I am being pulled in a hundred different directions. Staying on top of my business, keeping in contact with current clients, managing all of the details that come with sellers who are anxious to sell and buyers who are anxious to buy. Continuing to prospect for new business no matter how "busy" the rest of it seems so I can keep things consistent. Helping my team members to grow and expand their own businesses. Implementing business plans and team plans that have been established.

Taking care of my family, from my extraordinarily patient and kind husband who never gets enough attention, to 3 active and growing young boys who all need something different (and yet need the same love and attention) from me all at the same time. Two crazy dogs who are like bulls in a china shop, plus a geriatric old dog who can't hardly see, can barely hear, struggles to move around, and gets me up every night in the middle of the night to go out. Then there is the elderly cat who for years was an outside cat until she just plain got too old, and so now has a cozy "condo" set up in our basement bathroom where she can snooze the day away in warm comfort, only no one else in my house seems to know what the litter box scoop is and me and one of the crazy dogs who loves her are usually the only ones who remembers that she is there.

Enter extended family caring for an aging parent for whom I manage his household too. He gets so excited when he gets those scam letters in the mail about money that he calls and wants to bring them to me right away. Paying his bills, managing his money, making sure he has food. An aunt who is like my mother (she is my mother's sister) who is overrun by fear of cancer and illness. We've worked through her bouts of it recently and before, and with whom most every conversation is a run-down of doctors' appointments and asking me ten times if she "will be okay".

My people do a good job of all of us working together to care for our household only I'm usually the only one who can see things laying on the floor or counter no matter how often they pass by (remember that suitcase episode on Seinfeld?), or even though you are hard pressed to be more than 5 feet from a trashcan at any given point in my house trash still doesn't seem to be able to make it in the proper receptacle.

Even maintaining the group here. My head is full of ideas and thoughts to share, but some mornings NOTHING wants to come out. There's more, but I'm tried just writing it all out.

Who else can relate to this? I'm guessing most all of us here. My friend Kara Macdonald just recently out of the blue (which was, of course, perfect timing) shared with me a strategy she uses to keep it all in check. She wrote a personal value statement for herself, and when it comes to taking on more things, or even just dealing with the day to day she will think back to whether or not it fits within her value statement, and therefore whether it is worth her energy or not. I really like this idea. Do you have a personal value statement?

March 22, 2017

Yesterday I posted this on my personal page ... "the bitterness of poor quality remains long after the sweetness of low price is forgotten". I found it courtesy of a friend, another small business owner. We've probably all had this experience before. The inexpensive play clothes I would buy for my kids that only last for 1 or 2 washes and wears before they would literally start to fall apart. Of course, when I am unhappy about having to throw away the clothes I'm not thinking about how happy I was to pay the cheap price for them. Not realizing that I have indeed gotten what I paid for, but by then, it's too late.

Our industry can be brutal. Public perception can be not only inaccurate, but downright rude. We work HARD to make money to support our families. We work HARD to represent our clients to the best of our abilities to ensure that they are protected during the most expensive and important decisions they will make in their lives. Most people only buy or sell a handful of homes in their lifetime, many fewer than that. It's a big deal with a lot of liability and risk. They have money on the line from day one. We work for weeks and months for the clients for free until settlement, putting out our own dollars up front for marketing, gas, and more. No one would want to or expect to walk into work being told that they are going to do the exact same job they did the day before but for ½ or ⅓ of the income. Yet it happens to us often.

As our market gets stronger, I feel like our value gets questioned more and more. Take your eye off the ball (or in this case, the client relationship) for a second, and there are many more agents, lenders, title companies, etc. ready to jump right in and take your place. And even when you don't take your eye off the ball in this climate there are competitors everywhere vying for attention and business, even your business. The business that you think is "yours", that you are sure is yours based on past relationships, conversations, even based on strategy sessions or appointments when you are just waiting for the signatures to come back are gone in a second when someone else offers to do the same job for less, says the "right thing" that the client really needed to hear, or was just there at the right place at the right time.

I've seen this happen before and it will happen again. Our market can be a roller coaster, up and down, up and down, sometimes over the course of years or sometimes just months. What I know for sure is that as the market adjusts over and over again, I'll still be here. The other professional career agents I know will be here. Will you? Know your value. Focus on the big picture. Shop at Walmart or shop at Nordstrom ... both have their place in the marketplace, both are valuable. Know which one you are, embrace it, don't apologize for it.

March 24, 2017
Across all of our Monthly Meet Ups yesterday (we had women meeting in 10 different cities), we heard quiet a few consistent challenges/themes when it comes to prospecting ...
-Not knowing what to do
-Not having time/making time to prospect
-Overthinking/trying to make it perfect
There were so many great takeaways and ideas, I'll share a few of mine here.

Don't over think it. It is not for us to judge if we are calling someone too early or too late or too often, or if they will or won't want to receive our mailer or email. Allow them to choose if it is right for them by not answering the call, discarding the mailer, unsubscribing from or deleting the email, not coming to the event. Even if they do all of those things, you've still achieved a big part of your purpose which is to remind them that you are still here, you are still in real estate, and you are still ready, willing and able to help them.

It doesn't have to be perfect. Nothing is. Start with something and do that consistently. Edit and improve it as you go. It is better to send or do something that is not perfect than to do nothing at all. While you are waiting to get it just right, many others are out there doing it, calling, mailing, emailing. Even though you may be someone's realtor of choice that they have worked with on their last several transactions, chances are they are receiving marketing from others via Facebook ads, geographic farming, and more.

The biggest change for me and key for me when it comes to prospecting is having a system. Developing a system or a plan for what you will do and when solves the not knowing what to do and not having/making time issues. For 10+ years I did the same every other month postcard drawing mailers, and annual calendar magnets/holiday cards with a few pop bys sprinkled in (by the way, the pop by was the most common form of prospecting talked about yesterday in my group, ⅔ of the 36 women in attendance do them consistently!). It was a simple system and was easy for me to execute because I knew what I was going to do. Over the past 2 years I've really stepped up my prospecting as has my whole team. Last year Vicky Noufal and I wrote out an entire plan for all of 2017. We already know (thanks to Edyta Simmons) what our 3 pop by choices will be for each quarter, what postcard is mailing on the first of each month, that an email is going out on the 15th of each month, and the dates for our call nights and client events are already scheduled. We've "automated" it the best we can, and while there is still work and activity to be done for each "step" it is much less overwhelming because we know the what and the when.

Whatever you do, do it consistently. Start now ... plan out what you will do for the rest of the year, put it in your calendar and do it. Start with something. Maybe it's just 3 calls per day. Maybe it's 2 notes per day. Start somewhere and build on it.

April 3, 2017

On my very first day in real estate, July 15, 2002, I spent the day (and several of the subsequent days) with a man in my office named Tim Schutte. He was rather new as well, just a few months into the business, but he taught me some of the very best lessons right out of the gate, which I use to this day.

First, treat (and call) everything an appointment. Whether I am going to the dentist, have dinner planned with my spouse, or volunteering in my child's classroom it is all an appointment and if a client asks to meet during that time, I simply say that I already have an appointment scheduled.

Second, never say "when do you want to meet". Always give the options, be the leader. Say, "how about today at 2 pm or tomorrow at 10 am" (or whatever). I have found that 95% of the time the client or prospect will choose one of the options I offered. If neither work, then I try again. When meeting or getting to know a new client, I will sometimes ask what their schedules are like, are there days of the week that are better for them, etc. so that I can get a feel for what will work best. Still, I provide the options first. This sets the precedent and expectation that I am a professional and treat my schedule as such. They then tend to treat me the same.

April 14, 2017

I love this quote by Marianne Williamson, "Everything we do is infused with the energy with which we do it. If we're frantic, life will be frantic. If we're peaceful, life will be peaceful". There are times in my life, some that feel like entire large time periods, when I felt frantic ... and so my reaction to everything, even the littlest of things was frantic. There have been periods driven by fear, and so I have acted (or rather reacted) accordingly.

Have you ever been on the other side of a transaction with an agent that you can tell needs it more than everyone else (their client included)? There is a desperation level that you can feel coming. Your energy speaks for you long before you open your mouth. Be conscious of yours. If are in a period where you are struggling, take time to focus on finding peace and gratitude within yourself. It will change your energy, and the situation/challenges that you are facing will change.

April 19, 2017

Earlier this week I was listening to a podcast featuring community member Christy Belt Grossman and one of the things that Christy said which really resonated with me was that she doesn't just get up in the morning and go haphazard about her day. Everything she does from the moment she gets up is intentional and designed to ensure that she sets herself up for a great day.

Several years ago, I became a convert in this area and started getting up early for what I call my "quiet time". Even on weekends when I don't need to be up quite as early, I still factor it in to ensure that I can have an hour to ready myself mentally and spiritually for the day. Drinking my coffee, writing here to you and reading positive messages help to establish my mindset to launch into my day before other people have a chance to affect it.

Then I get my kids up and out the door, get myself ready and start the day. At some point, either during a walk or while driving I'll listen to business or motivational podcasts to help to keep me in the right frame of mind. When I sit down at my desk, my to do list has already been started so I know what to do and my day has direction. This has all been key for me in managing my time and in being productive, not just busy. This quote from Zig Ziglar is a good one on this topic, "People often complain about lack of time when the lack of direction is the real problem." Do you know your direction?

April 21, 2017

This has been the absolute craziest week. I've had 3 different offers come in on 3 different listings, none of which worked out. I've signed 4 new listings but lost another that I was sure I had based on a prior relationship (those always sting the worst). I had a buyer (my buyer) default on a contract (which has never happened to me before), that could have turned ugly but thank you to a gracious seller and listing agent, everyone is moving on. I have 2 other buyers who have been in a holding pattern for a while that are now finally ready to go. I had a great referral that resulted in a terrific listing appointment, and I'm hoping a beautiful new listing in the next few days. This business (and life too) is full of ups and downs, yeses and nos, crazy highs and crazy lows.

As it pertains to business, I've found that the key to not getting (as) upset about the losses is the confidence that comes with consistently doing your marketing and prospecting activities. It's easier to shake off the one that got away when you know that another opportunity is right around the corner.

I've had a few conversations this week with a friend who is going through a significant life challenge. Significant isn't even a strong enough word to describe it. More like devastating, heartbreaking, gut wrenching. We've been talking about advice that she was given to just keep walking. No matter what is going on, you have to just keep walking. No matter how painful the steps are, no matter how slow or small they are, keep taking them. Eventually they will take you through the difficulty, possibly to a new one, but eventually to the other side of whatever has been ordained to be next for you.

April 26, 2017

The internet is truly a fascinating thing, isn't it? 24/7 we have access to an incredible amount of information, people, connection all right at our fingertips. It also offers some "protection". You can "say" things to someone that you would likely never say to their face, and probably shouldn't say in either circumstance.

I'm proud to say that in the nearly 3 years since I founded this group there have been less than a handful of times that I have had to delete a post because the commentary was becoming hateful (reminder ... no personal promotion posts, advertising of other groups or in person events, no selling or posting listings ... those posts are deleted practically on a daily basis). The women in this group are largely very respectful of one another and that comes through in the way we "talk" to each other here. I love that when a post or comments are not in keeping with the theme of the group that instead of 100 people chiming in on the post and arguing back and forth, my phone starts blowing up with members reporting it so it can be stopped. We should be able to have differing thoughts and opinions and communicate that to each other civilly.

That doesn't always seem to be the norm in the world at large these days, but it will be in my little world and in this group. Insulting someone else because they think differently or do something differently than you is just plain mean and inappropriate. There is a way to say things when you don't agree to still make your point without personally attacking or being just plain nasty.
2017 marks my 15th year in real estate. I spent the first 6 ½ years on a team with RE/MAX and it was a wonderful experience. There came a time that it was no longer the right fit for me, and I moved on. That doesn't mean that the RE/MAX brand, team, or office that I worked for was "bad" or not a good place to be, it was just no longer for me.

From there I spent almost 6 ½ years (that seems to be a trend for me) with Century 21 with the majority of that time as an agent selling, and a portion as a managing broker. It too was a great experience and exactly what I needed at the time. Same as before ... the time was right for me to move on, but that in no way is an indicator of the quality of where I had been. It doesn't mean that I am better than anyone who is there and vice versa.

For the last almost 2 years now I have been with Pearson Smith Realty. My first time not with a national brand or franchise, and it has been a truly incredible experience. This is exactly where I need to be for me and where I am in my career. Is this where I will be until I retire from the industry? Maybe, maybe not.

Over the years I've interviewed with Prudential (now Berkshire Hathaway Home Services), Long & Foster, Weichert, other RE/MAX offices and Keller Williams. I know, like and respect many agents at those firms and enjoyed my conversations with those representatives, but they weren't the right fit for me at the time. That in no way is reflective of those companies or agents as a whole.

Personally, I believe that as you grow and change as an agent and move through the various stages of your career that your brokerage needs will change as you go. That is why for me shifting brokerages has been the right move. I know other agents who have spent their entire careers with one brokerage, one office and it has been absolutely the best decision for them personally. The key here is personally.

I can appreciate enthusiasm for your own view and the company that you work for, but that is not an excuse or valid reason to attack, put down or talk badly about another company or another person because they work at that company. You only know your specific needs and experience, not that of anyone around you, no matter how much you think you know about them. To the new licensee who was asking for advice (and the response to which inspired this post) ... the best news of all is that there are so many terrific options available to you. It can seem overwhelming. Identify what the priority is for you right now. Is it training, camaraderie, accountability, commission split, location? Start there. Interview with as many different companies as you can. It is not only the brokerage and offerings themselves that will be important to you, but it is the people as well. You want to be in an environment where you are free to ask questions and not be lambasted for it.

Don't just take the brokerage representative's word for it. Seek out an agent or two at the company you are considering and have a conversation. Once when I was trying to decide between companies I stopped by open houses and chatted with the agents I met there. Trust your gut, find your right fit, and go for it. Know too that if at some point you realize that it is no longer the right fit you can make a change. It will not impact your business negatively no matter what anyone tries to tell you. Make the decisions that are best for you.

April 28, 2017

Have you had times in your life and your business when you have tried to do good things, you give, and give, and give only to be taken advantage of? You work hard to provide something valuable, only to be fussed at and criticized when it doesn't happen perfectly? I sure have. When it happens, you have a choice. You can throw your hands up and say never again. Quit. Stop being helpful. Stop giving. Stop whatever it was that you were trying to accomplish. All in the name of protecting yourself, your time, your heart.

Or you can keep going. Keep giving. Keep helping. Keep offering. Keep doing. Perhaps that person taking advantage of your time and generosity has been hurt themselves and doesn't fully know or understand how to receive and reciprocate. In fact, it is most likely because of past hurt that they are responding to you and treating you in that way. I've spent time, lots of time, getting easily stirred up, fired up, pissed off at the slightest injustice. I felt like I was in a heightened state of upset. When I think back, I was hurting and fighting to control those feelings. That impacted how I responded to others.

Now, I just let it go (for the most part, we all have those days!). I keep giving. I keep doing good things. I keep offering grace to others for I have figured out that when I do, that grace, that forgiveness, that love will go out and multiply and eventually come back to me in spades. Perhaps I won't feel it now in the transaction with the nasty bully of an agent who yells and fusses and criticizes, but if I keep offering that person grace, perhaps they will behave differently to the agent they are working with in their next transaction (if they ever have one ... oops, see, old habits die hard). Imagine how different our jobs and lives would be if we all treated one another respectfully, gracefully, if we sought to give more than we take?

May 1, 2017

When I graduated from high school many, many moons ago I chose to attend a community college. Partly for financial reasons, partly for relationship reasons, partly due to fear (see relationship reasons). When I graduated with my associates degree, I decided to enter the workforce instead of continuing on to earn my bachelor's degree, essentially for all the same previous reasons. I had a great administrative position at a pharmaceutical company in the marketing department. I enjoyed the work and was promoted relatively quickly, but I also hit a dead end quickly. The other positions above mine required a bachelor's degree in order to be considered.

One day when meeting with the HR representative she asked why I didn't go back to school. Our company had a tuition reimbursement program, and I could get nearly 100% of my expenses covered. My concern was the time. I was working full time hours, had a nearly 2 hours per day commute to and from work, and I volunteered practically full-time hours evenings and weekends as an EMT for our local fire-rescue. I would only be able to take maybe 2 classes per semester, taking four or more years to finish. She told me that the time would pass anyway. At the end of that time I could have my degree, or I could be in the same place. I'll never forget our conversation or how eye opening her advice was. (Thanks to her I did go on to complete my degree, and due to a "life experience" program I was able to earn more credits faster than I thought and finished in just over 3 years.)

Is there something that you are putting off because of the time it will take? Considering getting your license in a neighboring state but think it will take too long? Tired of buying leads but think it will take too long to build your business and database by referral? Dreaming of getting your broker's license, opening your own firm, building your own team? Everything in life takes time. There are no short cuts or instant, overnight successes. If you start today on your dream, imagine where you would be a year from now? The time will pass anyway, have it pass in your favor.

May 8, 2017

My wise friend Beth Donahue says that she learned a few years ago that she didn't have to attend every fight she was invited to, and it was that realization that really changed her entire state of being (Beth is now one of the most "zen" people I know). There are people in this world who will intentionally try to provoke you, they love to spar whether in person in snide comments or gossiping or online. We all know those people, don't we?

Then there are others who I don't think have a clue, but as a result of their rudeness and general lack of respect for others, their time, our industry as a whole they can provoke you just as much. If not more. I encountered one of those last week. I'm not altogether sure that he did it intentionally, but his ignorance and lack of professionalism shone through, and I was provoked. The first couple interactions I was composed, professional and "cool" (as in not overly friendly) in demeanor, but by the final rounds I had just about lost it and was ready to battle. Then, I remembered what Beth said, and knew I needed to share.

Life is short. Our lives can change in an instant. Children grow in the blink of an eye. Businesses ebb and flow. We only have so much energy to expend. I have realized the stronger my business becomes that in order to perform at a high level and to serve my clients well I must be as streamlined and efficient as possible. I cannot afford to "waste" my energy in places or on people that don't matter in the scope of my world. I've realized too that the ones who provoke out there, the ones that pick a fight and post incessantly, they don't have much else going on. They can't possibly or they wouldn't have time for those shenanigans.

Guard your energy. Spend it wisely. The "cost" of interactions is not equal. A negative interaction will take 3 times the energy from you than a positive one, which is actually most likely to increase your energy. As my 5th grader learned in the D.A.R.E. Program, just walk away. When it's online, the unfollow button is your friend. Choose your interactions, your friends, your colleagues, your partners, how you spend your time and energy wisely. For once it is spent you can't get it back.

May 12, 2017

Earlier this week while having lunch with Caitie Solomon we were talking about kindness and saying thank you. How different people we have encountered lately in service professions (customer service representatives, nurses, etc.) seemed somewhat genuinely taken aback when treated kindly and offered a sincere thank you.

Is it no wonder then that often when you call a service provider for help (how many people like calling their cell phone company?) that those on the other end of the call are often flat, no energy, certainly not "smiling through the phone", or seeming to offer much of anything more than the bare basics of the job? Can you imagine the verbal beating they take every day from people who are calling in, frustrated?

We need to be the change that we want to see in the world. Imagine if we took an extra minute, were kind and said "thank you" to those that we encountered. Perhaps then they would carry that on to their next call or interaction, and it would carry on and on.

This is so true in our industry. I feel like a broken record talking about it so much. When the market is strong, new agents come out of the woodwork. There's nothing wrong with new agents, we were all new once too, and new professionals help to keep our industry and profession (anything really) fresh and growing. It's a good thing. It's not a good thing when "dabblers" decide to try out a transaction or two not really trying or caring to do it correctly, or maybe that is just what we see on the outside. Perhaps they've never been properly taught, they don't have a mentor or good broker supervision. Maybe they just don't know. Often when you are new at something, you don't even know what you don't know. Instead of fussing at them and grumbling to ourselves when paperwork is filled out incorrectly or incompletely (I've definitely been guilty of this) what if we took a moment to kindly offer a suggestion or tip? Or maybe offer to meet for a cup of coffee and have a conversation? I'm sure I can imagine many folks saying that it isn't their "job" to do this, but actually, maybe isn't it? We are all in this industry (life and world) together. How one person acts and responds impacts others around them, which then impacts others around them and so on and so on. If we just took a moment to improve one interaction, to help one person, that cascading effect would be incredible.

One thing I have learned from this business, and just from getting to know people in life in general, is that everyone has "stuff". Baggage, issues, things going on. What you may see on the outside is bright, happy, fun, smiling faces, but what you may not know is that they help to care for a critically ill family member or spouse. Perhaps they have a child with development challenges that requires special care or therapy. Maybe they struggle with anxiety or depression from past hurts. Give the benefit of the doubt. Be kinder than necessary. Give grace to those around you. Say thank you, genuinely. The ripple effect will carry far beyond you and can change everything.

May 15, 2017
Change is hard. Change is also a part of life whether we like it or not. Our world is constantly moving and evolving. Seasons change. Our bodies and health changes as we age. Children grow older and grow up, with routines and habits and needs that are constantly changing. Some change happens to us ... other change we need to do for ourselves. Adjusting eating and exercise habits. Changing work routines and schedules to allow for more efficiency and better balance. Sometimes changing those we work with and for is necessary for our continued growth. Maybe you need a mindset change to see things around you differently.

For me, I find that whenever I am trying to make a change in pretty much any area of my life I need to take one of two approaches ... rip off the bandaid and jump right in (and don't look back) or if it is a habit I am working to change starting with 1 small thing and as that becomes second nature, adding the next small thing. Either way I find that I end up with momentum on my side that pushes me along and past the scariness of the change right to the exhilaration of growing and doing something new.

If you are feeling uneasy, unhappy, unproductive in your life or in your business, something needs to change. Your habits, your environment, your approach, your mindset. As life goes on eventually the things that we have always done or have worked for us for a long time will no longer work. It may be time to change things up. Find a fresh approach. Do something a little differently. Fighting the change will only cause you more stress, more uneasyness. Embrace it and move forward.

May 19, 2017
My husband likes this program, "The Sports Junkies". Are you familiar with this? From what I understand it started as a radio show and is a group of guys talking about and critiquing sports. It kind of drives me crazy. As far as I know, these guys have not been professional athletes or professional coaches or managers but have made a profession out of critiquing those who are. Kudos to them for that, but isn't that sort of fascinating, and really quite pervasive in our world these days?

Social media is awesome in that it connects us in ways that just 20 years ago weren't possible. It also helps to make everyone a critic and most anyone can say they are an expert in this, that, and the other thing, without really having done that thing. Are you really an expert or should you be critiquing or questioning how someone is or should be doing something if you haven't actually done that thing yourself? And if you have, should you really be critiquing or questioning how someone else is choosing to do it?

Maybe I've just gotten grumpy as I've gotten older, or perhaps I just no longer have the patience for judgey-ness. We all only get 1 shot, 1 chance at this life. We have no idea what is coming and when, or what someone else is dealing with behind the scenes. There is ALWAYS more to the story, more that you don't know, and frankly, more that really isn't your business anyway.

Just do you. Unapologetically. Make the decisions that are right for you, for your family, for your business. Make them, own them and don't apologize for them or worry about the critiques from those who don't know what it is to live your one precious life. At the end of the day, at the end of your life, those people, those critiques, none of it will matter. What will is knowing that you lived and loved fully, with no regrets.

May 31, 2017

We had a great discussion yesterday at our Platinum Group Real Estate team meeting (we always do really, I love these women so much!). One of the things we were talking about was our progress towards a "taking action" challenge that we have been working on this quarter. It is a series of daily activities (my Daily Business Builders™!) that we do Monday-Friday (or all at once, one day per week, which also works). Something I heard again and again was the time it takes to do it, that there isn't time to do it.

Here's the thing (and this is true with a LOT of things in our lives) ... we spend more time thinking about why we can't do something or how hard it will be or that we don't know how, than the amount of time that it actually takes to do it! Seriously! In this case, these tasks are simple business builders that work. They have helped to transform my business. I had the same number of settlements in the month of May than I had in January - April combined ... and those 4 months were steady business (averaging 3 transactions each month) -- not a coincidence!. It takes less than 45 minutes per day of intentional focus on your business. Just 45 minutes and done!

I've struggled with this thinking and not doing thing over and over again. Take for example, the curtains in my master bedroom. When we bought our house, it came with custom fabric covered cornices in each bedroom. The ones in our room had a beautiful fabric on them, but not anything that ever matched any of our bedding. After walking into my bedroom multiple times per day for years, each time thinking, "I really need to recover these", I finally bought the fabric to do so (solid color linen tablecloths, on clearance at Target of course). That fabric then sat in a drawer in my room for at least two years. Finally, one day, I started. I did 2 of them one day, and 2 the next. It took me no more than 40 minutes total. I procrastinated for years to do something that irritated me every day and took less than 40 minutes to finish. When I think about all of the time that I wasted thinking about doing it over the years, that time added up to well over 40 minutes. Does any of this sound familiar to you?

So, here's the lesson in all of this ... we tend to rush through the day to day with no specific direction. We think we don't have time to do things because we are so busy. I'm here to tell you, none of us are that busy. We aren't lacking time, we are lacking direction, focus and boundaries. When we go about our day intentionally focused on what we want to accomplish, you will be amazing by how much more time we actually have because we are able to get it done, plus all the other stuff that keeps us busy each day.

Try it. Spend a few minutes this morning, no more than 5, with a pen and paper and your schedule for the day. Write down the most important intentions for today, and if possible, do those first. Then, when you get to the end of today, and that long list of things to do isn't complete (it never is), you will feel so accomplished because you did the most important things. I'm not talking about just the "tasks", the errands, the paperwork, I'm taking about intentional steps to grow your business. To grow your friend and family relationships. We think we don't have time for those things, but the time is there, we just need to use it to our advantage.

June 5, 2017

Last week my dearest friend and business partner Vicky Noufal lost her husband after a nearly 18-month brutal battle with stage IV pancreatic cancer. I've been pre-reading for her Sheryl Sandberg's book "Option B", and it was in it yesterday that I came across a quote by Viktor Frankl. A Holocaust survivor, Frankl said, "When we are no longer able to change a situation, we are challenged to change ourselves." There are many times that life is completely unfair, that it throws us a curveball, that it just plain sucks (you can also repeat that exact same statement as it relates to our businesses). Often, we are handed situations that no matter what we do, how hard we fight, we cannot change. And so then, if we are to survive them, if we are to thrive again, we must change ourselves.

Doing the things we have always done in life (or in business) is not meant to be the status quo forever, because the status quo changes. Sometimes minute by minute, day by day, year by year. Nothing stays the same, and so then why should we? What worked for our businesses last quarter, may not be as effective now, in a new season. The ways that we marketed and sold homes 10 years ago do not work as well now as they did back then. The way we lived our life 18 months ago is not going to be the way we can live it today, so we must change.

What changes can you be making, should you be making, in your life or your business today? Learn how, flex that muscle. Change now what you can, when you can. Eventually change will be forced upon all of us. Knowing how to do it will add to our strength when the stakes are higher, the losses deeper, the situations more drastic. Count your blessings (we all have them), tell your friends and loved ones what they mean to you, live passionately and joyfully every day that you can.

June 9, 2017

Yesterday I had a great conversation with Aliyah Dastour for her Loudoun100 project. We talked about a lot of interesting things, and have so much in common, but one question she asked me threw me for a loop ... "what would you tell your 15-year-old self?" Does that sting for anyone else like it does for me? There were even a few tears. What would I tell my 15-year-old self? I would tell her that she is enough. Just as she is. She doesn't need anyone else to validate her or to solidify her "enough-ness". I would tell her that absolutely everything she needs is already inside her, she just needs to let it out.

I would tell all of you that too. What is it about the world and the people around us that we (especially women, but men too) get the message that we aren't enough? Both personally and in business. Buy this car, these shoes, that brand. You need this lead general tool, this website, my leads. You won't be as successful without me, or anywhere else. We hear messages like this everywhere, even from people who love us.

Whatever the reason for all of that (I could write all morning on that topic), none of it is true. You are enough. I am enough. Just as we are. Do we work to improve ourselves, to learn new things? Absolutely. Growing is good, it helps to make us even more of who we already are. Know that just as you are, who you are, you are worthy and capable of love, friendship and success. No changes, ultimatums or modifications required.

June 26, 2017

I'm currently in the midst of a vacation with my family, and finally I feel like the fog is starting to lift and I'm starting to feel relaxed and refreshed. Do you have vacation plans this summer? In our business it can be hard to truly get away. You may feel like you are going to miss out on business opportunities, buyers might get away, sellers will be unhappy. I'm here to tell you, it's not true, any of it. My first year in business we had a vacation scheduled with extended family that had been scheduled long before I even knew that a layoff, career change and real estate was on the horizon. I was so terrified of missing an opportunity. I was brand new (as in just a couple weeks) and had a buyer I had just started working with. He ran me all over with no regard or respect for my time or schedule. Thankfully I wasn't working with anyone else at the time! We delayed our trip so I could take the buyer out, then I ended up cutting it short to come back and show him homes. We were gone less than 4 days, and those days were miserable as I was stressed and on the phone. The buyer never bought anything in the area (I stalked the tax records for a long time), and I learned several valuable lessons.

Since that time almost 15 years ago, I have routinely taken vacations every year, often a week or more at a time (this vacation is 2 ½ weeks), gone on my honeymoon, and taken 3 maternity leaves. I know for certain that my business is stronger as a result. I return refreshed, energized and ready to work. The key to that for me, is that while I am away, I am almost completely unplugged. My voicemail and auto email reply both reference my vacation and to contact my Client Care Manager in my absence. All of my current/active clients and agents that I am in a transaction with were notified before I left and given her information as well. I set up a keyboard shortcut on my iPhone, so if I get a text message all I need to do is type 2 letters and a text is ready to send with my coverage information, who to contact and when I will be back. Twice per day, usually in the morning and in the evening, I do a quick scan of my email. Trash is deleted, anything needing attention now is forwarded, and anything for me to address when I get back is moved to a "To Do After Vacation" folder ... that way my inbox stays clear and when I get back, I'm not greeted with over 1000 unread emails (that happened once, never again).

You can do this too, I promise. You are worth it, and so are your clients. Most of us have likely encountered the agent trying to work on vacation, responses are delayed or spotty, and good service is not being provided to anyone. Don't think you need a paid assistant, employee or team to make this happen. Partner with an agent that you trust, and cover for each other. There are no rules, work out an arrangement that works for you.

July 24, 2017

The last 2 ½ years have been crazy. Early 2015 was filled with uneasiness, hatefulness and drama. Then my mother, whose cancer was supposed to be in remission, suddenly fell ill and passed away. My heart was forever changed and things I would tolerate before, were clearly no longer worthwhile, or even on my radar screen. I launched into the new role of taking care of my father, essentially running 2 households. In his late 70s he had never paid a bill or managed money (my mom did all of that). To this day he still brings me his mail every couple days. The page in my book of life was turned for me, whether I liked it or not (I didn't).

A couple months after my mom passed, my aunt (her sister, who has always been a 2nd mother to me) was diagnosed with cancer. I was now attending all of her doctor's appointments and procedures. This was all too much. In the midst of this I left my position as a managing broker and went back to the field to rebuild my real estate business. A business that had essentially been shut down for more than 2 years. Time for me to turn the page on my terms. During a routine medical checkup for me about a month or so after returning to the field I had my own cancer scare. A large and fast-growing breast tumor. I'd actually had several of these in the past and had them removed (always benign), but my doctor was concerned that this one seemed different and more aggressive. It was while I was at the hospital one day waiting for my aunt to come out of one of those procedures that I was on the phone scheduling one of my own. A significant surgery with reconstruction and several weeks of healing. About a week before my surgery my business partner Vicky Noufal and I officially launched our team, Platinum Group Real Estate. Not just a new page, but a new chapter had begun.

In December of that year, just as we had started to breathe again, we were all hit with one of the most devastating blows imaginable when Vicky's husband was diagnosed with late stage, aggressive cancer, with no known cure, and a horrible prognosis. I'll never forget it ... I was standing in the Orlando airport waiting for my flight home with my family talking to her as we learned the news and through tears she said, "I quit my job, this is my job now".

The next 18 months were the lowest of lows, with a few great highs sprinkled in. Vicky became full time cancer cure researcher, holistic medicine expert, special diet food preparer and caretaker ... with some real estate here and there when things were good. I worked for the both of us, both our businesses and running the team. The pages were turning slowly, painfully.

On May 31, 2017, our world, the whole world, suffered the greatest loss when Joe passed. Have you ever felt someone else's pain so acutely, it is almost like it is your own? It isn't though. At the end of the day, I get to return home to my husband and "normal" life, Vicky does not. This can't be the end of the book, can it? It was never supposed to end this way.

And so here we are. I'm feeling restless, in between. Throughout all of this, the hard work, the emotions, the tears, my business has built and grown, and is back on track, almost as if I never left it. I'm on pace to outperform my best year ever as an individual agent (the year I stopped to manage). Thank God for bountiful blessings amongst the chaos of everything else.

So now what, turn the page again? New chapter? New book? I'm not sure. That is why I've been more quiet here the past couple months. Things are shifting again, my children are growing rapidly, my husband is on the just under 10-year countdown to retirement from the fire department. I'm not sure what's next, but I feel some excitement, and fear and trepidation as it approaches. I'm trying to sit here quietly in the middle, waiting patiently (not my gift), seeking an answer, praying, feeling it all out. I just finished reading Lara Casey's new book, "Cultivate", which focuses a bit on this same thing. A good read. Is this the valley or the mountaintop? I'm not sure. What do you do when you are waiting in the middle?

August 9, 2017

Last week my friend Aliyah Dastour was bullied. Publicly, via a comment on her own post that she wrote about a book she is writing. Essentially this person told her that she wasn't qualified to write a book, that she should stick to her "little mommy business", let the experts write the books, and on and on. If you are friends with Aliyah, you may have seen her emotional video response. Why do we do this to each other?

Bullies are everywhere. In my experience, the more successful you are, the farther along you are on the right track, the more likely they are to show up. Why any woman (or man for that matter) would tell another that they should play small and "stick to what they know" is beyond me. The "experts" in any field didn't start out as experts ... they started out like you or me with a desire to grow and learn and do more ... exactly what she is doing now, and I hope you are too.

It is sad how many people are driven by fear and lack in their life, and not only does that keep them from growing, but they also then try to keep others from doing the same. Success is not a pie with a certain number of pieces to hand out, it is infinite, I'm sure of it! Just because you are successful at something, doesn't mean that there is less for me and vice versa.

As I have experienced in my life, when the hate comes at you, it's sometimes there for you to rise above and to push you to the next level. It can sound hard to believe, especially when it is fresh, and you are in the thick of it ... it hurts (a lot!) ... but I can truly say that I am so thankful for mine. It opened my eyes to new possibilities, and the business, the true business, that came out of that has been such an incredible blessing. More than I could even have imagined.

Here's what I also loved about how Aliyah chose to address this (via a video) ... airing it out removes the power. When you have been attacked by someone (verbally or otherwise), there is great shame that comes with it, and part of that shame is with the secret, not wanting others to know. Fear of reactions if they knew. People who do these things count on that. Even though the comment was posted publicly, there is still a private shame and pain attached. She took that power away.

Aliyah (and many of you reading this right now), you are genuine, authentic and not afraid to act on your dreams and ideas, which is what will make you a target to those who are not and who cannot. Write your book, and I'll continue writing mine, and one day we can market them together. Everyone has a story to tell and a book inside them that should be shared.

September 22, 2017

Are you treating your real estate business like a business? It is a business you know. And a business requires consistent investments in time, effort, attention, education, and money to continue running. If your reason for being in real estate is for a fun hobby or a little extra spending money, I promise that it is not worth your time, money or aggravation. This business is HARD. We are often the verbal and mental punching bags clients who are frustrated with the market or their own bad decisions when things aren't going their way. We sacrifice evenings and weekends and often miss family events for people who often treat us as disposable. We can spend hours over the course of days, weeks, months, sometimes even years for a client who backs out of a transaction at the last minute or walks into a model home and buys a house without us, and then we are never paid for our hard work or expenses. This business is expensive, the fees alone on a yearly basis just to keep your license and tools of the trade active can add up to the cost of a small transaction. I've often been frustrated over my career, particularly during my time as a managing broker, watching agents refuse to spend tens or hundreds of dollars in investing in their business and marketing, saying it's too expensive, only to turn around and spend the same amount on a new pair of shoes. The new shoes will wear out in a season or two, while the connections you make from one month of prospecting can earn you hundreds of thousands in commissions over your career.

When you are running your business like a business you've got to keep your eye on the big picture and know why you are doing it. If you want to build a sustainable business for the long haul to support your family, put your children thru college, buy a retirement home, etc., then focus on that. Some months that may mean not going to Target or not buying the cute new pair of shoes so you can invest back into your business, your prospecting and marketing or maybe even childcare so you can work. The rewards of our business can be tremendous, but not without effort, not without hard work, and not without sacrifice. That sacrifice may mean missing a dinner at home with your family to show homes and write a contract, or it may mean giving up a $4 a day Starbucks habit and putting that money into marketing instead. Either way, it can and will pay off if you are focused, consistent and determined.

October 11, 2017

Let's face it, our industry is a competitive one. I've known many agents over the years that I have worked with, come in contact with, or even asked for help/advice who are afraid to share what they know or do in their business. Afraid that someone else will "steal" their idea and somehow take their business. A lot of that is just paranoia and a lack mindset ... the fear that there isn't enough. The real estate business isn't a pie with a limited number of slices, there is more than enough to go around. Sometimes it's warranted. I remember my first team leader telling me stories (from probably 20+ years ago) of how other agents in her previous office would go through her trashcan for information/leads (this was before everything was electronic). Most times it's not.

Sure, there are some things that are proprietary ... a team or brokerage agreement, for example. Otherwise, I'm almost always happy to share, and here's why ... you aren't me, and I'm not you. Even if I laid out step by step by step exactly how I do things, with the exact presentations, scripts and marketing materials your delivery will not be the same as mine (nor mine yours, if roles are reversed). The most beautiful thing about our business, our world really, is that no two people are exactly alike. No one is you, not only is that your superpower, but that is the unique value proposition that you bring to the table, and it cannot be duplicated by anyone.

So, the next time a colleague wants to meet for lunch or coffee or calls to "pick your brain", say yes! My guess is that through the conversation you will learn some things too. And don't be frustrated if you are following the same steps to success as someone else and aren't getting the same results. Her journey is her journey, and your journey is yours. There are many factors that affect how we perform, follow up, what we do. From mindset to personal history, it all plays a role in where you are going and how fast you will get there. The "you" factor in any of that is your superpower, know it, embrace it and use it. The faster you do, the further you will go!

October 20, 2017

We had some terrific conversations at our Monthly Meet Ups yesterday about systems! For me, systems are the difference between getting things done and working efficiently. Not only do they make my life and my job easier, but they also make it repeatable ... by someone else. By establishing systems in your business to make things run smoothly for you now, you then also make it easy for someone to assist you when you are ready to hire down the road. Systems also help you to combat "decision making fatigue". Not thinking about what I should do now or when should I do this; the decision was already made for you when you set up your system. You just implement.

For those who couldn't join in the meet ups yesterday, here are some of my key tips ...

1. Any task that you do more than twice you should establish a system for. Don't recreate the wheel every time. Even if you know what you are doing, how and when, eventually when you are very busy it will become easier to forget details if you don't have a set system for what you will do and when.

2. Take the time to write out your steps, from start to finish, that you do in each phase of a transaction. For example, I have checklists/task lists for when I sign a new listing, when that listing goes under contract, when the home inspection contingency is removed, when settlement is complete and when it is time to close out the file. Each phase has steps that I will complete, even down to the very basic like send a copy of the contract to the title company, and to the things that are important but will get skipped over when we are busy (like sending a thank you note to the agent who sent you the offer).

3. Decide where you will keep/how you will use these checklists. Maybe a paper checklist works best for you, I did this for many years. Eventually I started using Evernote for this, and now I keep track of my transaction tasks in DotLoop. The systems I use for client relationship follow up are in marketing campaigns in my Referral Maker CRM. At the Meet Up I hosted yesterday I heard others talking about using Google Docs, Realty Juggler, even Boomtown for managing their transaction systems and sharing that information with others.

4. Establish a system for your listing and buyer presentations. At all times I have 5+ packets ready to go at my office and at my home for my listing presentation. All I have to do is grab a packet, double check that I like the brochure samples inside (as compared to the type of listing I am going to), add my detailed marketing plan for that property and my comps and I'm ready to go. Do the same for what you will do after the appointment. How many times have you met someone for an appointment, had it go really well, but they weren't going to be ready to doing anything for several months ... and then

you forgot to follow up? I know I certainly have. Not anymore ... I have a marketing campaign template in my Referral Maker CRM that I launch when I get back from the appointment (or in the morning before I go). It then sets up a series of tasks for me to complete from jotting down notes about the appointment so I don't forget key details (like what the seller owes, the commission we discussed and the sales price I suggested), to sending them a thank you note, to reminding me in certain intervals to follow up.

5. Look for opportunities for things to be duplicate-able. For example, I set up keyboard shortcuts in my iPhone for phrases I type often, like directions to my office. I have an email signature (this could also be an email template depending on the system you use) set up and ready to go for my sellers for the first time we receive feedback on their listing. Instead of re-typing the same things over and over again, I just type a few letters or apply an email signature, and it is ready to go!

6. Systems work not just in our business, but in our personal life too! Every morning as soon as I get up, I throw in a load of laundry to wash, switch it to the dryer when it is time for me to get in the shower, and it will be done by the time I am ready to head out the door. The kids can then put it away when they get home. On Sundays I have my "Sunday Checklist" of tasks that I do (my whole family usually helps) to help me to be more prepared for the week. Things like filling the bathrooms with toilet paper, emptying all of the trash cans, prepping school lunches for the week (it is easier and faster to spend 10-15 minutes on Sunday making 10 sandwiches for use throughout the week vs spending 5 minutes every night making 2 for the next day), filling my car up with gas, refilling the dog food and treat containers, etc. These seem like silly things, but when you are running like crazy during the week they are not only irritating but seem to always need filling or doing at the most inconvenient times. Spend a little time at once prepping for the week, and your week will go more smoothly.

Don't discount the power of a system! Minutes saved here and there add up to extra hours in your week ... hours you could spend prospecting for new business, enjoying time with family, or even doing something for yourself! Don't underestimate the few minutes that you will save by using a system.

Invest the time upfront to set up your system, and it will pay off for years to come.

October 25, 2017

Sometimes, a lot of times, our business can feel isolating and lonely ... even though we spend much of our day meeting with or talking to people!
The same could be said of motherhood, being a wife or partner, being an adult child caring for older parents, and many of the roles that we play out every single day.

What we often need, I know what I need, is to just vent out the frustrations and feelings to someone who knows, someone whose been there, someone whom I know can relate, or just someone who I know will be a gentle and understanding ear. I know that getting it out of my head will "lessen" the pent-up worry and frustration that I am carrying around. The same way that voicing a secret, that thing you don't want anyone to know or that you feel ashamed about ... getting it out kills it power and it's hold over you.

I'm so grateful that I have been able to surround myself with a wonderful team of women for whom at any moment or situation, can be that ear.
Do you have someone or a group of people who can be that for you? If not, make it a priority to find them! Start within your current brokerage or company, maybe an agent that you worked well with on a transaction and connected with. Invite them to coffee or lunch. My guess is that it will be therapeutic for both of you!

November 16, 2017

It feels good to be back at work this morning, fresh off my team's annual business planning and goal setting retreat! We had so much fun and cried so many tears, the cleansing, releasing "stuff" kind and the laughing so hard kind.

We did something new this year with a symbolic "polar plunge" in the ocean to cleanse away the old as we get ready for the new year. We even surprised everyone with our own private dance party, bringing in a DJ who set up a night club complete with light show at our rental house so we could dance the evening away. We reviewed 2017, presented what's coming in terms of marketing, schedules, budgets and more for the new year, and shared our business and personal goals for 2018. It was invigorating and refreshing, but I am also, so, so tired today!

There were so many great take aways. One of my favorites came from Jackie Fields-Gleadall. One of her goals for 2018 is "don't anticipate, participate". How many times do we overthink things? It was a common thread for a lot of us. We don't send out our marketing pieces to our database or farm because we anticipate how the recipient will feel. As Beth Donahue shared, she can get a text or a message from a client that says, "the sky is blue" and she will interpret it as, "we hate Beth". How many of us do that? I certainly do. Instead, we are going to strive like Jackie to participate fully in our life and spend less time anticipating and over thinking. Just send the mailer or the email marketing piece. Don't pre-judge. If the recipient doesn't like to receive it, they can unsubscribe or let you know, or just throw it away without another thought. When you receive those messages that are unclear and you start reading into them, stop and ask the person what they meant. My guess is the answer is probably not what you thought. And if it is? The door is now open for an adult conversation.

November 22, 2017

If you have spent any amount of time at all around me or reading my posts here in the group, then you know that goal setting and business planning are two of my very favorite topics. I met my match 13 years ago when I met Vicky Noufal. It is quite possible that she loves goal setting, and striving to achieve her goals, even more than I do. So, you can imagine then how we have upped our game in this area since partnering together 2 ½ years ago to form the Platinum Group Real Estate team. It's like a whole new level of dreaming, goal setting, planning, (and the most important part) doing, and I am thankful for her and our team of 21 phenomenal women every.single.day.

Since founding Empowering Women in Real Estate almost 3 ½ years ago I've often been asked to share my processes and systems, to teach classes on the subjects, to write a book about it all (in progress!), and often I have. But now, it's time to take it to a new level too. We've worked hard. Diligently and consistently improving our process for goal setting and business planning for years. This year we developed a formula based on my own personal tracking data for identifying how many contacts you need to reach your transaction goals. Specifically connecting the actions and activities to the goal you've set. You can't reach the goal unless you know what it will take to get there and have a plan in place for how to do it.

And so, based on popular demand, we have now packaged our Goal Setting & Business Planning system and for the first time ever are offering it outside of our team. This system can be purchased for $99 and includes the worksheets and spreadsheets you need to document and analyze where you were business-wise in 2017, then take that data to help you to formulate your goal for 2018. With your goal set and knowing what you need to do in terms of contacts to get there, we also provide you with the framework for your marketing plan and budget so you can set yourself up for success now. In addition, we provide a video walking you through the steps. The system is simple and straightforward, and I know from personal experience, it works!

About that video ... the content has lived in my head for a couple weeks now since we decided we were going to offer this. Vicky wanted notes, a script, I said we were just going to do it. This is the same conversation and process that we explain to our team. So yesterday, literally amid chaos (we had 146 pies ready to go for our reverse pop by event at our office, which was due to start in about an hour, then the toilet in our one and only bathroom in our office started leaking) we put up a "filming in progress sign", shut the door to our office and pressed record on my laptop. Our goal was about a 15-minute video walking through the documents in the package and the process. About 10 minutes in my screen times out and my screensaver pops up! It takes a few seconds for me to unlock the screen, and we realize that the camera was still recording ... relief! We were happy with what we had done so far, and we were determined not to over think, so we went with it and our little blooper is permanently immortalized in the video.

Isn't that part of the lesson that we all need to hear? This time of year, and the goal setting and business planning process can be demoralizing and frustrating if your year wasn't great, and it can be incredibly scary if you had a fantastic year and now have the pressure to recreate and even surpass it. Nothing we ever do is going to be perfect. We can plan and prepare and research and try to recreate the wheel and become paralyzed in in-action and do nothing ... or we can take action. Take a first step, get it done. When Apple rolls out their new iPhones there are always glitches. Some known, some figured out as they go, but they release them anyway and improve as they go along. If it's good enough for Apple, then it's good enough for me! It's time for you to decide what your goals will be. Then commit to what it will take to achieve them, and then the success will come. Won't you join us?

December 11, 2017

This morning, I will go on my final listing appointment of 2017 (leaving for vacation tomorrow!). Over a year ago I shared a big goal here ... to go on 125 listing appointments from September 1, 2016 through December 31, 2017. I fell short of that goal, but still feel like I won the lottery! In that time, I have gone on 90 (!) listing appointments. Of those 90 appointments, I signed 67 listings and have 4 others that have committed to list with me in the new year. Of those remaining appointments, ¾ of them haven't listed at all, there are only a handful that I went on who chose to list with someone else.

So why am I telling you all this? Several things.

1) Accountability doesn't have to be scary! Set ego aside. If you reach the goal you declare for yourself, great! If you don't, no big deal! Those who love you and support you will love and support you no

matter what and won't look down on you. You shouldn't look down on you either.

2) Don't be afraid to set big goals! This was a huge goal for me, but I set it (and put it out there) anyway. In doing so, I was so much more focused on the listing side of my business (my preference), and I am certain that I did more because of that big goal.

3) Always look on the bright side. Did I reach my goal? Nope, not by a long shot ... but I did NINETY listing appointments, and signed the overwhelming majority, and that is something to be proud of. It doesn't matter to me that I didn't reach the big number, I am focused on what I did do, not what I didn't.

4) Tracking is a powerful tool. I feel like a broken record talking about this, especially to my team, but it's worth repeating again. How many of us have gone on appointments, buyer or seller, only for them to choose someone else? I certainly have. It's painful, isn't it? One of my "losses" this year was especially painful. It was one of my earliest clients from nearly 15 years ago, who I've done multiple transactions with. Friends. They were ready to sign, then decided to talk to a super discount, limited-service agent. They offered me the listing if I could match his deal (I was already giving them my "repeat client" discount), and I said no. It was painful, and a little ugly. I felt unappreciated, like all of the hard work I had done for them many times over was worth nothing. Then, I looked at my tracking list for this goal. When I realized how many appointments I had gone on, and more importantly how many people had trusted me to help them, this one suddenly didn't matter anymore. It can be very easy to get down and frustrated in this business, especially when you work hard and things don't go your way. For me, I've found that tracking is a quick and easy tool to snap me out of it.

5) Know your numbers. I've always been more of a "listing specialist", but I never had any idea how many appointments I went on or how many listings I would/could sign in a year. Now I have a baseline number to guide me with goal setting in future.

Now that this goal is over, I don't have plans to do another listing appointment goal for next year, but I do plan to continue tracking my appointments and signed listings. Do you have a big goal planned for yourself for 2018?

December 22, 2017

Ahh, I'm back, fresh from vacation. It is such a bittersweet feeling. Sad to leave behind a wonderful trip, but happy to be home, and feeling energized to get back to work. There is nothing better than taking a time out from work to fully let go and relax with family. I am a big believer in taking REAL vacations. And by real, I mean disconnected, phone off. I learned a hard lesson my first year in business when I allowed a potential client to ruin a family vacation (and they never bought a thing). Looking back, I'm grateful to have had that lesson so early in my career. Now, I take several unplugged vacations each year with my family, and I truly believe that my business is better and stronger for it.

Over and over again I've heard and seen agents who don't think they can take real vacations, afraid that they will lose business if their clients know that they are away. They feel guilty relaxing and having fun when they have listings that aren't selling, and buyers struggling to find a house. Trust me, I've been there with you, but it can and should be done, here's how I do it ....

First and foremost, you need a plan, a vacation "system" if you will, and to set expectations clearly. The main component of that plan is your back up person(s). It is a must that you identify one person to be the gate keeper. Depending on where you are in your business and how busy you are, that could be one agent (who you then cover for when they go on vacation), an assistant, or even a responsible friend who isn't in the business. You need someone friendly, professional and responsive who can take the detailed message when calls come in and then route them to the agent best suited to help. Perhaps you have one person covering all of your sellers and ready to present offers when they come in, and one ready to show property and write offers for your buyers. There is no one right way to do this, find what works for you.

Next (and this is key), you need to tell your clients and any agents you are currently in transactions with that you are going to be away and who they should contact in your absence. I typically do this via email the day before I leave and copy my "gate keeper" on the email. In that message I also clearly specify that while I am away someone will be presenting offers to them should an offer come in on their listing and also that someone (name them specifically, depending on how you put together your coverage) will be able to show them houses and write offers on your/their behalf. I also prepare a "while I'm away" email summary for those who are covering for me that provides a quick reference point for what may/will happen while I am gone (anything date specific), plus a sentence or two about each active client with their contact info and where they are in the process.

Now you need to let everyone else know with your out of office messages. Change your voicemail and set up an out of office auto email reply, in both reference who they should contact in your absence and when you will return. I also set up a keyboard shortcut for texting that says the same. Then when a text comes in, I can type 2 letters to populate my message and be done.

While I am away, I do like to check my email once or twice per day (usually first thing in the morning) to make sure nothing is missed and to keep from coming home to 1000+ emails (learned this one the hard way too). I set up a "to do after vacation" folder in my email and using my phone or iPad (I rarely bring my laptop along) I do a quick purge ... delete the junk, forward anything that needs a response to my person (just in case) then move everything that I need to address or follow up on to the to do folder for when I return. This way my in box stays clear (less temptation for me to respond to things) and I am less likely to miss anything important.

Whenever possible I try to schedule either one more "vacation" day at home once we get back to unpack and do laundry and at least work from home/don't schedule appointments for my first day back. This helps with "re-entry" and to give me time to follow up on what I missed and check back in with my clients.

Finally, relax! Enjoy your time away. Your business will be here for you when you get back. Don't listen to the stories in your head or from people who tell you that you will lose business. That is coming from a mindset of fear and lack. It can be done, I know it, I have done it over and over and over again for years.

2018

1-3-2018

Several years ago, we started a family tradition of setting goals together on New Years Day. This isn't anything fancy, I use the notes app on my phone or iPad, and we talk about things we want to do in the new year as a family. It is largely centered around experiences ... places we want to go, trips we want to take, etc. We also discuss family financial and relationship goals (mostly my husband and I, but good for the kids to hear), and then each person takes a turn setting a couple goals for the year. For one of my sons, it is to improve his hitting in baseball, for another being on the honor roll each semester, for the youngest trying a bite of new foods at dinner each night (this one was set for him, and he wasn't thrilled, but that's a story for another day).

This has gotten better each year as the kids have gotten older and more into it. This year we had more of a conversation about what we do to reach our goals. Some of the goals the kids set were the same as last year, and so we talked about the need to do new things to try to reach our goals. Doing the same things you have always done will not give you a new result. If you want to do something new, improve something, you have to take different actions. I think we all know this, but doing it is the hard part.

Isn't that true for so many things? If you aren't pleased with where your business is right now, doing the same things you have always done will not move your business forward. If you aren't happy with the current state of your health and fitness, following the same diet and moving the same way (or not at all) isn't going to improve how you look and feel, you need to do something different.

Likewise, when you have a problem ... whether it is personal, business, financial, whatever ... the same level of thinking that you had when the problem was created is not going to get you past it. You need to rise above it, think at a different level, ACT (key) at a different level, and then you can overcome it. This is also where and why having trusted friends and advisors are so important. It is often hard for us to think a new way, to try something different, especially when it is what we have always done or the way we have always thought. Having someone to confide in that may have new or different ideas or ways of thinking can help to open up your own mindset. What problems are you trying to solve right now in your life or business?

January 5, 2018

One topic we talk about a lot here is consistency. There are so many things in our businesses that require consistency ...
-Consistent follow up
-Consistent marketing
-Consistent prospecting

And so much more. Coming back to work this week after a 3 week break in my normal work schedule from vacation and winter break has reminded me of one more reason why consistency is so important in our business. When you aren't consistent, everything is HARDER.

Case in point ... my daily business building activities. These are a series of activities that I do each day, Monday through Friday to focus on my business. They are a combination of follow up and prospecting. On a normal day, they take about 45 minutes, maybe an hour. I started doing these consistently last year, only missing when I was on vacation or traveling.

For months and months these tasks have flowed rather easily for me. As long as I did them first thing in the morning (if they got pushed later in the day they were harder to complete with the daily interruptions and sometimes didn't get finished), the more I did them the easier they became. The words for the notes I would write came more easily. The reasons for the notes and the calls came to me more quickly. Giving referrals to my preferred vendors each day came in multiples.

Now this week, after several weeks off and out of my habit, it is SO HARD to get these done each day! It is taking me twice as long. I'm having to think longer and harder about what to say and to who. I've been less engaged, and so the referrals aren't going out as easily. Therefore, it is taking me more energy and more willpower each day to get this done. It's like I am starting over again from scratch.

So, the lesson and reminder here is to be consistent and stay consistent. This isn't going to stop me from going on vacations, but I will definitely allow more time when returning for these tasks, knowing that it will take a bit more time to get back in my groove. If you have a habit or routine that you are working to implement in your business, don't quit because it feels hard! I promise you that the more consistent you are, the easier it will become.

January 8, 2018

Did anyone else stay up way past their bedtime like I did to watch the Golden Globes? Oprah Winfrey's acceptance speech when receiving the Cecil B DeMille award was positively awe-inspiring. I've already seen clips of it making the rounds on social media this morning, so if you didn't catch it live, do yourself a favor an find a recording of it to watch today.

Getting up this morning was a little harder than usual, and it's (another!) snow day here. This all goes to say that there are lots of excuses NOT to do what I know I need to do today. We talked a lot here last week about consistency and getting back into our routines and habits after the winter break. I'm determined no matter the circumstances today to make that happen.

So, at 9 am this morning (the time I would usually be pulling into my office after dropping off the kids at school) I'll be sitting down at my desk at home. We do a quick support team meeting each Monday at 9 to go over plans for the week, and as soon as that is done, I will start immediately on my daily business builders. I will not check email, answer the phone or respond to text messages until they are done. What is your plan for today?

January 10, 2018

In this business we wear many hats ... real estate advisor, therapist, marriage counselor, and many more. If you've worked with even a few clients, then certainly you know what I'm talking about. Anytime you work in a service industry, working with, for and serving others, it is inevitable that you will see people at their best, but also very much at their worst. Buying, selling, even renting homes are stressful times. Moving is stressful. Often there are situations driving the clients need to sell or buy or move that are difficult, possibly rooted in some sort of financial or relationship turmoil. Maybe a job relocation that isn't desired. There are many factors that can make this business transaction a highly emotional one.

We are the gatekeepers. Part of our job, like it or not, is to as much as possible neutralize the drama and the emotion as we help guide our clients through the process. Oftentimes, that drama or emotional turmoil that our client is experiencing that affects the transaction becomes our problem too. It's so difficult ... I have several sellers right now in highly emotional, challenging situations. This drives their decision making and reactions, and as much as I try not to let it affect me, sometimes it does. The way I react when the client is reacting or responding emotionally is often the determining factor in how the conversations will go. As the 3rd party, I can see so clearly what needs to happen, how it should go to help them out of the situation they are in, but no matter how many different ways I try to explain it or get the point across, sometimes it just doesn't work. Has anyone else ever been in this situation? What strategies do you use to neutralize these emotional situations and help to get your point across?

January 12, 2018

Last night I was talking to a friend and colleague who was feeling upset about a situation that happened this week. After working very diligently to put a rental transaction together, she found out that her clients (the tenants) had misrepresented something to her, and everything fell apart at the 11th and a ½ hour. Naturally, when notifying the listing agent of the situation, they were very upset, and I'm sure the landlord was as well. Unfortunately, some of that became directed at my friend, even though she had done nothing wrong. This was so upsetting to her, and she found herself becoming very emotional about it. Although the issue wasn't hers, and ultimately wasn't something she could control, she felt responsible and so badly for everyone involved.

Has this ever happened to you? We work so hard for our clients, and sometimes, no matter what you do, things go wrong, or you find out that the client misrepresented something that affects everyone involved, and makes you look bad too. We do have many checks and balances in our industry, but at the end of the day, we are dealing with people, and sometimes people aren't honest. Whether they deliberately mislead us and others, or something happens to cause circumstances to change, it can be inevitable to find ourselves in these situations at least a time or two.

My business partner Vicky Noufal has a favorite saying, "not my monkey". Meaning that while we are impacted by issues and circumstances surrounding our clients, at the end of the day it isn't OUR issue. Often though, we do end up taking it on for ourselves, like my friend did. In some ways, I think that is part of what makes us good ... that we care so much for others and have so much empathy for their situations. It can be what sets you apart from those who are just in it for the numbers and the commission. But it can also be so draining to take on the emotions and the issues of others. Even though they aren't our monkeys, they still impact us and our ability to do our jobs. As much as you care, you still have to find a way to keep it separate and keep it from affecting you. Always care, but learn not to carry.

January 16, 2018

Are you a reader? I love to read, always have. For years I said that I didn't have time, but truly we all have more time than we think. There are small pockets of time and windows where a good book is very useful. I've taken to carrying mine in my handbag, so when I'm waiting for a client, or waiting at a doctor's office, dentist, car service, etc. instead of flipping through their old magazines, I have something of my choosing to read. For a long time, I thought my only opportunity to read was at night in bed, but after just a couple pages I would fall asleep, no matter how interesting my book. I'll do that sometimes now, but not as often. Some of my kids in middle school are supposed to read 20 minutes a day, at least a couple days a week, so we have started making a habit of doing that together.

Last year I made reading more of a focus for myself, with a goal to read a book a month, and by the end of the year I had read 14 books! This year, my goal is to read 2 per month as I have learned the art of "books on tape". There are many services where you can listen to books, I've heard of a free app called "Hoopla" which connects to the public library. I use Audible, a service through Amazon which connects with my Echo Dot (a smaller version of "Alexa", if you are familiar with that device). I have one in my bathroom, and I listen to a book each morning while I am getting ready for work. One thing I discovered about listening to books is that there are some books that I struggle to get through reading them, but I really enjoy listening to them. So far this month I've finished 2 books (1 reading and 1 listening) and I am part way through listening to another, and will start reading a new one today.

My favorite genre is non-fiction, usually some type of business of personal improvement. I haven't read a fiction book in many years. When I did, I would get so involved in the story that I literally couldn't put the book down. I'm not sure I have that kind of time right now, or the discipline to leave it when I need to, so for now I'll stick with non-fiction. What are your favorite kinds of books to read? Is there a book on a subject related to our business that you would love to read, but haven't found?

January 17, 2018

One of the books that I finished this month was, "What the Most Successful People Do Before Breakfast" by Laura Vanderkam. The book is actually made of up of 3 shorter books, and there were several great principles that she covers in each.

How often have you said, "I don't have time for that" or "I'm (so, too) busy")? Whether relating to a social activity, business tasks (like prospecting), taking vacations, hobbies and more, I'm sure that all of us have been guilty of that on practically a daily basis. I know I have. When you look at people who are high producers, efficient, very successful, it can be easy to think they somehow have more time or are sacrificing all of their "fun" or family time to work, but by and large, that isn't true. It's all in how intentionally you use your time.

We all have the exact same amount of time ... 168 hours per week. Now let's say that you sleep 8 hours per night, that is 56 hours total, and then you work 50 hours per week, that still leaves you a total of 62 hours each week ... that is a lot of time! More time in fact than you spend working or sleeping, so where does it go?

I realized the truth of Parkinson's Law ... work expands so as to fill the time available for its completion ... when I became a managing broker. Prior to that, when I was in the field, I would spend many nights up until 11 pm or later checking and responding to email, doing CMAs, preparing for appointments, etc. The tasks seemed to all take longer, and because I didn't establish any boundary or guidelines for my work, they could drag on for a day or more. The great thing about our job is that there is flexibility, we can work when we want/when we are able, often from anywhere ... but that blessing can be a curse if you don't apply discipline and manage your time well. When I accepted a management position, a big part of the reason was those late nights and wanting to spend more time with my family. As a result (and also because a certain amount of office hours were required), I intentionally determined that once I left the office each day that I would leave the work at work. Now, I still often ended up taking calls and responding to emails/texts all through the evening, but I was away from the office, and I wasn't doing any proactive work or working on projects. What I learned by establishing that end time each day was that I got so much more done!

When you don't have a certain time to finish your work by, that work can easily creep into more and more time, occupying more of your day. There is no "push" to complete it, so instead of just doing it, you end up checking Facebook for a bit. Then putting in a load of laundry or running an errand. Maybe researching some new pop by ideas. Then before you know it, the day is turning into night, nothing has really happened to move your business forward and you are up working late at the computer once again. I've been there, I lived this, I know the toll that it can take on your energy, your mindset and eventually your business.

Try establishing a target end time for your days. I've been back in the field now for almost 3 years and applying this to each day means that not only am I far more productive than ever with my business, but I am logging fewer hours too. I have found that this is much easier to execute when I go to the office each day. Then, when I go home, unless something urgent is happening with a contract that needs to be presented or negotiated, I don't even take my laptop out of my bag until I get to the office the next morning. Often, I have days that I need to work from home, and it is definitely more challenging to allow the work to creep into every hour of the day, but even then I will intentionally stop at a certain hour (usually when the kids get home from school, or right before dinner time) and won't go back to my desk until the next day. This habit has been one of the very best for me in terms of not only "balance", but also for my family, for my energy, and ultimately for my business. By having a shorter amount of time to accomplish what I need to, I am focused on productivity, which means I am focused on action. Taking action in my business makes things happen.

Be intentional with how you use your time. In the book, the author talks about spending a few days doing a time log. Jotting down how much time you spend on each task, business, personal or otherwise each day. The idea is that you will see where the gaps are in your time, what you are wasting time on, what your patterns are, and where your "golden hours" are. We all have times of day that we seem to be most energized and productive. Don't waste those hours on low value activities.

For now, I am working on "blocking" or segmenting my days. I find that I do best with appointments first thing in the morning or later in the afternoon/early evening. That gives me late morning/midday/early afternoon for prospecting, follow ups, paperwork, email and more.

January 22, 2018

When is the last time you helped a rental client? We had an interesting discussion on our team's check in call on Friday. Beth Donahue, a very experienced, consistent high-level producer said that she was focusing on working with some rental clients right now to help build her database. Now, she certainly doesn't "need" to ... she ratified something like 3 contracts last week, but she is intentionally choosing to. It is what she did in the beginning of her career which helped to build the business that she has today, and she intentionally chooses to focus on her business as a series of relationships, no internet leads. She knows that working with a rental client (leads from her own rental listings) will allow her to build a relationship that will add to her database and become a new source of referrals. Not to mention a likely buyer in a year or so.

If you have been in the business for a while ... remember what it was like when you were new? You were so excited (and a little scared!) when the phone would ring ... it could be someone who wants to buy a house! Showing homes was exciting. Open houses were exciting. Every.single.thing was so exciting! Then time passes, we realize what can happen when you work in a customer service industry, and you become jaded. Instead of "yay, the phone is ringing", it becomes, "ugh, what do they want". We get tired, sometimes burned out, we keep doing the same old things over and over again. Usually because they worked before, but maybe not as well (or at all) 5 years later. We stop learning, stop going to classes, stop seeking knowledge from books or others, stop trying new things, all because we are so darn busy.

You know what happens then? We become complacent. Less friendly, less excited, less willing to do what it takes to move to the next level. Too tired to care or to try. Does any of this sound familiar? Do you know what the fix is? Be willing to be a beginner again. Try something new in your business. Adjust your mindset. If you are feeling all of the above, maybe it is time for you to retire or exit the business. There is no shame in that if that is where you are, but maybe it isn't. Maybe it is time to engage your imagination and infuse it into your marketing. Maybe it is time to mentor or spend time with a new agent, their excitement can be contagious. Maybe it is time to attend a class, read a book, meet some new people (both clients and others in the industry). What do you do when you need to get your energy flowing again?

January 26, 2018

What is your why? We hear this again and again. I've heard it at many of the real estate conferences I've attended, read it in books, discussed in podcasts, addressed in blogs and on and on. But I have to say, it never fully clicked with me until I started reading Simon Sinek's book this week, "Start With Why".

I remember talking to a colleague a few weeks ago about her "why". She, like many of us I think, thought that your why had to be a grand existential motive. A beautiful expression of something huge and worthy. That could be true for you but doesn't have to be. Your why can be simple, it can (and should) change with the seasons of your life. Your why for wanting to lose weight could be to fit into a certain dress, or your why for wanting to build your business could be to pay off debt. Those whys will drive you forward, may even get you to your goal, but then what?

Have you ever known or seen someone whose why for doing something is purely driven out of anger or spite? We certainly all have. That hatred and vitriol will energize them in the beginning and keep them going for a while, but after a period of time it's no longer enough to keep the vision going and their purpose fades away. I love this quote, "Working hard for something we don't care about is called stress. Working hard for something we love is called passion." It's your why.

Last week on The Tom Ferry show, Tom talked about prospecting time. How many of us avoid it, shy away from it, will do anything we can to not do it. Part of that, he said, is that we associate it with something painful, something that we don't want to do. Instead, he suggested associating it with our why. For example, if part of your why or motivation for working and growing your business right now is to pay for your children's college, then instead of calling it prospecting time, call it (and write it on your calendar as) "Building Bill & Suzy's College Fund Time" or whatever. Associating that time and task with why you are doing it, why you NEED to do it, can help you to focus and do what needs to be done.

Our business is hard. Between working with a not always gracious or honest public, and the intense competition between colleagues, it can be hard to stay focused and motivated, especially if you don't know why (or fully believe in why) you are doing all of this. So, your assignment today is to take a few moments and really think through why this business is important to you. Is it simply to help as many people as possible or maybe it is to retire in 5 or 10 or 15 years debt free and on a beach somewhere? That can give you the nudge you need to make those calls that you don't want to make. Whatever it is … think about it, visualize it, write it down, maybe even post it in your office or on your desk so the next time you feel like giving up, or you don't feel like doing what you know you need to do, your why will be there to remind you, and if it's really strong enough, will help push you forward.

January 29, 2018

One of our favorite family activities when the weather is cooler is putting together puzzles. I'm usually the one who gets started by putting it out on the dining room table, and my husband and three sons join me on and off to work on it. Saturday, I started with a 1000 piece puzzle of an old fashioned winter scene. Lots of snow, evergreens, trees without their leaves, some children sledding, a house and barns, a horse drawn sleigh. I always start by laying out all of the pieces, and then putting together the border. The straight edge pieces are the easiest to find and assemble.

As I am doing this it seemed extra hard. I was certain that I was missing pieces. It just didn't seem to be coming together. My husband had joined me by this point and when I told him that I thought pieces were missing he said, "you have everything you need right in front of you" (damn it). I continued on, and I had the majority of the border finished, except two spots where I just didn't seem to have the right pieces. I found that I kept getting frustrated. When I start something, I like to complete it, and I could only work for about 15-20 minutes at a time, then go do something else, and come back later. Definitely an exercise in patience. I found that when I would come back to it after a break, I would almost immediately find pieces I couldn't before and start making much more progress. After a while, that progress would wane, everything would start looking the same again, and it was time for another break.

My family would come in and out and join me at the table, but I was the only one working on the puzzle. Still, it was nice to have them there with me, each of us doing our own thing, but still there for each other. I decided to start working on one corner of the puzzle that was full of evergreens. Just focus on the green pieces, I thought. Only no matter how hard I tried; I couldn't seem to get any pieces to come together. Then the house started to come together, then the children sledding. I really wanted to finish one section before moving to another, but other pieces would jump out at me, and I would work there for a while before bouncing back to another spot. Throughout the weekend I piddled away and will likely be working on this still for a couple weeks before I'm done.

Part way through this process I realized that there were two pieces, one on each side of the border where I couldn't get things to work that were in the wrong place. At first glance it appeared that the pieces fit together, but on closer inspection, they weren't the right fit at all. Once I discovered this, I was able to make the adjustments and finished the border. Seems like my husband was right about having all the pieces all along (damn it again).

So why the long story about a puzzle? As I was working, I thought what a great metaphor this is for our life and our business. At any given time, you and I have everything we need. It's right here in front of us, within us. We just need to stop and recognize it. Things don't always go the way we want them to, in the order that we want them to. We often try and try, struggling to make something work, and when we stop fighting and move in the direction we are being prompted the pieces starting falling together almost effortlessly it seems.

Often, we think something is the right fit, but the more we work with it, the more it becomes obvious that something isn't right. Trust that feeling and investigate, you may find that some adjustments are required. Having those you love around you is the best part. Family, friends, just having them near to support you, even if they don't understand or necessarily want the exact same things you want is far more valuable than going it alone. Patience in anything is a must. This is extra hard for an impatient girl like me. We can't get everything done on our timeline. Sometimes it's better to go slow, take breaks. When you are frustrated and getting tired, it's better to take a little break. When you come back to what you were working on it will be with fresh eyes.

Life is like a big puzzle. Take your time. Savor it. Feel the frustrations. Take breaks when you must, but forge ahead, chipping away towards your goals, your purpose. It will be finished in due time, far faster than you think.

January 31, 2018

I really don't have too many other words today other than these. Working with people can be so hard. Especially when dealing with huge life transitions like moving and buying and selling homes. Some care only to point fingers at others, demand this and that for perceived "wrongs", never looking at the big picture or the others perspective. When you have those people on both sides of the same transaction it becomes especially toxic for all involved. Good people turn nasty on a dime. And who is left running interference, trying to solve and soothe while those causing the chaos continue pointing and sulking and fussing and screaming and are busy being hurt and concerned, so concerned? We do.

It's just business some may say. To an extent, yes, it is. But it is also people, and their lives and emotions and our livelihoods. "Just business" doesn't care about or take into account the people. It is what people in charge or control say when they want to pretend that their actions or decisions don't affect others, but they do. Every. Single. Time.

February 2, 2018

At my business networking group meeting last night we were talking about marketing. One of the topics we discussed was the importance of the words that you use in your marketing. For example, one person was talking about the importance of the keywords that you use online. Someone in the automotive industry may use the words "vehicle" or "auto body repair" to describe what they do, when actually the consumer would be more likely to search for "car" or "auto repair shop". It is important to speak the language of your target audience.

This reminded me of a story I read in "Start With Why" by Simon Sinek. Many years ago, a company came out with an MP3 player. They marketed it for what it does, a certain amount of memory or gig-something (obviously not memorable or connectable, I can't even remember it to explain it). Then 2 years later Apple came out with the iPod (also an MP3 player), which they marketed as being able to carry 1000 songs in your pocket. Guess which one was more successful? The iPod wasn't the first, and possibly wasn't even the best, but it was understandable. The consumer easily knew from the marketing not only what it was but why they would want or need the product.

Think about this next time you are preparing your marketing messages. What words do we use in our industry that the consumer is not as likely to understand or connect with?

February 5, 2018

Several years ago, when my mom died, I spent the next many months filled to the brim. Filled to the brim with grief, sadness, uncertainty, and overwhelm as I took on responsibility for dealing with the aftermath, and taking care of my father, his home and financial situation. This was all added on top of very demanding work (I was a managing broker at the time for 2 offices and over 125 agents), plus all of my other responsibilities caring for my home and children and family.

At any moment the slightest extra thing would cause a "spillover" of emotion. This wasn't necessarily in the form of tears or sadness. Sometimes anger, often lack of patience, frustration, short tempered-ness and even downright meanness. The simplest thing, extra traffic, not getting the answer I wanted in a customer service situation, a request from someone for something simple, even just my shredder jamming was enough to throw me into a fit. I wasn't always the nicest, friendliest, kindest or most patient person during this time. For those who didn't know what I was going through, and those who "forgot" (this went on for months), I'm sure I came across as a less than nice person, and they probably assumed that I was just a jerk.

Here's the thing ... everyone is dealing with something. Grief, loss, health issues, financial burdens, issues at home with a child or spouse. No one is immune. When you come across that person who cuts you off in traffic, the clerk at the grocery store who seems rude or unhelpful, the client who goes from zero to 60 in terms of anger in the course of a conversation, remember that they are likely dealing with something that you can't see or know. They are full up with their struggle, and you are seeing the spill over.

I read in "Braving the Wilderness" by Brené Brown that it is the people who act up, seem the least kind, who are the ones that need the kindness from us most of all. Remember this the next time you encounter someone who is having a bad day. It's not personal or directed towards you, even though it may feel like it is. Sure, some people are just big jerks who have complete disregard for others, but most people aren't. They are just dealing with difficulties that you cannot see. Give them the benefit of the doubt. Offer kindness, even if you don't see the return right away, the next person they encounter may. All because you took a moment to be kind.

February 9, 2018

Did you watch the winter Olympics last night? We caught a little bit of the men's skating. Several of the men were struggling with their routines, routines that they have likely practiced flawlessly hundreds of times. The amount of work, dedication and sheer sacrifice that it takes for the athletes to make it to this level is truly awe-inspiring. One of my favorites parts is watching and learning the stories behind some of the athletes. Last night there was a piece on American skater Nathan Chen. His 3rd grade teacher was interviewed, and she said of the children that she teaches that all of them are brilliant, but only some of them are producers. Other are non-producers.

I thought that was fascinating. We witness that in our business probably more than most. What is it that sets people apart? A willingness to learn? To try new things? To keep their eye on the big picture? A strong work ethic? I think it is all of the above, and most importantly the willingness to DO. Having great ideas is wonderful, we all have them from time to time, but you have to be willing and able to execute them. That means that you have to be willing and able to fail. Perfection is not attainable. If you wait to produce your mailer or your newsletter or your whatever until every single detail is absolutely perfect, then chances are you won't do it at all. It is the willingness and ability to do that sets us apart.

February 14, 2018

It is easy to get fixated on the things that we are struggling with, the things that we don't like ... both in our lives in general and in our businesses. But just as in life, in business it is not all bad (at least I hope it isn't, or perhaps it is time for a different type of re-assessment ... life is too short not to spend time doing what you love).

In honor of Valentine's Day, let's spend a little time today sharing what we LOVE about our businesses! Even in the midst of the hardest and most difficult days there is always something, even a tiny little thing to love, enjoy and be grateful for.

For me, there are many things that I love about my business, and it has certainly evolved throughout my nearly 16-year career. The biggest thing for me now is that my business allows me to design my life the way I see fit. I can be creative and make my own decisions. I'm able to work hard, be rewarded financially and with great satisfaction in helping others, but also be there for my family the way I choose ... driving my 3 sons to school, attending their events, volunteering in their classrooms, picking up from school some days, taking multiple fun trips and vacations each year and more. I work hard and a I work a lot, but I am able to design that work around what is most important to me, which is ensuring that my family knows that they are most important to me and that I am always there for them. This time with my children is so fleeting, the years seem to pass in the blink of an eye, I want to be there to fully enjoy and maximize all of those moments (even the ones where they are driving me crazy!).

February 16, 2018

How often are you asked to do things that you don't want to do, and you end up saying "maybe" (or worse yet, "yes") when you don't have the time or interest when really all you want to say is "no"? If you are like me, this has probably happened to you a lot more than you would like. I was taught from a young age to be a "good girl" and learned very early to be a people pleaser. It took me a really, really long time to learn that I can say no to someone else's request and still be a good person. Saying no isn't rude, or bad, or mean. We have so many demands on our time in this business, really in life in general. It is impossible to be all things to all people all the time.

When the phone rings in middle of dinner with your family it is okay to say no by not answering it and checking your voicemail later. When a potential client tells you that they want bottom of the barrel pricing and white glove service, you can say no if that is not your business model. When you are called (over and over again) by the website trying to sell you ads or the grocery store wanting you to advertise on their shopping carts, you can say no when you know that is not a pillar that supports your business. The more confident you are in yourself and in your business, the easier it is to say no when something doesn't work for you or won't help to support your goals. Like many things, it's a muscle that gets stronger over time. The more you understand yourself, are clear about your goals, and take the time to track and fully understand your business, the easier it gets. You owe this to yourself.

February 21, 2018

Recently I was listening to "The Brian Buffini Show" podcast and he was interviewing Casey Lohrenz, the first female F-14 Tomcat pilot. Casey said that her favorite quote was, "those who tell you that you can't, and those who tell you that you won't, are the ones who are most afraid that you will."

I love that quote. Has anyone ever told you that? It makes total sense to me. I've certainly had people who told me I couldn't or wouldn't, that I wouldn't be able to do it without them. Looking back, it makes sense that they are the ones who would be most afraid that I could and would. And guess what, I did. The conversation pretty much ends for me the moment someone tells me I can't do something. Especially if it is accompanied with some sort of ultimatum to stay in place, to not grow on my own. That is my non-negotiable and the fastest way to show me who you really are. No longer my friend or ally or advocate, but just another person putting his or her own personal agenda ahead of my own personal development and growth.

February 23, 2018

Earlier this week I saw a post in an online forum about what made you successful in real estate. This got me thinking about my own career, and what has been most helpful to me. Starting out, almost 16 years ago, I joined a rainmaker style team (a team where the leads are provided by the team leader, and all business and marketing is recorded under that person's name) under Sherry Wilson. This was a critical time for me in laying a strong foundation. I was exposed to a high level of volume, learned the value of systems, honed my work ethic, was taught the importance of goal setting and tracking, how to provide a high level of customer service, and so much more. The experience was invaluable, and I talk about it and refer back to that time often.

Speaking of work ethic, not being afraid to work, and work hard has been key. In the beginning, I spent every day, 7 days a week, for months in the office learning from others, listening to others on the phone, and being ready for any and every opportunity that came my way. Being there and being present opened up many opportunities. It didn't matter what it was or where it was, I jumped on it. As I grew in my career and went through changes both personally (giving birth to 3 sons, a few surgeries and tragic losses) and professionally (including "quitting" to become a managing broker because I was burned out, and then restarting my business 2 ½ years later) having the work ethic and discipline to do what needed to be done, even when I didn't feel like it has made the difference between having a strong business and no business at all.

At some point along the way, in the past couple years primarily, I really learned the power of doing. Grant Cardone says in his book "The 10x Rule" that when you have an idea or a goal you need to focus on action, not figuring out all the details, and I have to say that I agree. If you wait to implement something until it is perfect or until you have it all figured out the world will pass you by. Thinking and planning and organizing (two of my favorite things) won't get you where you want to go, only action does. I've learned that even when it feels uncomfortable, you have to put yourself out there and promote yourself. This doesn't have to be over the top or "cheese-y", but it is vital to the success of your business if you want people to think of you as their go to. Otherwise, you are just a secret agent and they aren't thinking of you at all when they or their friends or family need real estate assistance. Instead, no matter how much they like you as a person, they will connect with one of the many, many other professionals vying for their attention. It's not that they don't care about you, it's that they don't even know that you care about helping them.

Lastly, I'd say that possibly the most important thing for me has been connecting with a support system of people who truly and unconditionally care about me, support me and my business, and push me (ahem ... Vicky Noufal and Jackie Fields-Gleadall) even when I'm super comfortable and don't want to be pushed. Having these people who I know have my back gives me confidence to try new things, put myself out there, and be less afraid to fail. They brainstorm with me, get excited with me, and laugh with me when things don't work out. For me, this support system has been being a part of or having a team, but it can also be a group of colleagues that you know, like and trust. It can be an assemblage of your preferred vendors who support your business and vice versa. It can be agents in other brokerages, even in other cities or states, just find your tribe, and when you do, hold tight to them, no matter what.

April 9, 2018

Today, I would like to tell you a story about underwear. Stick with me here, I promise there is a message!

One morning last week as I was getting ready for work, I pulled a pair of underwear out of my drawer that I had only worn maybe once or twice (past due on laundry!). They were beautiful, excellent quality, a little expensive, and even though I have had them for at least 2 years they always get pushed to the bottom of the drawer because they aren't very comfortable.

After getting dressed I immediately regretted wearing them. I was uncomfortable all morning and it seemed as the day went on, the more uncomfortable they became. I found myself being crabby and having trouble focusing. Finally, I couldn't take it anymore ... I went to the bathroom at my office, took them off and threw them away (luckily, I was wearing pants that day!). Immediately, I felt better. What had I been waiting for all this time? I was now able to focus and had a great, productive afternoon.

This got me thinking ... how many times do we hold on to things that aren't working for us? I didn't get rid of those underwear before because I spent a lot of money on them (thinking I would like them, I originally bought more than one pair in different colors). Every day I would see them in my drawer and move past them to something else. Feeling a little guilty each time, thinking that maybe one day they would work for me.

Does this sound familiar? How many things are you dealing with in your life and in your business that you know aren't working for you? You know it's a bad fit, you know it was the wrong decision, but you hang on to whatever it is feeling badly that you spent the money and time on something that doesn't work. You try to convince yourself that the problem is you, and maybe one day when you do or are "x" it will work for you. In the meantime, you bog yourself down with extra stuff, guilt, and clutter. Holding tight to what doesn't work.

Just let go. One day is now, it is today. Let go so your hands will be free to pick up something else, something that will work for you. When you let it go, you will feel so much lighter, so much better and then be able to focus on being productive and moving your life and your business forward. You aren't the problem. Accept that whatever it is ... the wrong CRM, the wrong planner, the wrong lead generation tool, the wrong client, the wrong brokerage, even the wrong underwear ... is just that, wrong. For you. That doesn't make it bad or mean that it isn't great for someone else. It just isn't right for you, right now. And that is all that matters.

April 11, 2018

Have you ever found yourself saying no to a dream or an opportunity because of the time it will take? Many years ago, when working in my former corporate career I was meeting with our HR representative talking about benefits at the company and future roles for me. She encouraged me to return to school to get my bachelor's degree (I had an associate's degree at the time). I resisted, telling her that it would take years for me to finish between my full-time work schedule, and basically full-time volunteer EMT schedule. She told me that the time would pass anyway, and at the end of that time I could either have earned my degree or I could be in essentially the same place I am now. I was really struck by her comment (and I did go back to school and earned my BS in Business and Marketing!) and have never forgotten it.

How often do we see an opportunity or have a dream and think, "no, that's not for me" because I'm too old, too far along this path, too set in my ways?? Big things, dreams, accomplishments take time. Everything takes time. There is no overnight success at anything, even though it may appear so on the outside, you can be sure that likely years worth of preparation and hard work have led up to the current success. I've learned that it is less about the destination and more about the journey. It doesn't really matter how long it will take you to achieve something because getting to that something isn't really where the joy and the magic happens. It is in the day to day, learning, growing, doing, becoming, and that takes time. What are you saying no to because of the time it will take?

> **DON'T EVER LET A DREAM FADE BECAUSE OF THE TIME IT WILL TAKE. THE TIME WILL PASS ANYWAYS.**

April 16, 2018

Last week at the end of the Monthly Meet Up that I hosted in Leesburg, VA, the always kind Jan Kahl spoke up at the end of the session and offered some wonderful and complimentary words to me about the group. As we finished and were all preparing to leave, the very wise Liz McDonald asked me if I heard what Jan said, because she didn't think I heard her. She kept repeating this, and I realized what she was trying to get across was did I HEAR her. Of course I heard the words she spoke, but did I really HEAR them. Did I absorb it, take in, accept the sweet words that she offered. Which of course, I hadn't really.

Does this sound familiar? How often do we brush off compliments and kind words that are offered to us? When someone is speaking positivity into us about us, we rush them along, brush them off, wave them off. Why is that? Why is it uncomfortable to hear nice things?

I would say that most (if not all) of us crave words of affirmation, but when they actually come in our direction, we are suddenly unable to really hear them. Do you think maybe that is because we don't say enough kind words to ourselves? Is it that our inner dialogue is full of so much criticism that we seem unworthy of the compliments, and therefore can't receive them?

Productive criticism and critiques are very helpful, but none of us deserve them 24/7. They should be balanced with a healthy dose of acknowledging what you are doing right, that you, just as you are, are enough. Be more gentle with yourself. It is important, necessary, and very needed. I'd like to challenge you that the next time someone offers you kind words, take a moment, look them in the eye, listen fully, and then very simply, say thank you. And mean it.

April 18, 2018

At my team meeting yesterday, we had a lengthy discussion about rest. It has been a particularly busy spring market, and many of us are feeling overly tired and worn out. One person said that she is totally exhausted and needs 2 full days to rest and renew. Someone else said that it is important to push through as much as possible right now as the spring season truly builds 75% of our business for the year, and that come late summer/fall she will be happy to have pushed through during this time. I think both are right.

Rest is extremely important to our overall health, happiness AND productivity. If you are consistently worn down it will show in your energy level, in how much you have to give to others and in what you are able to accomplish. Sometimes (most times) the best thing you can do for your productivity is to take a rest.

Anyone who knows me well knows that I love (and thrive with) routines and habits. One thing I've learned over the past 6 months is that I need to be more flexible with those routines and habits, that they need to change with the seasons. The routine and rhythm that I had with my work and family life in the winter season when business was heavy on planning and planting seeds and the boy's basketball season only had us going to 2 games per week (plus practices) that were usually close to home is not going to work now when I am in the thick of the spring market, have active listings in the multiple double digits and almost the same amount of contracts pending, and baseball season is ramping up at home with several games (and practices) per week with more driving between them.

I've learned that I need to take advantage of the business season that I am in, but also be more flexible of my definition of rest. The last couple weeks have been especially busy for me, and my energy is feeling quite low. Right now, working from home on Mondays so I can take a late morning yoga class feels luxurious to me. Going to the grocery store at 8:45 am after dropping off the kids when the store is practically empty takes half the time. When I finished up with my team meeting and brokers open yesterday, I took a 20 minute nap on the couch in my home office and woke up feeling energized and able to tackle the most important things quickly and enjoyed a great dinner at home with my family. I'm being more intentional with conversations in the car with my kids on the way to school in the morning to make the most of that time since everyone's evening is much busier. Asking for (and sometimes paying for) help is key to survival this time of year.

Take it from me ... someone who burned out so badly five years ago that I quit ... learn to rest. REDEFINE your definition of rest for the season you are in. Be flexible with yourself and give yourself a healthy dose of grace. This season and time will pass, and the next season will offer its own challenges. The faster you can learn to adjust and flex, the easier it will be.

April 20, 2018

Last week at our Empowering Women in Real Estate Monthly Meets Ups our discussion topic was "Establishing Your Circle of Success". I learned very early in my career that part of being successful is having a group of people around you ... your circle of success ... to help you grow your business and flourish. Being a business owner or entrepreneur can feel very isolating, especially in our highly competitive environment. Family members and friends may not understand what we do and why, and so it can be difficult to find people out there who can relate to our challenges (and even our successes). This is where your circle of success comes in.

Your Circle of Success is likely (or should be) made up of people in these categories:
- Mentors/Trusted Advisor/Coach
- Colleagues/Teammates
- Trusted Vendor Partners
- Assistants/Employees

Having a solid, trusted mentor is key to business and personal growth in my opinion. A mentor can be someone who has already done what you want or has been where you are going, or someone who is a trusted advisor who understands your business or industry and can provide a listening ear and sage advice. To find your mentor, seek out other experienced professionals to collaborate with and look for your right fit. You can also be mentored by others through books and podcasts. I would consider Brian Buffini a mentor to me even though we have never met. I've followed his programs and systems for as long as I've been in business. I've been mentored through his seminars and conferences, courses, books and podcast. Hiring a professional business coach may be a good fit for you.

Being a member of or having a team is a great way to build your circle of success. Hopefully your team is made up of like-minded individuals with similar ideals, work ethics and drive. These should be people that you can trust not only with your clients, but you can also trust on a personal level for advice, suggestions, or even just to vent frustrations. If you are not on a team or don't want to build your own team, you can also find support from colleagues. Have you done a transaction recently with someone that you really felt comfortable with and would like to know better? Invite them to lunch or coffee. You could establish your own mastermind group, a group of individuals that you can collaborate with on a regular basis to share ideas and talk through challenges and successes.

In our business there are a number of vendors that we work with on a regular basis ... lenders, title company, movers, contractors, photographers, designers. The list goes on and on. Establishing relationships with people that you work with again and again can not only help your business, but it can allow you to be more efficient and provide a higher level of service to your clients. I work with the same few contractors again and again. They always provide great service to everyone, but because of the volume of business that we have together when I have a need for service for one of my clients, I am often able to get it addressed quickly (especially helpful for last minute urgent issues). Many years ago, I went to my preferred title company and requested to use the same processor for all of my files. Now I never have to wonder who to contact, everything is handled by one person. She understands how I do business; I understand how she does things, and as a result we work together far more efficiently than bouncing around to different companies or processors. I've learned in the last few years especially that Business to Business Networking can be a powerful tool to grow your business, but even if you never receive referrals from your vendor partners, having the attention and high-quality service that comes as a result of that relationship will pay many dividends in your business and the experience that your client will have.

If you are wondering when you will need to hire your first (or subsequent) assistant or employee, then that means you need one now. This is one of the questions I get the most. Finding the right fit can be hard, but once you find it, it is absolutely priceless. Don't be afraid to look outside the box. We found our Marketing Director right amongst our family, our Client Care Manager from Craigslist, our Client Care Coordinator through a friend of a friend, and our Real Estate Assistant/Runner through Facebook. There are many different ways to find the right person. To start you must identify exactly what you want that person to do. What are the daily tasks that you perform that could (should?) be done by someone else? Use this information to form a profile of who your best hire would be. Someone with social media marketing experience? Flexibility to run lockboxes and brochures in the afternoon and on the weekends? A high level of detail for managing contract files? As you develop this profile, you can put together a job description and go in search of right person for you. Include a qualifier in your application instructions. For example, when hiring our Client Care Manager our ad required that they go to a website and complete a (free) DISC profile and submit it along with their resume. Probably 75% of those who applied did not complete this step! Immediately we discarded their application. If they couldn't follow instructions in the application process, then we knew the attention to detail that we were looking for wasn't there to begin with. There is a saying, be slow to hire and fast to fire. Take your time to make a quality hiring decision, but don't be afraid to make a quick decision if things don't work out.

It takes time to establish your circle of success. Like everything, including success itself, nothing is over night. Your circle will shift, change and evolve as you move through your career and that's okay too! We change, our lives change, our businesses change, it is only natural that our circle will change. Who is part of your circle of success?

April 25, 2018

Have you seen the movie, "Black Panther"? I realize we are a little late to the party here. My middle son saw it early on with a friend, so we had planned to wait to buy the DVD to watch all together, only my son couldn't stop talking about it. So yesterday we took my oldest to see it for his birthday.

The movie certainly lived up to the hype, and it is easy to see why it has been so successful. It has all the great things you would expect from a movie … a great storyline, strong characters, action, adventure, drama, a little romance, a little humor. For Marvel fans there are several tie ins to other movies. The cinematography was amazing, and the scenery and wardrobes are beautiful.

The thing that struck me the most throughout the movie were the strong female characters. While the roles would be considered "supporting" roles to the King himself, there were many from the Queen to the guards, and these women were incredible, each one. Strong, beautiful, smart, confident. There was no doubt that these women knew exactly who they were and what they were capable of. They carried themselves with such strength and power, I found myself watching and wanting to be like them.

This is what I want for you, and for me. For all of us. That we know who we are, why we are, and carry that out with complete strength and confidence. That we stop looking to other people and things for validation, worthiness and happiness, that we find it within ourselves and in the image in which we were made. Whether in your business or your personal life, I hope that you will recognize your strength, your power, your beauty. It is something that we all possess. The more we see it in ourselves, and take the time to recognize it in others, the better we will all be.

April 27, 2018

Did you catch my recent Facebook Live Coffee Chat here in the group with Christina Daves of "PR for Anyone"? We talked about many things, but one of my favorite topics was about being a community ambassador. I really love this idea. I have always believed firmly and truly that one of the keys to success is in how you care for and treat others and in your generosity.

This is most clear to me in the area of geographic farming (marketing to a specific neighborhood or area). Many of us do it, it is a long-held marketing strategy in our industry. What I've found is that the way to have the most success with geographic farming isn't in just sending postcards a couple times a month, or sponsoring a community event, or having your face on the shopping carts at the local grocery store. It is a mix of all of those things. Getting massive results comes from being connected to your community, being visible, being available, being helpful.

Sure, if you only do one thing you may have some success, but when you position yourself as a fixture of the community, as THE person to work with in that neighborhood or area, that is when the business really flows. The good news (or bad depending on how you look at things) is that you can't just buy yourself into that position. Yes, financial investment is needed, but so is an investment in time, with people and on your community as a whole.

Do you consider yourself a community ambassador?

May 4, 2018

Once upon a time, many, many years ago, someone called me the "queen of losers". It was meant as an insult. I've always refused it as that, and instead will take it as a compliment.

People are not winners or losers. Some are not better than others. We all have different gifts and talents. Sure, some of us may be better at a particular something than someone else, but that doesn't make that someone else less than.

Everyone has potential. Everyone. What I have found is that some of us (many of us, maybe even most of us) need others to help us see the potential within ourselves. We need someone to believe in us. To help prompt us forward. Some need just a little nudge; others need a lot of pushing and shoving. Sometimes (oftentimes) we can't see the goodness within ourselves, we need someone else to point it out to us. I certainly know that I do, and I bet that you do too.

I believe in giving people a chance. A chance to do great things, to rise to the occasion of who they really are. If that makes me the Queen of Losers, then that is a crown that I will wear proudly. And I hope you will too.

May 7, 2018

It's Monday! Which in our business, doesn't mean much. This could be your "Saturday". For many years in the early part of my business Monday was my day "off" without appointments, the one quieter day of the week. Or maybe this is just another day in a string of many days of consistent work and appointments without a break. I hope that it is more of a true "Monday" for you, and you were able to take some time for rejuvenation this weekend.

How are you feeling this morning? Good? Happy? Excited to go about your day? Or are you overwhelmed, stressed, depressed, and tired already? No matter how you are feeling, there is one thing that is certain ... you can't just work on the days you feel good. The phone still rings, the emails come in, clients and potential clients need tending to whether you feel like it or not. We don't get "sick days" or "vacation days" or paid anything days for that matter. That can feel stressful.

Or that can feel like a beautiful thing. There is no one who says what time we have to be at the office, or what time we have to take our last appointment. Suddenly find yourself with a morning or afternoon with no appointments? You can go home, go to the spa, take a nap or binge Netflix and not have to ask for permission or even tell anyone. It is that freedom which can make all of the risk and uncertainty worth it, but only if you put in the time and track and prospect consistently so your business is strong and consistent. Only if you work on the days when you don't feel like it. How do you feel today?

May 14, 2018

We all talk about wanting more business, finding more leads, even often pay for leads, but there is gold right within our own database. This was the focus of our conversation topic during our Monthly Meet Ups last week.

Try this exercise:
-How many people are in your database? (example 500)

Many experts say that 10% of the people in your database should result in a closed transaction each year by doing business with you themselves or referring someone to you who does.
-What is 10% of your database? (example 50)

How many transactions did you close last year that were a result of your database? (example 35)
-Now, subtract your database potential (50) from your database actual (35) and multiply times your average commission per transaction (example $10,000).

This number (example $150,000) represents the amount of business that was potentially left on the table last year from not fully optimizing your database!

Here are the tips that I shared last week:
1. First things first ... do you have a database right now? If not, you need to start one immediately! Start with your holiday card list and build from there. Make your initial goal a list of 100 people. It is not just 100 people who you think will buy a house from you, but also who would refer you.

2. Identify where you will keep your database. The right answer is the system that you will actually use. It does no good to assemble your database in a program and then let it sit there. You actually need to INTERACT with it if you want anything to happen. Excel spreadsheet, old school rolodex, your phone contacts, or ideally a CRM. Whatever it is make sure that it works for you, is easily accessible anywhere, and has a method for automatic follow ups and reminders.

3. Sort and qualify your database. What makes sense to you? Is it a ranking system (A, B, C, D, etc.) for quality of contact or whether or not they have done business or referred to you? Is it based on geographic location or maybe

source of the relationship? Pick something that makes sense to you and go with it. You can always modify later on.

4. How do you grow your database? I've learned to grow mine from most any interaction. When I meet a new person, parent at my child's school, connect with a new vendor or service provider at my home, that is an opportunity to add to my database and then follow up our interaction with a note. Get in the habit of asking new clients/referrals for their mailing address, email, etc. to ensure that you can round out their contact information.

5. But … it doesn't need to be perfect. Do you only have their mailing address? Start with that. Only an email or phone number? That's okay too. Enter them in your database with what you have. It's a starting point.

6. What about out of state clients/friends? I say keep them in your database! I recently received a local referral from a past seller who moved to Connecticut. Just because they leave the area doesn't mean that they sever all contacts with their friends and family in this area. Especially with the benefit of social media there is a high likelihood that they will still have opportunities to refer to you here. Plus, over the years I have had many of my sellers that moved away call me when they are ready to move back.

7. Now that you have established and are continually working on growing your database, when is the last time you edited it? It is worth going through it a few times a year to pull out those that no longer belong (they did business with someone else or fall into the "D" category), and update contact information for those who you have helped to move, etc. Part of my file close out procedure for settlements is to update contact information in my iPhone contacts and CRM to help keep everything up to date.

Your database is a living, breathing, life-giving entity. All of your success comes through your database. Like it or not, it is the principal system for a profitable and consistent business, and so we need to treat it as such. The more you can get and stay in the habit of building, growing and nurturing your database the easier it will be. Set a goal this week related to your database … organize it, edit it, maybe add a certain number of contacts, or even just start one altogether!

May 18, 2018

Yesterday I received an offer on one of my listings. Contingencies checked in the offer as being included weren't included. Critical boxes were not checked, selections were not made. Portions were not initialed off by the buyers (even though they were meant to be), a part that was to be signed by the buyer's agent wasn't, entire portions were not filled in.

Those who know me best know that this Drives. Me. Crazy. Seriously, completely crazy. When I taught new agent classes and spent time as a managing broker, I emphasized this and taught and presented on the proper (and complete) way to fill out a contract, the same way that I was taught. Contrast yesterday's experience with an offer I received on a different listing of mine over the weekend. It was beautifully and perfectly complete. When I called the agent and complimented him on this (we used to work together) he commented that he knew if he was sending an offer to me that it better be right, lol.

The sad reality is that I see and have seen poor quality of work and attention to detail not just from new or inexperienced agents, but also from those who have been around for a long time (sometimes the worst offenders). Why is that?

There are many important and complicated facets to our job, but perhaps none is more important than the contract and paperwork that we prepare for our buyers and sellers. These are legally binding agreements, they deserve proper care and attention. The boxes you check (or don't check) or the sections you complete (or completely omit) can be the difference in negotiating power for your client or in the outcome for your client in the event of a void or default contract should an attorney become involved.

Yes, marketing is fun. Spending time, effort and money on generating leads, blogging, doing videos and websites is important ... but it will eventually stall if when it comes time to put pen to paper and do the actual job if it isn't handled properly. The basics are not exciting, but they are fundamental, the foundation of what they do.

As a listing agent, I will judge the quality of the buyer's agent and their ability to work through a smooth transaction to closing based on how well written their offer is. In a multiple offer situation, I share this information with my sellers, and it will be a basis in determining which offer to choose. It only takes a few extra minutes to ensure everything is right and to complete everything properly. When in doubt, ask someone! A trusted colleague, ideally your broker. Fill out "practice" contracts and paperwork and have them reviewed for accuracy and completeness before you start practicing on actual clients when their funds and property are on the line. It is not the listing agents' job to correct your errors or complete sections you leave blank, nor should they. As much as it pains me to leave these mistakes in offers, I also won't make a correction if doing so changes the power position for the client that I represent. Instead, I will identify that weakness for potential use for my clients benefit later on if needed.

Take the time to ensure that your contracts and paperwork are completed correctly. If you aren't sure, ask someone. It is better to be vulnerable to your broker or trusted colleague, than to put less than stellar work out into the world (where you will develop a reputation for this) and put your clients at risk. I don't often rant, but when I do, it is usually on this subject. Thank you for letting me get it all out.

May 21, 2018

"Only take advice from someone you are willing to trade places with." I'm not sure where or when I first heard this quote, but I immediately wrote it down and put it on the wall in my office.

How often do we get distracted by the chatter in our world, our lives, our industry? Sometimes (oftentimes) the loudest voices are coming from those with the least experience, the fewest accomplishments. We allow ourselves and our decisions to be swayed by masses who are reacting to situations around us rather than those who assess the data, keep their eye on the big picture and lead.

When you are making decisions about your life and your business, don't listen to the chatter. Don't follow the pack. Make sound, direct and specific decisions based on actual data with the big picture in mind. Look to those with whom you would trade places with for guidance and direction. Lead if you must. Your future self and your future business will never regret it.

May 25, 2018

Oh, what a week this has been. I needed a little therapy session with myself this morning, which typically means writing to all of you. Feel free to move along to other, happier messages in your feed, nothing to see here.

I had a contract fall through on one of my listings. Not just any listing, but my brother and sister-in-law's listing. Their home and location is unique, and they are devastated. I know that we/I did all that we could to hold it together and are doing all that we can to find our "just right" buyer, but still. They are so upset, and being family, I am just as upset for them. What they have wanted for a long time was just within their grasp and now it is gone, and we are starting all over.

We had some wonderful, and a little unexpected, changes with our team this week and growth. So exciting, and all good things, but also a little stressful too making sure that everyone is well taken care of and they have all they need.

The scale has not been my friend this week (or since I turned 39 ... almost 6 years ago ... but I digress). When I don't like what the scale says I get frustrated and stressed. When I get frustrated and stressed, I eat. The cycle begins again. And again. And again.

There has been an unfortunate turn of events with a very complicated sale that has otherwise been going rather smoothly. The other agent thought I meant or said something other than what we did. What we did was to perform as to the letter of the contract. Now they think (and said) that my word doesn't mean anything. Ouch. I know we performed exactly as we were supposed to, and that I upheld my fiduciary responsibility to my client, but I really hate anytime someone thinks I didn't do the right thing.

I had a client interaction that left me feeling less than, out of my league, not good enough. Granted, I know this is 100% in my head. In my 16 years in business, I have personally helped well over 700 families. I've listed and sold $1500 mountainside properties and $2M estates and virtually everything in between. Over my career it has seemed that I have specialized in the strange and unique. I've had many clients who seek me out as a result of that experience. But still. Somethings, some days, and I feel like I can't.

Several challenging moments with my kids earlier this week, including rolling them out of bed at 6 am one morning to complete a chore that was supposed to be done the night before (taking out the trash). It was supposed to be done before they enjoyed their video game time, only when I got home from work upset (see 2nd paragraph above) I forgot and didn't remember until the next morning. I don't like being the mean mom, and while the lesson was good (and they have straightened up and stepped up to their responsibilities since) it doesn't always feel good to me.

I have a number of challenging listings and clients right now who I am allowing to stress me out. I know the scripts, I know how to handle them, but for whatever reason I allow them/it to cause me to question the things I already know.

The greatest irony of all of this is that much of my stress and feelings this week boils down to mindset, my mindset ... and I did a Facebook Live here in the group earlier this week talking about mindset and how it impacts us and our productivity. Perhaps I need to watch and listen to myself.

Phew. As usual ladies, you have done it again. Just being able to spit all that out I feel much better. Now I'll enjoy the rest of my quiet time this morning, get all my little people up and out the door and focus on solving problems and making things happen today.

May 29, 2018

Last night I was watching an episode of "The Crown" on Netflix. If you are not familiar with it, it is the story of the British monarchy, and about Queen Elizabeth as a young woman and young Queen. It is rather fascinating, though certainly not completely historically accurate. In the episode I was watching last night, Queen Elizabeth was meeting President John F Kennedy and First Lady Jackie. There was much buzz about the beautiful, intriguing, young (though she was roughly the same age as Elizabeth) First Lady, and everyone at the palace seemed to be taken with her and couldn't wait to meet her. The Queen was feeling less than, like she didn't measure up, maybe a little intimidated. While certainly Jackie Kennedy was an amazing woman in her own right, Elizabeth was THE QUEEN. There really isn't much status to be held above that position. Funny that she would feel somehow less than.

But don't we all from time to time? Twice last week I had conversations with community members about "imposter syndrome", which seems most likely to afflict those who are successful. We feel like we've "faked" our way to success, like a fraud, like we will be figured out, like we don't have anything of value to share, like we don't belong.

Does anyone else feel this way? The way we often treat and respond to one another certainly doesn't help. We are all uniquely qualified to do, succeed and to achieve. Whether it is a new listing you are working to earn, a buyer in a price range or neighborhood that you are still learning about or mentoring other women in the industry, you have unique values and gifts to bring to each of those situations. You cannot be an imposter, as there is no other you.

May 31, 2018

I've been sitting here for quite a while now trying to figure out the right words to say, but truly, there are none. It was one year ago today that my dear friend and business partner Vicky Noufal lost her husband after a ferocious battle with a brutal and unforgiving cancer. There are no perfect quotes or quips to describe the past year or the 18 months before it. Nothing to do justice to an incredible life that was well lived yet finished too soon.

So instead, I will simply say this ... embrace fully the life that you are given today. It may not be perfect. You may be in a season of difficulty, overwhelm, frustration, but you have this day. Find a moment to be grateful for, to feel a spark of happiness, to truly see and connect with another person. Do all you can to fully live all the moments of your days before you have used them all.

June 15, 2018

We live in an extremely competitive world. Consumers have information available 24/7 at their fingertips via their smartphone, which has changed the face of many service and product-based businesses, especially real estate. In a competitive marketplace, how do you not only survive, but thrive?

This was part of the topic of our Empowering Women in Real Estate Monthly Meet Ups yesterday and here are some of my tips for handling the competition:

1) Set yourself apart through outstanding customer service. Doing your job well is basic, it's the minimum standard. You've been hired to do a good job, anyone else can (and should do a good job). This is the expectation, so what would be the next step above that? The better you know your client or customer, the easier this becomes. The more invaluable you become to your client, the less likely they are to fall prey to your competition.

2) Identify your specialty and capitalize on it. If you specialize in solving a specific type of client problem (i.e. – selling historic properties, working with investors, etc.) or in a specific area or neighborhood then you become known as THE person to work with for that need or location. This basically eliminates all other competition. My business has primarily been focused on a specific rural part of our area, and part of that area includes unique and unusual homes. Several months ago, I was contacted by a potential seller who reached out to me specifically because she has regularly seen my signs (and my sold signs) on those unique properties, and wanted me to sell hers. One appointment, listing agreement signed, they didn't even reach out to anyone else. Competition eliminated.

3) Understand that you are not a commodity. When the focus of your business becomes strictly based on the price of your goods or services, you are a commodity. Pricing is important, but it isn't everything. If your sole value proposition is that you are cheaper than the competition, then you have set yourself up for others to come in and undercut you. Your clients will only see your value as you being the least expensive. When someone else is cheaper, they will see no reason to stay with you, they will simply work with the cheapest option. To avoid becoming a commodity, focus on your quality, your experience, what sets you apart. Yes, there are some customers or clients that you may lose because you aren't the cheapest, but in the long run your

business will be better for it. When your low pricing becomes your marketing plan, you set yourself (and your business up) for the most difficult competition there is.

4) Make learning new information and education a priority. Stay relevant in your field. In an ever-changing world avoid becoming a fading winner. Just because you were or are successful now, does not mean that you will be able to maintain or continue to grow that level of success without making changes and adjustments. Perhaps that means embracing technology, connecting with others in your industry, adding a new pillar to your business. What you have done to get you to the level of success you have now, isn't going to get you to the next level, and eventually will not even be enough to keep you where you are. You have to increase your efforts just to stay where you are and the best way to do that is being aware of what is happening in the market around you, learning new things and adjusting accordingly.

5) Are you pursuing your own clients/database? We tend to get complacent when it comes to our past clients. We make assumptions that they will always be there for us and return to us. However, they are being pursued constantly by our competition. Make sure that you are pursuing them too. Pursue them through your marketing efforts, client care initiatives, calls, notes, pop bys, lunches, coffees. Specific acts of kindness. Make sure that they know that you value them, and also that they don't forget about you. Also, don't pre-judge. Don't decide for them that they don't want to hear from you, that they would be bothered by your call or pop by, that they won't find your mailer informative. Let them decide for themselves. They can choose not to answer the door or the phone or to throw the mailer away. The point is that they see you, they don't need to respond. I would venture a guess that a good 90% of my sphere and database marketing efforts go unresponded to IN THAT MOMENT. However, when that client contacts me months later because they need to buy or sell a home or have a referral, then they respond. It is the keeping in touch that makes it okay for them to contact me when they are ready.

June 20, 2018

Summer is officially in full swing! No school, more daylight, warmer temperatures, and vacation season is fully upon us. This is a wonderful time of year, but it can also be a challenging time in our business. If you're a mom, summer presents a unique challenge with childcare, or just keeping your children busy. Listings tend to sit around a little longer in many cases, and new business opportunities may be slower to come in. And hey ... you deserve to have a little fun in the sun too, right?

This is why you need a summer business plan. It can be fun to stay up later and sleep in, spend more time outside, and not work as much when things are quieter. You should do all of these things, but whatever you do, don't completely take your focus off of your business. It is the work and effort that you put in during these summer months that you will be paid for in the fall and winter. It can be too easy to take it easy this time of year while your commissions and settlements are still happening from spring and feel like everything is great! But if you totally check out now, come September, October and November you will be feeling the pain, and probably a lot of pressure.

A summer business plan may not sound exciting, but trust me on this, a gentle routine or rhythm to your days will help you to enjoy your time now and enjoy the fruits of your labor later. I'm still working on what this will look like for me. My youngest son has been out of school for 2 weeks now and my older two for a week. This week is our first full week with our new schedule, so I am still figuring some of it out. What works best for me is prioritizing my prospecting. I know, I know, that isn't what you want to hear, but it is what you need to hear. I've talked before about my "daily business builders" or daily tasks that help to grow my business. A combination of calls, notes, pop bys, giving referrals, adding to my database and having face to face appointments with clients or my database. My preference is to do these things in the morning so I will "win the day" and then I have the rest of the day (depending on how busy my business is at the moment) to enjoy however I see fit! Maybe sitting by the pool or swimming with my kids, going on a little outing, taking a walk, sitting on the porch ... I can enjoy this time guilt free because I've already spent some time moving my business forward.

June 22, 2018

Can you relate to this? Sometimes I feel like my brain is going a million miles a minute on a thousand different topics, and then by certain points of the day it (and I) just turn to mush.

Between my own personal real estate business, ideas for my team to grow and increase their own business, caring for my husband, my children, my household, my father's household, clients, other family members, friends, pets and more it is sometimes all just a bit much.

When my mind is spinning this fast and overwhelmed, I tend to like to retreat a bit. This is sometimes good, sometimes not. Taking a little time today and this weekend for myself should help to clear out the clutter a bit. I also like to do a "brain dump" where I write out everything I am thinking about or worried about onto a sheet of paper. Get it out of my head, identify the to dos (because they usually relate to things to do) then figure out what I need to do, what I can delegate and what I should just delete.

How do you handle it when your brain is too full?

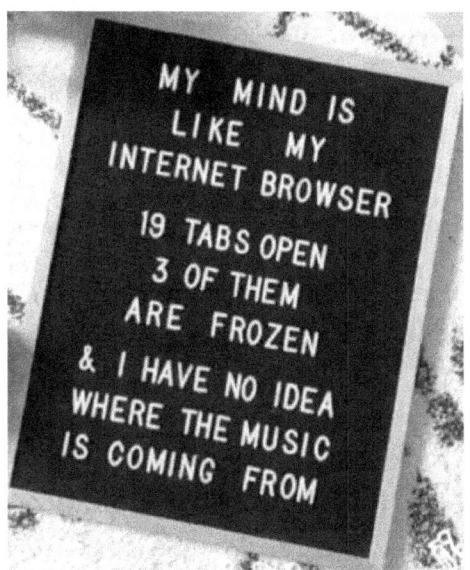

June 25, 2018

There is no such thing as an overnight success. People ask me all the time how I got here, and I tell them that it has been 16 years of hard work. I spent years, more than 6 to be exact, paying my dues on a rainmaker team. I was what you would call a "good hire", working 6-7 long days per week, averaging 50-60 transactions most years for what averaged out to be a less than 20% split on listings, all in my team leader's name. It was a tremendous amount of hard work, with a small immediate financial return, but years I wouldn't trade for anything. During that time, I built the foundation of my business. I learned and honed extremely valuable skills which I continue to use to this day.

Then when I moved on to a different brokerage as an independent agent, I took on all the responsibility for my own business. Yes, I earned more, but I was also chief cook and bottle washer ... meaning I was responsible for everything. Marketing ideas, design and implementation. Generating leads, going on appointments, closing the deal. Every facet was not only my responsibility from a "work" point of view but also from a financial point of view. There were certainly months while the market was recovering when I didn't have the money to pay for my marketing, but I found a way and did it anyway, because I knew that if I stopped, my business would stop.

Now, as a team owner it may look easy on the outside. I have help to run my lockboxes and brochures, to design my marketing materials, to manage my transactions. I also have more responsibility than ever before ... creating (with my business partner) a quality marketing program not just for myself but also for our team of 17 agents, being personally responsible for rent and multiple salaries which will always be paid before I am ever paid.

When I receive a lead or a referral, it doesn't just appear out of thin air (neither do yours when you receive them, by the way), there is always a price that has been paid. Whether it is a lead you pay for through a lead generation source, a lower split and/or higher referral fee through a corporate source (like relocation), or years of nurturing with both time and money. When I receive a lead in my geographic farm it is because I have spent many, many years investing thousands upon thousands of dollars in sponsorships, community events and marketing. When I receive a lead from my sphere or my database it is a result of years of focused, intentional, consistent nurturing, connection and a countless number of calls, notes and pop bys.

So naturally, with the investment I have made for this many years in my business I tend to be "pickier" with what I choose to work and what I choose to pass. Part out of necessity (it is not possible to produce this much and run a team and also run all over with buyers or far away listings) and part because, quite frankly, I've earned it. One of the greatest benefits of consistent investment in your business is choice.

Over the years I've had opportunities to meet and spend time with hundreds of agents. There are two things that drive me crazy ... 1) not connecting the value of the consistent activities and investment (both time and money) with the results or having a stable business, and 2) the expectation that it (quality leads, success) should just be handed to them. This is true of basically every profession. A doctor doesn't just get their degree and then proceed to immediate, unsupervised patient care. A musician doesn't write one song and immediately have a top hit. Dues are paid. Consistent, diligent hard work and investment in time, effort and money has to occur again and again and again. And when you do make that consistent investment in yourself and your business, I find the results are more than worth it.

July 2, 2018

Can you believe that we are now halfway through the year? The older I get (and the older my children get), I swear the time seems to go faster and faster. Have you checked in with your goals lately? It's time to do a mid-year meeting with yourself. With my team we call this the "State of the Union" and it is scheduled for next week. This is when we take a long hard look at what has transpired during the first half of the year, do some year over year comparisons, and address what needs to be done to finish out the year strong and reach our goals.

I'm a big believer in doing this with your personal and professional goals. When we set our goals in the new year we tend to be motivated and excited, then real life reality sets in and it can be so easy to lose track. Before you know it, the year is almost over, and you've lost sight of where you wanted to be. It isn't enough to just set the goals, you need to connect them with the activities as well. Want to lose weight? Just saying it or writing it down won't make it happen, you need to take specific actions. Plan to grow your business? It won't happen on its own, you need a strategy for marketing and prospecting, and you need to act upon it consistently.

Set aside a little time with yourself this week, or even better with a colleague, friend or mentor and review your goals and your progress together. Analyze what you have done (or not done) so far this year to get you where you are and determine if continuing on that track will get you where you need to be or if you need to make some adjustments. "Wishing" your goals into reality doesn't work (I wish it did!) ... it takes focused, purposeful, consistent action and activity. It often takes trying new things, moving outside your comfort zone. It takes work, plain and simple. There is no shortcut.

July 4, 2018

Is there something (or someone) holding you back from realizing your dreams? Are YOU holding you back from achieving your goals? Limiting beliefs. A nagging self-conscious telling you that you aren't good enough, that the success that you want is for someone else. Setting the bar too low for yourself, playing small so you can achieve it ... and then hitting it with amazing accuracy when so much more is available to you.

Today is a great day to declare YOUR independence! Let go of the negative messages from the past. Refresh, reset, and charge forward knowing that whatever it is that you want to achieve is available to you. You just need to rise up, do the work, and claim it!

July 6, 2018

Yesterday on my Instagram stories (I'm @karen.w.cooper) I was talking about learning something new every day. I am frequently asked about what I have done to achieve my level of success in real estate (July 6th and about to ratify my 40th transaction of the year!). Learning and education is definitely a big part of that. I make time each day to listen to, watch or read something that will help me to improve myself or my business.

That all sounds great, right? We all want to learn more, but the reality is who has time? Well, I do, and so do you. It is all about what you prioritize and finding little pockets to fit it into your day.

Here are some of my favorite ways for fitting a little learning into each day ...

- Be an early riser. For the overwhelming majority of my life this has not been my thing, at all. I was always a night person, more productive late, then struggling to get up in the morning and usually letting my kids be the ones to wake me up. I so wish I knew then what I know now. During the school year my alarm goes off at 5:20 am and during the summer 5:45 am (I usually hit the snooze button once or twice). After taking care of a couple little chores, I take a seat in my favorite chair with my favorite hot beverage and the next hour or so is ALL MINE. After writing to you I spend the rest of my time reading my favorite blogs, and now that the mornings are a little slower, I have taken to sitting on my porch for a while with a good book before I need to get moving for the day.

-Listen to audio books. There are many ways to do this, my favorite is by using my Amazon Echo Dot (aka "Alexa") and using Audible. My Alexa lives on a shelf in my bathroom. I typically spend about 20-30 minutes each morning getting myself ready, and Alexa reads to me while I am putting on my makeup, getting dressed, fixing my hair, etc. My favorites books to listen to are ones that I have read before and love and that are read by the author (my favorite is "Year of Yes" by Shonda Rhimes) or books that I want to read but seem a little "heavy" (a good example of this is "The 10x Rule" by Grant Cardone, I couldn't get through the book version but LOVED the audio). When a book is especially good, I will often then continue listening to it in my car between appointments or on the way to the office.

-Listen to podcasts. I love the Podcast app on my iPhone, and I typically listen to a podcast every time I am in my car. My favorites on iTunes are The Brian Buffini Show, Pat Hiban Interview's Real Estate Rockstars and Real Deep Dive with Kara Macdonald.

-Take a "video break" during the day. Many days I find myself eating lunch at my desk or taking my lunch outside. I like to take a break during this time, so I will usually watch a video on my computer or my phone. I like Tom Ferry's video blog for this. Most entries are between 10-20 minutes long, the perfect length to watch while I take a break and enjoy my lunch. This is what I was doing yesterday when I recorded my stories on Instagram.

-Read before bed. In order to get up early, you are going to need to get to bed early ... at least I do! I need a good 7-8 hours of sleep in order to function at my highest level. During the school year that means we typically go to bed when the kids do, and I am in bed between 9-9:15 pm. During the summer it is usually 10 pm. I enjoy reading for a few minutes before I fall asleep, so I purchased a little clip-on book light at Target so as soon as I start feeling sleepy I can just switch off the light and put the book on my nightstand. Admittedly, I can usually only get through a couple pages at night before I start dozing off, but that still counts!

-Keep a book with you at all times. I almost always have a book or magazine in my bag, so I am ready anytime I have a few minutes. Our days are often spent waiting on other people ... waiting for a client to arrive, waiting for a home inspection to finish, waiting for a doctor or dentist to see us, etc. How do we fill that time? All you need to do is look around you the next time you are in a public place waiting and you will see everyone head down looking at their phones. You can do that too, or just people watch or stare into space (could be a good option) or you can take that time to learn a little something by reading. I promise, you have more time for this than you think! Even with my busy work and family schedule I still usually read or listen to 2 books per month. Those few minutes here and there add up! I've read 13 books so far this year!

July 25, 2018

I'm closing in on the final few days of a 2-week vacation at the beach with my family ... while of course there has been the usual sibling fighting, whining kids over who does and doesn't want to do what, and a few rainy days here and there, overall, it has been glorious.

If you have ever asked me about traveling, I would say that I don't like to do it, except to certain places that I like. I've done a lot of reading on this trip, and in one book ("Slow" by Brooke McAlary) the author talked about her travel style of "deep vs wide". Instead of visiting many places or exploring as much as she could of a place in one trip and not returning, her family prefers to take their time while visiting a location and instead of trying to see and do all the things, they focus on exploring a few spots really, really well.

I realized that I do like to travel ... and this is my style too! Those who know me best know that my family tends to find a location that we like and revisit over and over again for a number of years. We love really getting to know that location ... coming to know the shops, the restaurants, the local customs and shortcuts. We will do this again and again with a location until we feel satisfied and then move on to a new area. While we may travel to fewer locations, the ones we visit we get to know really, really well.

I was thinking that this concept of deep vs wide applies to our businesses as well. Now, I'm definitely not saying that you should have only one stream of income or one pillar of your business (i.e. - sphere or cold calling) but that you should identify a few and really home in on those areas. For me it is my sphere/past clients/referrals, business to business networking, social media and my geographic farm. I focus consistently in those areas and go deep in each one versus skimming the surface of many.

There are so many distractions in our business. It seems that on an almost daily basis we are targeted to buy into this lead generation tool or that one, all promising to grow our businesses. Ultimately, it is up to us to grow our business. To identify our ideal customer or client (Kara Macdonald calls this our avatar), to get clear on who it is that we want to do business with and how, and then focus our energy, effort, and investment of time and money in that/those area(s). That is when the magic happens.

August 3, 2018

I returned last weekend from a wonderful 2-week vacation away with my family. When I go on vacation I pretty well completely unplug and have a system that I have established that helps me to do. After a very hectic spring market, it was wonderful to get away and relax. It was 2 weeks of sunshine (and a little rain), walks on the beach, hunting for shells and sea glass and shark's teeth. Two weeks of reading and card games and puzzles. Staring at the ocean, cocktails at 5 (or before! and after!). It was peaceful and quiet (as much as it can be when you have 3 sons) and wonderful.

However, I noticed when I got home last weekend, that not even 24 hours home I could feel the pressure descending on me like a wet, heavy blanket. I suddenly found myself in tears trying to write out the meal plan and grocery list for the week. Crying. Over groceries. And I don't cry. After some thoughtful introspection, and a bit of an intervention from my dearest friends Vicky Noufal and Jackie Fields-Gleadall I've been able to clear out some of the mental clutter and identify much of the source of my own pressure.

Me.

I struggle to stay in the present, either thinking about the past or worrying about the future. So. Much. Worrying.

I set big goals for myself, always a stretch goal, which I like to do, but always raising the bar higher and higher and higher without taking into consideration all of the other goals and responsibilities that I have for driving my business, my team and this group forward beyond just my transaction number.

I am everyone else's problem solver, which means I tend to take on their problems. Friends, family members, clients. I relish in solving problems and finding creative solutions, excel at it even ... but I have forgotten how to distinguish between listening to a problem (venting) and taking on that problem as my own to solve.

I aim to please, to serve, to provide, to produce. As a young girl how many of us were taught to be a "good girl", and being a good girl meant smiling no matter what (even when you were hurting), saying yes when asked to do something, and taking care of everyone else's needs first? I sure was. That also means then that when I want/need to take care of myself, do something for myself, I feel selfish. Like deep down I must be a very selfish person, and that means feeling guilt, which then leads to more pressure.

I strive for efficiency in everything. That means lots of thinking and overthinking about what is the best move and when, where to go, how to do. In some ways, this is great! I get shit done. A LOT of shit done. But it also means that I can tend to take it too far and the striving for maximum efficiency only leads to more pressure.

Literally just this week, Vicky, my dear friend and business partner, gave me "permission" to take it easy a bit, to lower my goal and to ease the constant striving and pushing. Now, I don't need her permission for this, both she and I know this. But what I did need was for someone to say it out loud so I could give MYSELF permission, she knew this instinctively and it was perfect.

Something tells me that many of you here can relate to much of this. As women, we tend to take on the weight of the world. We are nurturers, I think, by nature, and that takes form in many ways. In the way that we care for our families, our friends, our clients. It is often what sets us apart and makes us SO GOOD at what we do. The challenge though, is that we sometimes forget to nurture ourselves. I tend to do and do and do and do and perform and perform and produce and produce and get great results. Which means I get asked a lot to do more, to help more, to perform more, to produce more. This is great, but what I often want (and struggle to ask for and give up control for) is for someone to just take the reins. To say, "I've got this", whatever this is ...

planning the meals, delivering the pop bys, scheduling the back-to-school physicals, whatever. The problem though, is the more we show how capable we are, the more we can produce and do and achieve, the less others are likely to step up to do this (or anything) for us without our explicit instruction. That just leads to one more decision, and it is the endless, constant decisions that wear me out.

So ... I will continue to strive and produce and to care for others and to be the problem solver, it is my nature. It is what I love. But I will be working on doing so in a kinder, gentler way that doesn't involve depleting every piece of myself to do it.

August 8, 2018

Looking for success habits? Here are a few, specifically for women in the real estate industry ...

1. Prospect. Daily. We've talked about this a lot here and at one of our recent Empowering Women in Real Estate Monthly Meet Ups. Prospecting doesn't just mean cold calling and door knocking. It also means note writing, open houses, calling past clients to check in, social media "hunting" and more. To have a successful business you must work a little of this into every workday.

2. Consistency, consistency, consistency. I want to scream this from the rooftops. Think about a success that you have had in your life ... losing weight, graduating from high school or college, securing a great listing. More than likely that success came from little things added up that you did over and over again (eating healthy, exercising, studying, marketing, follow up).

3. Don't judge your success by the success of others. Over the years I've seen many agents who get hung up on what others are doing. Deep down they have a fear based or "lack" mindset and when they see someone else being successful, they almost take it personally, in a negative way. Instead of viewing another's success as inspiration or proof that they can do it too, they somehow feel let down or discouraged and find excuses for why that person was successful, other than just good old consistent hard work. Stay in your lane. Focus on your goals. If someone else seems to be speeding past you on the path to success, acknowledge the years that it has taken them to get there. You don't know their sacrifices or reality behind the scenes. Be motivated by what they are doing, they are carving a path for others. Maybe you don't want what someone else is achieving, and that's okay too. We are all running our own races, there is no right or wrong answer when it comes to achievement for each individual. Align yourself with those whose goals are similar to yours and help each other to rise.

What other success habits would you add to the list?

August 17, 2018

Ah, summer. While the heat may stick around for a bit, the seasons are changing. You can feel it in the air in the early mornings and evenings. The sun is going in a little earlier each night, and the late summer bugs make the most glorious noises here in the country. My kids go back to school soon, and with back-to-school activities starting, summer is most definitely wrapping up.

Sometimes when I feel melancholy, nervous or anxious I like to look through the photos on my phone. It is a nice reminder of fun times and activities and where we've been. It's been a fun summer with a long and restful vacation, lots of pool time, porch time, fun activities and memories, with plenty of work woven in, around and through it all. I like to say that real estate is both the most flexible and the least flexible of all, but it is this time of year especially that I am truly grateful for what it does offer. It is not always easy. The uncertainty, frantic pace, ups, downs and frustrations, but it is always worth it.

August 20, 2018

A gentle reminder for your Monday morning ... no matter how slowly, just keep moving forward! Rome wasn't built in a day. Success doesn't happen overnight. Take teeny, tiny baby steps if you must. Take bigger steps when you can. All of that forward motion will move you towards your goal. What doesn't move you toward your goal? Standing still. Self-defeat. Overthinking. Fear. Striving for "perfect".

While at the beach this summer my family and I visited a sea turtle hospital. We learned that there are around 100+ eggs in a nest, but that it is estimated that only 10% or less of hatchlings ever survive to adulthood. Many are taken by their predators (crabs, birds) between the time they hatch and emerge from the sand and the time it takes them to reach the surf, which then presents a whole new set of challenges. The only way they can make it is to keep moving. Slowly, awkwardly. Moving forward.

August 22, 2018

Late summer market for me has been quiet and has been the perfect "break" after a crazy first half of the year. I've been doing some work each day, but also enjoying some of the last bits of summer with my kids (back to school for two of them tomorrow!) and working on clearing out my house.

For me, physical clutter is draining. The busier I am the less time and energy I have to deal with it, and then things pile up, decisions get delayed, and before I know it closets and cabinets are full again with excess stuff. It feels so good to go through things to giveaway, donate, sell. I've always loved moving furniture around and freshening things up (even as a kid, I would regularly rearrange my room ... signs of my future career in real estate and helping my sellers with staging perhaps?).

I always loved back to school as a student, the fresh notebooks and school supplies. New backpacks and clothes. Getting into the groove with a new routine. I suppose this focus on freshening and decluttering is my adult version of back to school! Going through this process at home helps me to feel lighter, and daily tasks to seem easier. It gives me the adjustment I need to reenergize and jump back into fall market full steam ahead.

August 24, 2018

If you know me at all or have been following along here in the group for any length of time, then more than likely you know that I am a big fan of routine and systems. After a very busy first half of the year, I've taken a bit more relaxed approach these last few weeks of summer to regroup and enjoy time with my kids. I've been working a here and there, that doesn't completely stop, but I've put aside my usual routines and time spent going into the office.

You know what I've discovered? Building, growing and maintaining a real estate business that is successful and consistent REQUIRES routine. At least it does for me anyway. Without the routine of getting in the shower and getting myself ready before the kids get up means that some days the morning completely escapes me, and it is afternoon before I realize that if I needed to run out to see a client or to show a property unexpectedly that I'm not prepared to do it.

Without the routine of going into the office after I drop the kids off at school means that unless I have a meeting or specific reason to go in, I've barely seen the inside of my office in several weeks. Without the routine of sitting down at my desk to start my day around 9 am and opening my CRM to get started on my daily prospecting and client follow ups, well, that means it has barely been happening. Without my daily work routines, my productivity has dropped significantly. Yes, I'm taking care of anything time sensitive and ensuring that my clients are all taken care of, but that's about it. My email is overflowing. Critical business tasks (like prospecting) keep getting pushed aside day after day, and it shows in the slowdown of my incoming leads and referrals.

This is no way to run a sustainable business. Running a business REQUIRES routines and rhythms and systems to ensure that it is moving forward. The ability to work from home is a great perk of our business, but it can also distract us from the actual work part. As my youngest goes back to school in a couple days I'm looking forward to re-establishing my routines. I still like to work from home some, but being in the office is typically what works best for me. I've enjoyed this time with my boys and will likely do it again next summer. Time marches on, and before I know it, they will all be off to college or out on their own and summer break or back to school won't hold the same meaning. For now, I'll enjoy the last couple summer days at home with my littlest guy, and next week will launch back into my routine with a full heart and spirit, and ready to make great things happen this fall.

September 5, 2018

Negotiations are so much of what we do in our business. For our buyers, for our sellers, for ourselves. There are many different "strategies", and like most things in life, no one right way.

Many, many years ago I learned from my dear friend and incredible realtor Jeanne Cooper that often in negotiations "he who speaks first loses". Meaning that sometimes we can talk our way right out of whatever it was we were trying to negotiate in the first place. Not only that but listening ... really listening ... to the needs and concerns of the other person without judgement, or without waiting to reply can provide valuable insight. Make your point, put it out there, and then be quiet. Don't be tempted to fill the silence. I've used this again and again and again and found it to be a strategy that works really well for me. What is your favorite negotiating strategy?

September 7, 2018

Once a month I lead a business networking group in my town. This is a group of business owners from a wide variety of businesses. Last night we had an organizer, a fudge maker, a yoga teacher, a social media person, a doula and a travel agent. Other times we have had general contractors, landscapers, house cleaners, junk haulers and more. It is nice to have such a diverse group together.

Last night I asked each guest to share the current biggest challenge in their business, and every single one said, "spreading the word". AKA marketing and prospecting. What is so interesting to me is that earlier this week when I posted a survey here in the group the majority of you also said that your trouble spot is marketing ... how to, who, what, when. All the things. Clearly this is a problem that plagues small business owners across the board.

One of the comments last night from one of the guests as I was discussing my marketing plan was that she had tried something similar to one of the things on my list but didn't get any results, and so she stopped. This is a common misconception and something I hear often. The best and most effective marketing will be designed to "hit" your database or your target market in more one way, more than once. There are many things I do which I can rarely or never have a "direct" tie back to a new lead or referral ... expensive festival sponsorships, charity auction baskets, some postcards, email drawings, etc. However, many people need to "see" you multiple times before they call. The best thing you can hear when you ask a new lead why they contacted you is "I see you everywhere". It is the combined effort of seeing my banner at the festival, then maybe a few days or a week later they see a post on social media, then they see my sign on a listing in their neighborhood. It is the compound effect, and in my experience is the best and most effective way to market. Does this take a lot of time, effort and money to provide the consistency needed? Yep, sure does, but few things worth doing come without a price.

September 12, 2018

I have a love hate relationship with water. Specifically large bodies of water. Dark water. Water that I can't see the bottom of. The more water, the bigger my issue. On one hand, I'm absolutely terrified by it. I was practically a teenager before I learned how to swim, and I consider myself somewhat mediocre at it. Yet I have an in-ground pool at my home and have never doubted my ability to do what I needed to do if one of my children had an issue.

Big, expansive bridges that go over large bodies of water cause me weeks of anxiety before trips (I'm looking at you, Chesapeake Bay Bridge). What if the car goes over the side? How will I save everyone? This one didn't really start becoming an issue until I had children.

Boat rides aren't my favorite. I could go the entire rest of my life never going on a boat again and it would be okay by me. This is a struggle though when you have a husband who loves to be out on the water and enjoys deep water fishing. Again, how am I going to save everyone if the boat crashes or starts sinking? I will go along under some protest and can usually muster up reasonable courage to be calm during the ride, but before and after my mind and body are on high alert.

On the other hand, I love the water. The beach, the lake, the river. For spring break we visit this beautiful home on Lake Anna with a screened porch that overlooks the lake, my favorite morning spot. We spend much of the day on the dock fishing or in a hammock relaxing nearby. Our favorite summer vacation is the beach. Walking by the water each morning, sitting on the beach, wading in the water (about thigh deep is my limit), listening to the waves. Fewer places I'd rather be.

So, what gives here? Same bodies of water, two different mindsets or types of experiences. I think that what much of it boils down to is control. My fears that I can't control a situation. Water is bigger and more powerful than I am, in the event of an emergency (in my rational thoughts I know that the likelihood of a problem is very small) there is likely little that I can do.

Truly though, most everything is out of our control. Control is an illusion. The only thing we have complete control over in our lives is our mindset. The way we view experiences, the way we view things that are happening to us and around us.

I love this quote, ironic that it has to do with sinking ships … "ships don't sink because of the water that is around them, they sink because of the water that gets in them." It is so true though. Don't let what's happening around you get inside you and weigh you down. Mindset is the difference between driving yourself (and those around you) crazy with fear and anxiety over things you can't control, or that you can but you doubt yourself right out of taking action and making things happen ... and understanding that a certain part of success in life requires surrender and complete gratitude for your experiences. No matter the experience, there is always something to be grateful for.

September 17, 2018

We all have daily habits. Those things that we do every day, often automatically without even thinking about it. Drinking our morning coffee or tea, brushing our teeth, having dinner with our family.

But what about daily habits for your business? That's a tough one, isn't it? Real estate is so unpredictable. You can have your day beautifully planned out either for a day "off" or neatly scheduled appointments and then, the phone rings/an email comes in. A buyer needs to see a new listing ASAP. A seller is ready to sign their listing paperwork right now. A home inspection contingency addendum comes in on your listing that needs to be presented. You're just about to head home for the day at 7 pm on a Tuesday when an offer on one of your listings shows up in your in box. Suddenly, the day shifts and your plans change.

It can be really hard to establish daily habits in our business when so much of our day is, and needs to be, fluid. When I talk to successful agents or read/listen to their interviews, one of the consistent things I hear over and over is about their daily habit in their business. Prospecting every morning from 8-10 am, an "immovable" appointment. Previewing every day. Writing 5 personal notes a day. When your day is crazy, how do you even fit that "extra" stuff in?

The thing is ... that "extra" stuff is often the most important stuff. You may be super busy right now with all of your transactions in process, but in another couple weeks after those transactions close, then what? Spending that regular time tending to your database, "hunting" for new business is what will keep your business consistent week after week, month after month, year after year.

September 19, 2018

I have to say ... getting older brings some mixed feelings, except for this one. Without a doubt, as the years tick by I do become more clear about who I am. Unapologetically. Part of it I think comes naturally from the aging process, more years means more experience and more experiences. Part of it though has definitely been a conscious decision brought about by taking the time and making the effort to learn and try new things. The more I learn, the more I try, the easier it is to discern what works for me and what doesn't.

The real estate business is hard. There was a stat I saw floating around yesterday from Tom Ferry that there are something like 1.4M real estate agents, but only 3% of them (43,000) have done more than 25 transactions. Those are some pretty astounding numbers. One of the benefits of experience is being better able to discern your place in the industry, what type of business works for you and what doesn't. When to fight to hang on, and when to let go. That in and of itself is a beautiful thing.

September 24, 2018

A couple weeks ago on our Friday weekly team call, one of the agents on my team was sharing about what a rough week she had been having. Difficult clients, losing a transaction, plus family things on top of that. We've all been there, and the longer you've been in business and the more business you do, the more times you've had weeks like that. She was looking for ways to change her energy and her mindset, so she could go into the weekend and some special family events without carrying the crap from the week with her.

I suggested that she spend some time that day being generous, to give something away. There is no better way to change your outlook than by helping someone else. So, you know what? She did. She took to social media, gave out several referrals to great local companies as well as a few gift cards, just because. And it worked. Like a charm.

Today, I'm letting you in on my dirty little secret. I love to give to others. Sponsoring community events, donating to weekend food programs at my children's schools and more. Many of these things I do get recognized for, but there are many more that no one knows about. Giving anonymously to families in need during the holiday season, sending food and supplies to those who need it most, giving supersized tips at restaurants when I feel prompted, paying for the groceries of someone in line ahead of you who doesn't have enough cash (super bonus points when your kids get to witness these experiences) and more. Not all giving has to involve money either. Many instances involve giving time and energy, sharing experiences when agents reach out when they need help or advice.

When I see a need, I like to fill it because I genuinely like to help, but also because it helps me. There is no better way to improve your mood or your day than by giving to others, with no expectation of receiving anything in return. Yes, you may be making someone else's day, but I guarantee you will be making yours too.

September 26, 2018
One of the things that I really love about this business is that it is a relationship business. We build relationships with our clients before, during and after transactions which are some of the biggest milestones in their lives ... which when done right will lead to referrals and repeat business. We build relationships with our most trusted and preferred vendors which can sometimes lead to referrals, but also the priority status and care and concern that they will in turn show to our clients.

We build relationships with other agents through groups like this, within our brokerage offices and local associations, through networking events and in cooperating together on transactions. Those relationships can lead to referrals, but also bring tremendous value in terms of learning, support, and simply in helping to make a transaction go more smoothly. We build relationships with our communities, investing in the people, businesses, economy and culture, which leads to more business but also a tremendous sense of satisfaction.

These are all great benefits of relationship building, but as we all know, it doesn't always come easy. In my market it feels like every fifth person has a real estate license (and the true statistic probably isn't that far off). Competition is fierce, and while strong relationships have the best chance of standing up to that, it doesn't always which can lead to tremendous hurt. Anyone who has lost a client for any reason, no matter how strong the relationship, knows exactly what I'm talking about.

September 28, 2018

When are you your most productive? For me, hands down, it is the day before I leave to go on vacation. I feel this urgent need to wrap up projects, clean out my email inbox and more.

I'm heading out of town in an hour or so, and so true to form last night I was knocking out work left and right. In a relatively short timeframe, I completed multiple things that I had been procrastinating on for weeks. Once I got focused and "in the zone" (and with my phone and email turned off) it felt relatively quick and easy. What I thought was going to take me so much longer only took a fraction of the time.

The bad news is that I stayed up far later than I wanted to and am only running on about 4 hours of sleep today. The good news though is that I am off on my trip with a clear mind, to do list and in box (to be fair, quite a few things are moved to my "to do after vacation" folder to deal with when I get back, but at least my in box is clear!).

Can you spend some time today creating your most productive environment, at least for an hour or two? Turn off your phone, your email, all your notifications. It is okay to be unreachable for a short period of time. This will help you to catch up; to have time (and mental space) to be creative and you too can move into the weekend with clarity and peace.

October 8, 2018

This week promises to be a stressful week for my household. An emergency tooth extraction for my least cooperative child today, a full day of chemo on Wednesday for my father-in-law, a major surgery for me on Thursday with recovery for at least a couple weeks after. Add in all the other, "normal" stuff with kids and family and household and it is easy to get overwhelmed.

Yesterday we drove home (15 hours!) from a magical 10-day vacation. I had lots of thinking time during the drive, and the worry and anxiety would start to creep in ...
-What if Tyler won't let the dentist pull his tooth? When will I find time to get him to the other (further away) dentist that can do the nitrous?
-When will I get groceries?
-Ben needs to get an outfit for the Homecoming dance.
-Tuesday night is likely the last baseball game of the fall season for Ben and Ryan that I will be able to go to. It's late and far away, who will sit with Tyler?
-I need to make sure that I have x, y and z ready for my surgery on Thursday.

-The kids have a combined 5+ doctor/dental/orthodontist appointments scheduled for while I am down (including getting braces for one of them). Need to make sure none of them get forgotten.

I would even let far off worries start moving in ... what about that big presentation at the end of November? Will I be ready? Have I prepped enough for our team retreat? I haven't found a physical therapist yet. What about my follow up procedure early next year? How will recovery be from that?

Each time the chatter would start, I would stop and consciously make a decision that I am only going to deal with one day at a time. My only goal/focus/thoughts for yesterday became just getting home. Today I will spend a little time making sure I am prepared for what I need for tomorrow, and then will focus only on the kid's appointments today, unpacking and going to the grocery store. One day at a time is hard for me. When I put things off, procrastinate, I feel stressed, but looking too far ahead when there are so many unknowns or things that haven't happened yet I think is worse.

This affects all of us in our day to day lives. The further out you focus, the less control you have. Focus on what is most important for today. Do a "brain dump" on paper to get all the "stuff" out of your head and identify what is truly most important for today or that needs to be prepared for something later this week. Identify what you should do, delegate or delete. If it is something you should do, just do it today or figure out which day it should be done. If someone else can help you with something or do it for you, let them! Delegate without hesitation (still hard for me, especially at home). What on your list really isn't important at all? Delete it. Let it go.

October 11, 2018

I'm headed to the hospital this morning for a mastectomy. It has been a truly challenging last 6 weeks or so. Many (well meaning) folks gave me the advice not to share publicly my current struggle at all or at least until it was over for fear of how it may affect my business or be "used against me". That didn't feel right to me. That felt like hiding and didn't feel authentic.

So, I chose to share publicly, and I've included my personal post here below in hopes that it may help some of you with your own messaging should you ever need it. We all have struggles, and whether you choose to share or not, at the end of the day we are all just people. And most people truly care and want to help each other. I'm truly grateful for this group and community that has been built as a result.

Today is the day, I'm on my way ...

To Reston Hospital for a mastectomy. Yes, it sucks. But it's going to be okay. Maybe not off to great places in the traditional sense, but my doctors are truly great. My mountain is for sure waiting, and I'm at peace with it ... and ready to climb and conquer.

I have a long history of breast issues (the right one, for those who are curious and will struggle to make eye contact with me the next time you see me while you try to figure out which is which) and rare tumors. This is my 7th surgery to treat this issue, with the most recent not quite 10 months ago. I've averaged a surgery just about every other year for the past so many years, so I am truly grateful to see this come to an end.

Initial pathology on this one was scary, but the second opinion was less sure, and for that I am grateful. I'm going with the latter until proven otherwise. We won't know for sure until it is out. Either way, I am incredibly grateful that surgery is my cure, with possibly some radiation (won't know for sure until later). Reconstruction will be completed with a final surgery early next year and I will be good as new ... or at least better than a 45-year-old woman with 3 children. I'll be very grateful for that result.

A long post for this morning, but this is the most efficient method to spread the word ... and you know I love efficiency!

It also needs to be said, that while I may be down for a couple weeks recovering, my business isn't closed! I have been truly grateful over the years to have been entrusted by so many of you to serve you, your family and your friends with your real estate needs. Your continued trust and referrals are more important than ever. Please don't hesitate to reach out to my office. They are amazing and will help get anyone started until I am up and about in a few short weeks.

My family is overwhelmed with quite a lot currently as my in laws are dealing with some health challenges as well. Those of you who know have reached out and we have been continually blessed with delicious meals, help moving the Cooper boys from place to place with their activities, and more. Josh and I are not likely to be able to be responsive the next couple weeks, so I would request filtering any offers, thoughts or needs through my truly wonderful and dearest friends Vicky Noufal, Jackie Fields-Gleadall. They will know what we need and how to help.

My 2018 word of the year is grateful. That has sure been a struggle at times, but I feel it now more than ever ... truly, truly grateful.

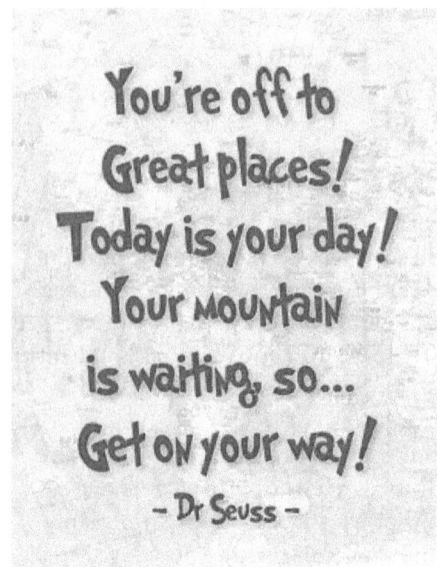

October 15, 2018

Four days post op, things I am grateful for ...

-Family and friends. So many deliveries of food, yummy treats, balloons, books, flowers.

-Aunt Coo Coo (Shirley Sanbower) has been toting my kids hither and yon, doing her best to make me edible soup (cooking is not her gift), and brought me (most likely Uncle Reggie made) my favorite applesauce cake that we only have at Christmas.

-Cute new Halloween pajamas.

-My "recovery pouch" little apron thing that holds my drains and my cell phone ... super convenient! I may try to bring the apron back after this.

-My favorite chair, my Sleep Number bed, mindless TV.

-My incredible Platinum Group Real Estate team who has jumped right in and taken amazing care of my clients without missing a beat.

-Ben who squeezes my lemon into my warm water in the morning. Ryan who checks on me frequently. Tyler who ever so gently covers me up or rubs my arm.

-Joshua Cooper who somehow manages to make me feel attractive even though I am pretty sure I smell bad (yesterday was the first time I was allowed to shower, and it was hard) … even while he is dumping the blood and stuff out of my drains twice a day.

Yes, I'm quite lopsided at the moment, but things aren't nearly as scary looking as I thought. I look like me, just smaller and with this weird thing making odd shapes under my skin (it's the spacer, phase 1 of reconstruction). The swelling and general weird skin and yuckiness under my arm makes me grateful that it is fall and we are fully into long sleeve season. It's all only temporary.

Mostly, I am incredibly grateful for a smooth surgery and for the immense calm and strength I felt on that day. I know for sure that it was a "God thing" and due at least in part as a result of the many thoughts and prayers from all of you.

October 18, 2018

I'm still in full on recovery mode over here, but as I am feeling better and stronger and weaning off the pain meds, my head is feeling more clear and is beginning to swirl with ideas.

More than ever our world seems to be an instant gratification world, but that isn't necessarily a reality … and definitely isn't a reality in our business. I struggle to think of anything in our business which gives instant results. Probably the closest you can get is an open house … you sit the open, you meet potential clients. But even then, they are not likely to buy something that day, and even if they did, it still wouldn't close for several weeks.

Our business is about planting seeds, nurturing, watering, weeding, waiting for them to sprout and then grow. The work we are doing now is what we will be paid for 30, 60, 90 days, maybe even a year from now. It is ESSENTIAL if you want to succeed in this business and build a sustainable, consistent business that you keep the big picture in mind. Always.

You will spend money now and next month and the month after, maybe even for a year before you see results from marketing to your geographic farm. But when it starts to work, just 1 closed transaction will cover your costs for multiple years.

You will take less on a transaction now, knowing that it will pay off in the long run. Let's say you get a lead as a referral from another agent or your brokerage that has a hefty fee attached. Instead of making $5000 or even

$10,000 if you had generated it yourself you will only make $3000. But now you have a new (hopefully) raving fan in your database. In a years' time it is reasonable to get 1 closed referral from that client, which you would have personally generated, so that's another $10,000. Now you have 2 potential new raving fans in your database. Another year goes by, and they both refer 1 closed new client to you, that's $20,000. This continues to compound again and again. I have multiple clients in my database who have sent me multiple referrals that have closed over the years, not to mention clients who themselves have moved 2-3 times. While sure, it sucks that you make less on that initial transaction, the potential return on that investment is massive.

Nothing is a quick fix. There is no such thing as an overnight success. True sustainable success takes time. Plant your seeds, focus on the big picture, and before you know it you will be reaping the rewards!

October 19, 2018

I do NOT have cancer.

The best way to say it is just to say it! My initial diagnosis on August 28th from a needle biopsy was a "periductal stromal sarcoma", a very rare malignant tumor. Shocking. Terrifying. Heart wrenching.

It was around 10 days later than a 2nd opinion on that pathology revealed that it could be that, or that it could be a non-malignant version of a phyllodes tumor (also rare, but I've had 4 of them before). Since hearing that possibility I've had 100% faith that it was the latter, not the former, and we were right! God is so good.

My big tumor (5.1 cms) and all of her baby tumors (essentially all my tissue was "diseased", no wonder I have had so many recurrences) were borderline (not benign, but also not malignant) phyllodes tumors. Surgery was my cure, and given the size of this tumor mastectomy was my best course of treatment, malignant or not.

There was one small area very close to the skin where my surgeon was not able to get clear margins (meaning the diseased area was still present at the edge of what was removed), but my chance of recurrence is not much higher than had it been negative. We are electing a "wait and see" approach. No more mammograms on that side, but I will need to be vigilant with self-exams so if a lump appears it can be excised.

I'll admit ... as thrilled as I am with my final diagnosis, I was disappointed that my chance of recurrence (with negative margins or not) is still in the 20-30%

range. I had hoped this would be it, but that's okay. I'll take this "annoyance" over the alternative any day.

Overall, I am exceptionally grateful for this entire process. I mostly feel as well as (or better than) can be expected given what I have experienced. We have been overwhelmed (in a good way!) with love, support, meals, kiddie carpooling, and pretty much daily deliveries of flowers, gifts, books (so many books ... you know me so well!) and more. The pain is more like discomfort and no longer requires medication, my drains may come out on Monday (please, please, please!), and my primary complaints are extreme fatigue, a weak right arm (physical therapy will follow), and trouble getting comfortable enough to sleep at night. The next phase of my reconstruction (inflation of the expander) is also likely to start on Monday, which I have been told is unpleasant, but this too shall pass.

Long post again, but so many of you have reached out to me and others to check in, this is the easiest way to spread the good news.

Now ... is that Power Ball lottery thing still going on? I'm thinking I should probably buy a ticket.

November 5, 2018
While I've been home recovering from my surgery, I've watched a lot of TV. Probably more TV in these last 3 ½ weeks than I've watched all year combined.

One of the few "regular" shows that I record to watch each week is Grey's Anatomy. On one particular episode, Dr. Miranda Bailey, who is an incredible talented, strong, driven wife and mother, and the Chief of Surgery was talking to a colleague about her stress.

She has struggled lately (or the last many episodes) with stress, having physical responses like chest pains and more. She took some time off, and even most recently temporarily stepped down from her coveted and long fought for position as Chief.

She remarked to her friend that she started focusing on her health (diet and exercise) and still felt stressed. She took time off, and as soon as she returned, she felt stressed. She appointed an interim Chief to handle her position while she focused on an easier practice, and she still felt stressed. She was working on a medical research project that she loved and was exciting, and yet she still felt stressed. (The plot line is that her stress comes from her husband's new-ish job as a firefighter, but let's put that aside.)

As she was talking about her stress and all the things she was doing to prevent it (to no avail), I had a thought ... everything that she was attempting to do to alleviate her stress was outside of herself. Some she can "control", some she can't, and so still she was stressed. Does this sound familiar to any of you? I know it did to me.

What if instead she (and we) focused inside of herself (ourselves). Instead of trying to control all the things and adjusting things to make the stress go away we instead focus on our individual response to it. It is our response that determines whether or not we feel stressed.

I know this is easier said than done, this is certainly a struggle for me on a daily basis. I've come to learn that stress, pressure, worries, struggles, are unfortunately a part of life. Perhaps they are even meant to teach us something. What exactly I'm not sure, but I do think there is a bigger picture purpose to all that we experience. I've been inside of literally multiple thousands of people's homes over the years, between my 10 years as an EMT and 16+ years in real estate. Just about everyone is dealing with something, it just doesn't always show. The most beautiful looking home (and life) from the outside, can be a huge mess on the inside.

Just some food for thought on what is a chilly, rainy Monday morning here in Northern Virginia. I don't really have any solutions to offer, I'm still figuring this one out myself.

November 12, 2018

Yesterday marked 1 month since my mastectomy. It's been a bit of a ride since that date. I've been re-learning how to do all my usual things with a strange feeling foreign object (a tissue expander) in my chest. I still sometimes (oftentimes) need to trade an hour or two of activity for an hour (or two) of rest. Taking a shower and getting dressed is still my most dreaded (and most tiring) activity. I suppose it is something about those particular movements, and of course the reality check of seeing and touching what I am dealing with.

Still, I am so grateful. One of the most powerful lessons that I have learned during this experience is being fully present in whatever moment I am in. This has always been extremely difficult for me. I'm a worrier by nature. I'm a planner, always thinking two (or three) steps ahead. I've learned that looking, thinking, working too far ahead only serves to rev up my anxiety to a fever pitch.

The day of my surgery you would have expected my anxiety to be at an all-time high. But it wasn't. Quite the opposite. I felt an immense calm, indescribable almost. I know that much of that can be attributed to those who were praying for me, to God's presence, and the rest came from me being fully present in that exact moment. Sitting in the chair in the waiting room. Chatting with the friendly nurse technician. Changing into my gown. I didn't let my mind wander beyond that immediate moment.

I did the same after I woke up from surgery later that day and in the days that followed. If being in the immediate moment was too uncomfortable (sometimes painful or feeling nauseous) I would pick out the next "big" moment (one that was just a few hours away) and focus on that ... the sun coming up, going home, having dinner. This felt manageable and allowed me to stay calm.

As I started to heal, I found myself back in the same pattern. Worrying about household tasks, things that needed to be done, work that needed to be prepared for. That period was one of the more difficult ones thus far as my mind was swirling around all the things that needed to be done, but my body and stamina wouldn't cooperate with doing them.

I'm certainly not suggesting that procrastination is the way to go, and that putting things off is the key. I've been there before, and that is a sure-fire way to send my anxiety through the roof. You need to take specific steps to plan and prepare for your work, your day, your week, but don't linger in that space. Do you struggle with worry and anxiety like I do? How do you cope?

November 14, 2018

Last week I spent a couple days away with my team for our annual retreat. Imagine 24 women sharing a (huge) house ... it's like one big slumber party, only with a purpose. We spent lots of time laughing, crying, laughing until we cry. The time we spend together is always restorative, and we come back inspired and ready to go.

One of the things that I heard repeatedly from different team members as they were sharing the review of their year, and their goals was a struggle with self-confidence and self-esteem. I can certainly relate to this, and I bet many of you can too.

I've learned that oftentimes it is the person who appears the most confident and "in charge" on the outside, who struggles the most on the inside. But why is that? The little voices in our heads that tell us we aren't good enough, or that we don't deserve the good things that are happening in our lives, or that we are flawed in some way have generated from some outside force ... an experience as a child, something someone you love (and you thought loved you) told you you were, and more. An experience as an adult or someone else's actions that we interpret as "our fault" or as occurring because of something we did or didn't do, or simply because we weren't enough. For some reason we hold on to these words and experiences and they become a little loop that plays over and over again in our brain telling us we aren't good enough, strong enough, talented enough, attractive enough, or just enough, period.

Life is too short to spend at war with yourself. Pick one of those stories or experiences and re-tell the story in a way that doesn't have anything to do with anything that is wrong with you. Keep telling it and re-telling it to yourself until this new story becomes the little voice in your head, then move on to the next one. This isn't easy. I have plenty (tons) of first-hand knowledge in this department, but it is worth it. Not only for yourself, but for your business and everyone around you. The more you know, love and respect yourself, the more you are able to show up for others in a bigger and better way. No matter what anyone else says, especially those lying little voices in your head, you ARE worthy, you ARE talented, you ARE valuable, and you ARE ENOUGH.

November 19, 2018

One of the very best things about our business is that we get to work with and serve other people. That is also one of the most challenging! My "specialty" has always been working with sellers, and my geographic area of expertise (and choice) is a rural area, and my "niche" is unique or unusual homes. All of this to say that days on market is typically 30+ and it would sometimes seem that the more unique the property, the more unique the situation ... and often the more unrealistic the seller!

No matter your area of focus in your business, we all deal with clients in difficult situations from time to time. Many times, not their "fault", oftentimes the result of their own poor choices. In either case that problem usually leads to unreasonableness and unrealistic expectations of value based more on what they "need" than on the market conditions.

One thing I've often struggled with is separating myself from my client's personal drama. I remember once many years ago a client who was recently widowed and in financial distress. We worked like crazy to prep her (very messy) home for sale, spending hours myself and several of my colleagues organizing, cleaning and staging. She would call me anxious almost daily about selling the house, then would decline showings. A few weeks into the listing we scheduled a sit-down meeting at the house; she was angry with me that the house hadn't sold and I couldn't understand why she was declining half the showing requests ... if you don't show it, you can't sell it. As soon as I walked in, I realized why ... against my advice she had decided to repaint one of the rooms in her house by herself. The room was full of a ladder, paint, drop cloths, etc. and she had undone a good portion of our staging.

It was maddening. I could see so clearly what she needed to do and be focusing on, and no matter how I explained it she just couldn't get it. Out of complete frustration during our heated conversation I started to cry ... and I never cry! (Okay, obviously not never, but most certainly rarely, and not in front in clients) We parted ways the next day, she relisted, and the house finally sold many months later as a short sale (which it wasn't when we started). I was so sad for her, she couldn't see how to help herself, and wouldn't allow those who could to do their job. Have you ever been in a similar situation? I like this quote, "not my circus, not my monkeys", but putting it into practice is often easier said than done.

November 28, 2018

Over the years I've had many, many agents ask me for advice on how to get started in real estate, or how to build their database, or even how to rebuild their business after a hiatus or lull. I've given out many suggestions, but one has been consistent: rentals.

This is not always popular advice (and I know in some markets that agents don't work with rentals at all), but it works. I've done it myself, more than once ... It worked when I was brand new, 16+ years ago, and just getting started, my very first transaction was a rental. It worked 9 years ago when I left a rainmaker team to go out on my own as an independent agent, some of my first deals at my new brokerage were rentals. It worked nearly 4 years ago when I returned to the field after "quitting" for 2 ½ years to be a managing broker, my first deal back was a rental. And it works now ... after scary health news this fall and being out for a couple months handling that and recovering from my mastectomy surgery, my first appointment when I returned, and my first transaction back was a rental.

Rentals allow you to get some relatively quick cash in your pocket while you are building (or re-building) your business. They allow you to build your database; those renters will almost always turn into eventual buyers and in the meantime, they know plenty of other people they can refer you to. Rentals allow you to build your confidence, especially when you are new, and to learn the ropes with showings, scheduling appointments, and managing paperwork.

I'm not the only agent that this has worked for. On a recent Facebook Live here in the group I had a conversation with Chrisie Pekala who has done just that. We talked about how she took leads from one rental listing when she was brand new and turned them into something like 25 closed rentals in just a couple months' time, and she has been reaping the rewards from that experience (and others) ever since, having her very best year ever in 2017 ... with nearly all of that business personally generated from her database and referrals. It was a great conversation!

December 3, 2018

This past Friday I had the opportunity to speak at the Virginia Women's Business Conference about "Time Mastery" ... one of my favorite topics to discuss! Every single one of us has the same 24 hours in a day, but then why is it that some people seem to be able to accomplish so much more, not just in their day, but in their lives? It is because they know how to master their time.

The reason I am so passionate about using my time wisely is not just because I want to be as productive as possible and to accomplish as much as possible ... it is actually because I place a very high value on down time (or any time really) with my family. I love my work, I need to work, I'm very driven, but I also crave, and thrive on, my quiet times with my favorite people. Being efficient with my time, making it work for me, is the way that I can do both.

It's quite funny, and very ironic, that in the week leading up to my presentation I was pretty frazzled and didn't do or forgot several bits of my own advice ... and paid the price for it. Instead of saying yes to working on my presentation I chose to do online Christmas shopping instead, which left me scrambling with last minute preparations. Instead of setting the alarm on my phone I overslept which left me grouchy and running behind the whole day. Instead of setting the timer on my phone so I would know when to leave the office I forgot, and wound up being late to pick up my youngest son from school (which of course when I pull up he and the aftercare teachers are waiting outside the door and he greeted me as soon as he opened the car door with, "where were you?").

I realized too that not only was I not as productive as usual last week but that I had a constant feeling of "running behind" ... and what came along with that was extra stress. And I don't know about you, but I for sure don't need any extra stress in my life right now.

The best advice I can give you when it comes to being a master of your time is two things ... 1) be clear on what is most important/highest value to you, and 2) know where your time is going. Also, be prepared to be flexible. What works for you in your schedule right now probably didn't work for you 6-12 months ago and probably won't work for you 6-12 months from now. This is especially true when you have children at home. Things are constantly changing, and so you have to be open enough to adapt to those changes instead of fighting against them.

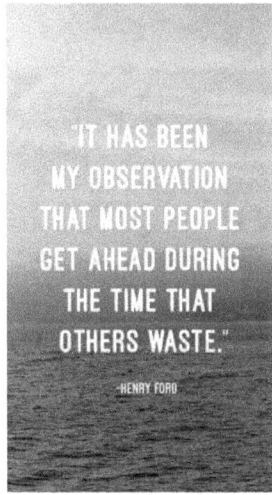

December 5, 2018

Last week I had a really great conversation with a friend (actually, she's the therapist I started seeing before my mastectomy, but she is a friend of a friend, and she reminds me of my friend, and so talking to her feels like talking to a friend. Anyway.). We were discussing Brené Brown's book "Daring Greatly" and the idea that we play to our critics.

I had been working on my presentation that I was giving last Friday at the Virginia Women's Business Conference for weeks and was struggling with the flow of it. We were talking about my anxiety surrounding my preparation and how I was struggling with my content ... even though I had given this presentation before. Through our conversation I realized that my audience this time was different (women in business, not necessarily people in real estate) and I was feeling insecure. Like maybe I wasn't really qualified to be sharing with them, and that my presentation (I) wouldn't be worth their time. Then my friend said something so profound ... critics will be critical no matter what.

The reason my presentation was feeling so uncomfortable was that I was playing to my critics. I was spending so much time focusing on people who may not necessarily enjoy what I had to share, who would be critical of it no matter what, instead of focusing on giving and sharing a presentation for an audience who would surely appreciate it and ensuring that they had the best experience possible.

For the record ... I have no idea who the critics are. My presentation went off without a hitch (well, not exactly without a hitch, there were some technical issues and no podium which threw me off a little, but still), the only feedback I received was kindness, appreciation, and positive. The critics existed purely in my mind.

Now that isn't to say that the critics don't exist in real life, I've certainly had my fair share of them, but the key take away here is that we tend to spend so much time, effort and energy trying to please and pacify a very small number of people who cannot be pleased.

We do this in our homes, in social settings and in our business. Yes, it is important to strive to be better and to be constantly learning and improving, but upending your entire way of being or doing, censoring yourself, just to try to please those who ultimately don't care about you at all and will be critical and judgmental no matter what ... well that is a never-ending battle.

December 10, 2018

My word for 2019 is Brave. Not necessarily brave like daredevil brave ... jumping out of airplanes and the like. More brave like facing down hard things and moving forward, fear or not.

Bravely having difficult conversations.
Bravely facing exciting (but also scary) shifts in my business.
Bravely forging ahead with another surgery in the new year and some difficult family challenges

Brave can also be committing to taking better care of myself, stepping outside my comfort zone, allowing myself to be more open. When the word first came to me, I was a little disappointed. I didn't want brave ... or rather maybe I don't want to BE brave, but the more I sit with it the better it fits.

I've chosen a word for the year ... my "theme", if you will ... for the last several. My word in 2018 was Grateful, and while I don't always feel like I embraced it, I sure put it to use the last half of the year and have truly been grateful. In 2017 my word was Simplify, and I feel like it was truly transformative and helped me to put aside all the extra "stuff" and focus only on what was most important to me. My 2016 word was Faith, during a year that it was desperately needed.

To help me to stay connected to my word, I will buy a couple little signs featuring my word or even frame a printout of it. I make sure I have one on the stand in my bathroom, so it is the first thing I see each morning, and another on my desk or on my wall at work. It's a fun tradition for me to put together the right ways to display it before the start of the year.

December 12, 2018

Yesterday my team had our final meeting of 2018 and closed out the year together with our annual holiday potluck. To end our meeting we went around the room, and each shared our biggest takeaway or lesson from 2018 and the thing that we are most looking forward to in 2019. We had several recurring themes in this group of 24 women ... a desire for more calm, and a concern about getting too wrapped up in our clients' issues.

Do you think these themes are unique to women in our industry? In all my years I don't think I've ever heard a male agent say that one of their biggest struggles is caring too much about their client's situation. In my opinion, it is that empathy, that high level of care and concern which makes us GOOD at what we do. It is the trait that causes us to be sought out and allows our clients to refer to us. They know that we care about them as people, not just the digits in the commission.

So how do we protect ourselves from getting dragged down into the mess (and if you've been around for a while you know that some of these situations can be really messy ...) when we do care deeply about helping?

Two things.

1) Set boundaries. If you allow your clients to contact you at all hours of the day and night ... and by responding you are teaching them that it is okay ... then you will not be able to separate yourself from the drama long enough to refresh. Unless you are in the midst of time sensitive contract negotiations, or you have clients in another time zone, there is no good business happening at 9 pm or 10 pm, or even 6 am. It's okay not to respond or to respond to say, "I'm settling into bed (getting ready for the day) and will give you a ring first thing in the morning (in 2 hours)." This works and it will be okay, I promise.

2) Know when to call it quits. Some client situations are such a mess, and some clients in such a bad place, that there is nothing we can do to help. When clients are in an ugly divorce or separation and are more interested in battling it out with each other ... with you firmly planted as the pawn in the middle ... than they are in doing what is necessary to get the house sold you need to know when enough is enough. Yes, walking away means losing that

commission (if they can even get it together enough for the house to sell) but how much are you losing while working with them in terms of both your mental health and other clients? Say, "It seems that there is more happening here that needs to be worked out before the property can be properly marketed and sold. I am not going to be able to continue with you until x, y, z is handled". Then refer them to someone else or send over a listing withdrawal. I've done both. Your business will be better for it.

December 17, 2018

Have you started working on your goals yet for next year? The time is now! Don't wait until January to get this done. Take some time now so when January 1st is here you are ready to hit the ground running.

Here is my simple formula to not just setting goals but making them actionable and achievable.

1) Understand where you have been. Look at your data from 2018. If you didn't intentionally track anything (and I strongly encourage you to in 2019) then at a minimum you should be able to pull your sales history from the MLS or get a report from your broker. Identify the source of each transaction ... sphere, referral, open house, postcard, etc.

2) Identify your goal. This year we set goal ranges with our team. Your minimum is the absolute bottom line that you must make to get by in 2019 or the minimum that makes it worth it to you to be in this business. Calculate this by first figuring out your average net per transaction, then divide your bottom-line income number by this and you will know how many transactions you need. For your "maximum" or stretch part of your goal, what do you really want from your business in 2019? What would change your life for the better? These two numbers represent your goal range.

3) Get clear on the actions you need to take to achieve your goals. If in step one you identified that 5 of your closed deals came from open houses this year, and you sat 25 open houses, then you know you need to plan to do the same or more. If 50% of your closed business came from repeat clients and referrals, and you averaged 2 "touches" per month, then you need to plan to do at least that many next year. Break that down into monthly and weekly action steps.

Now go out and do the things ... and while you are at it, track them so this process will be easier next year.

There is so much more that I can say about this process, but these are the basics. Don't just pick a number by pulling it out of the air. Pick a number that makes sense for you and connect your actions to your goal.

December 31, 2018

Can you believe that today is the last day of 2018? In some ways it feels like a year passes so slowly, but yet so quickly. So much can change and happen in a year's time. Do you take time to reflect back?

One of the things I notice with myself, and you may notice too, is that we push, push, push to achieve and accomplish, but rarely take time to fully feel, appreciate and CELEBRATE our accomplishments. Are you guilty of this too?

As I was thinking about my year of 2018, it is easy for me to think negatively about it based on some of my experiences in the 2nd half of the year. However, when I take the time to look back through my year as a whole ... yes there have been major struggles ... but there were many good things too! I've seen others keep journals where they write down highlights from each month, but for me the easiest way for me to do this "look back" is to scroll through the photos on my phone or even through my posts on my social media accounts. It is a great reminder of fun memories and can help to put much in perspective.

Here is a snapshot of my 2018 ...

-I read 31 books ... probably my most ever in a year since BK (before kids).
-Earlier in the year I reached a milestone "Lifetime Achievement" award with my current brokerage, one of only 2 people at the time to ever do so, with $50M in sales in my time with them (3 years). Huge! Especially considering that when I joined this brokerage I was coming back to the business after a 2 ½ year "hiatus".
-This year I served as the leader of the Lovettsville Business Network, presenting on business topics to a group of local business owners each month.
-My youngest son settled into the proper medication/dosage to treat his ADHD, which has been transformative for him both in terms of academics, but also in becoming "more" of himself. It has been amazing to witness.
-We purchased our first investment property this year ... a huge family goal. The best part though is that the 2 families that we have rented to thus far have both been known to us, and this rental has filled a huge need in their families too ... a wonderful and unexpected benefit.
-I personally helped 50 families this year with their real estate needs ... and the very best part of that was helping my brother and sister-in-law to sell their

home and buy a home closer to our families. This is transformative for our overall family as a whole as we are now able to share hosting duties for family events, as well as just being closer to all of us day to day.

-My middle son played his last ever Little League baseball game as he "aged out" this year. It was a memorable season with my husband managing his last team. He also got braces later this year, was selected to an All-Star baseball team, and started playing Babe Ruth baseball in the fall on his older brother's team, which was a lot of fun.

-Our family discovered and fell in love with a new beach, Topsail Island, NC. We ventured past our usual VA/DE beaches hoping to find something new that could also double as a future retirement location. Two weeks on the island and we were sold! We just booked our trip for 2019.

-I was interviewed on multiple podcasts this year (Real Estate Deep Dive with Kara Macdonald and Pat Hiban's Real Estate Rockstars, plus another that hasn't aired yet), as well as presented locally on real estate topics to multiple groups.

-We paid off our credit card debt, which was a much bigger task than I would care to admit, after nearly 2 years of careful budgeting and planning.

-My oldest son started high school (!!!), and we ventured into the world of football games, Homecoming dances and girlfriends. It's been a strange transition with my first "baby", but a fun adventure, nonetheless.

-My family went on many fun trips to some of our favorite places. Lake Anna for spring break, Great Wolf Lodge for one of their birthdays, the beach, Williamsburg at Christmas, and of course, our all time favorite, Disney World.

-I received a cancer diagnosis at the end of August, which then became a "maybe" diagnosis, which ultimately turned out to be a "borderline" tumor following my mastectomy in mid-October. The roller coaster was intense, and the emotional effects have been further reaching than I anticipated. On my surgery day I was remarkably calm ... truly a gift from God. The outpouring of love and support that I have felt through this experience has been nothing short of remarkable. Photo below taken the day after surgery after being released from the hospital carrying my "pain purse" (attached to my back with a catheter) and wearing my drains in an apron.

-The universe pushed me along (forcibly?) in making career adjustments with my business and here with Empowering Women in Real Estate, which will be bringing much growth and excitement in 2019.

-My team, along with my business partner Vicky Noufal, grew to 24 women strong this year and helped 414 families with their real estate needs ... an amazing accomplishment for us! We celebrated our 3rd year together, had our best retreat yet at Lake Gaston, NC, and we were all also featured in NOVA Real Producers December issue where I shared more about my personal story.

-Just 7 weeks post-surgery I spoke at the Virginia Women's Business Conference ... a longtime goal.

(My husband had many accomplishments and challenges of his own this year, but is more private, so not sharing here.)

I've always hated New Years Eve (even though I love New Year's Day), can't really explain why, but writing out some of these highlights and accomplishments helps to "lighten the load" so to speak and brings the excitement of the New Year a bit closer. My focus today will be on celebrating all that 2018 brought with it, good and bad, I hope you will do the same.

Wishing you all the most joyful, happy, healthy and prosperous New Year!

2019

<u>Milestones:</u>

6-12-2019 – Launch of Empower Coaching (now, the Inner Circle) monthly membership coaching program

11-6-2019 – First episode airs of Empowering Women in Real Estate - The Podcast

January 2, 2019

A few weeks ago, before the holiday break, I had to call my dad to come to my house in the morning last minute to stay with my youngest son who wasn't feeling well until I could wrap up my appointments and get back home.

As I was preparing to leave the house with my older boys, I heard an exchange that gave me pause. Dad wished one of the boys a good day and as part of the conversation I heard him say, "every day you have is a good day".

Dad turned 80 in the fall, and while he is in overall good health, he is having trouble seeing and hearing which causes a lot of challenges. He has always been incredibly active, and this coupled with financial issues, and the loss of my mother 3 ½ years ago has left him lonely and depressed a lot of the time.

To hear him say that every day is a good day was a bit surprising at first, but then made total sense. Much of the reason for his longevity I have no doubt is a result of this positive outlook. His overall view is positive, even when much of what he is dealing with these days is not.

My boys go back to school today, and so I will go back to work too. It has been our family tradition to take a holiday break while the kids are off school between Christmas and New Years, and while we've had a wonderful time it will feel good to get back in the routine of things.

Will you have a good day today? Certainly not everything you will experience today is likely to be good. Heavy traffic, frustrated clients, things that break, illness are just a few of the things that affect us on a day-to-day basis. Don't let those moments impact the view of your day. Find the good today, enjoy those moments, and you will have a good day.

January 9, 2019

At the start of each new year, I find myself doing a lot of reflecting and planning. Reflecting on the past, both personal and business. Reflecting on what did and didn't work for me in the previous year. Planning what I will do this year to shake things up in all areas of my life. Planning ways to improve myself, my relationships, my business.

I loved this quote as soon as I saw it … "The past is in your head. The future is in your hands." It is good to reflect on the past, but not to stay there. The future IS in our hands. We don't have to stay in the same patterns, the same old way of doing things, getting the same results. We can make different decisions, take new actions, try new things.

I've been guilty of saying, "that doesn't work for me", "I'm not doing that", "I've already tried that" when it comes to doing something different with my business (or, okay, fine, my life in general). A wise friend said something to me last week that stopped me in my tracks. She said that just because something worked for me or was manageable by me a year, three, or even 5 years ago doesn't mean that I will get the same results or have the same experience or be able to handle it now. Not because there is anything wrong with me now, but because I am a different person than I was a year, three, and for sure five years ago.

Think about that for a moment. How many more things do you know, how many more experiences have you had, how many more things have you learned in the past year, three, five? There are things I would have tolerated then that I most certainly won't now. There are things that didn't work for me then, in part because I didn't know what I know now, that very well may work today. There were also things that worked for me then, that won't work for me now … because I know more, know better, am in a different place.

I've been frustrated since my surgery in the fall that I seem to be struggling to accomplish as much, to produce as much, as I used to. I have always thrived with a frantic, busy pace, juggling multiple things at once. That doesn't seem possible for me anymore, or at least right now. Or maybe it's just not what I want for myself, my life, right now. The funny thing I have noticed since making this observation and giving myself more focused time on important priorities is that I am being very productive, and I'm doing it in a more intentional and "calm" way, if that makes any sense. What used to work for me doesn't anymore, and that's okay. So, I'm giving myself (and you) permission to grant myself (yourself) grace. It's okay for things to look different, to feel different. It's okay to want different things. It is all of the experiences and changes that I have made over the years that have gotten me here, and more experiences and more changes will get me where I am going. What used to be was great, but I don't want to relive those years over and over and over again. I want to grow and learn and try new things. This is where I am and what will get me where I am going, and that is a great feeling.

January 14, 2019

I decided to sleep in today.

We got about 10 inches of snow this weekend, and so it is a snow day for us here. With the kids out of school today I decided that I would set my alarm for an hour later, and even then, when it went off, I decided to turn it off and sleep for another hour. I suppose my body needed the extra rest today.

How often do you listen to what your body (or your heart or your mind) needs? We go, go, go and we push, push, push, when sometimes what we really need is just a little rest. A little break. A time out. A deep breath (or two, or ten). When you are in the thick of it (I'm talking to you, spring real estate market) it is easy to believe the lie that you can't take a break. There is too much to be done, there are too many opportunities to take advantage of, now is not the time. So, you press on and on, well past the point of exhaustion until you burn totally out.

I've been guilty the last few years of going so hard and so fast the first half of the year, that it pretty well takes the majority of the second half of the year to fully recover. And then the cycle starts all over again. I'm no longer sure that is the best way to live.

What if we did something different instead? What if we rested when we were tired. What if we took breaks to refresh ourselves, spring market or not?

I think we ... and our businesses ... will be better and stronger for it. Is it possible that we may lose a client if we aren't available for them upon demand? Possibly. But if you set the expectation clearly and (here's the key) confidently, and you have a contingency plan (an agent to refer to when needed, someone to help with showings) it WILL be okay. Your value is far greater than simply your availability.

Building a strong, thriving, consistent business for the long haul is a marathon, not a sprint. Stop treating it as such. Listen to what you need, what you really need, and respond to yourself with kindness and grace. You, and your business, will be better for it.

January 21, 2019

"Faith is taking the first step, even when you don't see the whole staircase" ... one of my favorite quotes from the late, great Reverend Dr. Martin Luther King, Jr. Seems very fitting to share today.

When I think about the experiences in my life that have been the most life-changing, the big chances that I have taken, not a single one of them was clear. I didn't know where they would lead, I didn't understand everything that would happen, and I didn't know who I would need to be in order to be successful.

But I did know that I needed to take the chance, make the change, move in that direction ... and so I did so in faith. And with each step ... some smaller than others, the next step (or 3 or 5) would sometimes slowly, sometimes quickly, come into focus.

When I took that first step, almost 17 years ago, into my real estate career I had no clue where it would take me. I simply wanted, needed, to make a living. I didn't know that it would be a source of great sacrifice, but also great flexibility and opportunity. I didn't know that it would provide my family with great financial gains, but also times of near financial ruin. I didn't know that I would be building a business ... my business ... that would be a great source of pride and joy, but also exhaustion and depletion.

If I had known all of the ups and downs, would I have continued up the staircase? Who knows. I was a different person then, than I am now, and I have the journey to thank for that. Perhaps that is why we can only see the first step and need to move forward in faith, if we knew all the bad that goes along with the good maybe we wouldn't take the chance at all.

January 22, 2019

I had my day all planned out.

-Morning routine

-Meeting with a team member
-Lead team meeting
-Guest host in "Next Level Agents" for Pat Hiban
-Film a video for an upcoming event
-Walk thru a listing I have coming soon
-Pick up my son from school

My planned post for this morning was going to be all about daily routines, something some of my team members and I have been discussing lately. I started prepping some of it last night to go through my typical day with you, and was planning to share snippets throughout the day on Instagram Stories. A "day in the life", if you will.

But then we got the call last night for a 2-hour school delay due to the extreme low temperatures this morning and my whole plan went out the window.

So instead ...
I'm doing my morning routine, just a little later.
My team member meeting was moved to Thursday.
My team meeting was moved to Friday.

I'm still guest hosting today.

I'll still be filming the video, doing a walk thru with my seller and picking up my son. I'll do the daily routine post and "day in the life" Instagram stories another day.

In the meantime, how often is it that we have a great plan, but things change outside of our control? All. The. Time. I'll admit, I didn't necessarily handle it gracefully when we got the call last night. I had everything planned out and was committed to executing my plan, there wasn't room or time to shift things around.

As usual though, when I took a step back, identified that which HAD to take place today and shifted around what I could, I recognize that it's still going to be a great day.

Stay committed to your decisions, your goals, your plans, but be flexible about your methods.

January 24, 2019
When is the last time you tried something new?

"New" used to terrify me. I strongly disliked anything different, any change. I loved the sense (and it was truly just a sense) of control I had over what I did.

Then one day, years ago, when I was reflecting back on my accomplishments and my most fun and exciting memories from the year, I realized that they all involved something new that I tried.

Once I made this connection it was like my eyes opened to a whole new world of possibilities.

By no means am I an "expert" here ... I still like to think that I am in control, and being in control, in part, means feeling comfortable, and feeling comfortable typically equates to not doing new things.

It does get easier though. It's like a muscle. The first few times you work it, really work it, it is uncomfortable. You may be sore for a couple days, but the more you use it the better and stronger it becomes. The easier it is to use and push.

So now, I love to try new restaurants, I'm no longer adverse to trying new foods, and I love to stay at new resorts when my family vacations (keep in mind, they are usually at the same destination, but still ... baby steps).

And so, with all this practice in "little" things, trying new things in my business are now a breeze. I'm able to move forward confidently with new ideas, in part, because I've learned to trust myself. I know that if I try something new and it doesn't work or it doesn't fit, that I can change it. I can fix it. No harm, no foul. The best thing about it is that even if my something "new" doesn't work out, I don't end up going back to the old way, because trying something new usually leads me to a better way that I never would have thought of in the first place.

January 28, 2019

What motivates you, propels you forward toward your accomplishments?

A lot of people may say, "my family", "having a goal", "winning", even "making money", but stop and think about it for a moment ... when you are making a change in your life, when you are growing and accomplishing things, when you are being propelled forward, is it because a problem is pushing you in that direction, pushing you to take action, or are you being led there by your dreams?

Really think about that for a moment. When I look back and think about my experiences and the times that I grew the most, there was a significant period of my life where I was more often being pushed by my problems. A problem/situation/issue in my life had become so uncomfortable that there was no choice but to act, to move, to take a step in another direction. As a result, these experiences were sometimes painful, lengthy, long and drawn out, and not usually welcomed ... until I got to the other side of course and realized what it was all about.

Then when I think about the times that my dream or my goal led me to act, progress seemed ... easier. Not that there still wasn't hard work involved with the change, but it didn't seem to be as painful, it was joyful even.

I suppose there is no right way. Both approaches will eventually get you in the direction you are supposed to go, but I do think that when your dreams are leading that you will go farther, faster ... and maybe even more enjoyably.

Can you see how this principle has been at work in your life? Do you tend to be pushed or led? Are you experiencing something right now that feels like pushing? Instead, why not stop a moment. Think about the direction you are moving in, change your internal dialogue about that experience and visualize or dream about how it could be different. Then instead of being pushed by the "problem" that "started" it all, let that dream lead you. I have a feeling that it may make all the difference.

January 30, 2019

Have you ever found yourself dealing with the same problem over and over again?

Maybe not the *exact* same problem, but the same "category" of issue again and again ...

Clients who don't respect your boundaries.

Missing out on listing opportunities.

Buyers who "cheat" on you and buy a house without you.

Clients who make bad decisions (maybe even against your advice), then blame you every step of the way as you work to clean up the mess.
Do you think that it is possible that the problem won't go away until you have learned the lesson?

The clients who call and text at all hours will continue to do so as long as we answer the phone or respond.

We don't seek feedback or look objectively on our processes and presentations when we lose, and so it continues to happen.

Buyers get nervous when expectations aren't established clearly and end up visiting model homes and open houses without us.

Do you blame your doctor when you get sick? Of course not. So why is it allowed (and even expected) when our clients blame us for their situations?

I'm not saying that we can prevent every issue, but I do believe that we can learn from them.

What is the most valuable lesson that your business has taught you?

February 5, 2019
Going to a four-year college after high school wasn't an option for me and wasn't a priority for my family. So, I went to community college to earn my associate's degree and was fortunate to find a civilian position on the nearby army base that paid well and allowed me to work full time during all breaks, and part time when school was in session.

At some point after graduating, I was hired as a market research coordinator for a pharmaceutical company. It was a good position, but without the bachelor's degree my advancement opportunities were limited.

One day while meeting with the Human Resources director she encouraged me to enroll in their tuition reimbursement program. I could have virtually my entire education paid for by them, which was huge!

Would you believe that I was hesitant? I remember expressing to her my objections and my concerns of how long it would take. Then she said something to me that I have never, ever forgotten ... "the time will pass anyway". At the end of the 3 or 4 years or whatever it would take I could have my degree or be in the same place I was then.

I took her up on that, finished my degree, and moved up to several higher-level positions in the company before the layoffs started and I found myself in the wonderful world of real estate.

Still, that lesson that she taught me changed my perspective on time forever. How many times do we say no to opportunities because of the time it will take, or because we are too impatient to get what we really want, so we settle for what is right in front of us?

The time will pass anyway. You can use it to make a difference, or you can live through it and be in the same place over and over again. The choice is yours.

Take the chance. Do the thing. Your future self will thank you!

February 7, 2019

I have two words for you today ...

Bless and Release.

Last week during a breakfast meeting with my business partner Vicky Noufal and our dear friend and mentor Jackie Fields-Gleadall we were chatting about challenges and difficult clients, and Jackie told us to bless and release. We can't control every situation. Clients will be unreasonable. We just need to bless them (or the situation) and release it.

It's my new favorite.

Difficult client who doesn't take your advice, and is then upset later when they understand the consequences of that? Bless and release.

Rude coop agents who try to prove their worth by belittling you? Bless and release.

Listings that won't sell.
Buyers that won't buy (even though you've shown them the right house 10 times over).
Renters that drag their feet.

Bless and release.
Bless and release.
Bless and release.

I could go on and on. There are a million and one applications for this. Try it, it works!

February 14, 2019

It's Valentine's Day!

This may be a day that you love, or a day that you dread. Either way, let's put aside the romantic notions for a moment and talk about other things that we love.

Me, I love words.

I love the spoken word ... listening to others who are eloquent speakers, and speaking them out loud myself. Sometimes I'll say words that I didn't think I knew, but suddenly they come out of my mouth at just the right moment to fill just the right sentence.

I love the written word ... reading them and writing them. Sometimes they flow so easily from my fingers as I type that I truly have no idea where they are coming from. There is a spot in my brain that seems to engage, and everything makes sense.

I've joked with friends that words are my spiritual gift. I've often been known by those I work with as the person to come to when you need wordsmithing or spinning when working on marketing pieces, handling difficult situations, language to use in contracts and more.

I love to use alliteration when naming programs or classes. I love words like ancillary, fatiguing, plethora, bravado. Fun to say, fun to type.

This is my thing. Words are my jam.

Now tell us, what is something that you love? Not people, or places or pets, but a something, maybe intangible, maybe unusual, that you love.

February 19, 2019

The universe has quite the sense of humor.

I was SO tired this morning. Sitting in my favorite spot with my favorite mug figuring out what to write to you before 6 am and all I could think was, "I'm so tired".

Today is a jam-packed day, no room for error. Appointments at 8:30 am, 10 am, 12 noon, 3 pm, 4 pm and 6 pm.

As I was sitting this morning thinking of how tired I am, I started to smell something. Something unpleasant. Something I've smelled before. I stayed in denial for a few minutes, then it was obvious.

Both dogs. Sprayed by a skunk. At 6:15 am.

After a momentary pity party, my husband and I went to work. Separating them. Bringing them in through the unfinished side of the basement. Barricading them one by one in the basement bathroom for their baking soda-hydrogen peroxide-Dawn dish soap baths. Have I mentioned that they hate baths? They are 80 and 100 pounds each. It's like wrestling a whiny, shaking, smelly bear to get them into the bathtub (my next house will have either a dedicated doggy shower or no dogs ... the verdict is still out on this one, guess which way I'm leaning this morning?).

The dogs were clean and sleeping in their crates by 7 am. We have little bowls of vinegar all over the house to help trap the residual odors. I'll repeat the baths tonight for good measure.

But guess what? No longer tired.

That'll teach me.

February 28, 2019

I'm taking a sick day today.

The last few weeks I've been SO TIRED. I've been fighting what seems like the same cold over and over again all winter. I'm usually someone who only gets sick maybe once or twice in the whole year, but I've had the sore throat/runny nose/congested/earache thing on and off since December.

My body has been telling me to rest, and I haven't been listening.

So today, I'm listening. I'm clearing my schedule. I'm sure I'll catch up with some work on my computer, but I'll be doing it from bed.

I take care of other people and their needs like it's my JOB. My household, my husband, my children, our pets. My dad, my aunt, my friends, my team. My clients. My vendors, local businesses, my community.

You know who I don't take care of? Me.

By the time I'm done with all the other things there is no time, or energy, or mental capacity left to take care of me. So, I'll throw little band aids on here and there to placate the situation. A monthly massage, a pedicure. Buying a new top of two (always on sale) or a new bag or pair of earrings. A handful of cookies or M&Ms with a cup of tea. A glass of wine. Maybe two. None of it done intentionally. Often as an afterthought. Sure, it brings some momentary pleasure, but it doesn't last. And sometimes the hole feels bigger after than it did before.

Raise your hand if you can relate.

So today I'm going to listen to what my body has been asking for and take care of me. I'm still going to take care of some things that need to be done for others ... put the finishing touches on some new listings that are coming on tomorrow, call the insurance company for a couple of issues, plan out some things that need to be done, but mostly, I'll rest.

Is self-care a priority for you? How do you take care of yourself?

March 4, 2019
How are your habits? We all have them, good and bad.

My good habits? I consistently complete my prospecting tasks every week. I do a load of laundry every morning. I get up early. I write to you every day.

My bad habits? I've been hitting the "snooze" button a lot more lately. I need something sweet every afternoon. I linger in my favorite chair too long on the weekends.

You don't know how deeply ingrained a habit is until you try to break it.

I was talking to a wise friend about this last week, and she suggested making "micro" changes when you are trying to break or change a habit, or to start a new one. If you want to form a habit around exercise, instead of starting with jumping right into an hour a day, start with a 5 minute walk each day. Keep that going until it becomes a habit, then tweak again, maybe going to 10 minutes.

When it comes to bad habits, try delaying them. Instead of hitting the snooze button today, decide that I will do it tomorrow (Mel Robbins talks about procrastinating your procrastination in her book, "The Five Second Rule"). Instead of having my sweet treat when the habit hits around 2 pm, decide that

I will instead have it at 3 pm. Maybe I'll still want it then, or maybe I'll be so busy doing something else that I won't even notice.

Habits are funny things. They drive our subconscious into doing things good and bad. Most of my habits are centered around some sort of self-soothing. My prospecting habit? Soothes my anxiety that I'm not doing enough for my business. My laundry habit? Calms my feeling of overwhelm. My weekend chair habit? It feels so good to relax and enjoy time to myself that I don't want it to end.

March 6, 2019

Recently I was watching an episode of Super Soul Sunday with Oprah Winfrey on the OWN network.

She was talking with Bradley Cooper about his experiences with the movie, "A Star Is Born". This was a relatively new experience for him, something he worked on for several years, writing, directing, and acting in the film.

Oprah asked him how he thought this would change what he did moving forward. What he said was so powerful.

He said that this has expanded his view. That prior to this experience he tended to operate in one way, doing what he was comfortable doing, and staying in that space partly because of fear. Pushing outside of his comfort zone showed him what more was possible, and expanded his view of what he could do in his career.

Isn't that awesome?!

How many of us stay stuck in the same pattern year after year after year? Because it's comfortable. Because we're afraid to try something different. Because we are afraid we will fail. Because we are afraid we will succeed.

Imagine though if we do push outside of our comfort zone. Imagine how much more of the world will be opened up to us? I've seen this in my own life and my own career. Every time I have pushed past the fear to try something different, to go in a different direction, to try something a little bit new, not only have I often succeeded, but more importantly, my view of what was possible for myself expanded. And those times when I failed, I learned so much, and it opened up so many more possibilities to me that it never felt like a failure, or at least not for very long.

March 11, 2019

I was reading a book recently about success and one of the concepts the author talked about was the importance of taking action.

The problem though is that we often become so overwhelmed with the idea of all we need to do in order to accomplish our goals that we freeze. Instead of doing something, making progress, we do nothing.

Does this sound familiar to you? It sure does to me.

Instead, identify the next step (and only the next step) that you need to complete in the progression towards your goal, no matter how seemingly obvious or small.

For example, is your goal to start a postcard campaign to your geographic farm? Your next step (assuming you have already identified your farm) is to select a printing company to print and send your postcards. You could even further break this down to "post on local Facebook group for printing company suggestions".

Maybe your goal is to have a client appreciation party. Your next step would be to decide what kind of party you are going to have.

Perhaps your goal is to sign your first listing. Your next step may be to put together the components of your listing presentation.

Or maybe you just need to get yourself in for a haircut! Next step, write down "call salon" on your to do list. Sure, you could just make the call right now, but you are probably feeling a bit too overwhelmed by everything, which is why you haven't done it in the first place.

No matter what it is that you need or want to accomplish, there is something so powerful about simply identifying your next step. Forget for just a moment about the 15 other steps, and just focus on the one next step. Identify it. Write it down. Then do it. Then repeat.

What is just ONE next step that you can take today to get you closer to where you want to be tomorrow?

March 14, 2019

My oldest son, a high school freshman, is now playing on his high school's JV lacrosse team. This may not sound too exciting, lots of kids play high school sports, but he has only been playing lacrosse for about a month.

See, he has always been a baseball kid. He has been participating with the baseball team doing winter workouts every day before or after school or for several months now, and even signed up for and completed an "optional" (and expensive) Saturday training program.

While he loves baseball and works tremendously hard, he is not the strongest player, and he knows that. Making the team at our school is a little political, and very competitive. There were at least double the number of kids trying out for the spots available, so at literally the last minute (less than 2 weeks before try outs) he shifted gears.

His priority was belonging to something. His priority was playing for his school. So, when he learned about the opportunity to try out for the lacrosse team (they were actively recruiting new players) he jumped at the chance.

Never mind the fact that he had never played lacrosse in his life.
Never mind the fact that he owned zero lacrosse equipment.
Never mind the fact that he didn't know the first thing about the rules or strategies of the game.

Still, he jumped all in and he LOVES it.

As he played his first official game of the season last night, I was thinking of the courage required to try something that seems so big and so different. For him, it doesn't seem to be a big deal to try something ENTIRELY different. For me, the thought seems overwhelming.

Is it the age difference? Am I just too jaded as a 45-year-old woman and he is too naive as an almost 15-year-old boy?

Maybe he's got it right. Look at your big picture, be clear on what you want to accomplish, and just jump right in and go for it.

When is the last time you tried something new?

March 19, 2019
While on a listing appointment yesterday I was reminded of one of my favorite pieces of advice ever, "he who speaks first, loses" ... courtesy of my very wise friend Jeanne Cooper.

During the "close" portion of the appointment the seller became quiet when I asked if he was ready to move forward. The silence was awkward and seemed to last forever.

But I stayed quiet and waited. And waited. And waited.

Finally, he said that he was ready to sign.

I could have filled the silence with chatter. I could have offered "outs" to stop the awkwardness, but I learned long ago the importance of knowing when not to talk. It is just as important as what to say when you do!

March 20, 2019

Today is the day we've been waiting for ... it's the first day of spring!

Depending on where you live, the spring real estate market may have been going strong for weeks now. You may also live in a place where snow is still not off the table. But at least now the calendar is affirming for us that bluer skies and warmer weather is on the way.

At our team meeting yesterday, we were saying how amazing it would be if we could work hard 6 months of the year then take a month or two off. Wouldn't that be amazing?

Unfortunately, our business doesn't work that way. When we stop engaging with our business, the business stops coming in. It's important to continue with the consistent cycle of prospecting, following up, keeping in touch, and putting yourself out there. It can be exhausting, a little frustrating and a lot defeating to think that you can put in weeks, months or years worth of work and the moment you step away it dissolves very quickly.

So, what's the fix? Systems. Having a system and a plan for follow up can go a long way towards keeping your business going as automated as possible. Do you have a system, or is this a pain point in your business?

April 2, 2019

I have long understood the power of generosity. The more you give, the more you will receive. Some call it the law of the harvest. I call it common sense.

There is a catch though. If you are giving only with the intention of receiving, it's just not going to work. There is an unspoken energy that follows when you're being generous to others. When that generosity comes with expectation, the energy flows differently.

Being generous is more than just giving money. You can be generous with your time, your energy, your love, and your kindness. All are equally, if not even more, valuable.

What you give out in slices will come back in loaves. I know this to be true.

Can I challenge you to be generous today? Give something to someone else. Maybe it's money to someone who could use it, clothing, toys or household goods. Perhaps you will give your time to help someone in our industry who is newer or struggling who could use advice. You could give your ear and your energy to a friend or a colleague who just needs to vent.

April 8, 2019

As I've been reading, "Girl, Stop Apologizing" by Rachel Hollis along with our Empowering Women in Real Estate Book Club, there have been many great take aways. My favorite so far is the concept of striving to be "centered" instead of balanced.

How many roles are you juggling on a daily basis? It can feel like a constant struggle to balance all the things, but balance is a facade. It is impossible to give equally to all the things all the time.

Instead, I love the idea of focusing on being centered, grounded. If I am centered and at peace with myself, I will be better able to manage all the roles and people and moving parts. If I am firmly grounded then I can give as needed, when and where without losing myself ... and my sanity.

As I am about to embark on an incredibly hectic week, I am holding onto this idea and using it to stay calm and "in control".

April 10, 2019

There were so many great take aways yesterday from the She's Unstoppable Live! women's real estate conference! My favorite came from Bravo TV's Anna Brent, star of "Buying It Blind" and real estate team owner in Atlanta, Georgia. Anna blew us all away when she asked if we had 10 (or insert 3, 5, 15, 20) years of experience, or if we have had the same year 10 times.

Ouch.

Are you seeing growth in your business or are you hustling, bustling and running yourself into the ground only to have the same year over and over again?

She is so right about this. Have you been in the business 10 years (or 3 or 5 or 15) or have you been *working* your business for that many years, actively engaged in your business and your market? There is a very distinct difference.

I love this thought. Either you are growing and changing, or you're dying. There really is no in between, is there?

April 22, 2019

I'm baaaccckkk! Did you miss me? (Did you notice I was gone??)

I had a wonderful vacation last week with my family for spring break. It was a whole lot of peace and quiet (my favorite), sitting in the sunshine, looking out at the water, watching my boys' fish, and plenty of reading. Taking time away from my business and taking time to reflect helps me to come back much more clear. More clear about my purpose, my goals, my next steps.

Having this clarity is truly priceless. Without it, it is far too easy to continue day to day, week to week, even year to year doing the same things over and over again out of habit, not necessarily out of desire or purpose, and definitely not with the big picture in mind.

One exercise I did last week to help me to get clear was doing a vision board. I put together a vision board using Canva (but you could use any photo collage app) and then had several copies printed in 8x10 size at my local Walgreens that I picked up when I came home. My board was a simple collage of photos with a photo of my family at the center, my word of the year (Brave) at the top, a couple quotes, and then photos that represented what I most want ... health, energy, my favorite places to visit, my long-term vision for myself, what I want my work to look like. I will post a copy by my desk at home, one at the office and one on the wall in my closet where I will see it every day.

Having clarity allows me to feel more confident in taking action. Taking action is the only way to change the things I wish to change and to get where I am going. Lots less thinking and talking, lots more action.

April 30, 2019

Did you know that whenever you or I have a success or a win, that there is almost always at least one other person that we can credit with that win? Think about it.

Win a listing appointment? Who are the people that you shadowed on appointments or the broker or manager who taught you how to present or the podcasts or videos you watched to learn to be a proficient listing agent?

Ratify a contract? Those buyers certainly played a role for putting together a great offer, plus the lender whose conversation with the listing agent helped them feel confident with your offer.

Lose 5 pounds? Did someone in your household support you by buying or preparing healthy food or how about the friend or neighbor who went for walks with you?

I just finished reading, "Wolfpack" by Abby Wambach, Olympic gold medalist and retired professional soccer player. In it she talks about this quite a bit. She says that with any win ... yours or someone else's ... you should be either rushing or pointing.

When someone else wins, you should be rushing towards them with support and congratulations. When you win, you should be pointing at all of the people who contributed to that win.

I love this idea. Success is sometimes thought of as this solitary practice, but really it rarely ever happens alone.

May 7, 2019

Did anyone else watch Brené Brown's Netflix special? You can be vulnerable and strong at the same time. In fact, the two go together.

I love her quote, if you aren't in the arena also getting your ass kicked, I'm not interested in your feedback". So many people love to weigh in, give their two cents, comment, criticize and pick apart. And usually when they do it is from a place of not doing. I'm working, striving to grow and do something different, and the loudest critics aren't, have no interest, are too afraid to do for themselves so instead they pick at others.

I'm happy to hear thoughts, feedback, constructive criticism ... but ONLY if you are out there pushing hard, growing, and doing it too. Otherwise, I'm not interested. And you shouldn't be either.

Don't play to the critics. They will be critical no matter what.

May 9, 2019

Have you ever stared at a word so long that it no longer makes sense? Like you aren't even sure it is spelled correctly, and you're not even sure what it is.

Brave. That's my word. It's my word of the year, you know. When I look at it too long it doesn't make sense to me anymore.

I'll be brave though. I'm off to the hospital this morning. Almost exactly 6 months to the day of my mastectomy for my "exchange" surgery. This is where they replace the hard, rigid, sometimes pointy feeling around the edges expander that has lived in my breast since my last surgery with an implant and then work their magic on the other side to try to get some sort of symmetry.

A friend asked me if I was going for "Ariel" or "Jessica Rabbit" (total Disney reference for fellow fans). I actually don't know. I've had so many surgeries on this side (this will be my 7th or 8th, I've lost track) that there are limitations for what can be done.

So, it's totally going to be a surprise. I'll wake up to breasts I don't know on a body I no longer recognize. *Surprise!* None of this was my choice, and it doesn't feel exciting or fun. I am beyond immensely and eternally grateful that I do NOT have breast cancer (I have a long history of a rare type of tumor called a phyllodes tumor). Still, it's a lot.

Recovery is estimated at 2 weeks. I'm hoping for less than that. The physical pain and discomfort I can work through. The emotional pain though, that is different and creeps up and appears out of nowhere and I've learned often looks like exhaustion and no energy and a short temper, particularly with those I love the most.

So off we go. I've prepped a post or two for you here in the group that have been scheduled out, and more than likely will pop in to write some things here and there because words are my happy place. And also, because, brave.

May 31, 2019

Let's talk about pain for a moment, shall we? Many of you know the physical challenges I've been through of late. A mastectomy in October (I am forever grateful that I did not have cancer) and the completion of my reconstruction 3 weeks ago.

After each surgery I was always struck a little bit by the medical personnel who cared for me that seemed to be constantly seeking to completely eradicate my pain.

Now I'm certainly no masochist, and there have been many moments when I have absolutely, positively needed help with the pain. But there were many others where I was uncomfortable, but okay.

There are many different types of pain. Physical, emotional, spiritual. The kind of pain you feel when you step on your kid's Legos in your bare feet, and the kind you feel watching a beloved friend contend with her own pain.

Some is fleeting, some is more long lasting ... lifelong even. Some is easier to brush past or push down, some requires you to stop and pay attention.

Sometimes, it's okay to feel the pain.

Without the pain, we would press on and try to do too much when we really need to rest, reflect and care for our bodies and our minds.

Without the pain, we would amble on from activity to activity, day to day, without fully noticing, appreciating or ever "feeling" our life.

Without the pain, there would be no benchmark for joy. We are able to recognize (and appreciate happiness) because we have known pain.

Sometimes the pain comes first, then the joy. Sometimes it's the other way around.

Just some rambling thoughts this morning. While I don't wish for or look for pain, I've learned to accept, and even appreciate it, because it means that something or someone was worth it. That there was joy and love and happiness, and that was worth the pain.

June 12, 2019

empower

verb em·pow·er | \ im-'pau(-ə)r \empowered; empowering; empowers

DEFINITION OF EMPOWER
transitive verb

1: to give official authority or legal power 2: ENABLE 3: to promote the self-actualization or influence of
(Source: Merriam-Webster)

I am so excited to announce Empower Coaching by Karen Cooper ... powered of course by Empowering Women in Real Estate!!!

Since first creating this group in July 2014 my mission has been to empower women in the real estate industry. I've worked to help you to see your power and capability and what you bring to the table. I've worked to enable you to build a strong business AND a happy life. Empower Coaching is a natural progression, and something that you have asked me for again and again.

Ready to learn more? Here we go ...

Empower Coaching will be delivered through a monthly membership group and will be based on the systems that I have implemented with my real estate team (31 women strong!) and in my own personal business. What I've learned over the past 17 years (and over 700 families helped personally) as an individual agent, managing broker and team leader is that not only do women in our business need coaching, accountability and a feeling of belonging, but they also need a clear sense of direction. And I'm here to deliver that, step by step.

My coaching system will include a Plan of the Week to help set your direction with specific steps for engaging with and building your database (based on my team's highly successful Client Care Program) and personal branding so you can continue to grow your business. There will be clear how tos for the various components of the program so it will be easy to implement. We will have 1-2x monthly Facebook live group coaching and Q&A sessions, and more ...

*Comprehensive marketing plans delivered weekly
*Monthly group coaching Q&A sessions
*Monthly Meet Up video recordings
*Annual online goal setting workshop
*Access to our private Facebook mastermind community

*Step by step "How To" guides for each facet of the program
*Group support and accountability

Empower Coaching (Author's note: now called the Inner Circle) membership is now live on our website, EmpoweringWomenInRealEstate.com and ready to join. Whether you join this week, next week, or next month the program is comprehensive and continuous so you can jump in anytime. I hope you will join me!

June 19, 2019

I love this quote by Nelson Mandela, "may your choices reflect your hopes, not your fears". I feel the truth of it very strongly, but it is perhaps one of the hardest things to do.

When you are making your choices and decisions in your life and your business, what drives them? Is it your hope for a more abundant business, a happier experience, or is it your fear of something new, trading something that may work better for something that worked in the past?

For me, when I have based my decisions on fear, it has always left me "stuck" and pushed me further and further towards misery until I reached the breaking point and was forced to make a change. But when I make those choices based on hope and optimism, everything seems to flow, almost effortlessly, in the right direction.

Next time you are faced with a decision, take a moment to really evaluate what your decision making is based on. If it's hope, charge forward confidently. If it's fear, take a deep breath, know it will all be okay no matter what, and challenge yourself to move with hope. You won't regret it.

June 21, 2019

Today is the first official day of summer! No school, more daylight, warmer temperatures, and vacation season is fully upon us.

This is a wonderful time of year, but it can also be a challenging time in our business. If you are a mom, summer presents a unique challenge with childcare, or just keeping your children busy. Listings tend to sit around a little longer in many cases, and new business opportunities may be slower to come in. And hey ... you deserve to have a little fun in the sun too, right?

This is why you need a summer business plan. It can be fun to stay up later and sleep in, spend more time outside, and not work as much when things are quieter. You should do all of those things, but whatever you do, don't completely take your focus off of your business. It is the work and effort that you put in during these summer months that you will be paid for in the fall and winter. It can be too easy to take it easy this time of year while your commissions and settlements are still happening from spring and feel like everything is great! But if you totally check out now, come September, October and November you will be feeling the pain, and probably a lot of pressure.

A summer business plan may not sound exciting, but trust me on this, a gentle routine or rhythm to your days will help you to enjoy your time now and enjoy the fruits of your labor later.

I'm still working on what this will look like for me. My boys are 15, 13 and 9. Too old for a "babysitter", but not really old enough to be left to their own devices all day, every day (boys = all the fighting). I set up a workspace for myself downstairs so I will have a quieter space to work. I'm working from home more days, and when I do go into the office or are out on appointments, I try to limit how long of a stretch that I am away. I've also figured out that I need to start work much earlier than usual, as just when I am getting my groove, people start waking up, asking about breakfast (lunch and dinner, boys think about food constantly ... anyone else have this problem?), what our plans are for the day, etc.

This is just week 2 with our new schedule so I am still figuring some of it out, and tweaking as I go. What works best for me is prioritizing my prospecting. I know, I know, that isn't what you want to hear, but it is what you need to hear. I've talked before about my "daily business builders" or daily tasks that help to grow my business. A combination of calls, notes, pop bys, giving referrals, adding to my database and having face to face appointments with clients or my database. I've shifted this a bit this year, as I have found that for me in this season what works best is having weekly prospecting goals vs daily.

Instead of writing 3 notes per day, my focus is on 15 per week. I still chip away at these things a bit each day, but in a more fluid way ... maybe I only wrote 1 note yesterday but write 5 today. My preference is to do these things in the morning so I will "win the day" and then I have the rest of the day (depending on how busy my business is at the moment) to enjoy however I see fit! Maybe sitting by the pool or swimming with my kids, going on a little outing, taking a walk, sitting on the porch ... I can enjoy this time guilt free because I've already spent some time moving my business forward.

Do you have a summer business plan? Does your routine this time of year differ from the rest of the year?

June 27, 2019

A couple weeks ago I noticed that a sunflower is growing in my yard (thank you little birds for planting it!). It hasn't bloomed yet but is getting close. I can see it clearly from my favorite chair and my porch, and love watching it grow. I've noticed that depending on the time of day the "head" of it seems to be "facing" different directions. I realized that it is deliberately facing towards the sun.

Isn't that lovely? For nourishment, in order to grow, the sunflower adjusts to take in the rays of the sunshine. What a great metaphor for so many things.

There is a lot of negativity in our world. Lots of industries make their living ... their riches ... by feeding our fear and our insecurities. If one look at a beauty magazine, the evening news or your local paper isn't proof of that I don't know what is.

What if, instead of facing the negativity, the hatred, the fear head on, we turn toward the light. Towards those who are making a positive difference in the world. Towards hope and possibilities and love.

If I've learned anything in this business (17 years and counting) and in life, it's that taking action will cure anxiety. Turning towards the light is the best first step of action that you can take, no matter your circumstances.

Worried about your pipeline? Not enough business? Unsure what to do next? Take a step of action. Write a note. Call a client. Have coffee with a colleague.

Turn towards the light.

July 11, 2019

Earlier this week I went on a listing appointment. Nothing unusual for me. In my 17-year career (primarily as a listing specialist) I'm sure that I have gone on close to 1000 of these appointments, if not more. But this one was different, and I left mad. Big mad.

I knew going in from the initial phone call that this seller was going to be difficult. I was VERY firm with him on the phone. So much so that my husband, who overheard the conversation, commented on my directness (as it pertained to commission). I didn't want to go, and I should have listened to myself.

The walk through of the property went okay, but the presentation part, not so much. I had listened to him go on about the house for an hour, but he couldn't stand to hear my presentation for 5 minutes. Constant interruptions, "I already know that", "I read that about you online", blah, blah, blah.

Then we had a "discussion" about how my industry is going away. That the role of the Realtor® isn't important and once you figure out how to handle getting people in homes, that we will be obsolete. He basically saw zero value in anything that I would provide and took my detailed marketing plan for his property and essentially just pointed out the professional photos and said that was all that really mattered and was all it took to sell the house. Now this may be true in some markets and for some types of property, but not for this one, and my comps and market data (which he would barely listen to me review) showed that.

He's probably not alone in his thought process. There are media outlets and some in our industry even who are putting all their stock in technology and bypassing the people. The sky is falling as they say, and we best get out the way.

Yesterday I watched Brian Buffini's Bold Predictions. As usual he did a great job of sharing NAR and economist data and interpreting it. One statistic that I couldn't help but pay attention to ... of all of the transactions done last year, only 0.2% (that is two tenths of 1%) were done through an "iBuyer" or similar type format ... you know, that technology that is on the precipice of running us all off the cliff. In addition, the number of transactions that were done without a Realtor® were at an all-time low.

Something else that I loved ... when looking at survey results and statistics of people polled about optimism with our economy and the housing market, those in rural areas had the highest levels of optimism. Why is that? Brian's answer was because those in rural areas tend to have more limited access to media. The media that tells us that we are becoming obsolete. The media that last year was all abuzz in the real estate industry about an impending recession. The naysayers that want us to believe that technology will replace people and yet while today's consumer is more sophisticated and has access to more information, more consumers are using professionals than ever before.

Good news doesn't sell. Bad news does. Fear is a powerful thing. It sells newspapers and tickets and systems and apps and so much more.

Don't believe the hype. Be informed, be involved, pay attention, but don't start cowering when the cries of "the sky is falling" start swirling about. Focusing on that instead of focusing on your business will derail you faster than anything else. Yes, change will come. It always does, it always has. In what form, who really knows. What I do know is that people will always need a place to live. The way people look for homes, absolutely that has changed. When I started in business when the buyer said, "I found my new house myself", that was really saying something. Now, of course they did, they're supposed to (Brian said that, by the way). Will a computer completely replace a Realtor® in the future? I don't know. Did the automatic dishwasher replace your need for a kitchen sink? I can't really see it.

Stay engaged. Keep an open mind. Try new things. Respect your colleagues and the industry. Know your value. If you don't, no one else will either.

July 17, 2019

For much of my life I have been chasing happiness. Happiness with myself. Happiness with my real estate business. Happiness with my family and friends. Happiness with how much money I have. Happiness with how my home looks.

I thought that happiness meant being happy all the time, and that if I wasn't constantly happy then clearly something was wrong with me and my life. This endless pursuit of happiness actually left me feeling much less happy, often down and depressed, and anxious. Everything but happy.

Then one day I suddenly realized that happiness is not a constant state of being, happiness comes in waves. And that is perfectly okay.

Life is full of ups and downs. Highs and lows. Mixed emotions. Beautiful experiences, and desperately tragic ones. In our business alone we can go from furious to frustrated to disappointed to elated in the span of an hour (sometimes less!). If that isn't a microcosm of life, I don't know what is!

My message today is the same one I gifted to myself. Go easy. Release the expectation that everything needs to be perfect and that you can be happy 24/7. Instead strive for peace. Calmness. Self-assuredness. Then, you can thoroughly enjoy the happiness when it comes at the crest of the wave, and when you are at the lowest point, in the trough, you can hold strong knowing that this too shall pass.

July 24, 2019

One of the things that I have noticed about myself, and my business, is that in order to speed up ... make big things happen, have a breakthrough or idea ... that I first need to slow down.

I tend to run at a go, go, go pace. Constantly running, going, doing, accomplishing, producing. And the more I stay in that state of being the lower my creativity goes. My brain can't take any more. I no longer feel enjoyment in reading, can't focus when listening to my favorite podcasts, bounce from one thing to the other in a state of frenzy. I feel it, my friends and family feel it, I'm sure my clients feel it. All of that is a sign that I need to step back, and slow down.

It is such an oxymoron, but truly in order to produce at a high level, in order to be super-efficient and effective, you have to slow down. Whenever I do, whether it is for a few hours, or a day, or even a 2-week vacation like the one I am on now, I come back refreshed, renewed, excited. The ideas flow more freely. Things that felt stuck ... the difficult client relationship, the listing that wouldn't sell ... I can see with fresh eyes and take new action which almost always moves things forward.

One of your tasks on the Plan of the Week this week is to "treat yourself", but really, it's to take a little break. Give yourself the gift of a little time without the incessant demands of others. Turn off your phone. Walk away from the computer. Sit outside. Take a walk. It will make a difference in how you feel, and those around you will feel it too.

July 27, 2019

While spending our last few moments on the beach early this morning before packing up and heading back home to Virginia, I was thinking about changes. When walking on the beach once or twice each day as we do, you notice the power of the ocean ... one morning big shell beds, that evening they are all gone. Large ledges develop along the beach overnight. Where things were once flat with soft sand are suddenly differently shaped with hard, firm sand. The landscape is constantly changing.

Just like life.

Each day we would adapt the route for our walk based on the changes along the shore. The faster we can learn to do that in life, the better we will be, I think. Change is inevitable, and like the tides, we cannot change it. You can spend your life fighting the changes, trying to push back, or you can open your heart and your mind, and learn to ride the waves. I'll choose the latter.

July 30, 2019

We've just hit a big milestone with Empowering Women in Real Estate ... yesterday was our 5-year anniversary as a group! It's been 5 years since I founded this group, really out of loneliness and the desire to fill a need. At the time I had left the field after 10 years of successful sales to be a Managing Broker. What I found was that I missed the camaraderie of working with and associating with a group of women who understood. Women who understood what we go through on a daily basis to support our clients, build our businesses, and still manage to take care of ourselves and our families.

I realized it one day while I was in the shower, dragging my feet to get ready and get on with my day, that if I was feeling this way then certainly other women in the industry were feeling this way too, and Empowering Women in Real Estate was born! Through this group I've learned again and again the importance of speaking my truth ... because someone else out there needs to hear it too.

Yesterday should have been a great day to celebrate this milestone, but instead I wanted to cry. It was a rough day. My first day back after a wonderful 2-week vacation and mid-morning my internet went out. If you haven't noticed, we rely heavily on the internet in our work, and with a massive to do list and a spotty connection on the hotspot on my phone the day was one frustration after another. My kids were yelling and fussing, and the dogs barked all.day.long. Nonstop. Then I see a notification of an FDA recall of many different types of implants (you can read about my mastectomy last October and reconstruction this past May in the group) and had to dig on the specifics of what I have and what was recalled (some types from my manufacturer were part of the recall, but gratefully not the style that I have). In the midst of phone calls my 80-year-old dad stops by, peering in my windows (doorbell isn't working, see no internet above) to drop off his mail from the past 2 weeks for me to take care of and is weepy as he stopped by after visiting my mom's grave at the cemetery. More fussy kids, more barking dogs. Sellers who are frustrated with slow traffic and market conditions. More things to add to my list. Can't print documents I need (no wifi, no printing) and on and on and on. Frustration was running high. I know you can relate.

I could have stayed quiet. I could have pretended all was well. I could have posted the shiny, happy posts that we all do from time to time, even when we aren't feeling it. Instead, I've decided to share the struggles of my day with you, because it's the truth, and I know that someone else needs to hear it.

These days happen to all of us. It doesn't matter how long you've been in business, how many clients you have, how well established you are and how much you have figured out, we all have those days, those moments when it feels like nothing is working or going your way.

So yesterday I took a walk. I had wine with dinner. I may have had a handful of chocolate (I definitely had the handful of chocolate!). I had a tough conversation with one client and scheduled a face to face with another. I counted my blessings.

I am grateful to have a bountiful business, even when it is stressful and clients are difficult.

I am grateful to be able to work from home when my kids are home for the summer, even when they drive me crazy.

I am grateful that more surgery is not in my immediate future, and I can continue healing from a challenging health season.

I am grateful for this group. It has grown and developed beyond my wildest dreams. We went from a strictly online forum to an active and helpful group full of likeminded real estate professionals. I'm proud that we have little to no drama, and I can count on less than 1 hand the number of folks I've had to remove from the group for being disrespectful and the number of posts that I have had to remove because comments became ugly. We have Monthly Meet Ups in a variety of cities around the country so we can further the conversations on the topics we cover here, and now we have Empower Coaching, our monthly membership group coaching program. I'm able to connect and teach in an even deeper way with those of you who choose to participate in the program and share the marketing systems that have helped me to grow my business and that of my team.

Today is a new day. My internet is still down, but the service provider will be out to the house this afternoon so hopefully a resolution is in sight. I'll be out this morning with my boys as two of them require a quick in office medical procedure which will hopefully give us some answers towards easing their discomfort. It is sure to be dramatic and unpleasant, but afterwards we will do a little back to school shopping (which they are strangely excited about) and my dad will be at my home to meet the internet folks (and "being useful" always helps him to feel better). Then I will get to wrap up the day with my team's Summer Client Event, which is always a fun time.

Thank you for being here. Thank you for contributing to this community. Thank you for giving me a platform to speak my truth, because as I've learned over the years, it is often yours too.

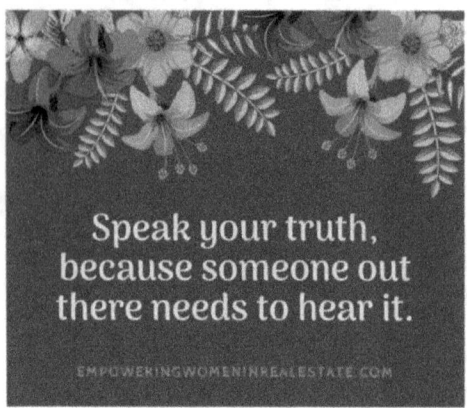

August 1, 2019

How many times do we spend our time, effort and money on something that seems like a waste of time? The marketing idea that promised lots of buyers. The open house that no one came to. The meeting with a buyer that is years away from buying.

I strongly believe that nothing is ever a waste of time. Whether that action results in a success or a failure, either way the end result is growth.

One idea leads to another. We need action to grow. Don't be afraid to put yourself out there, no matter the result, it will put you one step closer to your goal!

August 8, 2019

For a while now I've been reading the book, "Atomic Habits", by James Clear. I'm finding that I can really only absorb it in small bits, so I usually only read a few pages at a time.

One of the concepts that the author talks about in the book is an "identity change" vs just focusing on a new goal or habit. He says that by focusing on changing your identity and identifying with that which you are trying to accomplish, that you will experience better results.

I have to say, I think he's on to something. I'm someone who struggles to get enough activity in my day. I don't love (or let's be honest, even like) exercising or working out. There have been seasons of my life where it has been enjoyable (Running, who even was that girl? I'll tell you who. A girl with no kids, that's who.) or felt more doable, but this isn't that season. To tell the truth, the last many haven't been either.

For years (literally) getting more activity has been on my to do list, my goal list, my habit list, and any other list you can think of that I might create. I bypass it again and again for other things that I enjoy or prefer.

Then, we went on vacation. Every day while we are on vacation we go for a walk on the beach. Sometimes twice a day. No thought or extra effort involved, it's just what we do. I was thinking about this while we were on the way home and how it is my part of who I am, part of my identity to take a walk daily at the beach, but it's not when I am home, so I decided to change that.

I am someone who takes a walk every day. It may only be 10 minutes, but it's a walk, and it's just what I do. Making that shift in my identity means that I have taken a walk every day for 25 straight days (of course I am including those days that I walked at the beach, because, duh, who doesn't need a little boost when doing something new?!). Naturally I'm tracking this, and of course I have an app for that. (It's called "Done" and it's free.)

Making this identity shift has made this dramatically easier, and I'm even enjoying and looking forward to my walk each day, go figure.

I imagine this can work both ways. What negative "truths" do you identify with? I'm lazy. I'm not good an open houses. I just don't like making phone calls. (I totally identify with that last one.)

Instead of trying to change your habits, or setting another goal, or putting something on your to do list again and again, instead try shifting your mindset around your identity. It just might make all the difference for you.

Now if anyone needs me, I'll be taking a walk. It's what I do.

August 9, 2019

Earlier this week I found a new series called "Undercover Billionaire" on the Discovery channel.

EMPOWERING WOMEN IN REAL ESTATE

The show features Glenn Stearns, a billionaire businessman and entrepreneur who built a hugely successful business. Mr. Stearns grew up in a challenging home situation, fathered a child at age 14, and barely graduated high school. The point of the show is that with determination, sacrifice and perseverance (I'm paraphrasing), anyone can build a wildly successful business.

Mr. Stearns is "dropped" in Erie, PA with a duffle bag of personal items, a cell phone with no contacts, a pickup truck and $100 cash. His mission is to build a $1M business in 90 days. He did not know where he was going to be taken and cannot use any of his connections to help.

The show is very interesting, and within hours of landing Mr. Stearns researched on his phone the cost of living for the area and determined how much money he would need for food/lodging/living expenses and his focus for the very first week becomes to earn enough cash to cover those expenses for his entire 90 days.

Why? He said that if he is focused on survival, he won't be able to focus on building a business.

Does that strike anyone else? How many of us are so busy just try to get by, just trying to survive, it's no wonder we struggle with consistency in our business.

When you know that your basic living needs are taken care of, you can make better decisions and act bravely when it comes to your business. I've often heard and said to those considering real estate as a career, that before you start it is best to have 6 months, ideally a year, worth of living expenses covered. Otherwise, you will be making decisions about the direction of your business based on fear and survival, instead of focusing on where you want to go and investing in what it takes to get there.

If you watch the first episode, you'll see that when it comes to covering his living expenses, Mr. Stearns is talking about the very basics. Food, shelter (and he often sleeps in his truck). That's it. No new clothes. No fancy coffees. No eating out.

Here is some tough love for you. Have you ever made the decision not to market to your database because of cost? Maybe you decided not to send out a mailer this month because you didn't have the money. But did you stop and get your coffee at Starbucks? Did you go out to lunch with your friends or dinner with your partner? Did you buy the cute new shoes that were on sale? If you have ever made those decisions, then maybe real estate isn't the career for you. No one likes an inconsistent business. Being on the roller coaster of having business this month, and then none the next two, then back up again really sucks. It's painful. It's frustrating. It is a lot more work than taking consistent action in your business. But if you are choosing to spend on the extra comforts in your life instead of investing in your business, then you are choosing the roller coaster.

If you want the $4 latte every day more than you want a consistent, thriving business, that's okay. That is your choice, and you get to make it. But if that is what you want more, then you need to know and understand that you are choosing the inconsistency in your business. Acknowledge it. Be okay with it. If you aren't, then invest in your business first, and learn to make the latte at home. Make that sacrifice enough times, and in time, you can buy all the lattes you want without a second thought.

August 13, 2019

For many, many weeks now I've been lamenting the state of my front flower beds. Whatever the opposite is of a green thumb, that's what I have. So, we hire a landscaper or gardener to help take care of our beds, weeding, pruning, etc. This year, we are working with a new company, and unfortunately gardening doesn't seem to be their forte either.

For weeks (months?) the bleeding hearts in my front beds have needed to be cut back. They died off long ago after their beautiful blooming period this spring and have been waiting to be cut back so they can re-emerge next year. Each week I've hoped that the gardener would take care of it. Each week I've been disappointed. Every time I would sit out on the porch or look out my front windows, I would get frustrated. Finally, I'd had enough, and this past weekend I took matters into my own hands.

Armed with multiple sets of clippers of varying sizes I cut back the bleeding hearts, and just about everything else in my path. Overgrown and tired out rose bushes, things that maybe were plants but don't bloom. All of it, cut down to the ground. And guess what I found ...

Underneath all that stuff that was long past its prime and ready to go was a flowering pumpkin vine. Now if you know me at all, you know that I love fall and everything about it. I felt like finding that vine that just may produce a pumpkin was my reward for finally taking care of business and getting rid of all that stuff that was long past needing to go.

Are you noticing the parallels? What are you holding on to that no longer serves you? Something good may just be waiting there beneath it!

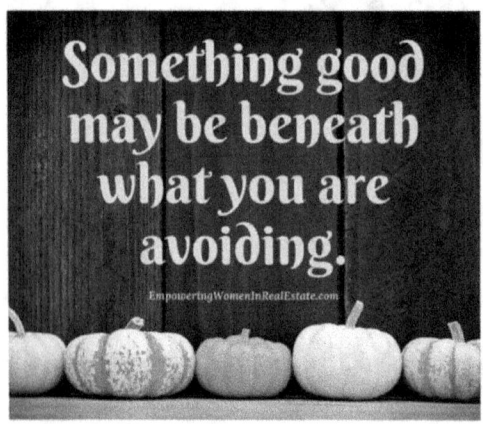

August 20, 2019

So, I've shared here before recently about my daily walks. As I read in the book, "Atomic Habits", I've made part of my identity someone who takes a walk every day. I even snap a photo each day to share in my Instagram and Facebook stories for accountability. I'm on a 37-day streak, by the way.

The other day as my husband and I were on the last bits of our walk, which are mostly uphill, I noticed something. It was hot, I was tired, and the hill felt extra hard. Usually when we are walking, I have a tendency to took down. Partly because we mostly walk on a gravel road, and I need to pay attention. Partly because when the walk is hard, putting my head down and just doing the work, trudging through, feels like the right thing to do.

Then I realized that my husband was getting further ahead of me and as I looked up, I noticed that I was moving faster. The hike uphill felt a little easier. Keeping my head up and focusing on where I was going and what was ahead helped me to move faster.

Where can you apply this in your life? So often we trudge along, head down, doing our work not fully focused on where we are going, and it's hard. It makes what is hard anyway even harder. But when you have a goal in mind, a direction to move in, a clear vision for your path, it truly does pull you along. Stay focused on where you are going, not just on the steps to get there, and I bet you will get there faster.

August 21, 2019

I feel like someone needs to hear this today ... it's okay to make mistakes and it's definitely okay not to be good at everything.

In fact, the more you "put yourself out there", the more you try new things, the more you push forward, the more mistakes you are likely to make. And learning from those experiences is part of what will make you great.

Earlier this year I made a foolish mistake. I've sold many, many hundreds of homes in my 17+ year career and I made a simple, silly mistake. One I certainly knew better than to make and have processes to keep from making ... but, alas I made it. So, I bought a microwave, we closed on time, and all is well.

It happens. Don't beat yourself up. Learn, learn and learn some more. Take responsibility when the mistake is yours and chances are you will never make it again.

August 22, 2019

It is hard to believe that summer has come to a close and my kids are off to school today! Once again, this year I have 3 kids in three different schools ... a 10th grader, an 8th grader and a 4th grader (he doesn't start until Tuesday).

A couple years ago I started driving my boys to school on a periodic basis, then it became more consistent when my youngest switched to a school that does not provide bus service. I quickly found that while this adds a good bit of extra time in my day (with traffic, from the time I leave my house until the time the last one is dropped off and I get to my office it easily takes 90 minutes, sometimes more), that I really value this time. It gives me and the boys some time to chat in the car, and after the younger two are dropped off some one-on-one time with my oldest, which can be hard to come by. I've decided to continue the tradition this year. This time next year my oldest will be driving, so this will be the last year before this particular season comes to a close.

I'm a creature of habit and find that I do best when I have a routine, so over the course of the next week I'll be playing around with my daily schedule and figuring out what will work best this school year. Do you adjust your schedule for the seasons of the year?

August 27, 2019
One year ago today, I was excited that it was my youngest son's first day of school, and excited that all 3 of my boys were now back at school and we were back in our routine. A morning, really, just like today ... only last year, after taking my youngest to school I headed to an appointment with my breast surgeon to talk about my recent biopsy results. Much of this was "normal" for me and super annoying. I'd had 5 or 6 breast surgeries up to this point thanks to a rare (but not for me apparently) tumor that seemed to occur again and again, despite being cut out again and again.

This time was different though. My doctor told me that the tumor I had was cancer. I really wasn't prepared for that, even though the evening before on the phone she told me that the biopsy showed that I had periductal stromal sarcoma, a very rare type of tumor. When I asked her on the phone if it was cancer, she said "it is not breast cancer", and I realized sitting in her office how carefully she had chosen her words. Though the tumor was in my breast, it was not a type of breast cancer.

I know many of you in this group have been through this in one way or another. I don't need to tell you what that day or the days following were like. If you don't know personally (and I pray you never need to) it was horrible.

So horrible. For over a week I cried on and off, suffered anxiety attacks (nighttime was the worst) and made appointments, had scans and second opinions and tried to figure out what was next.

And then, a miracle. The pathology second opinion was not so sure that the diagnosis was correct and thought that it actually could be another type of the same tumors I'd had before. The initial treatment either way was mastectomy, and it was scheduled for 5 weeks later. Only then would we know for sure.

But I had what I needed to hear. Hope. Hope is an interesting thing. Once I heard that there was a chance that it may not be cancer, the way I felt was night and day from the days before. I decided that I would focus on the "positive" outcome and went with that, never looking back. Thank God, that second opinion was right, which was not cancer. I was incredibly lucky. For that, I am eternally grateful.

It's been a crazy year. Cancer, not cancer. Removing my breast. Reconstruction. Finding out I still have a 30% chance of reoccurrence. For many (many) months I didn't recognize my body, felt disconnected. Still do most of the time. The same day I was diagnosed my father-in-law was diagnosed with cancer (he is responding well to treatment a year later; he's the primary caregiver to my mother-in-law who has Alzheimer's, so this has been extra difficult).

I've always loved this time of year ... Back to School, fall, pumpkins, Halloween ... the whole nine yards. I'm already enjoying it so much more this year after not having that chance last year.

This experience woke me up (again) to the importance of being in the moment. Each moment is precious and special, and the next one is not promised to any of us. These moments are far too precious to spend them unhappy, unfocused, and playing smaller than what has been placed in your heart.

What is the dream that you have for your life and your business? What does it look like? How does it sound? Where does it exist? Identify that vision, focus on it, and take steps ... no matter how tiny ... to get yourself there every day.

August 28, 2019

"Be crazy enough to think you can do anything in life." You can you know. Maybe that makes me crazy, but I tend to think that most anything is possible ... for other people.

Do you dream of being a ballerina, dancing with the Russian ballet? Never mind that you are a lady of a certain age and have never taken a dance class, I'll be right here cheering for you and believing it will happen. In fact, I'll even help you shop for the best leotards and research flights to Russia. I believe in you and your dream that much.

But for me, setting aside my personal sales to focus on helping my team to grow and thrive and building my own coaching business to serve women in real estate in a bigger way sometimes feels a little nuts. Never mind that I have over 17 years of experience. Never mind that I have held most every position in the industry (independent agent, agent on a team, team leader, managing broker). Never mind that I have personally sold over 700 homes. Never mind that I have successfully coached and mentored hundreds of agents in my career. Never mind that I have an amazing team of 31 truly incredible women who already serve many hundreds of families every year. Never mind that I am already serving more than 80 Realtors® in my coaching program who are learning and growing and implementing in their businesses each week.

Let me tell you a secret, sometimes, when it comes to my own goals and dreams and aspirations, the further they stray from my "norm", the less likely I am to think that they are actually possible for me. Now that, my friends, is crazy.

What is your dream?

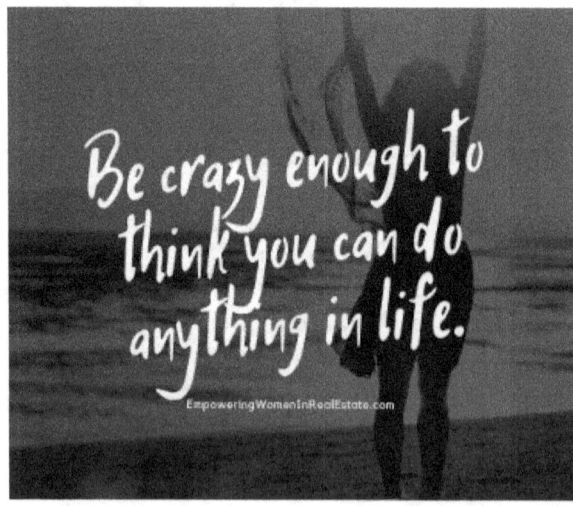

September 5, 2019

The other day I was listening to a podcast (The Ed Mylett Show, episode featuring Jenna Kutcher ... so good!) and I heard the most interesting thing. Women don't often go after their dreams, or even try, because they don't think they can compete with someone who is already doing what they want to do, and so they don't do it.

I would say that this is true for many of us. This has definitely been me before. I see someone doing something really well and just assume I can't compete, so why bother?

But here's the thing ... what I bring to the table, what you bring to the table, they are different things. If not different in "product" they are different in delivery. We are different in personality, we are different in energy. Who is to say why someone may choose to work with you over me or vice versa?

This is why I have never been afraid to share what I do in my business. How I serve, my processes, my systems, my materials, all of it. Even if I give you step by step exactly what to do and how to say it (which I do, by the way, through Empower Coaching), the reality is that you will deliver it differently. That doesn't make my way better or worse than your way, it just means that there is ROOM for BOTH of us!

There is enough business to go around. There are people who will want to work with you, you need to let them know that you want to work with them too. We need to spend less time comparing ourselves, judging one another and deciding that we can't because she can.

You can. I can. She can. We all can. Believe it, and in helping another woman to see that along the way you will both get there faster.

September 11, 2019

Today my littlest guy turns 10! What a huge milestone, and one we don't take lightly. September 11th is a date marked by great loss and tragedy in our country. September 11th is a date that marks great loss and tragedy in the lives of many individual families for a variety of reasons. As does yesterday, and tomorrow, and next Wednesday, and so on.

The day that Tyler was born I will never forget the nurse coming in to turn down the monitor on my belly that was capturing his heartbeat. There had been a loss in the room next door, and they could hear my child's heartbeat while theirs was absent.

Many years later I met and connected with a wonderful friend who I found out lost her precious daughter on that same day, that same year, in that same hospital. She was not the woman in the room next to me, but another family whose life had changed forever.

My sweet boy has some challenges, including a rare genetic defect that he also shares with one of his brothers ... making our family extra, extra unique to have two in one family (it's called Kartagener's Syndrome, and includes situs inversus, or "backwards" organs). I remember when it was confirmed feeling this overwhelming sense of ... relief? Gratitude? Like we dodged what could have been a much bigger bullet? It was a reminder that anything could happen, and nothing was promised.

Our lives are a gift. Each day is a gift. No one knows what life has in store for us and you never quite know what someone else is dealing with. Be kind to each other, more so than necessary.

As is our family birthday tradition, we will be springing our sweet boy out of school midday and spending the afternoon as he wishes, which will probably include a trip to Target and more than likely some new Pokémon cards.

Rejoice in this day that you have been given. Smile at a stranger. Leave an extra-large tip for no good reason. Leave a big, beautiful, generous mark on the world while you can.

September 20, 2019

Yesterday, along with my longtime friend, mentor and preferred lender Jackie Fields-Gleadall, we started facilitating day 1 of Brian Buffini's Pathway to Mastery Essentials course.

Throughout my career I have taken and facilitated Brian's 100 Days to Greatness (Sherry Wilson started me on the path to learning early!) and Peak Producers courses multiple times. This style of learning works for me, and the foundational aspect of each course helps to recenter me in my business each and every time.

In the session yesterday Brian was talking about plateaus, and how what happens when we hit a plateau in our business is that what was once our goal becomes our standard.

I love that! Once your goal becomes your standard though, in order to grow, you need a new and bigger goal. That can also be stressful. Once what was your goal becomes your standard, you are constantly holding yourself to a higher standard. You know all the work it took for you to get there, and so you know a bit of what it will take to both stay there, and also get to the next level.

That can be overwhelming to many of us, and that is where I often see agents quit. Quit trying, quit growing, quit learning, sometimes even quit the business altogether.

If this all sounds familiar to you, say "I".

I've been there. My struggle was often getting to a new place and then having no idea what to do from there. Where to go, who to turn to, what to try. It is then that I would start falling prey to all the "shiny objects". The things that I could pay for that would magically make it all better. Spoiler alert: that doesn't work.

Brian said that when you hit a plateau you are trying to push through, that what you need most to invest is your TIME. Learning, trying, testing, tracking. That is what will help you to bust through. That is what will help you to understand what you need next. Sometimes that will mean investing in a new product or system or coaching program. Sometimes that will mean re-adjusting the infrastructure of your business. Without investing that time, you'll never know.

No great solutions, inspirational quotes or aspirational edicts for you this morning ... I just wanted to share something that spoke to me. Food for thought, if you will. Have you ever hit a plateau in your business, and if so, how did you push past it?

September 26, 2019

My family adopted two kittens yesterday! I haven't had a kitten in over 20 years. We are all so excited to welcome these two rascally brothers into our family. Being big Disney and Marvel fans, they have been named Thor and Loki … after the God of Thunder and the God of Mischief, also brothers. (If you know, you know.)

My family has been trying to talk me into kittens for YEARS. When my son and I went grocery shopping last weekend we noticed signs for an "adoption event" at the adjacent pet store, so we walked in, just to look. That is where we met Karen.

Let me tell you about Karen. She was one of the volunteers with the rescue organization that was putting on the event and was one of the best salespeople I've ever seen.

-She wasn't pushy.
-She noticed my son and I looking and after a few minutes took an interest in us and asked questions.
-As we answered her questions, she would casually pick up this cat and that kitten, making comments about them that complimented the things we said.
-She "took it away" … when I said we really weren't looking to add to our family, she suggested fostering instead.
-She told me about the adoption process, what I would need to do, how long it would take, how much it cost.
-She gave me her card.

Our entire interaction probably only took 10 minutes (or less) but was obviously very effective.

How are your sales skills?

-Are you pushy or are you too aloof?
-Do you notice, pay attention and ask questions?
-Do you make suggestions based on those answers?
-Do you ever "take away" to check motivation?
-Are you clearly explaining the process and what is involved?
-Do you hand out your card?

These seem like simple things, but they are the foundation of our business and without strong sales skills you will struggle with consistency. Which of these areas do you struggle with the most?

September 27, 2019

Money has never been a motivator for me. Yes, I do enjoy making money, and I love the freedom that comes from a comfortably sized bank account, but it isn't what drives me.

I've never set out to do something (or not do something) based on what it will cost me or what it will make me. Now I have many friends and know many wonderful people that don't necessarily share this view. I'm not saying that I'm right or wrong or they are right or wrong, but I know that this is what feels right for me.

For me, I'd rather give first and figure out the rest later. I'd rather focus on the action or the person and trust that I will be taken care of. And you know what? I always have. Even in times of a difficult market when I have struggled financially and experienced a lot of stress as a result, it has always been okay.

What I know for sure, is that when I focus on giving, on being generous, focus outside of myself, the reward is and will always be tenfold. What you give out in slices will come back in loaves.

October 4, 2019

What percentage of the time are you happy with your business? Not just happy with how much business you are doing, but what is your happiness level with your day to day, the actual "work" of your business?

Someone asked me this question yesterday, which I thought was really interesting. No one has ever asked me that before. After thinking about it, I can honestly say that I am happy a good 80-90% of the time.

I love my work, my team, and our Empowering Women in Real Estate community. There are challenges each day, some far less fun than others. There is a lot of stress and responsibility that comes with owning and leading a team. We have 4 full time employees and several part time. Every week it is our responsibility that they are paid, no matter what. There's rent to be paid, supplies to be purchased, and client events to pay for.

A business in real estate means no ceiling, which is amazing ... but there's also no floor. The rewards are great, and the risks are high. It's too hard and too expensive to be halfway in. Commitment is required if you want to succeed. And at the end of the day, no matter how tired, no matter how long, I'd choose it all over again.

October 6, 2019

Last year I wrote 836 notes. Yep, 836!

You know what makes that more fun? Fun notecards and fun stamps! I brought out the jack-o'-lantern stamps for my October birthday and "home-aversary" notes today.

You can order all sorts of fun stamps from the US Postal Service online (I rarely go into the post office). I always buy the forever stamps in case I have left over seasonal ones then I can save them for next year. Shipping is only $1, totally worth it!

October 8, 2019

Hi (new ... and "old") friends! I've been so fortunate to make so many new connections here since founding the Empowering Women in Real Estate group (now with over 10,000 members!) 5 years ago, that I thought this would be a good time to say hello and nice to "meet" you!

I'm a wife and proud mom to three rapidly growing boys, ages 15, 13 and 10. We have 2 dogs and 2 new kittens (that are dominating my IG and FB stories lately) and we are obsessed with all things Disney. I love that I never left my tiny little rural hometown where there is more than one road sign with my family names on them. I love fall and Halloween, and anything seasonal really. Real Estate is my passion and has been for 17 years and counting. I've served in just about every role there is in the industry ... agent on a rainmaker team, solo agent, managing broker, and now a team owner and real estate coach, learning new things about myself and this business all the while.

Most of all, I'm an encourager. A cheerleader. The person who believes in you when no one else does … and not only tells you that you can do it, but helps you figure out how. I see potential and possibilities in everyone and everything, and despite some pretty crazy anxiety at times (who doesn't have that?), I strive every day to choose faith over fear. A recovering control freak, I've learned (and am still learning!) to master my time and have been asked to speak or write on that topic in a variety of forums from large-scale conferences to local real estate publications.

I'm also all about the numbers. I track ALL.THE.THINGS. I've personally helped well over 700 families in my 17+ year real estate career. I teach and inspire (I hope) daily to you and the 10,000 other women in this group. I co-own a top producing real estate team consisting of 31 amazing women and 1 very brave man. I've gone on well over 1000 listing appointments as a listing specialist, and while actively selling real estate averaged selling 50-60 homes per year. I wrote 836 personal notes last year and did 389 pop bys. I've given more than 50 referrals this year and received 133. My team will help well over 400 families in 2019. We have 6 client events per year and mail more than 25,000 postcards. I coach and mentor 83 women (and a few good men) through my Empower Coaching program. I've read 20 books so far this year and am about to embark on my 14th trip to Walt Disney World with my family.

Helping women to grow flourishing real estate businesses on their terms without sacrificing their family or quality of life is my mission.

October 10, 2019

Do you have clients who "misbehave"?

What about rude agents, hateful colleagues, those who are spiteful or negative who drag you down and through the mud?

How many times do you turn the other way from the rude comments and ungrateful attitudes?

How often do you bend over backwards and give, give, give until you have nothing else to give to others who want more and more and more?

This happens to you too, right?

What if instead, we had open and honest conversations? Tell others when we aren't happy with something. Dispel misunderstandings by asking questions.

These conversations are hard. I suck at them, but I will get better at speaking up. It's worth it, because when you tolerate bad behavior, you are teaching people how to treat you.

October 11, 2019

One year ago today, I checked into the hospital for what was then my 7th breast surgery, a mastectomy.

My anxiety should have been through the roof. I should have been crying as I was wheeled into the operating room (as I was for surgery #5).

But I wasn't.

I chose to share my experience publicly, and that decision turned out to be one of the things that made the biggest difference for me on that day.

I know for sure that it was the thoughts and prayers from family, friends, colleagues and so many of you here that allowed me to feel so calm on that day. Perfectly calm.

My husband and I had a nice chat with the technician about our local sports teams and his teenage son playing football. My nurse had on the prettiest earrings and the color of her scrubs was so gorgeous against her skin tone. The anesthesiologist came in and put the catheter attached to my pain "purse" in my back, and everything from then on was a happy blur.

I woke up in more pain than I had imagined and that was scary, but the surgery was over, and I was relieved. The next morning, I woke up on my husband and I's 16th wedding anniversary ... and when the sun came up we realized that my room overlooked a town center area where we had stayed before for our anniversary. Not quite the same experience. It's okay though, we will make up for it with a little trip this weekend.

This week one of the tasks on the Plan of the Week was to make a difference for one person, and all of this is why. So many people are struggling with issues that you may or may not see or know about. All of the calls, notes, messages, meals and gifts that I received during this time last year made a tremendous difference (and positive impact) on me and my family. Unless you have been through something similar you may not realize the impact that the smallest gestures can have.

Interrupt anxiety with gratitude. It works, every time.

October 15, 2019

I'll preface this post by saying that I don't know much about baseball, so please don't hold me responsible for any technical things I get wrong here. lol

Last week my husband was watching the Washington Nationals during a playoff game. I was sound asleep when I woke up to screaming from him in our room and my two older kids across the house when one of their players, Howie Kendrick, hit a grand slam home run (which scored 4 runs, and essentially secured the win).

Wide awake then (grumble, grumble) I was trying to go back to sleep while listening to the game with one ear. When it was over a reporter was interviewing Mr. Kendrick and he said something that got my attention. "There is no success without effort or error."

How true is that?

In the pursuit of success, you will make errors and mistakes, but each time you will learn something that will help you to move forward.

In order to succeed you must put forth effort, significant effort. In fact, the level of success you achieve is directly proportionate to your effort.

On the road to success, each day will most likely involve a little of both.

October 25, 2019

What does a productive day look like for you in your real estate business?

I was tagged in a post on this topic a couple days ago in the Lab Coat Agents group and couldn't help but talk about it here. If you've been around any length of time, you know that productivity, time management, balancing real life with real estate and scheduling are my jam. I could talk on and on about these topics. I love finding ways to be more efficient and productive with my time ... and of course then sharing it with you!

So, what does a productive day look like for me? I'll preface it with this ... what works for me today did not work for me 6 months ago, and definitely not 6 years ago. The key that I have found is constantly testing and tweaking to find a rhythm and a formula that works for you in your current season.

Right now, I'm in a season that is a little different as I am shifting from my own personal sales into more time spent managing and supporting my team of 32 incredible women (and 1 very brave man!). My kids are in 3 different schools this year, so mornings are hectic ... but I know this time is coming to a close as my oldest will be driving next year (Jesus, take the wheel. Literally, take the wheel!)

Here is a little peek into what my day looks like currently ...

5:30-6 am - Up and at 'em! As I've been staying up later watching the World Series this week (actually, my husband is watching and I've been using this as a chance to catch up on work), it's been more like 6 when I get up.

6-6:45/7 am - Start the tea kettle. Dogs fed and let out. Kittens fed. Throw in a load of wash. Unload the dishwasher. Morning "quiet" time. What fills me up during this time varies. I always check in here first, sometimes reading, check in with my favorite blogs, a quick email scan to delete the junk and forward anything that can be delegated, maybe some journaling.

7-8 am - THE MOST DIFFICULT HOUR OF THE DAY. Get myself ready. Help the 10-year-old to get up, ready, fed, medicated, etc. Make sure the teenagers are moving. Try to keep them from talking to each other as explosions often ensue as a result. Do my best to limit any yelling, name calling, crying and physical violence (let's be real, sometimes we get all of these in a single morning). Help with breakfasts and lunches. Forget to eat breakfast myself. RUSH out the door late for the first drop off.

8-9:15 am - Mom's Taxi Service, at your service! With traffic and 3 stops involved, it takes over an hour to deliver everyone to their school and then get myself to the office. So why do I do it? Because this time is precious to me. Kids are more likely to talk in the car (why is that?). Don't get me wrong, it's definitely not precious every day, but I know this time is fleeting so I will enjoy it while I can. After the boys are dropped off, I return calls, brainstorm with my business partner, or listen to podcasts until I arrive at the office.

I am not a rigid time block person, so there aren't specific times that I do things during the majority of my day, but I do like a particular rhythm to my day.

Upon arriving to the office my first tasks are my daily business building tasks. Writing a certain number of notes, making a certain number of calls, give 1 referral, and add 1 person to my database. For a long time, I would do 1 pop by per day, dropping it off during my drive in when possible. Now I outsource delivery.

If I've gotten this far, then I consider the day a big win! When scheduling client appointments, my preference was either first thing in the morning after dropping off the kids, and/or around 2-3 pm. Then I use the time in between to manage transactions, prospect, support my team and more. Now my day tends to be more time spent on team initiatives (the last many weeks have been full of retreat and 2020 prep) and on my Empower Coaching business.

I like to make my time "work for me" (as in serve double duty) whenever possible. If I am lunching alone, I eat at my desk and watch a video or listen to a podcast to learn something. I have a folder in my email called "brain food" where I keep things that I want to watch or read later. If I am lunching with someone it is almost always a business lunch where we are planning or working on new marketing strategies.

One of the most powerful things I learned to implement in my business 6+ years ago when I was a managing broker was to set an end time. This will vary depending on your day and if you have late appointments. At least two days per week I have to leave at 3:15 to pick up my youngest from school. The other days I can stay later. I know based on the day what time I plan to wrap up. Just knowing that time, and that I don't want to do any proactive work when I get home (I'll still take calls, respond to messages, etc. as needed) I find that I am much more productive during the day knowing my "deadline".

Evenings these days involve some sort of sports practice or game or toting a teen or two to an activity and back. I prioritize dinner around the table with the whole family together as much as possible. Sometimes that means eating early, sometimes not until 8 pm, but we try to do this more nights than not.

When my schedule was heavy with client appointments, I would not miss dinners at home two nights in a row.

Most nights I go to bed when my kids do (or at least when the youngest does), usually around 9-9:15 pm.

Photo from one of our morning "commutes".

October 30, 2019

Turns out that today is National Checklist Day! Second only to my listing presentation, I've had more requests over the years to share my checklists than anything else.

Here's the story of how they were created ...

I was about 7-8 years into the business (but only about 1-2 years of being an independent agent) and my business was BOOMING. Great news, right? It was, but I was also struggling big time to keep everything together. I didn't have an assistant, so I was doing everything on my own. After a couple of nights in a row of waking up in the middle of the night panicking that I had forgotten something ... and actually forgetting to order a pest inspection until the day before settlement on one of my transactions, I decided to formalize my process.

See, I knew what to do. I'd been selling real estate for many years and sold hundreds of homes, but everything was in my head. So, I spent a couple hours one afternoon documenting my process for each scenario or type of transaction. I would then "apply" that process as we got to it.

Signed a new for sale listing? I started working through my checklist for that part of the transaction. When that listing went under contract then I applied that checklist. When the home inspection was removed then I applied that checklist, and so on and so on.

I'll tell you; this was a GAME CHANGER for me. I've worked with these checklists in Evernote. I've printed them out and put them in files, and now I use them in DotLoop.

The really nice thing about these checklists is that when I have hired assistants, I was able to insert them right into the process which really helped to streamline training and the learning curve.

Taking just a little time to document my process into a checklist has paid dividends and saved me time for years to come. (All of my checklists are shared with our Inner Circle members!)

Happy Checklist Day!

November 14, 2019
Yesterday at our team retreat we reviewed our year of 2019.

We shared our numbers, discussed how they compared to our goal that we set, and shared our biggest struggle from the year, and the thing that we are most proud of.

There were LOTS of tears.

The recurring theme? The pressure we put on ourselves to do more, to be more, to produce, to be all things to all people. The fears that we aren't good enough. The worry that we aren't providing enough for our family, that we aren't always there for our children.

Why do we do this to ourselves? Every season is different. Some years, you can do more, produce more. Others, your focus will need to be elsewhere. What you did 3 years ago is not necessarily what you should be able to do this year. Circumstances change. Our lives change. And we change along with it.

After the review, and the tears, and writing a letter to ourselves 10 years in the future, we CLOSED OUT the year. Done. No more thoughts or worries about what we did or didn't do. No more talk about it wasn't enough. The year is done, and we are moving on.

This year we celebrated with a cocktail designed especially for us by the amazing Dianne Buckley of Staged Envy (check out her "Saturday Sips at Six" on her social media channels!) ... and I'd like to share it with you!

Here is the "Fig-Et About It ... You Got This Martini", it's as awesome as it sounds! Salut!

November 15, 2019

Do you have non-negotiables for your life and business? Yesterday during the goal setting portion of my team's retreat we shared our goal ranges (we set a goal range ... the low end being the minimum that we MUST do to stay in business/support our family and the top being our dream/stretch goal), the things that are non-negotiables for us ... that which we would NOT be willing to do in order to reach our goal, and then we shared our BIG, FUN goals!

Why a non-negotiable? When you are setting your goal, it is very important to understand what it will take to get there ... and what you aren't willing to do to get there. For example, if you want to sell 25 homes this year, but aren't willing to do an open house every weekend, what other methods will you focus on or even 10x in order to get there?

Some of the non-negotiables shared yesterday were things like, not working both days on the weekend. Not working with rude or disrespectful clients. Only working certain types of business (and referring out the rest), and more. What are the non-negotiables in your business?

December 3, 2019

Chances are you've heard of Rachel Hollis, right? Author of the crazy popular, "Girl, Wash Your Face" (selling over a million copies), and more recently, "Girl, Stop Apologizing". I've read her books, listen to her podcast, and she is all over social media and the speaker "circuit" in addition to leading her own events.

The thing is, before last year, I'd never heard of her before. Like many successful people who have a breakthrough, it seemed like she came out of nowhere.

But of course, we know that isn't how it works.

A couple weeks ago I stumbled across one of her videos on YouTube, and of course fell down the rabbit hole. Here is the fascinating thing, Rachel was putting out consistent videos not just this year and last, but the year before that and the year before that. Her oldest video that I found was 5 years ago. Her themes were often consistent, and the frequency of the videos were too. It was interesting to see the "progression" of how well done the videos were from then until now.

It was a nice reminder to me that success comes with consistent effort. Again, and again and again. Even when it sometimes seems that no one is watching or listening, even when you feel like you want to give up.

December 4, 2019

Over the weekend I started listening to a new book, "The Traveler's Gift" by Andy Andrews. It started out kind of slow, and the author (who reads the book) does some funny sounding (to me) voices, but now I'm totally hooked.

In the book, the main character is at a very difficult time in his life. Bankrupt, lost his job, losing his home and with a sick child and no money for surgery. He is taken on this traveler's journey through time meeting several significant players who each have a lesson to teach him.

At one point he is taken back to a Civil War battlefield and his "guide" is a former schoolteacher, turned Colonel. They are in the heat of battle and having lost most of their men and nearly all of their ammunition, with the enemy rapidly ascending on them, it would seem that their outcome was certain death.

The Colonel then repeated his personal mantra, that he is "a man of action". He said that he would rather die while taking action in battle than to be shot in the back doing nothing. (Spoiler alert: He calls for his men to grab their bayonets and to charge. They do, and the enemy stops in their tracks, then retreats.)

I can't stop thinking about this story. How many times are you paralyzed by fear. Frozen in place, overwhelmed, not sure what to do next, and so you do nothing. I've been there. I still sometimes find myself there, and I bet you have too.

What if instead we chose to take action? Just one tiny step changes your energy, and literally moves you in the right direction. Is there an action that you can take today that will help you to become "unstuck"?

December 19, 2019

It's the most wonderful time of the year! We hear that so much around this time, don't we? For many, this is the most wonderful time. The shopping. The presents. The trees. The lights. Parties. Time with friends and family. Celebrating the birth of baby Jesus.

For many though, this is one of the hardest times of the year. For those who have lost loved ones, are struggling with personal and health issues, who don't have strong family ties, this can be so hard. I've seen the posts floating around Facebook about this, and I certainly do feel this acutely this year, but that's not my point here.

The peace, love and joy and general merriment that we tend to share and experience this time of year, why do we limit it to once a year? So many of us go crazy this time of year trying to get it all done, to meet a certain standard, for what? A day or two of get togethers and celebrations?

What if, instead, we take that desire to help others, to be present with family, to celebrate a power greater than us, and apply that principal all year round? There are so many wonderful charity events this time of year, the toy drives and coat drives, the food pantries receiving a higher-than-normal amount of donations. But aren't there still children in need, people who are cold and hungry other times of year? What if instead of cramming it all into a few days, weeks, a month, we make this a part of our very way of being and doing? How would that change your life, your children, your family, your community?

Nearly everyone I talk to; we are so BUSY. Busy, busy, busy. I've come to hate that word. We piss away our days doing what? Rushing from one task to another, from point a to point b. Grumpy because we're tired, there are too many things to do, we've set an impossible standard for ourselves.

My thought today ... challenge yourself to find something good, intentionally have a little joy, connect with your people (family, friends, clients), give to others not just once a year, but every single day. See something that you know a loved one would enjoy? Don't wait until Christmas or their birthday, buy it, wrap it beautifully (or don't), and give it to them. Don't wait until once a year to prepare a special meal for family and friends, when the mood strikes, do it. Develop a relationship with your local support services and do what you can to help others throughout the year.

Another day, another month, another Christmas ... it isn't promised to any of us. Find a way to enjoy each day, each moment. The joy is there, you just need to look for it.

December 26, 2019

How was your Christmas? We had a nice day, and I received many wonderful presents, including a beautiful necklace from my husband.

My favorite gift was a set of wine glasses from my sister-in-law. They belonged to her, and I've admired them for years. They are super old, with a winter scene etched on them and a gold tone rim. Every holiday we visit them I would comment on how much I loved them. She looked high and low to buy me a set of my own but couldn't find anything even remotely similar.

So, she gave me hers.

I was (still am) so touched that she would gift them to me. Fancy presents, expensive gifts, they sure are nice, but truly it is the thought that counts.

2020

Milestones
3-20-2020 – Offered Empower Coaching for free during the pandemic.
4-10-2020 – Launched first professional website.

January 7, 2020
Fun (little known) Fact: My senior year of high school (way back in 1991) I was awarded the Outstanding Member of the Year award by the Future Homemakers of America club.

This is an extra fun fact (and quite ironic, as my husband likes to remind me), especially given that I'm not a great cook (hardly even a passable cook), and while I can decorate and de-clutter with the best of them, cleaning not so much. Spreadsheets, marketing plans and business strategy are more my jam.

What I've learned though is that homemaking is less about who cooks the meal and makes the beds and more about who allows you to feel welcome and secure in your home, just as you are.

January 21, 2020
Do you want to know the truth ... most likely you don't need to look for something new or better to solve your problems in your business. Chances are, you just need to work what you already have.

How often do we all do that? We are constantly in search of the latest and greatest tool and trick, the easy button to solve whatever it is that we are struggling with at the time. But the real trick is that there is no easy button, there is no magic tool or website or lead generation system that will get you to where you want to be, only you can do that.

Everywhere you look there are people trying to sell you something to solve your problems. Need more leads? Buy them on this website, put your face and name on a shopping cart, invest in these other worldly expensive predictive analytics so you can (hopefully) focus your contacts and efforts on people who are "likely" to move, purchase this or that CRM. The truth is, all of these things work, but getting them to work isn't as simple as stroking the check or importing your database. You have to do the work.

Paying for leads won't get you business unless you are quick to contact and consistent in your follow up efforts to convert that lead. Advertising on the shopping cart at the grocery store isn't going to get you business unless it is part of a complete and consistently executed geographic farming strategy whereby it is just one more way that your target market "sees" you. Predictive analytics won't magically make the gold in your database or geographic farm appear, you still have to reach out, make the call, and be consistent in your efforts. The CRM isn't going to add richness to your database and streamline your follow ups unless you log into it multiple times a day and actually make the calls, write the notes or do the pop bys.

When things are hard, we tend to look outside ourselves for help, for a solution, but really, we already have all we need. This is true in business and in life. We have the ability to pick up the phone and make a call. We can write a note or connect with our community via social media. Yes, there are many tools to help make our business processes more streamlined and efficient, but we need to actually use them, work the systems, in order to see the results. If not, we stay frustrated, and keep looking for bigger and better, easier ways and time savers. And while we are busy searching our businesses are slipping away, and we are being passed by in favor of those who are out there, present, engaged, and doing.

Do you have a tool or system that you have invested in and not fully used? What is holding you back?

January 31, 2020

My husband is a gem. Kind, thoughtful, caring, respectful and sensitive. A fully engaged husband and father. He treats me like a princess (even when I don't deserve it), and he even makes our bed every day, so I don't have to.

I know that much of the reason he is this way is because of his mother. She taught him to honor and respect others, especially women. As a boy (an only child) she took him with her to exercise classes, art classes, and they did lots of shopping together. I know this is why he's a far better shopper than I am!

We will lay his mother to rest today, having lost her earlier this week to the effects of Alzheimer's disease. It's been a multi-year battle, and the last few months and especially weeks have been particularly excruciating.

It is a blessing that she is no longer in pain and no longer suffering. I've grown used to being a motherless daughter over the past 5 years. Now he will navigate what it means to be a motherless son.

No matter how much time you have, it's never enough.

February 18, 2020

Do you sometimes feel like maybe you are a little weird?

You set big goals; you work hard to achieve them. You strive and learn and grow and find tremendous value in those traits. You have learned that diligence and discipline, even when you don't really like or "have time" to do certain things (ahem, tracking ... double ahem, prospecting) is THE KEY to a strong, consistent business so you prioritize those things, even when you don't want to. You know that even though change was never your favorite and (not so) deep down is something that you fear, you've figured out that not only is it necessary, that it actually energizes you. You learned long ago that keeping your eye trained on the big picture of your business (and your life) is what will prevent you from tripping over dollars to pick up nickels.

I may have been typing "you" there, but what I really meant was "I". I'm just thinking that many of you can relate.

Does feeling this way about your business sometimes make you feel like you are the weird one? A little odd for being so driven, so diligent, so disciplined (if only I could figure out how to apply that in other areas of my life, but I digress), so focused on change, so big picture.

Maybe it's not you. In fact, I know it's not you.

It's them. They are the weird ones.

Actually, if you think about it, we are both a little weird. Set crazy big goals and do whatever it takes to achieve them? Weird. Set comfortable goals (or don't set them at all) and do just enough to do what it takes to get there? Weird.

What we need to do is find people who are our kind of weird and stick with them. When you do, you won't feel weird at all. In fact, you will feel totally normal. Fully supported in your weirdness. So much so, that weird is no longer part of your vocabulary.

Then your weird is no longer weird, it's actually your strength.

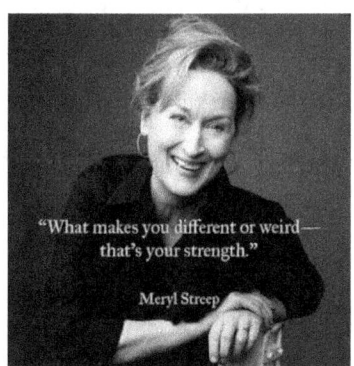

February 20, 2020

Last week Vicky Noufal and I were having a conversation with one of our team members who was feeling discouraged. She connected with potential clients through some marketing efforts she did last year, and they met to discuss listing their home this spring. She spent a lot of time going through the property and giving them recommendations and letting them know what they should be doing to prepare for market.

She followed up regularly and consistently with notes, calls, emails, and even a pop by during the holiday season. When she followed up again, they let her know that they decided to go with someone else.

She was frustrated, and tired of giving so much guidance and information away for free, only for the potential clients to use it and then hire someone else. Has this ever happened to you?

It's happened to me many times, and most assuredly it will happen again.

Our advice to her? Continue to give. Be generous with your knowledge, experience, and guidance. Most people will be grateful and will work with you as a result. There are some that won't. Bless and release and move on to those that you can help.

February 25, 2020

For Christmas I got Vicky Noufal a subscription to "Masterclass" online. Because I tend to like the same things she does, I got myself one too. Through this subscription we are able to watch a whole host of different courses taught by experts and celebrities. Really interesting things, and in small, bite sized episodes (our favorite kind).

We've both been watching one by Sara Blakely, the founder and creator of Spanx, on entrepreneurship. In one episode Sara is talking about goals. She was telling a story about this time that she and several other big business moguls (including Richard Branson) were on a reality show and one of their challenges was to jump off this cliff into the arms of their partner (both were harnessed, so even though it would be very scary to fall, it would be safe). Just about everyone failed the challenge. They would jump to their partner and their partner just couldn't hold on to keep them from falling.

Then it was her turn, she jumped, and her partner caught her! When the show host asked her afterwards how she did it she said it was because she aimed high. Instead of aiming for his arms or waist like everyone else was doing, she set her gaze and her aim on the top of his head. By aiming higher she actually landed closer to his arms and her partner was able to catch her.

The bottom line ... aim higher than you hope to go. When you aim for your just good enough goal you are less likely to hit it than when you aim higher.

February 27, 2020

This kid of mine. (Who hates when I take his photo, by the way.)

Last year, 2 weeks before spring sports tryouts as a high school freshman, he decided to switch sports and try out for lacrosse. Baseball had always been his first love, but he knew that with the number of kids trying out for the team that his chances of making it were low. His priority was wanting to be a part of something and playing for his school, so when he heard that the lacrosse program was in need of players, he switched last minute to a sport that he had NEVER played before. We spent an insane amount of money on equipment, and he got on the team.

It's been an eventful year since then. That very first night of tryouts last year he took a hard stick to the wrist and broke it. Only we didn't know it was broken. His supportive mother (that's me) picked him up that first freezing cold night and when he immediately started complaining about it, I told him what amounts to, this is only the first night, it's going to be hard, you need to toughen up. Oops. He played with that broken wrist for a month. It started to heal on its own, and then he re-broke it swinging a baseball bat. It was only then that we realized something was really wrong (in our defense, I was an EMT for 10 years and my husband is a career fireman ... he showed none of the usual outward signs that it was broken ... still, not our finest parenting moment) and we convinced him to get an X-ray (he refused to miss a practice for this). Even with his cast on he practiced with his team as much as he was able and never missed a game or practice.

He worked hard all through the summer, fall and winter. He went to camps, did extra tournaments and took every additional practice opportunity he could either on his own at home, with a few friends after school, or with organized practices. A note: NONE of this work ethic translates to anything around the house, just to be clear, lol.

This year, the team became more competitive. With the new freshman class many more kids (many more experienced kids) have joined the program. He saw an opportunity this fall for a need with a specialty position on the team ("the face off guy" for the other lax moms) and has been working hard for that spot.

Last night he made the JV team when many others did not. That's not the point of today's story.

Last night a friend that played on the team last year didn't make the cut. My son didn't think that was right. He felt that this kid had worked just as hard as the others. That he had taken the extra reps. That he had learned new things. That he had earned a spot. That he believed in and supported the team.

So, he and another teammate went to the coach to plead their case. And their friend was added to the roster. His coach said (and I'm totally interpreting from the few grumbled words I was offered from my almost 16-year-old) in essence, "all you really need in life is a couple people who have your back".

I'm more proud of him for standing up for his friend and for what he thought was right than anything else.

Life is hard and messy and complicated. Sometimes you will give more than you get. Other times you will receive possibly more than you deserve. We had an incredible meeting yesterday (a 3-hour lunch!) with brilliant new friends and we talked a lot about abundance. There is enough to around.

My long-winded message ... Go after what you want. Fight for what (or who) is right. Don't turn your back on those who have yours.

February 28, 2020

Do you know what tomorrow is? Tomorrow is leap day! We only get a leap day every 4 years, so it is most certainly a special occurrence.

So, for 2020 instead of the usual 365 days to make our goals a reality, we get 366 instead. I was thinking ... what would I do with this extra day?

Really, it doesn't feel like an "extra" day ... the kids still have sports, I'll still end up doing some work, the groceries will need to be shopped for, just a regular ol' Saturday. But what if it wasn't? What if it really was just an "extra" day to do whatever we wanted?

For me, I would love to spend that day at the beach or by the water. A walk in the morning, maybe some yoga. Extra leisurely coffee and reading. A walk around some shops or open-air market. More reading and some writing by the water. Probably an afternoon cat nap. A delicious evening meal that someone else prepares (and cleans up), capped off with a family movie night.

How would you spend your "extra" day?

March 10, 2020

Time. It's the thing we want most but tend to use worst. The amazing thing about time is that some people seem to be able to accomplish so much more than others. Think of people like Richard Branson and Oprah Winfrey. The level of accomplishment and productivity is unreal, yet they have the exact same amount of time … 24 hours in a day … that we all have. So how is that possible? It is because they have learned to master their time.

I've found that one of the most important keys to mastering your time is understanding the concept of yes = no.

Every time you say yes to something … happy hour with colleagues, a midday Netflix binge, you are saying no to something else … dinner with your family, prospecting or appointment time. It is critical to be intentional with your time and what you say yes to.

If you are like me, you have requests and demands for your time constantly. Clients, other agents and prospects calling, emailing, texting and messaging at all hours of the day and night. Invites for coffee and lunches, happy hours, brokers opens. And these are just the work-related things. Throw a spouse or partner, some kids and/or pets, and an extended family into the mix and your head (and schedule) are probably spinning on a daily basis.

While many of these may be really good things, they may not be a really good thing for you right now. Saying no now doesn't mean no forever. Prioritize that which is most important and most impactful and let the rest go. Know that when you say yes to something it is a "heck yes", and when you say no, it's okay to be a hard no or a not right now.

Our time is finite. It's your life, your schedule, your business. You get to decide how you spend it. Are you using yours wisely?

March 20, 2020

I have an idea. Now more than ever I believe strongly that we need MORE guidance, MORE communication, MORE positivity and MORE leadership than ever. So, I'm going to do my part.

Starting today I will be offering my Empower Coaching membership program for FREE on a temporary basis. Yes, free. (Don't worry about our current paying members ... earlier this week I announced that their payments for the program will be suspended for the time being as well.)

We are worried. Lots of us. Worried about our health, our families, our incomes and our businesses. The overwhelming majority of us in the real estate industry are commission only ... and as home sales slow due to economic changes and the need for people to stay in, our incomes will be changing (or even disappearing temporarily) along with it.

This too shall pass. I want you to focus on the health and safety of yourself and your family first. Then I want you to keep a continued focus and effort on your business, and I don't want you to have to prioritize paying for coaching over paying for marketing (or paying for household bills), so I am going to offer you coaching, support and step by step plans to keep moving forward at no cost to you.

I'll be offering the program for free for a month, maybe more depending on how things go with the spread of the virus and the impact on our economy and businesses. My hope is that whether you stay around after that with our program or not, that you will have received a great benefit in that time.

All that I ask is that if you request to join Empower Coaching that you will do the work. Nothing works if you don't work it, and this program is no exception.

March 24, 2020

Yesterday was a tumultuous day, like a lot of them right now, I suppose.

From finding out that schools will be closed at least through the end of the academic year (my kids are super upset about this, each one for different reasons) to learning that my state (Virginia) is one of the latest to "shut down" and having to determine whether or not our work in real estate is deemed "essential" (for our state, it is) and making sure our staff members and my team of agents will be okay.

It can feel hard to stay upbeat. But each day new, I start over and try again.

Yesterday a friend shared about her feelings after learning about our school closure. She described the feeling as "heavy". The pressure and responsibility now to not only learn how to continue to keep our businesses going in a new way (imagine if we didn't have the internet or smart phones?), but also to provide some education and daily structure for our children, plus caring for our households. Then there's that worry about who will get sick next, and whether or not the grocery store will have what you need when you do have to venture out for supplies.

It's a lot.

It's a lot for another friend too. Her husband is going on week 2 on a ventilator from COVID 19. She can't visit. She can't have a conversation with him (he is sedated, but the nurses do hold the phone up to his ear so she can talk to him). She has to wait for daily calls to find out whether he had a good night or a bad night. A good day or a bad day.

My youngest goes to a small, private Montessori school. This school has been a huge blessing to him and to us. The head of school shared with us yesterday that she is hoping to be able to weather the storm and keep up the rent payments so the school can reopen when able, but that is uncertain. Many of the families who would be paying tuition these last 2 months of the year now cannot afford to do so because they are small business owners experiencing some of what we are (or worse, shut down completely).

I feel like a bit of a downer this morning, but as it has been for the last almost 7 years, it feels good to share with you.

So seriously, here's my debate ... do I just need to let myself have a giant pity party and "get it over with" (if that's possible) or do I continue this back and forth during the day of moments of clarity and confidence, and then sadness and uncertainty? Literally, this was my conversation with God last night. Am I pouting too much? (I haven't received a response on that one yet, lol, so I'm asking you).

How are you coping these days? Share what is (or isn't) working for you!

March 26, 2020
One of the things that I really love about this business is that it is a relationship business. We build relationships with our clients before, during and after transactions which are some of the biggest milestones in their lives ... which when done right will lead to referrals and repeat business.

We build relationships with our most trusted and preferred vendors which can sometimes lead to referrals, but the biggest benefit is the priority status and care and concern that they will in turn show to our clients.

We build relationships with other agents through groups like this, within our brokerage offices and local associations, through networking events and in cooperating together on transactions. Those relationships can also lead to referrals, but their true give is that they bring tremendous value in terms of learning, support, and simply in helping to make a transaction go more smoothly.

We build relationships with our communities, investing in the people, businesses, economy and culture, which leads to more business but also a tremendous sense of satisfaction.

I believe wholeheartedly that these relationships are more important than ever before. If you've already been doing business this way, you have a distinct advantage right now. I've seen this to be true during other market shifts, and I think it will hold true even more so now.

Do you conduct your business relationally or transactionally? If you've struggled to build relationships in your business, what has been your biggest hurdle?

March 31, 2020

It's tough love time. How are you doing with your prospecting? Not good?

How about a few weeks ago when our world was "normal", were you prospecting then? Or were you too busy?

Here's the thing. The shift in our business is now. Maybe you've been able to eek along with an okay business by not prospecting (or not prospecting consistently), but with a shift upon us, that's not enough. You need to double what you used to do, just in hopes to do as much business as you used to do.

And if you weren't prioritizing prospecting then, and you aren't now, it may be time for a long, hard look at your business and what you are doing with it.

Just a reminder, prospecting is NOT just cold calling and door knocking or "pushy" sales techniques. I consistently sold 50-60 homes a year during my career and did not do any of those things.

Prospecting is keeping in touch. Reaching out consistently and intentionally. Calls, notes, pop bys, proactive social media. It could be open houses (when safe to do so again) or a comprehensive geographic farming plan. There are so many ways to do it, I know you can find a way that works for you and in your authentic voice, but you have to want to in the first place.

It doesn't have to be 2 hours a day (although right now, that would be nice!), but it does need to be consistent, repetitive effort. Not just on the days you feel like it. Not just on the days you have time.

If you do what is easy ... your life (and your business) will be hard to come by (especially now). But if you do what is hard, your life ... and your business ... will be easy, or easier at least!

April 2, 2020

How are you doing?

At my house we've been splitting our time between lots of work at home, afternoon movies on the couch every few days, and the occasional nap. When we have a beautiful sunny day like we did here on Monday I feel much more positive and optimistic. Then when we have overcast or rainy days like the last couple everything feels so much harder.

As tough as these days are, I am grateful to have a safe home, full of food and my favorite people, and for technology that allows me to continue to connect online with my friends, team members and clients.

April 7, 2020

I feel like I'm playing a never-ending game of red light, green light right now.

Red Light: Don't want to get dressed. Messy bun. No make up. Chart topping worry and anxiety. Overwhelmed. The couch calls to me (and all the carbs ...).

Green Light: I'm powerful and will make big things happen on the other side of this by laying the groundwork now. Fancy hair. Make up. Cute earrings. "Dressy" lounge wear. Mind flooded with ideas. Bringing them into fruition. Energized.

And this is just with my personal well-being and work. A similar game is constantly running with my kids, family, house.

The transitions between red and green are exhausting. There is no yellow light in this game. Trying to figure out how to create one.

That's how I'm doing today. How about you?

April 9, 2020
This is Abby.

Earlier this week I was on a roll.

In my groove.

Writing all the things.

Checking stuff off my to do list like a boss.

Then she laid on the surge protector and turned off my computer.

Whomp, whomp.

How's your work from home life going these days?

April 14, 2020
"Your actions are a consequence of your thoughts. Your thoughts are a consequence of what you consume. And in the modern age, what you consume is largely a consequence of how you select and refine your social media feed. Choose better inputs. Get better outputs." -James Clear

I had gotten into a bad habit of scrolling social media before going to sleep (I know how terrible this is), and I started noticing that as I scrolled, I was feeling more and more anxious. Almost like I was vibrating from taking in so many messages of uncertainty, worry, stress, frightening headlines.

Recognizing that effect, I've started reading my book at night instead (in all honestly, usually after scrolling for a few minutes ... bad habits are hard to break), and I've found that reading inspirational or helpful material helps me to feel more calm and in control.

I've been listening to more podcasts than ever right now ... while I'm getting ready in the morning, while I'm fixing my breakfast, when I take my walks to the mailbox and back a few times a day. Putting good stuff in is helping me to get more good stuff out.

April 21, 2020

Today's post has next to nothing to do with real estate. It is just pure and simple frivolous fun!

Yesterday I switched over my work bag and my handbag from winter to spring and included a boomerang about it on my Instagram stories ... and the number of messages I got about it was crazy! You girls sure like your bags, lol! I know I sure do.

So, just for fun, today I am sharing with you what I carry in my bags.

First up, my work bag. Here's what's inside ...
-My laptop
-Notebooks
-Approximately 12,000 pens and highlighters, plus some paperclips, sticky notes, note pads, tissues and my trusty name tag.
-Separate pouch with my laptop charging cable, plus extra chargers for my phone and usually a backup battery ... but my kids like to steal those.
-I always, always, always travel with stamped note cards, plus business cards and some gift cards to my favorite places. When I have a few extra minutes here and there I can scroll social media or write a note. The note doesn't always win (let's be honest), but it would never win if I didn't set myself up for success and carry them with me in the first place.
-Not pictured: my planner.

Next, my handbag. While I was never a Girl Scout, I could have been as I like to be prepared for anything (just ask my friends, if they need it, I usually have it).

Here's what's inside ...
-Wallet and "misc" pouch.
-Charging pouch with various cords, back up battery, etc. My kids tend to pillage this one too.
-Glasses, checkbook, notebook, Kindle
-Air Pods, sunglasses, phone and usually a bottle of water.

So that "misc" pouch, this is where my "must be ready for anything" anxiety takes hold. Here's what's inside ...
-Real estate "stuff" including my Sentrilock card and business cards
-Medical "stuff" including my husband's Epi pen, Benadryl (see allergic husband), various pain relievers, cold meds and cough drops.
-Just in case "stuff" like floss picks, tissues, band aids, more pens, nail file, lip balm and lipstick.
-Kid "stuff" including granola bar and pocket-sized games.

Yes, my bag weighs a ton. ;-) If you need it, I probably have it.

April 23, 2020

Inconceivable. I love this word.

A couple months ago (it feels so long ago ...) my business partner Vicky Noufal and I were at our weekly "leader lunch" doing our usual big picture planning and strategizing. As we were talking through where we've been and the things we have done, the word inconceivable came up.

Five years ago, when we formed our team, it was inconceivable that here we would be, 5 years later, with an incredible team of 35 women. It wasn't even a thought that entered our mind. All we wanted to do was make sure that our friends (our team members) were well taken care of and that we had a way that made sense to refer our buyer leads so we could focus on our listings. Oh, how things have shifted and changed!

Six years ago, when I founded this group, Empowering Women in Real Estate, it was inconceivable to think that here I would be 6 years later with a thriving coaching business as a result. Six years of near daily posts, organizing in person events, sharing, texting, messaging and getting to know hundreds, now thousands of women across the country ... when I really just created this to fill the loneliness I was feeling in my business.

Now, it's fun to think, dream, and plan for what our next inconceivable will be. What is your inconceivable?

May 7, 2020

Does your routine, habits and calendar mirror who you want to be? Huh. I had to think twice or three times on that one when I heard Dave Hollis mention this at the RISExLive virtual conference on Saturday.

Think about it ... who do you want to be? Who does your goals say you are?

A successful (you get to define what this means) Realtor®? A profitable business owner? A healthy, energetic woman? An exceptional spouse, a connected mother?

It is one thing to want all of these things, but quite another to make them happen in your life. And the only way to make them happen is to ensure that your routines, your habits and your calendar reflects that. This was a good reminder for me. How about for you?

May 8, 2020

Wealth is the power to choose.

Financial wealth is the power to choose how to spend money.

Social wealth is the power to choose who to hang out with.

Time wealth is the power to choose how to spend your day.

Mental wealth is the power to choose how to spend your attention.

Source: James Clear

Where in your life do you have the power to choose?

May 15, 2020

I read this yesterday in an email newsletter that I get from James Clear (which I highly recommend subscribing to, by the way) ...

The 3 Levels of Employees:
Level 1 — You do what you are asked to do.
Level 2 — Level 1 + You think ahead and solve problems before they happen.
Level 3 — Level 2 + You proactively look for areas of opportunity and growth in the business and figure out how to tap into them.

This reminded me of something that Rachel Hollis said during the RISExLive virtual conference a couple weeks ago. When you are hiring someone in your business you want to look for "yes, and" people. Meaning when you have an idea or want to try something or ask them to take a project you want to hear "yes" (I will do it) and also "and", meaning here is an additional step I'd like to take.

This doesn't just apply to the people we hire. This applies to us.

Which level employee are you in your business? Are you a "yes, and" person? Do you do just what needs to be done to get the job done for your clients or do you go one step further and think ahead to anticipate problems and cut them off at the pass? Do you go another step further than that and look for areas of opportunity and growth in your business? This is the road less traveled my friends, and it is when you tap into this that you really start to build momentum and see consistent success.

Let me give you a real-life example.

Earlier this week I did a "support local" post in my Instagram stories using a new tagging sticker and highlighted some of my favorite local businesses.

Then I created a highlight on my profile called "Support Local" and saved them all there.

Then I went the next step and created an actual post surrounding the stories and featuring the businesses (all tagged of course) so I would have a longer lasting impression than just the stories that disappear in 24 hours.

Then I went the next step and posted both the post and stories on my business Facebook page.

Then I went the next step and posted a version on my personal Facebook page. (each time tagging the businesses)

Then I went the next step and "liked" each of the businesses AS my Facebook business page so they will show up on my page.

Then yesterday I went the next step and posted an online review for each of the businesses.

Then today I will go one more step further and send a handwritten note to each of the businesses thanking them for supporting our community and including my calendar magnet.

The first step was good, right? Some may say good enough ... but the MAGIC is in the subsequent steps. Yes, it takes a little longer, but I am connecting the dots and with each step further increasing my reach and influence, AND further promoting, supporting and connecting with these local businesses that are so important to my community.

Trust me my friends. Take the road less traveled. It is rarely crowded.

May 19, 2020

Yesterday was not my best day.

The cats broke one of my absolute favorite trinkets that I found at an antique store and didn't think could be replaced (I did find it online).

My middle and youngest have taken over the dining room with Perler beads (created by Satan himself, I'm sure of it) which would be one thing, except the cats have figured out the joy of scattering them off the table and all over the floor. Little, tiny beads EVERYWHERE.

As I encouraged some help from the two oldest kids, fights ensued. Yelling. Name calling. Suddenly everyone who had been bored and pacing around the house trying to talk to me all morning had lots of work to do.

Clearly none of the "synchronous" learning that our school system is doing was happening in my house today. And realistically not much any other day either. I know the oldest two will be okay. They stay reasonably caught up despite what is going on, but the youngest is a mess. We try conferences with his teacher to set goals for the week (he goes to Montessori) but nothing is happening. He has some challenges already of his own, and I fear that I am failing him, and he is falling further and further behind.

So, we all took a time out. The cats. The kids. Even me. (The dogs were busy snoring somewhere, oblivious to all the goings on ... until the slightest breeze brushes past the window then the barking starts, but that's a story for another day.)

And it made all the difference. I chose the front porch for my time out, and between the fresh air, planning out my to dos for the week, and watching some real estate educational material on team building and leadership on my phone, within a relatively short period of time I felt like a new person.

This too shall pass. Some weeks it feels like I have more challenging days than I have good ones. I've learned though (and I often need to re-learn) that the best thing I can do is get quiet first, get outside, dump out my brain on paper, and immerse myself in some sort of learning. All easy. All free. There are so many excellent opportunities online right now, there is no reason not to.

What fills your cup when it feels like your day is coming apart at the seams?

May 29, 2020

Being in real estate is hard. The unpredictable hours. The unpredictable income. The challenging clients. The ever-changing markets, technology, competition. The good for sure far outweighs the bad, but you need to keep your eye on the ball.

Being a mom is hard. Whether you are with your children or not (and no matter their age), it doesn't stop. The worry. The unpredictable moods (with toddlers AND teenagers). Every time you get into a good routine and think you have "figured out" a stage, your child moves into another one. They are constantly growing and changing, every level brings a new devil. But ... the good for sure far outweighs the bad!

Now combine being in real estate and being a mom ... and in the middle of a pandemic and it can be enough to lose your mind! Trust me ... I've been in business for 18 years now, have personally sold 700+ homes, lead my team of 35 incredible women and I have 3 school aged children ... I know a little something about this firsthand! I've lived (I'll admit, sometimes barely) to tell the tale.

Over the years I've learned quite a few lessons that have worked, and quite a few that haven't. Every mom in this business has too. You can hear some of my best advice on Empowering Women in Real Estate - The Podcast, episodes 4 and 21. Are you struggling to balance your real estate life with your mom life?

June 11, 2020

Earlier this week I read a post from my friend Kelly Northcott that really resonated with me. Kelly is an incredible direct sales maven and now coaches other direct sellers from many companies all across the country. I'm in some of her groups because 1) I think she's awesome, 2) she's a past client and shares my love of the handwritten note (You know that story I tell about listing a house directly because of a note? It was her.), and 3) I find that a lot of what she shares is applicable to the real estate industry.

With Kelly's permission, I am sharing that post with you today. Replace customer/potential recruit below with buyer/seller/client and consultant with agent ...

"I saw this ($20 bill) in the middle of the street at the end of today's walk and I had the ethical debate of leaving it there in case the person who dropped it came back or picking it up so that I can stimulate the economy by celebrating Taco Tuesday.

If someone was around, I would have picked it up and asked them if they lost or dropped the money, and if they could tell me the exact denomination and serial number, I would have returned it to them (that part was a joke - I would have just asked for the serial number).

But no one was around.

I wonder if you debate about what to do when you find a customer or potential recruit that you think might be working with another consultant.

Do you walk away in case the consultant comes back? Or do you start serving her? Maybe even treat her to a taco if it happens to be a Tuesday.

I'm not an advocate of poaching, but I do believe that it's always the customer's choice whom she buys from and signs with.

I also believe that no one owns any customers.

And I know that when you serve your customers well and build a strong relationship with them, they're more likely to be loyal."

So, what do you think? We deal with this in our business all the time. I hear from agents who are upset because a past client bought a house with someone else (it's happened to me many a time). How well were you serving them at the time? Maybe really well and it just wasn't a great fit or they were just jerks (happens all the time). Or maybe you weren't serving them as well or staying in touch as much as you thought you were.

Food for thought.

July 14, 2020

You know what's not exciting? Repetitive tasks.

You know what helps your business grow? Repetitive tasks.

Listen, success isn't easy, and a lot of it isn't fun. You must be consistent in your marketing activities. This is why you see me talk about and do certain tasks repeatedly. It's not enough to do a great postcard or email once or twice. You need to do it over and over and over again.

I'm asked over and over again what was the key to my success, and consistency is right up there at the top.

Consistently following up. Consistently writing the notes. Consistently sending the mailers. Consistently executing my Client Care Program. Consistently engaging with my farm. Consistently showing up on social media. Consistently, consistently, consistently.

This is not an easy button. This is not sexy. But this is effective.

And I don't know about you, but I'll take effective any day of the week.

July 20, 2020

I took this photo a couple weeks ago of my youngest son at the beach. He wanted to "surf".

He's dressed for the part.
He has the tools he needs.
But he's not getting in the water.

How about you and your business? You want to be successful, right?

You're dressed for the part.
You have your lockbox key and your business cards.
But you aren't actually getting out there.

Your business works best when you get off the sidelines and actively engage.

You aren't going to find new clients, make new connections or hone your skills hanging around at home.

You need to get active. Preview property. Tour model homes. Participate in (and then take action on) various trainings (which you often can do from home!). Actively pursue and work with rental clients. Go on appointments with other agents. Visit broker's opens and even open houses.

Yes, COVID-19 makes some of this more difficult right now, but I know you can figure out different solutions based on what is comfortable and safe for you and your area. Maybe you can't preview properties in person, but can you do various MLS searches and study what you find to get more in tune with the market? You may not be able to go on appointments with other agents right now in order to limit the size of groups, but could you take an agent you admire to coffee (outside) or have a phone conversation to learn from them?

Where there's a will, there's a way. You have to want it, but EVEN MORE than that, you have to get in the water.

August 8, 2020

Wow! Thank you, Inman News, for including me in your piece on inspirational quotes from real estate coaches!! To have MY quote appear between icons Brian Buffini (who has been a model and coach to me in my career since starting in 2002) and Mike Ferry is pretty astounding.

If you would have told me 18 years ago when Sherry Wilson took a chance on me and hired me to join her team what this journey would look like and where I would be now, I never would have believed you. Not in a million years.

Thank you so much to my friends, clients, Platinum Group Real Estate team members, my business partner Vicky Noufal, and so many others for supporting me along the way. Most especially to my husband and my family who puts up with (and I think has learned to embrace??) my hard working and crazy ways.

To the 15,000+ members of this group AND to the 750+ amazing women (and few brave men!) from across the country who have entrusted me to guide them through my Empower Coaching program ... thank you for being on this journey with me!

September 25, 2020
Can I tell you something? Over the last few weeks, I have bought 2 different planners, 3 different weekly planning pads and 4 different wall calendars. I'm trying really, really hard not to buy a daily edition Simplified Planner.

I, the queen of planning and scheduling, have officially lost my mind. For whatever reason, right now I am feeling a strong need to update my system ... I've been feeling behind and overwhelmed and like I end up spending parts of my time being more reactive than proactive. I know I need to shake things up (this is great to do from time to time), but nothing is making sense to me. (Yet.)

A tip if you are like me and enjoy trying out new systems ... I buy "last years" model, meaning there is just a couple months left in the planner, but this way they are super, super cheap and I can try it out fully before committing to a more expensive version for the whole year.

September 29, 2020

Yesterday I was scrolling through Instagram and saw my sweet friend Jeni Harmon in her stories. She had on a really pretty blue colored top and looked beautiful. I commented and told her such.

Her reply, "I felt it". That gave me pause. I loved her reply so much but couldn't remember a time that I could honestly say that about myself.

It's become too easy to tear ourselves down. To nitpick apart what we view as the worst bits of us. It's become too easy for us to do it to others too. A simple request for opinions on which photo is better turns into a hotly contested debate over which one is less likely to get "inappropriate" attention. Which one is conservative enough and likely to be the least offensive to the majority of people. I've seen others post in the group their concerns about starting a real estate business because they have visible tattoos and wonder if that will hurt their business.

Many years ago, a friend of mine used to sell cars. There was a saying in that industry that "there's an ass for every seat". It's my favorite saying and applies pretty much everywhere.

My interpretation ... there are people who will be for you. No matter which photo you choose. No matter the outfit you wear. No matter the hairstyle, or piercings or tattoos or number of visible hairs on your chin (yesterday was an unfortunate day ...). I've lived 47 years in this world and have learned that it doesn't matter how covered you are or how shapeless your clothes, there are still those who will give "inappropriate" attention. That has less to do with you, and everything to do with them.

It is not possible to "neutralize" yourself to the degree that you will appeal to all people. You just can't, or at least I don't think you can, and I really beg you not to try.

Be you. Authentically you. Those who will be for you and want to work with you will do so because you are you. Those who don't? Well, there's an ass for every seat, and they will find the right one for them.

October 6, 2020

After over 18 years in this business (and personally serving over 700 families with their real estate needs) ... I KNOW that this statement from Marie Forleo is true; "Success doesn't come from what you do occasionally. It comes from what you do consistently."

It's not necessarily fun or exciting, but it's fact ... and it's where the magic happens.

Things I do consistently ...
-Write 5 or more notes per week. Almost every week without fail.
-Post 3 or more times per week on social media, mixed between my business and personal accounts.
-Email my database every month.
-Mail my database and geographic farm every month.
-Deliver pop bys every season.
-Add to my database (there were times when my target was 1 per day).
-Give referrals, my goal is 5 per week.

When I think about the things that have made the biggest difference in my business, it's these things right here. Done over and over and over again.

October 13, 2020

Yesterday my husband and I celebrated 18 years of marriage. This year I've celebrated 18 years in real estate, I started just a few months before we got married. Real estate was not always good for my marriage. This business can be really hard to understand when you aren't the one in it.

There were many years in the beginning when I would go nonstop, appointments 7 days a week, working late at night at my computer after we put the kids to bed that my husband didn't understand and was probably (not probably, was) more than a little bitter.

Can you blame him? My phone(s) (plural, when I carried my team leader's "lead" phone back in the day) was my constant companion that literally never left my side.

I learned early on the importance of boundaries ... first with taking a vacation with little to no interruptions, then taking 1 day per week "off" (which really just meant no appointments, the calls and emails never stopped), then being home for dinner with my family most nights and being home to tuck my kids in bed.

Each time I put a boundary in place I realized that it was okay. The world wasn't going to fall apart. My clients were not going to leave me. My business didn't deteriorate.

In fact, it got stronger. Every time.

Boundaries, like not responding to calls, texts and emails all hours of the super early morning and late at night, and giving myself a day "off" actually fueled my business. It allowed me to recharge and re-energize. It shifted my mindset into one of being a business owner making strategic decisions to grow, not just a minion at the mercy of everyone else.

Working less (and let's get real, "less" is still a crazy whole lot of hours), has actually allowed me to grow more.

October 22, 2020

I've been in real estate for 18 years, and earlier this week I had a first.

A longtime friend messaged me to apologize for not working with me several years ago. She felt like it hurt my feelings (it did) and wanted to apologize.

I'll admit, I kind of feel silly that this mattered to me, but it did.

Rejection is part of the business. I've had past clients, friends, new clients that I've met with choose to work with someone else many times over the years, and it will happen many more times in the future, I'm sure. This is the nature of the business.

Most don't hurt, this one did sting, and so to hear an apology really meant a lot. Has this ever happened to you?

October 30, 2020

Today I'll be pressing pause for a bit. Those who have followed along for a while know that I have a long history with a specific type of breast tumor (phyllodes) with many, many surgeries (including a mastectomy) to go along with it.

I've had a recurrence pop up, what feels like out of nowhere not quite 3 weeks ago, and today my surgeon will be taking it out, plus quite a bit of skin and my implant too. Which means starting the reconstruction process all over again. *sigh*

All will be well. My last tumor was a "borderline" (not malignant) and we expect nothing different from this one (pathology will confirm).

So just a little note here for two things ...

1) I'll be pressing pause on regular "live" posts here in the group for the next few weeks. Don't worry though, lots of content (including everything for my Empower Coaching members) has been pre-planned and scheduled out.

2) I'd appreciate all the prayers, good vibes and well wishes that you can give today and, in the days, to come.

December 15, 2020

This week my team and I are celebrating our year with our annual retreat ... only it looks a LOT different than in years past!

Usually, we are all together for several days at a gorgeous house on the beach or a lake. We have wonderful meals around a big table. We talk and share and laugh and cry while staying in pajamas most of the time. We have deejays and dance parties and fun games.

All of that has changed for us this year. Not once, not twice, but FOUR times. Which is why we have renamed this year's event Retreat 4.0.

We've turned it into a Retreat Week with shorter sessions each day, with take home bags of surprises and goodies, and even glittery pom poms so we can cheer each other on Zoom.

It's not what we wanted, but we've learned a whole lot about how to do things differently which will impact us positively for years to come.

December 22, 2020

Hi, it's me.

Things you may or may not know about me ...

-I'm a homebody, and I love nothing more than days with no appointments outside the house.

-Driving in snow and icy conditions terrifies me.

-I love a snow day at home with my kids.

So naturally I'll be starting radiation treatments in January ... every day, Monday through Friday, for 5-6 weeks.

During the time of year when we are most likely to have the kind of weather where I want to be home most of all.

2020 brought many lessons.

2021 is bringing me out of my comfort zone.

December 28, 2020
Here's my littlest guy, listening to a video on his iPad, surrounded by Legos, living his best life in all its winter break glory.

I'm living my best life this week too ... I LOVE the week between Christmas and New Year's.

This tends to be a quiet work week, and so I enjoy spending time cleaning up, packing up Christmas, organizing my office, de-cluttering stuff and files, and otherwise getting ready for the New Year.

How are you spending this week?

December 29, 2020
Simplify.

It was my word of the year for 2020 and turns out it was exactly what I needed.

I've simplified many aspects of my business, my team operations, my coaching program, and many parts of my personal life this year. Some by necessity, some intentionally.

This word has served me well. I used it a few years back and it was just as impactful then as well. This is one that I am sure I will return to again and again.

In what areas of your life do you need to simplify?

2021

Milestones
1-7-2021 – Our group hit 20,000 members!
1-28-2021 – Launch of the Empowering Women in Real Estate Educational Series digital courses
7-29-2021 – The first Empowering Women in Real Estate conference, 7th Anniversary Celebration
10-4-2021 – Empower Coaching is now the Empowering Women in Real Estate Inner Circle!

January 5, 2021
Purpose. It's my 2021 word of the year.

As I was working through my Power Sheets Goal Planner (highly recommend, by the way ... www.CultivateWhatMatters.com) and writing out what I wanted for my life I realized that I was writing the word "purpose" over and over again.

I want to live into God's purpose for my life.

I want to eat, move, spend, do everything with purpose.

I want to be purposeFUL in all I do.

Purpose. Feels right

January 7, 2021
Oh boy, oh boy ... look how far we've come!!!

Today, we hit 20,000 members ... TWENTY THOUSAND!!! It is an incredible milestone, and I couldn't let the day go by without mentioning it.

When I started this group, going on 7 years ago, it was designed to be a safe place for women in the real estate industry to come together and support one another. Over the years it has become so much more.

It has been my safe space (and I hope yours too) and respite as I went through the difficult loss of my mother, and writing to you all each morning felt like my salvation.

It has been the connection point for women in 19 cities all across the country to come together for Monthly Meet Ups.

It has birthed Empowering Women in Real Estate - The Podcast, one of my favorite things I've ever done.

It has become an extension of my business (a dream come true) with the launch of Empower Coaching in 2019.

It is a safe and positive place for women in our industry to support one another and to learn and grow.

Thank you. Thank you for being here. Thank you for listening to my ramblings and musings and thoughts and ideas as I've shared them 5-6 times per week for the last 6 ½ years. Thank you for supporting, encouraging and EMPOWERING each other.

November 11, 2021

"Givers need to set limits because takers rarely do." Boy, oh boy, does that resonate with me. I'm going to guess that it also resonates with a lot of you.

Boundaries are necessary in many aspects of our life, but in our real estate business they are what makes the difference between burning out (for some agents I know, this is practically on a weekly basis) and establishing a long-term successful business.

Our phones ring 7 days a week (if we are lucky, if they aren't ringing, you have another problem entirely). Clients, prospective clients and other agents texting early in the morning and late at night. Emails flood our inboxes nonstop. It can be exhausting. It IS exhausting. So how do you cope, keep it from taking over your life? You set boundaries, you set limits.

Now certainly not all among us are givers, and not everyone contacting us around the clock is a taker. Many times, they don't know any better. I'm quite sure that if they are texting us at 10 pm, or calling at 7 am, or sending an email at 1 am it has more to do with them than it does with us. Perhaps that is the first time they have had to sit down and send us a message, and that they will anticipate us responding the next day. Maybe calling and leaving a voicemail early while they are on the way to work is when it works for them to relay a message to us that they may not have a chance to do later on.

We, on the other hand, have been programmed to fear the loss of business, to fear providing poor customer service if we don't take the call or respond immediately. In our competitive market that fear is often justified. When someone calls you at 10 am because they want to view a house that afternoon, if you don't call back within a reasonable period of time, it is possible (likely even, depending on your relationship with that person) that they will contact someone else.

That call at 10 pm though? You certainly aren't going to be scheduling a showing in a few hours. Brainstorming a listing strategy that late at night isn't likely to be helpful to anyone as you are likely exhausted and ready for bed (and so are they ... tired = emotional, not rational). The problem though is when we answer that 10 pm call, that 11 pm text, that 1 am email we are teaching others that it is an acceptable time to contact us. In fact, what do we say? Their call or text may start with ... "I know it's late", "sorry to contact you so late", and how do we respond? "It's okay", "I was up anyway", "just sitting here at my computer cleaning out my emails". Then we wonder why they will continue to do it. We've given permission. We've shown that we will answer at that time of day/night. We are our own worst enemy.

You are a professional. It is not unreasonable to set boundaries for your business. In fact, I would argue that it is one of the most professional things you can do. "Real" businesses have office hours. Your business is a real business too, we need to treat it as such.

The key, however, is setting the expectations and doing what we say we will do. If you get a call or text late at night, maybe text back letting them know that you are settling in for the evening and will give them a call first thing in the morning. Then actually do it. It's when we don't call back or respond the next day that they start to think we aren't serious about providing them good service.

Do you set boundaries or limits in your business? Are there certain times of day that you don't answer or respond and how do you handle it?

January 18, 2021

In this business we wear many hats ... real estate advisor, therapist, marriage counselor, and many more. If you've worked with even a few clients, then certainly you know what I'm talking about.

Anytime you work in a service industry, working with, for and serving others, it is inevitable that you will see people at their best, but also very much at their worst. Buying, selling, even renting homes are stressful times. Moving is stressful. Often there are situations driving the clients need to sell or buy or move that are difficult, possibly rooted in some sort of financial or relationship turmoil. Maybe a job relocation that isn't desired. There are many factors that can make this business transaction a highly emotional one.

And we are the gatekeepers. Part of our job, like it or not, is to as much as possible neutralize the drama and the emotion as we help guide our clients through the process. Oftentimes, that drama or emotional turmoil that our client is experiencing that affects the transaction becomes our problem too.

It's so difficult ... over the past 19 years I've had so many buyers and sellers in highly emotional, challenging situations. This drives their decision making and reactions, and as much as I try not to let it affect me, sometimes it does.

However, I've learned (sometimes the hard way) that the way I react when the client is reacting or responding emotionally is often the determining factor in how the conversations will go. As the 3rd party, I can see so clearly what needs to happen, how it should go, what needs to happen to help them out of the situation they are in, but no matter how many different ways I try to explain it or get the point across, sometimes it just doesn't work.

Has anyone else ever been in this situation? What strategies do you use to neutralize these emotional situations and help to get your point across?

January 19, 2021

Karen Cooper, reporting for ... radiation?! Yep, that's me. And today is day 1 of 30 treatments to take place over the next 6 weeks.

(Background for those not familiar: I have a 10+ year history with a very usual type of tumor called "phyllodes" with 6 recurrences (plus others). After a mastectomy in October 2018, I thought I would be done, but fast forward to October 2020 and "phyll" was back, and so I had another mastectomy. It was also determined that I should have radiation to prevent another recurrence.)

Last week I went in for my radiation "simulation" appointment to ensure that the images lined up, etc. and it was like being inside of a spaceship. Blue lights in the ceiling, multiple big screens, things hanging down from the ceiling over the table. Truly like nothing I've ever seen before and that I struggle to describe. It was pretty intimidating, and rather unsettling.

Have you ever had a panic attack before? You know that feeling where it seems like you are right at the edge and if you can't reign it in you are going to spiral out of control and "lose it"? It was like that.

So, today's my day to start. If you are the praying kind, I would dearly appreciate yours, and if you aren't I would love all the good vibes and positive energy that you can muster. I'll be going in everyday M-F at 1 pm EST for the next 6 weeks for my treatments. The treatments themselves are very fast I am told, and the side effects that I have been told to expect are a "sunburn" like look/sensation on my skin and fatigue.

But I have 3 kids, own and operate 3 different businesses in the real estate industry and have a podcast ... fatigue ain't got nothing on me! I'm declaring now that THIS will be the final chapter in this particular part of my story, and I am so grateful for it.

February 4, 2021

You all know my love for Disney, right?

My friend Dinna Eckstein (who, by the way, is an incredibly talented designer who has been doing "remote" designing for clients all over the US since well before it became a necessary thing) loves Disney too. It's how we originally connected.

This week, she has been at our happy place. My last couple trips have been cancelled (#covidsucks #andsodoesradiation), so she had a pillow made of me and took me with her!!!

Can you even believe it? This is the funniest thing I've seen in ages, and I have laughed and laughed and laughed all week watching our "adventures".

She even got "me" a Disney button that says, "Celebrating Friendship".

Laughing is good.

Joy is good.

We all need a little more of it.

What is the funniest thing that you have heard or seen lately?

March 1, 2021

I'm a Sunday prep kind of girl. I like to spend a little bit of time making sure that I am set up for success in my week, both personally and professionally.

Here are the most important parts of my Sunday routine ...

First, I do a brain dump into my weekly planner to list out all the things I'm thinking of that need to be taken care of.

Then I go through my digital calendar day by day and write down appointments as well as any tasks or to dos that are related to those appointments.

Next, I assign any date specific tasks to those days, as well as assigning important to dos for the week.

This year I decided to also use a daily planner in addition to the weekly. My weekly is my master planner that has everything. Each day before wrapping up my work, I take some time to write out my tasks and schedule for the following day in the daily planner.

Yes, there's definitely some repetition in my process, but I find that this helps me to be more intentional and more clear about what needs to be done. I also like the clean-ness of a fresh page for each day, and it helps me to not overwhelm my day with too many tasks that just leave me frustrated when I can't finish them all. Both of my planners are The Simplified Planner by Emily Ley (EmilyLey.com).

Do you have a weekly planning routine?

March 4, 2021

Beauty is everywhere. It's there, I promise.

Today I'm wrapping up 6 weeks of daily (M-F) radiation treatments (yay!!).

Many things about it have sucked.

1, having the need to do it in the first place.

2, losing two plus hours every day in the middle of my workday in the middle of a very busy season.

3, burns, itching, pain, discomfort, tiredness.

There's been some beauty too ...

1, getting fully dressed down to the shoes, which hasn't always been the case this past year in the COVID work from home era. I'm reminded that I have lots of beautiful clothes and accessories that I enjoy wearing.

2, more time in the car for my 40 minutes each way drive has allowed for more time to connect by phone with my friends and team members. Taking time for conversations I haven't always "had" the time to do have made my drives more fun.

3, the people at the radiation oncology center I go to are wonderful. I truly look forward to seeing them each day, and we usually share a few laughs as we prep for each treatment. Agnes, Becky, Jan, Betsy, Mike, Mitzi ... their warmth, kindness, care and attention has made a difference in my life.

4, unbelievable support, love and prayers from friends old and new. Generous gifts, beautiful letters and cards. Even a friend that had a pillow made of "me" so she could take me to Disney. I've smiled, laughed and felt loved and supported again and again.

Beauty is everywhere. I promise. You just have to look for it.

March 15, 2021

You know what's hard? Re-entry from vacation. You know what I'm talking about. Especially if you got back home SUPER LATE the night before, like I did last night.

Laundry is piled up. You haven't unpacked. There's no food in the house, and before you can take a breath you are jumping right back into the fire and crazy schedule.

I have a few tips that I have used over the years on how to make this first day back a little more palatable ...

-Whenever possible, don't schedule any appointments for your first day back. Most likely you will need the majority of the day just to get through your email, to re-connect with your clients, and to get caught up on what happened while you were away.

-Do your laundry BEFORE you get back. Yes, that's right, I said before. The overwhelming majority of the time my family rents houses or condos when we travel, which means we have our own "in room" laundry facilities. The day before we leave, I do a load of laundry and pack back up clean clothes. This way when I get back home there is just a small bit of laundry to catch up on from our trip.

-Have a day or two worth of meal components already in your fridge, freezer or pantry for the first day(s) back. Meals planned; you just need to fix them.

-Schedule a grocery delivery or pick up for the day you return or first day you are back. Most grocery delivery services or online ordering for pick up (I use Harris Teeter) will let you schedule in advance or prep your cart to schedule as soon as you are back.

-Sssshhhh ... this one's a secret, but it's my favorite. Come back a day earlier than you tell everyone that you do. This way you have a day to re-adjust to being back home, to get everything put away, and to get yourself ready for the week.

Now, who's ready for a vacation?

April 13, 2021

"New goals don't deliver new results. New lifestyles do. And a lifestyle is a process, not an outcome. For this reason, your energy should go into building better habits, not chasing better results." I love this quote from James Clear, the author of "Atomic Habits".

Many of us, myself included, tend to think about or focus on habits as pertaining to improving our health or exercise ... but what about the habits that improve our business?

They are incredibly important, and in my experience when you focus on building better habits in your business that it helps to improve your life overall. (For more on this, what I call my "Daily Business Builders" check out episode 51 of Empowering Women in Real Estate - The Podcast.)

April 19, 2021

I feel like "hustle" has gotten a bad rap. You do need a certain amount of hustle ... drive, push, passion, willingness to do what it takes to get the job done ... in order to be successful. Especially in real estate.

But you can also take it too far. And the "hustle" can lead to stress, overwhelm, burnout. It's damned if you do, damned if you don't.

I've come to believe that you can do both. You can hustle AND rest. You can have a successful business AND a full "non-work" life.

Brian Buffini talks about this as the rest/run cycle. I think there is a book on this topic as well.

Last month I was very much in a "rest" cycle following my radiation treatments and with two trips during the month.

Now I'm in a "run" cycle, with lots of exciting plans and projects that I am pushing ahead. I know that part of why I am able to forge ahead with so much excitement and energy is because I had the period of rest.

What cycle are you in right now?

April 26, 2021
These are my Daily Business Builders ... an assortment of tasks that I have done for years and years and years to stay top of mind with my clients and to keep my business growing and thriving. It's my kindler, gentler way of prospecting.

The actual tasks have stayed largely the same, but my goal number for how many to do each day or week changes based on where I am with my business ... and what else is happening in my life!

I do these tasks, each day (M-F), without fail. As a result ... I consistently sold 50-60 homes per year during my career, and now I generate hundreds of leads each year for my team.

Here's what I am doing currently ...
-Calls (my least favorite!) - 3 per week
-Notes - 1 per day
-Database Additions - 1 per week
-Give Referrals - 1 per day
-Deliver Pop Bys - 50 per quarter

Most weeks I accomplish far more than this, but I am always sure to do this as a minimum. I'll add also that this is part of my larger Client Care Program that I implement throughout the year which includes mailers, emails, contests, events and more.

You can learn more about my Daily Business Builders on Episode 51 of Empowering Women in Real Estate - The Podcast.

What are your "no fail" tasks that you do each day (or week) in your business?

April 27, 2021
When's the last time you took a break? I did last week, and I'll tell you what, it made all the difference in the world! A whole day wasn't possible ... it was just a few hours of turning off the phone (and everything else) and it was just what I needed.

Could you do this for yourself at some point this week, or even TODAY?

May 6, 2021
I will say that I don't consider myself a super "tech-y" person, but I have learned the power of technology in helping me to conduct my real estate business and life more efficiently and effectively.

Here are a few of my favorites ...

1) DotLoop. My brokerage uses DotLoop for our transactions, and having the app on my phone allows me to create addendums, ratify contracts, get signatures and more with just a couple taps. If you don't use DotLoop in your business, check for an app associated with the program that you do use. It probably exists!

2) Referral Maker CRM. Many times, you've heard me extol the virtues of this CRM. It is by far the favorite I've ever used! While the app does leave a lot to be desired, it does have one feature that I absolutely LOVE, that is part of the Priority Action Center. It works with the GPS on my phone and will show me who in my database is "near" me wherever I am, and even shows their "rank" in my database. This makes impromptu pop bys a breeze.

3) Evernote. I've long said that Evernote is like my brain outside my body. I started using it 10+ years ago as my lead log. I still use it for that, but for many other things too. When you have an Evernote account you also receive a personal email, so I can just email things directly into it, and I can also tag them when I forward so they go into my pre-determined notebook. The search functionality is so good, making it really easy to find things, even when I can't recall all the details.

4) iPhone Notes App. This has fast become one of my favorites. I used the notes app to store all sorts of things ... "scripts" for repetitive emails or messages I need to send, lists of ideas for social media posts, goal tracking, and tons of "quick reference" notes.

5) Dropbox. My team uses Dropbox for our files, and having it sync across all of my devices makes it so easy for me to find documents on the go.

What are your favorite apps for your real estate business?

May 18, 2021
Earlier this month my team celebrated our 6-year anniversary, and I couldn't be more proud. Oh, the things I've learned as a Team Leader these past 6 years!

Here are a few of my favorite lessons ...

-Get yourself a good partner. Vicky Noufal and I push each other in the best of ways. Many of the areas where I am weak, she is strong, and vice versa. Yes, there are challenges that come with having a partnership vs making all the decisions on your own ... but you also don't have to make all the decisions on your own and that is a beautiful thing!

-Hire strong leadership and a top-notch support team. You need to surround yourself with people you can trust (this takes time), and with people who believe in and can see your vision even when you can't.

-There is no one size fits all. Our team is made up of 37 incredible women. Most are moms. Some are grandmas. All are amazing ... in their own way. Get to know your team members. Embrace their differences, as those differences will become your strength.

-You won't get it right the first time. And maybe not even the fifth. Being a team leader means constantly learning to grow, shift, pivot, tweak. Things that worked for us year 1 no longer worked in year 3 and for sure wouldn't work now. Get really comfortable with change and don't be afraid to make changes as you go.

June 22, 2021
Here's the thing about success ...

People won't notice the late nights or early mornings.

They won't see the self-doubt, the failures, the obstacles and risks taken.

No one notices the time and money invested. So much time and money.

They will only see your results and call you lucky.

It's not luck.

June 29, 2021

Is your spouse or partner supportive of your real estate business? Mine is! Today is his birthday, so is only seems right to shine a little light his way.

In all seriousness though, he wasn't always the most supportive of my business. My husband works in the fire service. His work, schedule, paid benefits, time off, and paycheck every two weeks could not be more different from my situation.

Even though I have been the bread winner in our family pretty much from day 1, he didn't always understand my business and the things I needed to do to be successful. And since he didn't always understand it, while he certainly was supportive of me, he wasn't always of my business.

For many years, in the beginning especially, he resented my career, most especially for the 24/7 nature of it. You know I am big on boundaries, but sometimes ... especially when you are just starting out and trying to get your business going or are in the midst of negotiations ... it just can't be helped.

I remember the looks when we would have family over for dinner or a birthday party for the kids and I was on the porch on the phone with a new lead or client.

The nights that we would do our bedtime routine with our very little kids, and then I would go right back to my home office and work until midnight trying to catch up.

Or how about the celebration dinner with his friends and colleagues for his big promotion and I kept excusing myself over and over again to take a phone call outside from one of my agents (I was a managing broker at the time) who was in the middle of a situation and needed help.

Thinking back over these experiences, it is easy to see where the frustration is. From my point of view whatever it was that I was doing at the time was more important. More important than being 100% present at my kid's birthday party. More important than spending an hour in the evening with my partner before we both crashed from exhaustion. More important than being all there for a big moment for him.

19 years in now, looking back, those other things WEREN'T always more important. Sure, sometimes there have been emergencies and time sensitive situations that needed to be addressed immediately, but more often than not those things could wait an hour or two for me to get to them. I wish I had learned this lesson earlier.

Eventually, I did catch on (it took a while, lol), and when I started putting better boundaries in place in my business his support for me also turned into support of my business. Because my work wasn't always more important, there was much more grace and understanding when it truly was in the moment. As they say, we've come a long way, baby.

July 1, 2021
There was something I read on Instagram earlier this year that I immediately took a screenshot of and emailed to myself with the subject line, "REMEMBER".

It was from Amber Lilyestrom, and she said that mastery is knowing yourself so well that someone else's wobble doesn't wobble you.

So good, right?

How many times have you allowed someone else's fears, self-doubts, "wobbles" in their business cause you to doubt your own path?

Listen, it happens to the best of us.

The antidote? Mastery. The more masterful you become in your skills, the more you master your vision, your processes, your systems, the less likely you are to be impacted by the wobbles of others.

A note though ... mastery doesn't mean that you know it all and that you aren't still learning and seeking to learn. For me ... I've mastered our contracts, my listing presentation, being a listing specialist. I'm a master at systems and checklists and making complicated things easy to understand.

That definitely doesn't mean that I know it all in those areas. I'm confident with my skills, my abilities, what I can do, but I am also constantly striving to improve and learn more to make it all even better.

What have you mastered?

July 5, 2021

Just a reminder to help you kick your week off on the right foot.

How do you talk to yourself?

"You're so stupid."

"You're not ready for that."

"You don't know enough to help them."

"Of course they will choose someone else."

"I'm not _____ enough (young enough, skinny enough, smart enough, pretty enough ... the list goes on and on) to be successful in this business."

It's not true. Any of it.

Instead try ...

"I have the ability to learn what I need to know."

"What I lack in experience I more than make up for in enthusiasm."

"No one knows everything. I know how to find out the answers."

"Some people aren't my people, and that's okay. There is plenty of business to go around."

"I am MORE THAN ENOUGH to accomplish anything I choose. If I set my mind to it and am willing to learn and work for it, I can do it."

The way you speak to yourself matters ... make it count!

July 14, 2021

It's Monday, are you ready? I'll admit, Monday morning is one of my favorite times of the week, but it wasn't always that way. Once I learned to take some time for myself to refresh and recharge, it made all the difference in the world.

What that usually looks like for me is that at some point Sunday afternoon ... around the time I start looking at my watch and realizing the day is passing quickly and I still have so much to do ... I force myself to stop, grab my favorite book and head to the porch.

Even just 20 minutes in my favorite spot is enough for me to take a breath. I can often literally feel the stress and tension leaving my body. An hour is even better.

Then, come Monday morning I'm up (often before the alarm) and rip rearing to go. It's one of my most productive times of the week.

What is your favorite way to refresh and recharge?

July 20, 2021

You know I love to write notes, right? In fact, so far this year I have already written nearly 500 notes! Part of my prospecting activities include a goal to write 5 notes a week, but as you can tell I typically write well more than that!

While my favorite and my used type of note is some sort of thank you, this one here is probably my next most often used ...

"I was on an appointment/showing homes/meeting with a client) in your neighborhood today and thought of you. Hope you're doing great!"

I include my business card and off it goes!

July 26, 2021

On Thursday we will be celebrating the 7-year anniversary of the Empowering Women in Real Estate community ... SEVEN YEARS!

To be honest, when I started this group, it was to fill my own loneliness. I had moved out of the field to be a managing broker and had really lost the day-to-day closeness I felt with the women I worked with.

I was surrounded by agents all day every day and spoke with them all day long ... but almost exclusively in the role as problem solver.

My other role was as a recruiter for my brokerage ... which meant when I did see or call other agents, they really didn't want to talk to me for fear of being sold to.

I had been following along on social media watching my friend Samantha Tunador experience Stella & Dot's "Hoopla" conference (Jessica Herrin is an entrepreneur that you NEED to follow) and I loved the show of camaraderie and togetherness and was feeling very envious (and a lot of FOMO) of that type of environment.

And then I thought, why not create it for myself and other women in the real estate industry?! Surely if I am feeling this way, others are too, and Empowering Women in Real Estate was born!

Now here we are 7 years later ...

With over 27,000 women as members from all across the US and many other countries.

With a podcast that has over 45,000 downloads and more than 85 episodes.

With a monthly membership program offering group coaching and systems specifically for women in real estate.

And here we are, celebrating with our 7th Anniversary Celebration Meet Up this Thursday, July 29th in Ashburn, VA with just SEVEN tickets remaining before we will have a sold-out crowd of 100.

Lucky #7?

Nah, purpose being fulfilled.

July 27, 2021

This is a hard one to hear, but you know what you need for success in your business? Patience.

Patience, coupled with consistent activity. I really don't know of any other way. Or at least any other way that works for the long haul.

Something I hear often from agents is that they are trying this and that and it isn't working. And when I ask how long they have been doing it I get answers like "2 weeks", "1 month", "3 months".

Have you seen that meme of the guy digging and digging and digging to reach the buried treasure, and then he stops and gives up thinking his efforts are fruitless ... only the treasure is only a few more shovels full of dirt away?

It's the same thing here. When you are working on new systems of lead generation or building new pillars in your business it takes time. At least 6 months, preferably a year, before you can really assess and say that it is or isn't working.

A week of workouts won't get you fit.

A full tank of gas won't get you from Virginia to Florida.

You need to repeat and refill again and again before you achieve your desired results. Patience, my friend, patience.

July 29, 2021

I really don't have a lot of words left for today, other than to say WOW! What an incredible experience celebrating 7 years of Empowering Women in Real Estate with over 100 of the best in the business!

Thank you to my incredible support team for all you did to make today a success ... and to our Platinum Group Real Estate team members for being there to show your support.

Thank you to our panelists Vicky Noufal, Sue Smith, Kathleen Stakem, Keysha Washington and Amanda Macy for sharing your stories, experiences and wisdom.

Thank you to all of our attendees ... 102 incredible women and 1 very brave man for joining us ... it is not lost on me that you would choose to invest your time here with us today.

And to my business partner Vicky Noufal and mentor Jackie Fields-Gleadall, who push me to do and be more every day. You believed and saw the vision before I ever did.

Many years ago, as Vicky, Jackie and I attended a women's conference and sat in a ballroom not far from where we sat today, and at round tables just like the ones we used, Jackie leaned over and whispered to me, "look around, one day it will be you with a room just like this".

Today was that day.

August 17, 2021
When I was little, I wanted to be an archeologist. I was (and still am) fascinated by history and past lives.

For a very long time as a kid I also wanted to be a secretary (like my mom) because I loved to type, and I really wanted to be a mom. I'd envision how many kids, what they would look like, and what kind of mom I would be.

As a teen I wanted to be a psychologist or therapist. I could see myself listening to the needs and challenges of others and helping them through it.

I've been blessed as a mom 3 times, and my career in real estate requires a lot of typing and admin work, a whole lot of therapy/counseling (lol) and I'm often revisiting how people lived in the past ... so I guess I've done/been all I wanted to be!

What did you want to be as a kid?

August 19, 2021
One of the things I like to do when I am on vacation is to dream about "what's next".

In my next phase of grown-up life, after my kids are grown and gone, I envision working in a bookstore or boutique in a little town by the water ... maybe even the same place we just visited on vacation.

Or maybe even in the Christmas shop at Magic Kingdom at Disney World.

What do you dream of doing in your next phase of life?

August 25, 2021
Today I'm giving a presentation to a large REALTOR® group on how to balance real life and real estate. A topic I'm well known for and have spoken on many times before.

The total irony of it is that the past handful of days have been extremely difficult. Overwhelming. In tears. Feeling insurmountable.

It doesn't matter how great your systems are, or how terrific things look on the outside, everyone has seasons that are just too much.

The answer?

Ask for help. The specific help that you need. Even if others try to shame you for it.

Be quiet, get still when you need to.

Give others room, space and grace. A time will come when you will need it too.

Here's to friends that get it, and love and support you no matter what.

Here's to taking the time you need, venting it out, and feeling better as a result.

Here's to a new day, and a chance to get it just a little more right, and to do it just a little more better.

September 20, 2021

Monday. There are 5000 things on my calendar and to do list for this week. And the next. And who am I kidding, the week after that too.

I've been making myself a little extra crazy lately with decisions. Which doctor for my next procedure? (Number 10, if you've lost count. I sure haven't.) Which reconstruction method this go round? The "recommended" one is quite intense, multi-phases, lengthy (very lengthy) recovery. I'm most certain I don't have the energy, the stamina, or the mental fortitude for that right now (maybe not ever). The other option has a higher rate of future issues thanks to my radiation (the gift that keeps on giving).

Did I mention all the decisions?

Trying to pick paint colors and bath fixtures and flooring and tile and a million other things for some long overdue home projects.

Starting the annual debate (and then planning) process for new products and services and updates for our team for the new year.

So.Many.Things.

Too many decisions and I start to become overwhelmed and paralyzed and just won't make any at all. That was me last week.

This week I'm ticking them off the list one at a time. Refusing the urge to change things just for the sake of changing. Listening to myself (and my body) over the "experts".

Monday. I'm ready, here we go …

September 27, 2021

Did you know that today is National Family Day?! Sure is, according to my "National Day" calendar, a fun Amazon purchase which always provides for a lot of social media inspiration.

Since today is National Family Day, I thought I would introduce you to mine!

My husband Josh is a career firefighter with over two decades of service. We've been married for 19 years, and while we have known each other since we were children, we consider when we met to be at the firehouse when I was taking EMT classes, and he gave me a tour of the ambulances.

My oldest son Ben is a senior in high school. I'm still not sure how that happened, yet here we are. He made the courageous switch his freshman year right before spring sports tryouts from baseball to lacrosse (he'd never played before) and the rest, as they say is history. It's all lacrosse, all the time over here, and he is actively engaged in opportunities to play at the collegiate level. We affectionately call him the "team mom" as he is constantly recruiting new players to his high school team, buying equipment for other kids and holding "clinics".

Ryan is our classic middle child who gets along with everyone. He loves to have fun, and while he is a talented baseball pitcher, he also plays basketball in the winter, and his brother converted him to lacrosse in the spring. They needed a goalie for the Varsity team, and Ryan stepped up with probably more than a little coercion from his brother. He's a noticer with a big, kind heart.

Our youngest is Tyler, who happily turned 12 recently. He is an atypical learner who just doesn't like to do things like everybody else. Moving from public school to then private school, to now a homeschooler attending a center for self-directed education has been a game changer for him. He is passionate about what he loves, incredibly creative, and throws around $10 words better than most 40-year-olds.

Our house is loud and messy, and usually a bit chaotic. We love our 2 old dogs, Annabell and Abigail, and our 3 crazy cats, Thor, Loki and Hela (can you tell we are Marvel fans?).

Tell me about your family! (Seriously, tell me! Message me on Instagram, I'm @karen.w.cooper)

October 4, 2021

I'm so excited to introduce you to the Empowering Women in Real Estate Inner Circle!

Our Empower Coaching group is getting a major glow up, and I can't wait to share more. We will now be your one stop shop for what you really need to grow your business ... marketing, direction, mentorship, community, and a (coming soon) top notch referral network!

As we migrate this month over to our brand-new educational platform website (which will make implementing and engaging with our content so much easier than ever before!), you can lock-in pre-launch pricing at just $79 per month ... less than $1000 annually for a program that can earn you TENS

OF THOUSANDS of dollars! Just like always, there are no contracts or long-term commitments ... cancel any time, no hard feelings!

I hope to see you in the Inner Circle! You can register on our website, EmpoweringWomenInRealEstate.com, click on "Inner Circle".

October 5, 2021

Can you believe that we are now in the final quarter of the year? When's the last time you checked in with your goals? If it was back in January when you set them, you're not alone.

That was me for many years. I'd start the year with fabulous intentions, excited about my goals, then real life would take over and the next thing you know the year is up and I'm realizing all the things I wanted to do that never even ended up on my radar screen.

This is why we do quarterly reviews with my team and with our EWRE Inner Circle Members (our review is coming up on Thursday!). It's a chance to stop, reflect, review, and then set a point of focus moving forward.

I'm also a big fan of the Powersheets Goal Planner by CultivateWhatMatters.com. I've used this goal planner for years, and not only does it have me looking at and reviewing my goals quarterly, but also breaking them down into daily, weekly and monthly action items as well. It has truly been a game changer for me!

What will your focus be for 4th quarter?

October 11, 2021

October is breast cancer awareness month.

As a "survivor" of breast cancer (or technically in my case, a cancer of the breast), I have mixed feelings about it all. Three years ago, today I had my first mastectomy for a stubborn recurrent phyllodes tumor.

On October 30, 2020 I had my second mastectomy when it came back again. I'm currently gearing up for surgery #10 as I make plans for reconstruction to bring this chapter to a close. Though thanks to my 30 radiation treatments earlier this year, that is much more complicated than usual.

I've heard Les Brown say before, "if you do what is easy your life will be hard, if you do what is hard your life will be easy". After that first mastectomy at my post op my surgeon said that in one spot she didn't get clear margins, and she could go back and remove more skin and tissue now or we could wait and see.

I opted for wait and see. I was exhausted, emotionally and physically, there was no way I could face another surgery right then ... but oh how I wish I had. If I had done it then, or a few months later, or when my first reconstruction was done perhaps, I wouldn't have gone through another recurrence. And another mastectomy. And then an excruciatingly painful liver biopsy (long story, all is well). And then radiation treatments. And now trying to figure out which of the reconstruction options are right for me right now, when none of them are great.

Long story, but here's the point ... advocate for YOURSELF. Listen to how YOU feel. ASK QUESTIONS. Then ask more. And then more again. You'll have to call and email doctor's offices repeatedly, and chase people down. It will be exhausting and frustrating and hard, but it is infinitely easier than the alternative.

October 14, 2021

"Do it with no expectations and watch God blow your mind" -Paraphrased from Tabitha Brown (her new book is AMAZING, btw!)

Seven years ago, when I founded the Empowering Women in Real Estate community I had no expectations. My goal was to find connection amongst like-minded women in the real estate industry, and for sure God has blown my mind!

We are now not just a national, but INTERNATIONAL group, with nearly 30,000 members.

Our podcast has over 55,000 downloads and will air it's hundredth episode later this month.

We've had meet ups in many cities across the US and are moving into larger scale events (stay tuned 2022!).

And now our Inner Circle group coaching program is teaching women (and a few brave men!) how to build strong, successful, consistent businesses by turning their small monthly investment into tens of thousands of dollars in annual revenue.

Seriously, mind blown. And we're just getting started.

October 25, 2021

Monday! Hefty mix this week of family things ...

-Eye appointments for 4 of us
-Hosting pumpkin carving party at my son's self-directed education center
-Driver's permit test for middle kid
-Field trip for youngest kid
-Last 2 baseball games of the season
-Fall lacrosse championship game
-Another kid doctor's appointment
-Family Meeting with center leaders

And about 12 other things including a birthday, pumpkin carving, aligning our schedules (and the sun, moon and stars) to get to a pumpkin patch, hippo therapy (horseback riding) for my youngest, and more.

And work things …

-Onboarding new team members
-Team photo shoot and lunch
-Last session of Pathway to Mastery and celebration lunch
-Strategy session with my coach
-Celebrating the 100th episode of Empowering Women in Real Estate - The Podcast
-Putting the finishing touches on the Empowering Women in Real Estate Inner Circle launch
-More 2022 marketing & services work
-Recording November podcast episodes
-Plan of the Week for November
-Write/prep/design/schedule November posts and newsletter
-Record November Weekly Quick Lessons and Review/Goal Setting session for the Inner Circle

Plus, a good 5+ meetings.

That silly "balance" thing we are all looking for ... what a myth. We are all already doing it ladies. Some days and weeks better than others, sure, but we're doing it. Ever wonder why you're tired, and your body aches, and all you want to do is sleep? This is why.

Now, where to buy 12 pumpkins this morning for this afternoon's party???

October 26, 2021
I had an interesting conversation with a friend recently about the law of attraction ... particularly as it relates to money.

Have you ever noticed, often in our industry, often in this group, folks will post looking for a particular service provider ... maybe a photographer or a stager ... and then specify that they are looking for someone inexpensive or cheap?

And then when it comes to payment for our services there will be frustration when our clients ask us for a discount or when the co-op commission is less than expected.

My friend said something I thought was very interesting ... when we devalue others, we devalue ourselves.

I'm certainly not suggesting that we overpay for products or services, but we can't expect to beat someone else up for their fee, or choose our vendor based solely on the fee, and then be upset when the same thing happens to us. What you put out into the world comes back to you. I've seen it happen over and over and over again.

November 23, 2021

Is your marketing style to "sprinkle"? You do a little something over here, try a little something over there, then mix in this new thing when you get a sales call for a bright new shiny object ... but you don't do anything consistently for any length of time.

Does this sound familiar?

It does to me, because this was me for a very long time.

Then I learned that much more important than sprinkling all over is consistency, and now my emphasis is on going deep.

Doing more and more of what works, expanding in depth more than anything else ... and in time moving out in width.

What is your marketing style?

2022

Milestones

8-23-2022 – Empowering Women in Real Estate® received a registered trademark from the United States Patent and Trademark Office

10-6-2022 – "Mastering the Juggle", the 2nd Annual Empowering Women in Real Estate® Conference

January 3, 2022

Happy New Year!

We were greeted with a winter wonderland here in Northern Virginia, a beautiful snow coming down, and schools are closed; looks like winter break for us is extended just a little bit.

2022 represents 20 years for me in real estate. TWENTY YEARS!

If you had told me when I started that one day I would be here ... 15+ years of personal sales (averaging 50-60 transactions per year), 2 ½ years as a managing broker, and now as a team leader of the 40+ phenomenal women that make up our Platinum Group Real Estate Team, I'm sure I would not have believed you!

It has been a crazy ride of some high highs, and some really (really) low lows. I've learned that consistency is key if you want a consistent business. Better to do a smaller number of prospecting activities each day/week and do them EVERY day/week than to do some big splashes every now and again.

Within my first few months of my career I got married, and by the end of my first full year in business I became the bread winner in my family (my husband is in the fire service), and before the end of year 2 my first of 3 sons was born.

Looking back, while I could have done without the hard years, I wouldn't change any of it. The lessons I've learned, the people I've met, the friendships and relationships I've built with colleagues and clients alike have truly been some of the greatest blessings in my life.

So, here's to celebrating 20 years in 2022 ... I'd say and to 20 more, but I'm not as young as I used to be! ☐

(Photo with my team member Yolanda Howard ... who started out as one of my clients from my first few years in business! We were cheesing hard in this photo as she was off to her very first settlement!)

January 6, 2022

Part of my morning routine includes a reading a devotional and some journaling.

This year the devotional I am reading each day is, "Live in Grace, Walk in Love" by Bob Goff, and I was really struck by this part from my reading this week ...

"Fail trying. Don't fail watching."

It reminded me of all the years that my boys played baseball. When it was their turn up to bat, if they were going to strike out, they wanted to strike out swinging the bat trying to hit the ball ... not strike out looking at the ball.

Failure is inevitable and a part of life. There are things that you will try that won't work. There are listings appointments that you will go on when you will not be chosen. There are offers that you will write that your buyers won't win.

There are also many times that you will succeed at that new thing you try. You will win the listing. Your offer will be accepted.

The only way you'll know which outcome you'll get is to try.

Me, I'm always going to go down swinging. Better to try and fail (and learn ways to succeed next time) than to be on the sidelines watching life pass you by.

January 10, 2022

This, right now, as I am writing to you is my favorite time of day.

The house is quiet, it's still dark outside, it's just me and the snoring dogs as I sip my coffee from under a blanket in my favorite chair.

The day is so full of possibility. My mind is never as clear as it is during this first hour or so. The phone isn't ringing, the text messages aren't coming in, I don't feel pressured to check my email.

I've become so addicted to this feeling, this time of day, that over the years I have gotten up earlier and earlier (5:30 am today) just so that I could extend this time for as long as possible.

In about an hour or so from now, my house will start to buzz with activity. Teenager's alarm clocks will go off ... and continue to go off, usually until I yell upstairs or go up there. There will be binging and bonging and banging and all sorts of noise as they start getting ready for the day.

As the sun comes up and the activity outside becomes more apparent ... cars driving by, neighbors walking or jogging, the local deer herd making their morning jaunt back into the thick woods across the street those snoring dogs suddenly hear and see everything, which means they bark at everything. Seemingly even just when the wind blows.

At 8 am I'll need to wake up the youngest to give him his medicine, and hope that he will go back to sleep for at least 20 minutes so I can get a jumpstart on getting myself ready.

It's usually around this time that the phone starts. Maybe a call, usually a text. I try to keep myself in the "zone" by listening to a book on Audible or a podcast while I'm getting ready in a desperate attempt to hold on to the peace and clarity. Some days it works, most days it doesn't.

'Tis but a season. Next year at this time there will be 1 less teenager in the house and his unanswered alarm will no doubt be annoying his college roommate instead.

So, for now, I'll write to you, sip my coffee, and enjoy the quiet.

January 11, 2022

Yesterday I was listening to the Empire Building podcast, and they were talking about disappointment. It reminded me of an experience I had last year.

My family has lived in our home for close to 18 years (our home is 22 years old). For many years, there have been things we haven't loved about it. One example … our master bedroom had never been painted … the only room in the house that had never been addressed, it had been builder grade white literally forever.

From time to time, we would do little projects (granite counters, paint a room) and big projects (in ground pool, replace fencing), but like many homes, as time goes on there is more and more to do. There were years that there was literally no money to do anything, and there were years that the money was there, but my energy wasn't, and the kids were young and destroying things anyway and so projects would get pushed.

For years I've thought what a relief it will be when "x" is done. How happy I will be when "y" is finished". I won't be embarrassed for someone to come in and see my dinged-up paint in the stairwell from the kids. On and on.

And so finally, late summer last year we hired a contractor to tackle the projects. One project turned into another, and then another, and before we knew it there was 3 months of construction. A full remodel for 3 bathrooms, replacing floor tile throughout the kitchen and laundry areas, painting the inside, painting the porches and metal roofs outside. On and on.

I couldn't wait for it to be finished. I looked forward with anticipation to completion and the day I could get up and start my routine without worry of interruption from contractors or losing access to certain rooms. I thought about how happy and relieved I would feel.

And then it was done ... JOY! Except, it wasn't. I felt ... nothing.

Talk about disappointment. I was so grateful to have been able to have these projects done (finally!), and I am happy with how things look and function, but that thrill I thought I would feel just isn't there.

It was a reminder to me (again) that true happiness and contentment isn't found in people, places or things ... and if it is, it is sure to be fleeting. When you are in a season of struggle (and we are deep in one right now), those feelings of happiness and contentment can be especially elusive. I've learned that when I am in that time of struggle, that is when I am most likely to try to look outside myself for what I need to ease the pain ... and that is when I am most likely to be disappointed.

Are you in a season of struggle? Feeling beat up by a challenging market? Been let down by a family member, friend or client?

You're not alone. Reach out, tell someone ... heck, message me if it feels easier than trying to explain it all to someone you love. Take a walk, get some fresh air. Take some deep breaths, pray, write about your feelings or write down the good things that have happened in your day. These are the best ways I have found to release some of the heaviness and to begin to embrace the season. Once you do, then you'll start to feel the happiness and contentment creep back in.

(Photo of my cat Loki enjoying my new bathroom shortly before it was completed.)

January 13, 2022

Early in December I had an emergency situation arise with my dad. He's 83, lives alone, has been extremely independent and healthy, but over the past 6 months or so we've started to see a lot more confusion and cognitive decline.

Then, this situation happens, and it has to be addressed immediately. I cleared my day, spent the majority of it on the phone, making calls, scheduling in-home assessments, making connections, and within just a few days that action produced a result that we needed (some part-time, in-home care) that provided relief.

Then I did what I know not to do, and I took my eye off the ball. I knew what I needed to do, continue with the action and the calls so we would be prepared to move into the next higher level of care (which was inevitable), but things seemed okay, so I kept putting off those important to dos. Life got in the way. A vacation, the holidays, work, illness. Not to mention the task itself isn't exactly one that I was excited to do. I can't tell you how many times I moved the task "Call Nursing Home" from day to day and week to week in my planner.

Then it happened again yesterday. Emergency. Must be dealt with now. Day cleared. Lots of calls, lots of action, and now today we have another assessment for him to get him the next higher level of care that he needs.

If only I'd kept on top of it, stayed in action, kept chipping away at this monumental problem I could have made continual, gradual progress and avoided some of this roller coaster.

We do this in our businesses too, you know. (You knew this was coming.)

Emergency! You have no business, the phone isn't ringing, your pipeline is anemic, so you get into action. Calls, notes, coffees, open houses, go, go, go, and it works. Relief!

Then you get so busy with life and work. You're serving your clients, everything seems great, so you put off what you know you need to do. The calls, the notes, the pop bys, the coffees, all of those prospecting and marketing activities that got you the business in the first place.

A couple months go by, and then, emergency! Again! Those clients have found their new homes, are under contract or have gone to settlement and you realize that you have nothing on the horizon. You've got your bills covered for this month, but what about the next?

So off you go again, action, action, action, calls, calls, calls, on and on and on, until the relief comes. This is the real estate roller coaster.

I've had enough of it, how about you? Let's get off.

(Photo of my cute Dad from a few years ago when I had listed the house next door to him and he wanted a photo with my sign, because let's face it, he's always been my biggest fan.)

Lawrence E. Wenner, Sr. 9-22-1938 – 1-30-2022

January 18, 2022

Last night at 9 pm as I was sitting at the kitchen table with my 12-year-old with unique needs while he was having an absolute meltdown, I couldn't help but start to cry too.

His fit started with a Scrabble game, and apparently, I threw gasoline on the fire when I had the audacity to put an empty fruit snacks box in the recycle bin (which by the end, he pulled out, reassembled and taped back together).

Mine started 6 months ago. Maybe a year. Probably 2. Who even knows anymore. It's been so long in this state of what feels like a continual loop of bullshit I've completely lost track of time.

But today, like every day, I'll plaster a smile on my face and keep going. I'll continue providing good care and service to my clients, my team, our Inner Circle members. I'll record podcast episodes on how to grow your business in between meeting the appliance repair guy and taking care of my 2 oldest that are still recovering from having their wisdom teeth cut out on Friday.

I'll be hobbling around on my stupid banged up knee (still) while I pack up my dad's things today, mostly in secret and in a hurry while my aunt gets him to the doctor for his pre-admission exam (we don't want to upset him further by watching this happen), and then tomorrow I'll be doing more of the same as I meet the movers and set up his new room at the nursing home … only we can't call it that because when he does have his moments of being lucid he is very clear that he doesn't want to "hang around with old people".

Is this just what midlife is? Just when you think you have something squared away and settled, something else pops up in its place. Maybe even two things.

But we keep going. There isn't a woman that I know that sits down and gives up, no matter what life continues to throw at her. It's just what we do. Although sometimes I wish we didn't have to.

January 20, 2022
Yesterday's move for my dad was a success, his room turned out super cute and cozy … as a friend said, you would think I did this for a living.

I was assisted by my preferred movers who did an absolutely incredible job and had us in and out in a jiffy. It was a reminder again that having close relationships with your preferred vendors is a must. Not only will they be there for your clients, but they will also be there for you too.

Things started off swimmingly, when I left dad had joined the other residents and was playing bingo, but within a few hours started going a bit downhill. Several phone calls throughout the evening and after midnight, each more confused than the next. To be expected … being in a new environment only adds to the confusion that was already there. I can imagine there will be more of this over the coming days as he settles in.

A funny story from yesterday's adventure … I was unpacking everything, and a gentleman came in to hook up my dad's TV. He noticed that there was some debris on the floor from the moving in and out and so he also went to get a vacuum and cleaned it up. I was attempting to make idle chitchat (not my strong suit) and said something to the effect of he must be the resident handyman extraordinaire. (My mother-in-law had been at this same place 2 years ago and I remember being helped by their in-house person.)

Turns out he was one of the new owners of the facility. Open mouth, insert foot. Oops.

January 24, 2022
This meme is pretty much how things work in my house.

I'm long past the phase of kids following me everywhere I go, now it's the dogs (or cats) following me around. It seems like at some point during the majority of our Empowering Women in Real Estate - The Podcast episodes you will either hear a dog barking (or more likely, snoring) or a cat meowing.

I call them my entourage. Heading up to the office? There is a trail of four-legged friends following behind.

Truth be told, they are some of my favorite co-workers.

> Me: *getting off the couch*
> I'll be right back.
>
> My Dog: I would really feel more comfortable if we went together.

January 25, 2022
Gradually, then all at once.

When you are gaining weight, it starts small, almost undetectable, then suddenly bam! Your clothes don't fit.

It's the same when you're losing. The lost weight at first seems so gradual that nothing is happening, then suddenly everyone notices.

Gradually, then all at once.

This is how it's happened with my dad. Over the past many months, really over a year, the changes in his cognitive state have been so gradual that you often second guess yourself that there is a problem. A little confusion here, some messed up words there, then all of a sudden emergency! And he requires round the clock care.

Gradually, then all at once.

We see this in our businesses too. You are working so hard. Writing your notes. Following up. Mailing postcards, posting on social media, open houses, pop bys, all the things. The progress is often so small that it feels like nothing is happening, nothing is working, and you go in search of the shiny object that will solve your prospecting woes.

Then suddenly, eureka! Calls come in out of nowhere. First one, then more. And before you know it your work has paid off and your pipeline is full.

(This works in the reverse too, when you stop engaging with your business).

Gradually, then all at once. Stay the course.

January 27, 2022

One of my favorite blogs to read and follow is "Modern Mrs. Darcy" (she writes a lot about books, one of my favorite things), and from time to time she does a post about "what's saving your life".

The idea being that when things are difficult, or it's a tough season (literally or figuratively ... cold and dark winters are hard for many people), what are the things that lift you up, bring you joy, "save your life" when things otherwise feel hard.

What's saving my life right now ... the flexibility and ability to "hibernate". It's cold (9 degrees here this morning), my energy for lots of people and conversations is extremely low.

I find comfort in my home and my people, and that's a gift. Working from home, sleeping in a little bit, taking the day at my own pace feels right at the moment. I'm still easily working 10+ hours per day, right up until dinner is ready (thankful for a husband that cooks), but it feels more gentle being able to do it this way right now.

Beautiful tulips from a friend (Melody Visser), displayed in a pretty vase also from a friend (Sandy Fletcher), a scented candle burning (a gift last year from a friend), and my under-desk heater keeps my work space comfy and warm.

I'm a few feet away from a sofa, so when it all becomes too much and I need a quick 20-minute nap (that was yesterday at 6 pm, still crashed by 10) I can, and my kitchen is downstairs with all my favorite coffees, teas, food and snacks (including some from my friend Sarah Cho).

This routine is saving my life right now. Are you in a challenging season? What is saving your life?

February 17, 2022

In February of 2019, the owner of our brokerage challenged our team at their annual awards celebration to close 1 billion dollars in real estate sales volume.

I'm pretty sure that he was just kidding, but Vicky Noufal and I took it to heart. Have I mentioned that we can be a touch competitive with ourselves?

We started using hashtags like #pgbilliondollarchallenge and #pgbilliondollarimpact. For months and months (and months) we would report our progress at each team meeting with a pie chart. Green represented what we had accomplished and red was the amount yet to go. It seemed like forever with red being the majority of graph. It was a sweet, sweet day when our pie chart had more green than red, meaning we were halfway to our goal. From that point on we could feel the momentum, and everything seemed to fast forward.

We did it!!! From the inception of our team in mid 2015 to the end of December 2021, our team has closed over ONE BILLION DOLLARS in residential real estate! Not only did we take our brokerage's challenge to heart, but we completed it!

Even better, these billion dollars in real estate sales volume sold represents serving 2,543 families with their real estate needs ... AMAZING!

This has truly been a remarkable experience, and tonight our team will celebrate with our Billion Dollar CELEBRATION!

You can learn more about our amazing team on Instagram, @platinumgrouprealestate.

February 21, 2022
"The fears we don't face become our limits."

I think like most people, I have a range of things that I am afraid of, big and small. I'm afraid of driving up really steep hills or driveways and will adjust my route or where I go accordingly. I'm afraid of driving in snow. I'm afraid of water, especially when I can't see the bottom. I'm afraid of a tumor recurrence. I'm afraid of frogs.

I'm often afraid that by doing the things I need to/know I should do in my business that it will work, and then I will have even more to do, and how can I possibly have more to do when my plate is already over full? (Listen to episode 131 of Empowering Women in Real Estate – The Podcast for more on the fear of success)

What are you afraid of?

February 22, 2022
I'm doing a training today for my real estate team on "How to Nail the Listing Appointment". It's a talk I've done before at women's real estate conferences, always with a great response and feedback.

EMPOWERING WOMEN IN REAL ESTATE

In today's competitive environment, having strong listing appointment skills can make the difference between having a consistent business and struggling.

As you can see from the slide below, this topic is well within my wheelhouse. There was a time I could do my presentation in my sleep, and I earned the listing far more than I lost.

This is my specialty.

When it comes to your real estate business, what is your specialty?

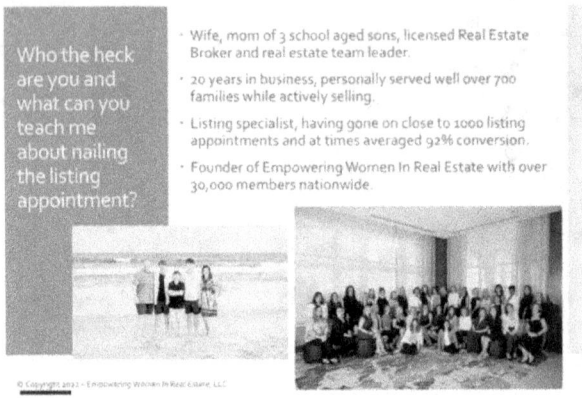

February 24, 2022

Five generations. These are the women that raised me. From left to right ...

My great-grandmother, Rilla Hickman. From the time I was a baby until she started showing more advanced signs of dementia when I was a teenager, Granny came to our house around 4:30 every morning to take care of my brother and I while my parents traveled to DC for work. Every single morning, she made me a pancake for breakfast. I spent most weekends with her too. She was strong, losing her husband when she was only 29 leaving her with 2 young children. She was a caretaker, taking care of many people and families. She was one of a few women that went butchering every fall with the men and brought home lots of yummy things (like scrapple, my fave!). She also loved to laugh. I remember her laugh more than anything.

My aunt, Shirley Sanbower. Also known as "Coo Coo". She has always been part sister, part friend, part 2nd mother to me. Always a bit wild and crazy, she loves to go out and have fun. If there is something going on, she wants to be in on it. She would bring boyfriends home and they would sit around the table and laugh and have a beer with Granny at night. When Granny was gone and Grandma was out with her boyfriend, I would spend weekend nights with her. She's the only one I have left.

My mom, Katherine Wenner. She struggled with depression and bi-polar disorder, but not many people knew it. Everyone around her saw her as a bright and positive person, someone easy to talk to. She would meet people everywhere she went. Once while at a surgical center waiting for a friend, she ended up meeting people in the waiting room that she talked to for hours. Then they were calling her later for updates. She was incredibly organized and detail oriented, which also meant that a lot of the responsibilities for others in the family fell onto her. She celebrated birthdays and holidays with a lot of emphasis, which made everything feel more special. She was the first woman in her family to graduate from high school.

My grandmother, Annabell Frye. We were the best of friends through my teens and twenties until her passing. She was TOUGH. No non-sense. Keeping her home was a job she took immense pride in. She worked and cleaned all day, with to do lists of what she wanted to accomplish. She had the mouth of a sailor and the appetite of a trucker. She could eat anyone under the table at dinner but was extremely disciplined all day as she went about her routine. The weekends were her time. After she was widowed, she dated and had a multiple decade relationship with a wonderful man that treated her like a queen (who was very much a grandfather to me). He would pick her up on Friday afternoon and we wouldn't see her again until Sunday night. They shopped and visited places and ate out and generally had a great time. She always dressed beautifully when she went out, with nary a hair out of place. I always thought I would have a daughter to name after her, but after 3 sons, it ended up being a dog instead. An extremely stubborn dog.

I see bits and pieces of each of them in me, and for that I am forever grateful.

May 5, 2022

Today is our anniversary! It was 7 years ago today that Vicky Noufal and I signed all of our "official" papers to formalize our partnership and our real estate team.

So much has happened since then. What started as just a few of us ... including Edyta Simmons and Jodi Hooper (still with us today) ... has now grown to an incredible team of 44 amazing women and moms. We've been through so much in these seven years. Heartbreaking losses and health challenges. Team member and role changes.

What hasn't changed is our commitment to each other and to our team, and our desire to accomplish big goals and to help our team members to do more business without sacrificing their quality of life. That is literally part of the core values in our team agreement.

We've learned so much, shared many laughs and a lot of tears. We've fussed at each other, been frustrated with each other, and at times the differences that have been so much of the magic of our relationship have seemed so vast like we are on two different planets. We've paid others before ourselves and worked more than we ever have in our entire careers. We've shouldered the burdens of each other's pain, and of the intense responsibility of building, managing and owning a team.

And yet, we'd do it all over again.

May 16, 2022
Good Morning Sunshines!

Just a reminder for you this morning ... your value is not determined by the way others treat you.

The client who has bought and sold 3 times in their life and is convinced that they know more about the market and strategy than you who has sold 10-100x that amount. You know the one.

The judge-y "friend" that makes "helpful" comments about how you parent or keep house or wonders aloud how that little "real estate thing" that you do is going. You know who I'm talking about.

The uppity agent in your office who has been around forever but doesn't dare share any of their advice or "secrets" for fear that they will lose their position at the top of the ladder. They'd rather look down than help pull you up too. You are picturing this person right now, aren't you?

It's a new day and a new week, what will you make of it?

May 17, 2022
Yesterday I had a bit of a surreal moment ... I had the opportunity to interview one of my mentors, Fabienne Fredrickson. You can listen to the interview on episode 159 of Empowering Women in Real Estate - The Podcast, as well as how it came about on episode 160.

I've been a fan and follower of Fabienne since first hearing her speak at the Virginia Women's Business Conference some 10 years ago. Having the opportunity to speak with her in this way was truly a pinch me moment.

One of my favorite quotes from Fabienne that I say a lot is "every level is a new devil". I see this over and over again in my life, my business, and in raising my children.

Just when you think you've progressed past one different phase or period and "made it" to the next, you may not have those old problems anymore, but you sure will have new ones.

I'll admit, I've let this fact about life get me down a bit that last year or so. It feels sometimes like the hits just keep coming. Every time I think I'm in the "clear" something new and different (and often harder) comes along to take its place.

It's kind of exhausting.

It's also life. I'm slowly figuring out that this is not going to change, but I can. My thoughts, my mindset, my approach. How I choose to handle (or not) the challenges that present themselves. Not everything is a problem to be solved. Some will solve themselves or other people will rise to solve them when I don't constantly try to swoop in and fix all.the.things.

Is this part of growing up? I think so. I'll be 50 next year, and honestly, I can't wait. My 40s have been a pill. A bitter, bitter pill. Amazing, wonderful highs, and traumatizing lows.

Those seeds that I've been planting for all of these past 20 years in my business have produced wonderful, consistent, abundant fruit. The seeds that I have been planting by way of relationships and pouring into other women in our industry for so long come back to support me and brighten my day when needed time and again.

The seeds I've planted in terms of not taking care of myself and pushing down the hard things, those are coming up too in the form of weeds that consistently need to be pulled. I'm learning to get the hang of that too.

May 26, 2022

Yesterday was not my best day. Anything that could go "wrong" in the morning, did.

My first task of the day was to call to schedule my annual chest CT. Don't let anyone fool you, "scanxiety" is absolutely real. Calling to make that appointment was enough to push me off the edge. Now to wait a little over a week until my appointment while I spiral with the "what ifs" over and over again. Then the agonizing wait after that feels like forever until my doctor calls with the results. There is no reason to think that the results will be anything other than clear, but as I have learned (and many of you have as well), that thing that comes out of nowhere and changes your life forever rarely comes with warning signs.

Add in tech challenges (I see you, mercury in retrograde) that caused much lost work (and time and effort) and lots of driving back and forth, back and forth when I was supposed to be doing my most focused work and I was just spent.

I needed a minute, so I took it, and took to the bed for a couple hours. Venting to a friend, sitting on the porch, a long conversation with Jackie Fields-Gleadall (she makes everything better) and I was good as new.

Well, not really good as new, but functioning and productive. I'll take that.

May 30, 2022

We see posts in this group all the time looking for lead sources, coaches (our Empowering Women in Real Estate Inner Circle is a good one, btw), tools and more that will lead to success.

Here's what I've come to know after 20 years in this business ...

Only you can make it happen.

There is no quick fix. There is no special tool. There is no CRM or website or product or coach who can make it happen for you.

Only you. You have to do the work, over and over and over again. Even when you find that great tool, product or coach, you still have to actually do the work and implement, or it won't work.

Surround yourself with like-minded people who build you up. (This group is a great place to start!)

Look at the success of others as proof that you can do it to, and learn all you can, all the time.

June 7, 2022

I had zero plans to knock anything off my 50 by 50 list so soon, but as I sat very anxiously in the radiology office late one afternoon last week, I couldn't help but notice that the woman sitting across from me was having a hard time too.

So, I took that moment to pray for her. I don't know why she was there, or what her struggle or discomfort was in that moment, but I knew that God did. I prayed that He would bring her peace and calm her spirit.

15 minutes later, I was back in the waiting room and having just had my own massive meltdown (constant crying on the CT table, sitting up just as they were about to start saying I couldn't do it ... I did ultimately go through with it and get my results, and they were clear, thank you God!), I saw a different

woman fussing at someone at the front desk. Clearly, she was frustrated and in tears over a physician's order gone wrong and an insurance issue.

I did not think kindly towards her, even though I had been in that position before and I know how badly it feels. In the moment I was too deep in my own pain to feel empathy towards her.

Hurt people hurt people.

A good lesson and reminder for me, and maybe for you.

One down, 49 to go.

June 16, 2022

Yesterday Vicky Noufal and I shared a brief text exchange with one of our team members who is currently away on vacation. She said that she was having an amazing time on her trip, and also extremely grateful to have a job that she is excited to come back to.

Have you ever felt that way before?

Happy and enjoying being away, but also excited to get back. That, my friends, is the sweet spot.

I'm happy to say that there have been many years of my career where I have felt this way. In fact, often, about halfway through my trip, it would be like a new creative level of my brain would kick in and I would be flooded with energy and ideas and I couldn't wait to get back and get to work again.

The truth is, I haven't felt that way in a while, but I'm working on getting back there.

The past few years have been a lot, both personally and professionally, and it zaps that creative energy and space like nothing else. Tell me I'm not the only one who has felt that way.

We don't have as much planned this summer in terms of fun family trips, for a variety of reasons ... mostly travel lacrosse tournaments, a chopped-up family beach trip losing both days and people during parts of the trip, surgery for me at the beginning of August, and then college move in for my oldest. When one more hurdle popped up last night, I tried to talk my husband into just canceling our trip all together and going in September with just our youngest (he's homeschooled, so we can go and do whenever). I didn't, and we aren't, but you know I'm a planner and this season is teaching me allllll the lessons on letting go and going with the flow. Both things I'm not good at.

One of my main goals for 2022 is to "embrace the season I'm in". 'Cause this season ladies, it's a doozy.

June 17, 2022
Today my oldest son graduated from high school! The days are long, but the years are short is an absolute understatement!

I was just under 2 years into my real estate career the day he was born, and now he's 18. I'll always be grateful that I was able to build my career while being a present mom, prioritizing volunteering in his classrooms, school activities, baseball and lacrosse games.

It was rarely easy. Racing from appointments to games, usually late. Sitting on the sidelines, talking on the phone to clients, or writing/ratifying contracts from the DotLoop app on my phone. Volunteering in the kindergarten classroom wearing a dress and heels because I had a listing appointment right after, trying not to get little fingerprints on me. Late nights and early mornings. Sneaking away from birthday parties to calm a difficult client on the phone. Hiding in the laundry room or my closet to take a call, while the kids screamed in another room.

There are many parts I wish I did better, and many more that I am proud of how I did them. Most he won't remember, but I will. Here's to a new chapter for him, and for me as his mom.

June 20, 2022

It's Monday! Who's ready for the week ahead? This week begins a hectic and busier than ever summer schedule for me. We are traveling 5 out of the next 6 weekends (some vacation, mostly travel lacrosse) … and if you know me, you know that I am not a great traveler.

All of that was supposed to be followed by my final reconstruction surgery the first week of August, but I got a call from my doctor's office on Friday that they need to reschedule. Finding a block of 10-14 days in my schedule to accommodate surgery and recovery is not easy in this phase of life (this will be my 10th procedure in this area/type … I find them both physically and MENTALLY exhausting and like to ensure I have the time I need to process and feel better), which means this is likely getting pushed to early December.

To say I am disappointed is an understatement. Keep in mind I've already been waiting a year plus for this to be done. This also further puts off additional imaging and a likely procedure for my knee, and while the discomfort is mostly mild, the swelling in my foot from it is not, and that affects my choice of summer shoes on a daily basis which does not make me happy.

This all too shall pass. I'm trying to soak up this summer with my boys, though I know it will pass in a flash.

So much talk and chatter about changes in my local market (we are in Northern Virginia, an hour-ish outside of Washington DC). The market shift we've been talking about for some time is here, which has many clients and agents alike making long term decisions with short term information … and largely out of fear.

Personally, my 20-year business has been through more than one market shift, and while yes things will change, I see this as a time of incredible opportunity … IF you stay focused and look for it. Aligning yourself with the right mentors is more important than ever.

How are you feeling about your business today?

June 29, 2022

Last night my husband and I went out to celebrate what we call our "special day". Twenty years ago on June 28, 2002, we were married by a justice of the peace in the living room of her small townhome in downtown Leesburg, Virginia. We didn't exchange rings, just vows. I wore a red skirt and top. I think he wore shorts. The plan was that it would be just the two of us, but he is an only child, and his mom was not about to miss it.

We kept the ceremony completely quiet, and only a very, very small number of family and friends and the State of Virginia knew. We actually had been planning for many months a beautiful wedding to take place in October of the same year, but something unexpected happened …

My real estate career. I bet you didn't see that coming.

I was getting laid off from my job in the pharmaceutical industry and was studying for my real estate exam. I had already committed to the team that I was going to join and was basically just waiting for my license and for the last day at my other job. Even though I was being kept on by one of the vendors we worked with to consult part-time on a project for a few months, my health benefits were going to run out.

A friend at the time suggested that we may want to move the wedding up. She'd been through some significant health challenges and thought that going without health benefits for 3 ½ months was pretty risky. That made sense to us, and so our special day came to be.

We still had that wedding on a beautiful fall day on October 12th, just as we had planned, and I forever get to joke that I married my husband for the health insurance.

You might say that this was the first instance of my real estate career controlling my life. The first, and definitely not the last. And you wonder why I'm such a big stickler about boundaries.

June 30, 2022

It's the last day of the month!!

Today I'm knocking 3 things off my 50 by 50 Joy List ....
-Read the "12 Week Year" (I will be implementing it 3rd quarter)
-Complete a full month of Yoga with Adriene
-Get a tattoo.

You KNOW I love a good checklist and even more so checking things off of it. My friend Edyta Simmons sent me this "font" sheet this morning for the word "breathe" that I am having tattooed on my left wrist/forearm. I'm really liking the script/cursive look, and the idea of making the "t" more exaggerated like a cross. My appointment is at 3 pm. I'll be sure to let you know how it goes.

Today is also the last day of the 2nd quarter, and we are in the throes of a Mid-Year Refresh with my team and all of the planning that goes into that. The market where we here has shifted, and it isn't done yet. That means lots of agents I know are worried. Their pipelines aren't as full, phones aren't ringing as much. And when people are scared or worried, there is a tendency to make long term decisions with short term information. I know. I've done this too.

Here's what I also know ... it's summer. In some markets (mine for sure) things slow a bit. Some of what you are feeling is that.

We are shifting into a "pros" market (my favorite!). Now is not the time to pull back and retreat. Now is when you lean in even more to your systems, your marketing, your community.

Does that mean your expenses may be higher and you are making less? Yes, yes it does. Especially at the start when everyone and everything is re-adjusting.

But, as we move further into this shift, those that have leaned in and doubled (even tripled) down on what works in their business will start to rise and their business will be even better by the end than it is now. I've seen it before. I've BEEN it before. And we will do it again.

I'm having the word "breathe" tattooed on my wrist because I need that reminder (there's a story), but right now, I think a lot of you do too.

Breathe. Do what you do. Do even more of it. Turn off the TV. Tune out the negative, fear-based chatter and lean into what you know works. Six months, a year from now you will be so glad you did.

July 7, 2022

I remember doing my first short sale.

It was late 2006, and I remember it so clearly because I was at the photo studio the day before Thanksgiving with my sister-in-law, my nephew and my 2 sons (the youngest wasn't born yet) having our annual holiday photos taken of the kids. I was wrangling a 2 ½ year old and an 8-month-old, trying to get them to smile, sweating through their outfit changes, helping them to be patient until it was their turn, when Wells Fargo called to negotiate the offer. Anyone who has ever done a short sale knows, getting the bank on the phone is not the easiest thing, so getting them to call back was not an option.

My client purchased the house in October 2005 (before we met, with another agent) and sold it in December 2006 for just under $100,000 less. I remember struggling with the listing. My client was in a difficult spot, the house had sat on the market for a few months at that point, and my colleague Jeanne Cooper suggested a short sale. While I had sold easily 100+ homes at that point, I had only been licensed for a little over 4 years and had never seen a shifting market. It was all new to me, but Jeanne had seen it before, and her advice was spot on.

When I first re-listed the property as a short sale it was one of the first of what would turn out to be many (hundreds) in our area. Other agents, who like me hadn't experienced this before, would call me asking what "short sale" and "third party approval" meant. That transaction and working with the bank was surprisingly quick, none of the others that I did were. I went on to do many, many short sales, some I negotiated myself, some I partnered with a short sale negotiator to handle. As time went on, they became more and more difficult.

Last week I was helping one of our team members who was going on a listing appointment for a family that had received a foreclosure notice for their home. She was concerned about the market value compared to what they owed, and just like Jeanne counseling me all those years ago, I was counseling her and we talked through the options for what to do when the bank has sent a foreclosure notice, and their options for a short sale.

While I don't think we will see as many of those now as we did back then, it reminded me of the importance of leaning into mentors. Those who've been there before, seen the market changes and fluctuations and know how to handle them. Every shift and adjustment is different, but the tools in our tool bag are often the same. What's old is new again, I suppose.

(Photo from that photo shoot back in 2006 … these two are now 18 and 16!)

July 8, 2022

I took a minute yesterday (okay, it was more like 90, lol) to sneak away from my desk to get a haircut and to get a pedicure. It's been a super busy week, next week is even more packed, then we are leaving for vacation, so I knew it was now or never.

Growing up in my little rural town of Lovettsville, Virginia the only things there besides farms and houses (and an elementary school) were a bank, a post office, a mini mart, and a High's. Anybody else know what a High's is? It's long since been replaced by a 711.

It was big news when Bonnie's Country Kitchen opened up! I remember my parents leaving me money so I could walk there for lunch once a week with my friends. My favorite song to play on the juke box was Whitney Houston's "Where Do Broken Hearts Go". Ah, the melancholy of pre-teen/teenage girl life.

Now in that same town we have a whole "town center", basically a strip of some commercial shops and restaurants, plus other amazing restaurants too, some that people come from miles around to visit. In that town center is my hair salon and my nail salon, right next door to each other. Let me tell you what a luxury it is to drive 10 minutes to these places, especially when the closest Target is 30 minutes away. My family's roots have been in this little town for literally nearly 300 years, back to the original settlers. There are several roads bearing the names of my ancestors.

Did I ever tell you that I was Miss Lovettsville? In 1992. It was a vvveerrryyy long time ago. I was on the Town Council too. At 19. The youngest elected official in our County.

Did I ever tell you that I am the #1 agent in Lovettsville? I have been the top agent by transactions for many, many years. And if not the top, then in the top 3 or 5.

I love my community. Supporting local businesses, the families and people here are a priority for me. It comes through in everything I do, including my marketing and how I stay connected. This is how I support my local community, and it in turn supports me. Do business smarter, not harder.

(Old photo of me being sworn in to the Lovettsville Town Council, and a parade appearance as Miss Lovettsville (I'm in the white gown), being driven by my dad in his old convertible!)

July 12, 2022

Yesterday my husband and I took our oldest son to his college orientation at Marymount University in Arlington, Virginia. This is a totally new experience for us. I earned my associates degree from a community college right out of high school, then went "back" to college while working full-time (paid for by my employer) to complete my BS degree in Business and Management. My husband was hired by the fire department not long after graduating from high school. Going "away" to college is not something we are used to.

When the students checked in for orientation, they were given name tags on cloth strings with their names and the name of their groups. It reminded me of the school bus shaped name tag with a similar cloth string that he wore the first few days of kindergarten. Remember those? The idea back then was so that others could help the little kindergartners to figure out which bus they needed to be on and which classroom they were in. The idea now was to help them to remember their group, where they belonged.

Do you remember where you belong? I'll tell you. You belong anywhere you damn please. You belong in this group, in this business, in this life.

You belong in rooms where big conversations are happening, with people who are smarter than you (my favorite kind of rooms). You belong at the table where decisions are being made, and your voice is being heard.

You belong. Don't forget. Even when it feels hard. Even when you don't think you measure up. All those people you see doing the things you aren't ... yet? They were once you too. Starting off unsure and uneasy. Struggling through the messy middle. Hitting roadblocks and stumbling over hurdles. I've yet to try or do anything in my life that didn't have components of all of the above.

You belong.

July 14, 2022

"She remembered who she was, and the game changed." These were my opening remarks at our team's Mid-Year Review & State of the Union on Tuesday.

It's been a challenging few months, a challenging couple years, has it not? When life gets extra hard ... personally, business-wise or a combination of the two ... you can feel beat down. I know I have.

You are feeling all of these external pressures literally squeezing the joy and the life out of you. External voices in media, from family, friends and colleagues telling you what you should be worried about, leading you to question that path that you are on that has worked so well for you.

You forget who you are.

I forgot. Over the past 2 years (maybe even longer than that) I've totally forgotten. When I had my last tumor recurrence in October 2020 it turned me upside down. In many ways the diagnosis for the recurrence before that one in late summer/early fall 2018 was worse, but I felt like in time I bounced back. But not this last one. More surgery, biopsy, tumor board meetings and recommendations, radiation. I powered through all.the.things. with a smile on my face. Or rather to say a fake smile on my face.

Inside I was withering away. Pile on top everything else that life throws at you, normal work and kid stressors, bigger struggles like an illness and death of a parent and I kept retreating further and further into the darkness. Do you want to know just how messed up I'd become? I've cried more for my cat that died than I did for my father who passed a few months before her. And my dad was (and will always be) one of the most important people in my life.

It's only been somewhat recently (thank you therapy and a patient husband and best friend/business partner) that I've come to realize just how not okay I was.

Instead of worry and fear and anxiety and hard things being a PART of my experience, it BECAME me. On the outside it looked like someone who could get all the things done, or maybe like someone who was short-tempered, aloof or withdrawn. The closer you are to me and my circle the more you felt it. Or maybe felt the wrath. From the outside looking it in all looked fine. Just fine. But my brain, my coping mechanisms, my central nervous system, my heart ... they were all shot. They were consumed.

I forgot who I am.

And then, I remembered. I'm not exactly sure when it started or why, but it was like a light being turned on by one of those dimmer switches. Gradually brighter at first, then all the way on.

I want you to remember too. Remembering is not only critical for you and your life, but it is also going to be important for your business as our markets continue to shift. No, this is not a crash, this is a shift. But some of you won't still be here on the other side. It's the Law of Equilibrium (read Gary Keller's book, "Shift"). I want you to be though.

You are strong. You are capable. You are more than the hard things happening to you and around you currently or have happened in the past. Do you want more hard? Then focus your energy on the negative voices and things that aren't quite right or don't measure up.

But if you want to break free and re-discover all that it is possible for you, you can. Remember who you are.

It's time to change the game. I'm ready to lead the charge.

July 15, 2022
#flashbackfriday To July 15, 2002!

Today marks 20 years in my real estate career! This is my very first business card. I remember so clearly heading to the mall to have that first headshot taken.

I'm honored and grateful to all those who have put their trust in me and supported me over the past 20 years and I look forward to the privilege of helping many more.

I'll always be eternally grateful to Sherry Wilson for taking a chance on me all those years ago.

July 15, 2022
This is Thor.

Thor loves treats.

He loves them so much that when he gets his bedtime treats, I have to quickly toss them in all directions so that I can run over and give his brother Loki his. Loki is a much slower eater, and Thor gobbles his down as fast as he can so he can run across the room to try to steal his brothers.

The other night as I watched him do his usual thing, I noticed something. When he jumped off the bed to go in search of his brother's treats, he left one of his behind.

The thing that he was rushing off in search of was right there in front of him. He couldn't see what he had, only what he thought someone else did.

Do you do this too?

I know I have.

The shiny object that promises to help you grow your business easier, faster, but distracts you from the good things that you are already growing.

And when you get distracted, you stop watering what's growing, and by the time you realize that the latest shiny new thing isn't right or working, what you had has started to wither.

Repeat, repeat, repeat.

What you need, what you are looking for, chances are you already have it. It is right in front of you, you just need to slow down and open your eyes to see it.

August 3, 2022

We got home from vacation on Saturday. We'd been home well less than 24 hours, when my husband said to me, "You're a different person on vacation".

This was a follow up to "Business Karen is back". And neither was meant as a compliment.

Ouch. It stung. Initially I felt hurt. Then I thought about it … and he was right. (Whatever you do, do NOT tell him I said that.)

When I am away from home, especially when we take our longer trips, I am a very different person. I feel relaxed. At ease. My anxiety level is way down. Each day is like a canvas before me to paint in any way I wish. The biggest worry is whether to go out, get takeout or stay in for dinner. My mind feels clear, problems feel easy to solve and I'm usually flowing with ideas.

But once I come home … the weight of my responsibilities hit me like a ton of bricks. Home, business, family, personal challenges to be dealt with. There is no escape here, and it feels daunting. I have to be "all business". There are things to do and to get done, many with deadlines. Commitments to be kept and prepared for, not to mention the day-to-day crap that if you don't keep up with it literally day to day it quickly spirals out of control and becomes an even bigger mess.

Can anyone else relate to what I'm saying? I bet you can. So, what's the answer? I'm not sure I know.

Actually, I do know. But the answers are typically things that I either don't prioritize or that I don't want to take time for because they feel hard too.

Spending time each day taking care of myself (sleep, eating well, yoga, taking a walk). I do enjoy my morning yoga practice, but some days I can barely finish 10 minutes ... my brain is swirling and so busy thinking about all I need to do that I end up bailing to get on with my day.

Asking for help is a big one ... also hard. Easier is just to power through and do the damn thing myself vs having a hard conversation with someone who isn't meeting expectations. Or just prioritizing getting the right help that I need in the first place. Taking the time to figure out exactly what it is that I need, finding and training that person. The problem is that all takes time and energy ... and when your time and energy are already depleted, it is extra hard to do the things that will help you in the long run because the short-term pain is too high.

And the vicious cycle continues. Round and round we go.

So, what to do? I'd like to say that today I will take action on some of this, but that won't be true. My to do list for today is long and full of important and time sensitive things that I have put off for too long.

I am going to give myself some grace though ... because Lord knows others aren't likely to give it to me. I am not in a season of life where Vacation Karen is a realistic way of life. Business Karen exists for a reason, and she's done a pretty damn fine job getting this far.

Maybe what I need to be striving for is something in the middle ... Zen Karen, Peaceful Karen, Soon-My-Kids-Will-Be-Back-In-School-And-Everything-Will-Be-Better Karen.

August 4, 2022

Earlier this week I had a follow up consultation with my longtime friend and client Melinda Rhoads, as now I am a client of hers and her healthcare practice for women at Rho Wellness.

A couple months ago we did a comprehensive series of blood and urine testing, taking samples at different times of day and under different conditions. We were finally sitting down together to review the results.

As we were looking at my cortisol ... or stress hormone ... levels, here is what I learned ...

I wake up with low to no stress hormone and within just a few hours it spikes dramatically, then crashes almost as dramatically. My stress hormones peak around 10-11 am each day, then crash around 1-3 pm, and as I think about my "patterns" of how I feel each day this couldn't be more accurate. (I shared these results with my business partner Vicky Noufal and after a little while she came back to me and said, "aren't our leader meetings usually around 11 am." Yes, yes, they are. lol)

My day always starts off strong with my morning routine, but as the morning creeps on the stress creeps in. Getting ready, getting kids out the door, rushing out almost always late, the phone starts ringing, the text messages and emails are pinging, and my first meetings or appointments of the day almost always start at 10 or 11 am. There is almost always a working lunch or lunch appointment.

After lunch each day, usually around 2 pm, like clockwork I start craving something sweet ... even though I'm not really a "sweets" person. It's my body looking for quick fuel to get through the rest of the day as by that time I have depleted everything I've got.

This explains why earlier this year after picking up my youngest from his education center and getting home I would crash and take a 20-minute nap almost every day before continuing my work day.

By evening I'm just done, and even doing chores around the house feel like too much. No wonder I never want to do anything in the evenings. After dinner I just want to sit on the porch or relax on the couch with an episode of our favorite show, just killing time until I can crawl into bed by 9:15 pm. Truth be told, most days I'd love it to be 8:15.

Fascinating stuff, right?

Sad, too. Nearly every woman I know in this industry is stressed beyond belief. Melinda works with many Realtors® and said that she sees similar patterns in their cortisol levels as well.

So, what can we do about it? We put together a plan that include vitamins, herbs and even some acupuncture (based on my total hormone picture, not just the stress hormones), and will revisit in 12 weeks to see how I'm feeling.

We talked about stress reduction strategies, the best times of day for me to exercise or do anything strenuous, and when I should be fitting in a snack with protein to ensure my body has enough fuel. I've learned more about my body, how it works and the impact of hormones in our 2 sessions than I have in all my years of seeing doctors … and you know I've seen a lot.

I'm excited to not only bring Melinda and her Stress Reduction Strategies to an upcoming training with my team next month, but she will also be our very first speaker of the day at our upcoming 2nd Annual Empowering Women in Real Estate Conference - Mastering the Juggle on October 6th!

We are kicking off the day … and our efforts to master the juggle … with health, because it is often last on our lists, if it even makes it there at all.

How are your stress levels these days?

August 9, 2022

A couple weeks ago my family had new photos taken while we were on vacation. The first photo below is from LAST year, 2021. The second photo is from this year, 2022.

I can't get over the changes in my middle son, Ryan (he's 16)! In the span of almost exactly 1 year he simultaneously shot up (he's over 6'2" now!) and thinned down. He looks like a completely different person!

You know who else is changing year to year?

You.

Me.

Even our businesses. Only not all changes are this dramatic and this visible. Recently I was re-reading Gary Keller's, "Shift", in preparation for my team's Mid-Year Refresh. In the book he talks about the shift between buyers' markets and sellers' markets, and how that in-between time of balance and stability is so fleeting that you often don't even notice it.

Our businesses are the same. You are always growing or regressing, there is very little time in between. Sure, you can grow to a point of great success and slow or stop all the activities that got you there and momentum will keep you going for a while, but momentum alone can only take you so far.

I saw this when I paused my sales business 10 years ago to become a managing broker. In the first year in that position the number of leads and referrals that I received reduced by 32%. A big number, but the number of leads were still a big number, so it still "felt" like a lot was happening, even though it was all sliding backwards. The following year those incoming leads and referrals reduced by 23%. Less of a regression, right? Nope. Less in terms of the number from the previous year, but if you look at where I started 2 years earlier my business was down a staggering 92%.

By the time I went back to the field 2 ½ years after I left, 2 ½ years after I withdrew, stopped engaging, slowed my "keeping in touch" to a paltry 4-5 times per year (if that), my business was essentially non-existent, and I had to start all over again.

Not all change is dramatic and visible. In fact, I would argue that most change isn't, especially not when you are in the middle of it. Thinking back over the past year the changes in my son didn't seem like much, it is only when seeing these photos ... a frozen moment in time ... that you can see how clearly just how much has changed.

Want to keep growing (or start!) in your business? Do the work. It is not the big splashy things that give you the most momentum or progress. It is the small, seemingly insignificant habits (read "Atomic Habits" by James Clear) and daily activities that add up to big, big things and can (and will) take you anywhere you want to go.

You just have to do it. Over and over again.

August 22, 2022
I've started this post to you three times now. The first time I wasn't feeling the message, so I set that story aside for another day. The second time was doing great until my husband asked me to check the date of something in my calendar, so I clicked away from Facebook to check, and when I came back my post was gone.

I suppose that is just how this morning is going to go, so I'm not going to force the issue.

Something similar happened yesterday too. Trying to get a vaccine booster, the pharmacy was understaffed, couldn't pull up my records (even though we've gone there for years), then my insurance wouldn't cover it (even though they just did for my kids 2 weeks ago). After about 45 minutes and issue after issue I said "enough" and left. Perhaps I wasn't *supposed* to have it yesterday for some reason.

I think sometimes when the universe puts hurdles in our way, it is for a reason. I've learned that it is often best to go with it and not push the issue. I remember hearing once that what first starts as whispers will eventually turn to screams if you don't pay attention.

This has happened in my life so many times. I don't always listen and will refuse to make the move or decision or adjustment until I become so desperately uncomfortable, the situation becomes so untenable that action is a requirement.

Oh, how much pain and drama I could save if I would just learn to listen to the whispers. Here's to learning to pay attention.

August 25, 2022
It is finally officially official …

Empowering Women in Real Estate is now Empowering Women in Real Estate®! Check out that registered trademark!

We've been building this community here, which in time has become a business, for more than 8 years.

We've been working on this trademark for more than 2 years.

Good things take time, and we are so excited for this one.

Now excuse me while we spend the next several days excitedly adding the ® to our name everywhere!

August 30, 2022

Did you watch the U.S. Open last night? I can tell from my feed this morning that many of you did. I'll admit I am not a big fan of tennis. But I am a big fan of Serena Williams (and her sister Venus).

When Serena announced her retirement from tennis earlier this year, she famously said that she wasn't retiring, she was "evolving" and I just love that so much. Shifting gears in your goals or your career isn't some sort of defeat or giving in or stepping back, it is (or should be) a natural progression. An evolving, not just of your business but of you as a person.

Last year I found Serena's autobiography "On the Line" at a used bookstore. It was a few years old at that point, but I absolutely loved it.

Here are a few of my takeaways ...

-There is a restorative, healing power to self-confidence. Amen to that. The conversations I have with women about imposter syndrome (had one just yesterday) are far too frequent. The number of times that I myself struggle with it are far too many.

-Words matter. Especially ones you say to yourself. Affirmations work. My friend and Platinum Group team member Leigh Anne Monk shared with our team last night a very real, very recent success she had with affirmations. Never doubt the power of the little things done consistently. Especially when they involve the words you say to yourself.

-"In times of stress and duress we start to resent what we love most." I'll just leave that one here. Raise your hand if you have experienced that. I'm totally raising both of mine right now.

Congratulations to Ms. Williams as she continues to evolve in her life, career and motherhood. She is truly one of the greatest of all time.

September 1, 2022

You knew it was coming ... September 1st. It's like my Super Bowl.

Never mind that it's still a high in the 80s most days. The mornings and evenings are cooler, the light is different, and you can feel fall in the air.

I'm thinking that after my Group Coaching Session with the Inner Circle this morning I just might spend part of the afternoon taking down summer and putting up my fall decorations.

Pumpkins and fall décor make me happy. Happy September 1st!

September 13, 2022

It's been 4 days since my knee surgery, and I am finally at my desk ... albeit sitting sideways so I can prop up my leg and ice my knee. My post procedure adrenaline has worn off (Am I the only one who has this?), and so for the past couple days I've felt pouty and quiet. I don't like not feeling well, and when I don't feel well, I can't think clearly, and when I can't think clearly everything feels overwhelming. And when I feel completely overwhelmed, I do ... nothing. Counter-intuitive, I know.

My planner is still on last week. I still haven't planned this week. I also have a sick kid which makes everything a little more complicated. But life goes on and I am back at my desk. Lots of work to do for our upcoming conference, approving signs and graphics, and editing our workbook.

I'm frustrated with myself for waiting this long to take care of this, but also super grateful to finally have it done (I tore my meniscus on both sides of my left knee ... while dancing. Last November. Oops.).

There are so many good things happening this fall ... fall lacrosse season for both of my older boys, our Empowering Women in Real Estate Conference on October 6th, a 20th anniversary getaway with my husband, attending the Lucketts Fall Market (it's on my 50 by 50 list!), hopefully participating in Walk 4 Mountains as a walker this year, not just a sponsor (a walk for breast cancer in my hometown), our team retreat in November and alllllll the planning for our 2023 Marketing & Services Debut for our Platinum Group Real Estate team and the EWRE® Inner Circle.

I'm looking forward to being able to fully participate in all these things without discomfort or limitations. What are you looking forward to in this season?

September 19, 2022

This gorgeous girl right here with Vicky Noufal and I is #roundhillrobin, aka Robin Gebhardt. Yesterday was Robin's 4-year anniversary of being a member of our Platinum Group Real Estate Team. She's a bright light of positive energy, full of ideas, and so focused ... she implements our plan nearly without fail. Even when at first it seemed like nothing was happening (you don't dig up the seeds as soon as you plan them), she trusted the process and did the work.

When she joined us 4 years ago, she was an experienced, good agent, closing $5M in annual sales volume (her best year ever). Since her time with us she has doubled, then tripled, now QUADRUPLED her business. She went from a respectable $5M in sales volume to having closed just shy of $20M in the past 12 months!

Robin, we love you so much. Your success is no surprise to us. Your kindness and care towards your clients and team members is top notch, and your positive energy makes our world a better place.

Here's to you, my friend!

September 22, 2022

I recently finished the book, "How Are You, Really?", by Jenna Kutcher, and there is a story she tells in the book (which I've also heard her share on her podcast and The Ed Mylett Show recently, both good listens) that I can't stop thinking about.

The story is about a Buddhist monk who is in New York City. The person who is guiding him says that they should take the subway to where they are going, that it will save 10 minutes.

Once they exit the subway, the monk sits down on the nearest bench. His guide says, "what are you doing?", and the monk says, "I'm enjoying the 10 minutes we saved".

You know I am all about efficiency, right? Doing all I can to squeeze everything possible out of every minute I have. I'm good at it.

I'm embarrassed to admit that what I haven't been good at lately is how I'm using all those minutes I save. Every minute saved gets put back in the work cycle to do more so efficiently that I get (or feels like I get) even more minutes. Repeat, repeat, repeat. I'm causing my own hamster wheel to spin even faster.

It's not often anymore that I use those minutes I've saved in a way that I can fully enjoy them. Yesterday I did, and it felt so good.

After dropping my son off at his educational center, I had 30 minutes to spare before I needed to head to physical therapy. Normally I would just go there and sit in the parking lot making work calls, responding to emails, maybe recording a podcast episode, or otherwise checking in.

Instead, I went to Lowes and enjoyed a little walk around the garden center, picking up some spring bulbs to be planted and a couple other things. It felt … refreshing. Efficient too, these were things I needed to get picked up, so I was using my time wisely, but it felt different.

When I arrived at physical therapy, I decided to tell the therapist that I only had 45 minutes for the day's session. I needed to be back for an online meeting, and I wanted to take the time to pick up a good lunch instead of hitting a drive thru. I'm learning to ask for what I need, and she was happy to oblige.

Instead of hitting a drive thru and racing back to my computer as fast as humanly possible, I stopped at Whole Foods instead. I didn't have time for a leisurely tour up and down the aisles, but I did grab a container of peaches that looked beautiful, milk (that was on the to do list), and picked up an assortment of foods from their hot bar to try for my lunch. I even grabbed a magazine to enjoy later. Only 15 minutes, but I left out of there feeling happy and free. Not my typical feeling these days.

How are you using all those minutes you save? Can you put them to work for YOU today, instead of you putting them back into your work?

September 26, 2022
Yesterday I was enjoying a slow Sunday morning by watching "slow living" videos on my iPad … at 1.25x speed.

I've been super intrigued lately by slow living/minimalism videos on YouTube, but I always watch them (and most anything else I watch) sped up.

Basically, I want to live more slowly and intentionally, and I want to get there faster.

Talk about an oxymoron.

Since starting physical therapy last week following my knee surgery, I've been trying to be really intentional about walking "correctly". I have some discomfort still in my knee and in my leg and it has been easier to sort of limp along, but of course then other things hurt (my hip, my calf) because I am compensating for my knee.

I realized that when I walk more purposefully, working to engage all the right muscles, not limping, while there is still some discomfort in my knee, it feels better overall.

The thing though is that I can't do that and walk fast. It takes energy and focus, and so I end up walking very slowly. Not cool for someone who has been a fast walker literally her entire life!

Don't we do this? We are so eager to get the results that we want, that we rush to get there. And it's often in that rushing that we make missteps or just miss the good lessons and good things along the way. I'm super guilty of this.

We do the work once, twice, a month or two, and want (expect) the results in our business right now. It doesn't work that way. Consistent, deliberate, and yes, often slow effort is what it takes.

The day you plant the seed is not the day you eat the fruit.

October 6, 2022

It's conference day!! Last night we welcomed our 15 VIP ticket holders from all over, some local to Northern Virginia, quite a few from West Virginia, two from New Jersey, and even one each from Florida and California!

Along with some of our sponsors, support team and top producers from my team, we enjoyed a beautiful dinner and even better conversation.

A topic that came up last night ... and the day before at another event ... was confidence. Specifically, women and confidence. We need it in our business, so much is outside our comfort zone, and how do we get it.

For me, it's 2 things ...

1) Confidence is like a muscle. The more you use it, the more it builds. You have to start by doing things that are uncomfortable to you, and the more you do them, the more that muscle builds and the easier they become.

2) You need a tribe to push you and cheer you on. Their support will help you to get over that initial hump to get going, and their belief in you will keep you going.

Today's event is a perfect of example of those two things at work.

Photo of Madi Harmon, our Program Manager for Empowering Women in Real Estate®, and her mom, Jeni Harmon, who planned our 2022 and 2023 conferences.

October 26, 2022

Yesterday I went to the fall family meeting for my son at his learning center. He has some special needs (don't we all really, when you think about) and the traditional educational models have not worked for him. Now he is home schooled and attends a self-directed learning center four days a week, and it has been absolutely transformative for him.

During the meeting yesterday, the entire point of the 45-minute session is to celebrate my son. His mentors at the center share highlights about Tyler, things they have observed about him, experiences and moments that they loved, ways that he has contributed to the community there. He gets to share his highlights too, and my husband and I share highlights from home as well. It is such a great experience. How often do we spend time "reviewing" others, talking about what they are doing wrong, where they need correction … and never just share what they do right? More thoughts on that one for another day.

One of Tyler's mentors shared that something she really appreciates about Tyler … and a big benefit that he brings to others in the community … is how clearly he expresses his boundaries. The community there is very open and accepting, and respectful of others and their feelings. An example they gave was during Minecraft class (lots of math happens in Minecraft!) some new members wanted to build together in the community realm which was different than how they have interacted before.

How many of us have issues when new people come in and want to change things up? And yet we don't express how we feel about that, our comfort level, etc. Yep, me too.

Tyler's mentor shared that he had no problem respectfully sharing his boundaries, what he felt comfortable with which she said was so important for a few reasons … 1) Tyler was able to express how he felt, what was important to him, so he could feel safe and comfortable; 2) By expressing his boundaries it was helpful to the others he was working with as they then knew and understood what to expect, the best ways to collaborate with him, and how that fit into what they were comfortable with, and 3) Clearly expressing his boundaries helped others to know that it was okay for them to have and express their boundaries as well.

You know where I'm going with this, right?

Do you set boundaries in your business? Most of us don't. I've come a long, long way over the years on this but still fall down from time to time.

We answer calls, texts, emails at all hours of the day and night. We jump up from the table in the middle of dinner with our families, we step away from our kid's birthday parties or other family events, we halfway cheer from the sidelines of games all to take what is almost always a non-urgent call from people that we are desperate to please and satisfy for fear that they will go work with someone else. (All of these above examples are things I've done. More than once.)

We allow our days to be scheduled to within an inch of our life. A block of "empty" space on the calendar … God forbid we use it for something for ourselves, "free" time or just time to think. If there is an empty box, we are eager to allow others to fill it … sometimes with good things, appointments that move our business forward and allow us to serve our clients well. Sometimes (lots of times) we fill it with appointments that serve someone else's agenda and needs without taking into account what we need.

Not checking and responding to emails at 9 pm is okay.
Not taking business calls in the middle of dinner is okay.
Not responding to text messages at 11 pm or 7 am is okay.

The number of things that will fall apart if it takes you an hour to respond is very, very few. Perhaps when we stop treating ourselves like a commodity our clients and the marketplace will too. The value that you bring to the table is so much more than your availability.

October 27, 2022

Yesterday I had my annual appointment with my breast surgeon for a mammogram on my "good" side and an exam on the other. Both were clear!! Thank you, God!

Two things that stood out to me from my conversation with her …

1) We were talking about the annual chest CT scans I've been having, which are also a source of tremendous anxiety (I had a panic attack this year, nearly refused the scan, tried to get off the table and cried the whole way through). She no longer feels that I need to have them done, and if I'm okay stopping them, she's okay with it. She said, "I don't want you carrying something you don't need to be carrying."

Right?! What are you carrying that you need to let go of? Resentments, past hurts. Worries, limiting beliefs. We carry them almost like a protective measure to not be hurt again, torturing ourselves with them again and again … but the truth is that they don't serve us, they only weigh us down and keep our arms (and hearts) so full that we aren't available for the goodness that is on its way to us.

2) I've been seeing this surgeon on and off since my early 20s thanks to my unique history. We were talking yesterday about what she has built. Literally from the first time I met her I can remember her talking about her vision for what she wanted to build for women under care for breast cancer. She wanted a place where you could go in for your screening/mammograms, then have the appointment with your provider right after. No more going home and worrying and waiting for the phone call, or (as I've had in my case more than once) having a terrifying appointment with the radiologist and then struggling to get your provider on the phone to get an appointment, make sense of it, and to develop a plan. It only took 25 years, but she did it. Now when I visit, after my mammogram a member of her staff takes me through the back door that connects her practice to the imaging center and right into an exam room to see her. It is an incredible relief and comfort.

I thought about our visit all day. How many times do we set a goal, develop a vision, and give up when it doesn't happen quickly? We love instant gratification (I do too), but often when it comes to the most important things, it just takes time.

Building a consistent business takes time. Getting your first client takes time. Growing from level to level in your business takes time. Consistent work and effort repeated again and again. It's what works. It's not sexy. It's not shiny. Heck, a lot of the time it isn't even fun. But it works. And the wait for what you develop, the relationships you will build, the life that you will create, will be worth it.

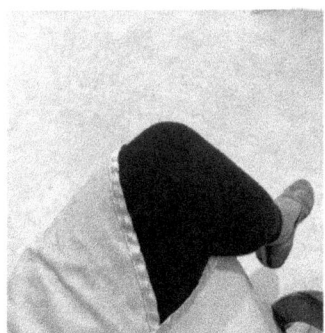

November 3, 2022

I heard a saying yesterday that really spoke to me …

"The top of one mountain is the base of the next."

As we go through life, we grow (I hope) through life. Just when you think you have it all figured out (the top of the mountain), the next moment reveals that you don't (the base of the next mountain).

Maybe you've felt on top of the world the past 2 years in your business, and now suddenly you're struggling to figure out where your next deal is coming from. A good reality check that I've heard shared is that we shouldn't be comparing our businesses to 2020 and 2021 … those years were an anomaly. You should be comparing them to 2019. As markets shift and adjust (which they do often, sometimes in more subtle ways than others), you need to be prepared to understand that what you thought you knew (top of the mountain) isn't the case anymore (base of the next). The way you manage that, how you align yourself, what you do now will determine if you will make it to the top of the next.

Sometimes life (or other people) will try to push you off the top of the mountain or even cheer when they think you are falling off. I find that is often in an effort to convince themselves of the accuracy of their own decisions. Someone has to be the villain in the story, and it's easier for them if they make it you.

Here's the thing … once you reach the top of the mountain, that resistance that you feel, the discomfort … you aren't sliding back down, you've just reached the base of the next.

Now you have a choice. Stand at the peak and try to convince those around you that you've reached the pinnacle.

Or you start to climb. I will always choose to climb.

> **BEING POSITIVE IN A NEGATIVE SITUATION IS NOT NAIVE. IT'S LEADERSHIP.**

November 14, 2022

Last week on a group text with my friends Vicky Noufal and Robin Gebhardt there was a conversation about our grandparents and the impact they had on us and our lives.

My grandmother Annabell was bold. Tough. She said what she meant and meant what she said. She was fiercely independent and incredibly stubborn.

(Vicky is nodding her head right now, realizing how much sense this all makes, lol.)

Educated only to the 7th grade, she was married and gave birth to my mother not long after turning 16. Widowed the year before I was born, she showed her love for her family by how she cared for and decorated their home and in the meals she prepared.

I remember the small scraps of paper with lists of food to buy (always tracking the sales) and lists of what to do (take down and wash the drapes, polish the floors). Her every day was filled with productivity.

She loved shopping and a good deal and took pride in her appearance and clothes. She was quick to tell you the sale price for her outfit when you complimented her. (This also sounds very familiar to my friends.)

She had a small, but tight, friend group, cursed like a sailor (but only around those she knew), and a quick and wicked sense of humor. She was all business (one of my kids literally just described me as that this weekend), but when she did laugh, she often laughed until she cried. (I do that too.)

While cleaning and cooking are not in my vocabulary, I very much demonstrate my love for my family in what I do and produce. The way I ensure they have what they need, and the fuss I make over the littlest of holidays to make small moments special.

I'm ridiculously independent and have worked hard to instill that in my children. I'm also horrifically stubborn. When I pick a hill, I'm prepared to die on it, right or wrong. There is no convincing me otherwise. That also means that I will make anything work, no matter what.

I give chance after chance after chance, forgive, tolerate and strive to make things work ... but once I'm done (applies to people, places and things), then there is no turning back. I also have no trouble saying the hard things. Some call that mean. I call it honest.

Growing up I didn't necessarily see that we are alike, but as an adult, her influence is everywhere on my life. And I am a better person for it.

November 16, 2022

Coming to you live from our team retreat at the beach! As per usual, my ride down with Jackie Fields-Gleadall and Vicky Noufal did not disappoint. We are known for getting into mischief on the way (mostly Vicky), and for laughing until we cry (mostly me).

Riding along, Vicky suddenly says, "oh, the gas light is on, and we have 19 miles to go"!!! And there were WAY MORE than 19 miles to go to our destination!

She hits the first exit, which seems a little sketchy and pulls into a 711 that was full of cars and people just standing around. We notice immediately that there is super loud music playing … to which Vicky says (also super loud), "it's a party" and puts our windows down.

Jackie and I put them back up, lol.

Then we notice that there is a legit DJ situation happening in the parking lot of the 711. On a random Tuesday afternoon in the middle of November.

Naturally Vicky is dancing while pumping gas, and Jackie and I can't get her in the car and out of there fast enough. There is a video. Not sure if she would be a fan of me sharing it, lol.

That's not the point of my story this morning. Also, on the way we took a picture of the temp settings on our respective sides of the car. Hers at 76.

Mine at 67. A true definition of our relationship ... and our co-working office battles.

As we were talking about life, business, goals and the future on our drive, Vicky said that like with our individual temperature settings, the "true" or "right" number is likely somewhere in the middle of our extremes.

So much of life is like that. We tend to operate in extremes. "My business is on fire right now." "My business is non-existent." Finding that happy middle ground of a strong, consistent flow of transactions month after month feels impossible to find.

But is it? I'm here to tell you that it is not. I enjoyed that consistent flow for well over a decade (after that pesky former market crash).

How did it happen? Consistently showing up. Day after day. Even when I didn't feel like it. Even when it felt extra hard. Even when I had 1000 other things to do.

Just like regulating our temperatures ebbs and flows, so does our emotions. And those emotions will make make everything easier or harder.

And that is where your habits come in. When you have good habits, strong habits, it is easier to keep going even when you don't feel like it.

My favorite books on this topic are "Atomic Habits" by James Clear (be sure to sign up for his email newsletter too!) and "The Slight Edge" by Jeff Olson.

What are your strongest habits?

November 23, 2022
Yesterday our Platinum Group Real Estate Team and I celebrated our 7th Thanksgiving "Reverse Pop By Event". We gave away 400 pies in two different locations.

For years we did this event at our very small office, and our amazing Support Team picked up the pies in multiple vans and cars. Over the years as our team (now 40!) and clients grew, the number of pies grew too.

This year we did two things that were a game changer for us … 1) We approached our preferred moving company about helping us to move the pies (we planned to pay) and they did so as a sponsorship for our event. HUGE! and 2) We rented hotel space for both of our locations. There was plenty of parking for our guests. We were able to spread out and sort the pies much more easily for our team members, and there was room for tables and seating for our guests who wanted to stay and chat or enjoy a bite to eat. The best part of that was limited clean up at the end … in years past a team member would stay after or come in late to clean up. Yesterday we just picked up our trash and any personal items, and we were done!

An added bonus … we had just a couple clients who ran super late and wouldn't make it before we closed up. We were able to leave their pies at the front desk to be picked up. Renting the hotel space for the afternoon was surprisingly economical and was made possible in part also to one of our event sponsors.

We love this event each year. It is relatively low cost and low fuss, for a big impact. Did you do a pie event his year? How did it go?

November 29, 2022
It's the most wonderful time of the year!

And also …

My plate is already over full with work (so much work) and kids and a partner who likes to spend time with me, and life and family stuff.

And now I am adding on top decorating, shopping, wrapping, writing, sending, giving. All good things that I love, but the other stuff on my plate doesn't intend to move over to make room.

So, I'm switching over from my regular everyday anxiety to my fancy Christmas anxiety, lol.

When I saw this quote yesterday, I had to share it immediately. Happy Holidays!

November 30, 2022

Late yesterday afternoon I was having a conversation with a friend, and she asked, "what keeps you going?" I stumbled through a very ungraceful answer of something like," I like to help people", but her question kept running through my head the rest of the day.

My fumbling answer was right, but didn't fully express what I meant.

Growing up, expectations for me were not high. I essentially needed to look cute and stay quiet. My opinions were not necessarily welcomed, and when offered not well received. Do the things, don't complain, take on other people's BS and clean up their mess. Repeat, repeat. I was to follow the line, not ask questions, and was taught by example (and sometimes words) that I needed to find happiness outside myself.

So, I did all that. I tried. I really, really did.

Then in the wee, early morning hours of a late September morning, the kind where the night is chilly, but the day is hot, I bore physical witness to a heartbreaking tragedy. I'd been an EMT for 5 years at that point. Run hundreds of calls and seen many (many) things, but this thing was too much. I still remember it in excruciating detail.

For a good 2 months I retreated and hid. I went to work, came home, and quite literally became afraid of the dark. Once the sun went down you weren't getting me out without a fight. And when I most needed support, I was let down. Really let down, for the millionth time. I finally realized that what I was taught was wrong. You can't find happiness outside yourself (though I do still try sometimes). Putting my feelings, my happiness, my everything in the hands of someone else to keep and protect is not the path to joy, it's the path to pain. When you don't respect yourself enough to give that love and care to yourself, you sure as hell can't expect someone else to.

In other words, I found my courage and I woke the F up. That was 25 years ago, and I've literally not been the same person since.

So, what keeps me going?

#1, proving to myself what I am capable of.

#2, proving to others what THEY are capable of.

What keeps you going?

December 1, 2022

It's time y'all. For 6+ months Vicky Noufal and I have been talking about #gamechanger and a bigger vision and reminding our team members (and ourselves) who they are.

During that time, we've hit dead ends, been disappointed, and tried to make round pegs fit in square holes in our pursuit of the future. We've also learned a lot. A WHOLE lot. About people, places and things. Some we already knew and was a blessing to have in the open. Some we had an inkling about and were sad to have confirmed. Others were a blindside. Those are the ones that hurt the most, of course. But those are also the ones that are the best teachers.

Four weeks ago today, the path to the future came into view. Since that time, it has become crystal clear. Many already know. Some think they know. Later today all will know.

Life is a strange and wonderful ride, and I'm so grateful for those who are on it with me. The future is here, and I'm so excited for this next chapter.

December 1, 2022

Making a move is a big deal.

It's a big deal for our real estate clients.

… and it's a big deal for our real estate team!

Vicky and I are excited to announce that the Platinum Group Real Estate team has moved to Real Brokerage!

When you've been in business as long as we have (nearly 40 years combined!) and sold as many homes as our team has (thousands and thousands!), it takes a lot to get excited about something ... and THIS we are excited about!

Through this opportunity we will be able to not only grow our team and serve our clients, but we can also grow our organization NATIONWIDE ... and even internationally. This is the perfect complement to our Empowering Women in Real Estate® community.

Thank you to Pearson Smith Realty for a wonderful 7 ½ years.

Here's to the next 7+ ... we can't wait to share with you all the wonderful ways that Real Brokerage will allow us to serve our clients at an even higher level and will help our team members to grow an even better business, and to provide for their family in an even bigger way.

December 7, 2022

On my drive home from work yesterday, I came upon a traffic stop. There is utility work happening on this one stretch of road I travel each day that has been going on for a week or so. The road is down to one lane for a certain part, and so they have flaggers at each end, alternating stopping and directing traffic through.

As I was stopped near the first flagger waiting for the traffic to come through, I noticed something. With every car that came by they were smiling and waving at the flagger, and he was enthusiastically waving, pointing and smiling at them too.

When it was my turn to go, he gallantly gestured for me to go through with a huge smile on his face and a wave. I couldn't help but smile and wave too. Then when I got to the flagger at the other end she was enthusiastically smiling and waving too. So of course I followed suit.

This simple interaction, which lasted just seconds, literally brightened my afternoon, lifted my energy, and made what was normally the most dreaded part of my commute on what is already an unpleasant road to travel … fun!

All because 2 people decided to add joy into their work, to make their time in front of others count.

Imagine if we did this as a practice in our work? How much more enjoyable would each day be? How thrilled would our clients be to work with us … and to tell their friends, family, neighbors and colleagues to work with us too?

It is truly the little things that make the difference. The attitude you portray, the energy you bring, it has more impact that you know.

December 16, 2022

I've spent this entire week, mostly in bed, recovering. I haven't talked to you all week, so this will probably be an extra-long one. I had actually planned for this. My work was done, no appointments scheduled. My home is ready for the holidays.

Only I wasn't recovering for the reason I thought. I was supposed to have surgery on Tuesday (the next step in reconstruction from my last mastectomy over 2 years ago). I've been looking forward to getting this done for SO LONG, I'm ready to slam the door on this chapter. Trying to schedule around work and events and family this year has been near impossible, and this was the perfect window.

But life had other plans. I ended up with a super nasty respiratory virus instead. It started with one of my sons 2 weeks ago and is currently making its rounds through our household. At first, we thought it would just be a cold, so when my symptoms started my doctor held another surgery date for next week just in case. It's been much more than a cold though, and I'm not cleared for next week either. So, I'll be looking forward to January 24th instead!

Here's the funny thing … my top goal this year, literally the one I put the most emphasis on, is "embrace the season you are in". I came into 2022 with apprehension, knowing this would be a year of transitions ... only far more transitions that I ever could have imagined.

Exactly one year ago we were in crisis with my dad, his health and dementia. It was a rapidly escalating situation, filling immediate gaps with home health care aids until we could find and make arrangements for him. Which I did in January of this year. Remember that story I did on my Instagram of his beautiful room set up for him? He died a week and a half later.

2022 was also a year of lasts and firsts for my first born. His last high school everything, graduating and heading off to college. My middle son would be the next driver in our home. My youngest would turn 13.

As someone who likes to control the things the world consistently shows me I can't, embracing these big changes ... and the feelings that went along with them ... I knew I needed to focus here.

The universe has the best sense of humor. I've needed to embrace far more changes this year than I ever could have imagined. Losing my dad, losing 2 beloved pets. Other major extended family changes, some good (my oldest nephew enlisted in the Army, he comes homes today before moving to his next post, we are so proud of him!), some not. Needing knee surgery and physical therapy. Dramatic changes in the market and our business. My real estate team looks very different now ... both in composition and in location (we moved to Real Broker a couple weeks ago) ... some of those changes have been fantastic and exactly what we needed, others have been sad and hard.

So, this year, especially this week, I've been learning to embrace the season that I'm in. Largely very imperfectly but learning all the while.

I've also been learning to trust. Did I mention my word of the year for 2022 is Trust? I should have known when I chose such a word.

I'm trusting the bigger plan. I'm trusting that even when I don't know how, and can't see how, God is clearing my path for the goodness that's to come. He's heard the conversations I didn't. He knows what's ahead that I need to prepare for. In every season that I have ever been in ... good and bad, plenty and want, He has provided for me. I'm not a great student. I often have to be made desperately uncomfortable in order to listen, trust and make the moves He wants, but in the end, it always comes together just as it should.

I'm ready for a new season, and you can bet that my top goal and word of the year for 2023 will both be a lot more light-hearted and fun!

December 31, 2022

2022. This wasn't my favorite year.

It was the year that started by single handedly moving my dad into a nursing home. Only for him to have a psychiatric/medical emergency a few days later, be admitted to the hospital, and die a week later.

It was the year we bought 2 more investment properties and did full remodels for 3. Including the home I grew up in that I had just moved my dad out of. The first 2 months of the year were such a whirlwind, I didn't know if I was coming or going.

It was the year my personal medical issues and traumas of the past few years caught up with me, and my body said pay attention and process this or else. I'm still working on this.

It was the year we lost 2 beloved furry family members, my cat Hela who was with us for just 8 months, but was a great comfort to me, and our sweet old dog Abby. We miss them both every day.

I killed more fish than I can count this year. I'm ending the year with a guppy that keeps having more (had her 3rd batch last night), so I think I'm up in the fish count by now.

We added a new family member, Luna the male cat, who was supposed to be a female cat. Who was also supposed to be my cat, but is really Tyler's, and Mom is really tired of taking care of people and pets.

This was a big milestone year.

Our real estate team celebrated closing over $1 BILLION dollars in sales volume. We also restructured, recalibrated and rebranded in a big way with our move to Real Brokerage.

Empowering Women in Real Estate® earned a registered trademark, The Podcast hit 200 episodes, and we welcomed our largest group yet at our annual conference.

My oldest turned 18, graduated from high school, got a "real" job coaching lacrosse and moved into college where he will continue his lacrosse career.

My middle turned 16, got his driver's license, probably played his last baseball game ever, refined his lacrosse goalie skills, and no lie, grew a good 6 inches taller.

My youngest turned 13, celebrated his birthday at Great Wolf Lodge, and has been maturing more and more.

My husband and I celebrated 20 years of marriage. Twenty years of ups and downs, of moving (figuratively) further apart and closer together again and again. Twenty years of committing to the big picture, even when it's blurry. Always committing to us.

2022 brings my 40s to a close. It has by far been the most difficult decade of my life. There have been wonderful moments, great highs, but also tremendous lows. This was the year that brought it all to a head. I lost any hopeful naïveté that was left, and my positive outlook along with it.

It's coming back though. As the door slams shut on this year and this decade of life, I can see the light of the future and it is shining so bright.

Goodbye 2022, don't let the door hit you on the ass on the way out.

Or actually, maybe it should.

2023

Milestones

10-5-2023 – "Align 2023", the 3rd Annual Empowering Women in Real Estate® Conference

January 17, 2023

We are now across the halfway mark of January, how are you doing?

I heard something interesting yesterday, that by January 15th many people have already given up on the goals, resolutions or new habits that they committed to for the year.

I would say that is often true, but it doesn't mean defeat, it often means a reset … and if you are one of those folks (I am too) who has stopped or put aside something new that they committed to for 2023, I'd love for you to view it that way instead.

Every year I do some version of this to myself. My morning routine is a perfect example. I tend to add too many things, which I quickly realize is overwhelming or too much, so within a few days or weeks I whittle it down to what makes sense.

This isn't a failure, its real life, and adjusting my life in a way that works for me while still progressing, improving and moving forward is the real goal.

Is there a goal or new habit that you've given up on already? Do you just need a reset instead?

January 27, 2023

Here is some frivolous Friday fun for you ... I aspire to live like the models in the J. Jill catalog.

They all look so happy, peaceful and relaxed. They look put together, but comfortable, and are often in locations near the water or on the beach. Every time I get one of their catalogs in the mail I can't wait to sit down and look at it, fantasizing about this ideal life.

I bet they don't have clients who call them at all hours of the day and night.

I bet they didn't get yelled at because the septic inspector put ruts in their yard.

I bet they didn't have to run over and clean trash out of a listing while dressed for settlement in their best suit and heels, sweating off their makeup and all the curl out of their hair at the same time.

I bet they aren't missing (or running late for, again) some family fun to squeeze in one more showing or to sit an open house where everyone seems mad to see you and to have to talk to you and signs in as "Mickey Mouse".

Do you get catalogs in your mail? Which is your favorite?

February 20, 2023

It's Monday, the perfect day for a fresh start!

I'm definitely moving into this Monday with fresh start energy, as I am finally having a breast reconstruction procedure that I have waited nearly 2 ½ years for. First it was delayed for radiation treatments. Then for insurance woes and the pursuit of finding a new surgeon, and then rescheduled twice in the past 2 months because I came down with a respiratory virus both times just a few days before surgery.

This is my 10th surgery in 15 years on this part of my body (except for the very first, which was way back in 1996). The photo below is of the expander that is getting evicted today. It is full to the brim with saline to stretch my skin and is attached to my chest wall in 3 places. Yes, it is as uncomfortable as that all sounds.

I'm so ready to bring this part of my story to a close (please Lord). I've moved from praying about it to begging and pleading about it. I'm not sure the anxiety and worry will ever go away completely, but I pray (beg and plead) that it will lessen over time.

When I'm quiet it's because I'm full up with sadness.

When I'm grumpy it's because I'm full up with anxiety and worry.

I'm more than ready to be full up with pretty much anything else. Joy, peace and happiness would be a great start.

I want to feel happiness and relief this morning to be getting this done, but the anxiousness that my doctor will find something else in there while he is doing his work is edging that out.

Either way, in about 6-ish hours I'll be waking up from a really nice nap, and I am trying to replay that moment where I get the all clear and hear that everything went great. If I'm extra lucky I won't need any drains today, but I'm prepared if need be. I spent pretty much all day yesterday panic prepping, doing all the things for work and around the house to ensure things will be easier for all my favorite people. I also set up my "recovery station" so I'll have what I need close by.

I hope that your Monday is bright and beautiful. May you have a big win in your business today, and the confidence to know that you are on the right track.

February 28, 2023

Yesterday a friend posted about confidence, and the struggle that so many of us have with it. Raise your hand if this is a struggle for you.

It absolutely has been, currently is, and probably always will be for me in one way or another. (Hello, imposter syndrome.)

Part of the difficulty here is that in our business, confidence is key. When you don't have it, aren't feeling it, it shows.

Have you ever walked into an appointment feeling unsure of yourself, your knowledge, your capabilities? You act different, you talk different, your energy is different. If you aren't confident in you, then how can the client feel confident that you are the person to help them?

Then you don't get the business, and your confidence takes another hit. This cycle can play out again and again.

This is not just limited to those of us who are newer or not as experienced yet. I can remember many instances throughout my career (I celebrate 21 years in July!) as an accomplished, experienced professional, confident in what I knew and what I brought to the table ... but every now and then there would be a client who came along that rocked that confidence. I would forget who I was and what I brought to the table. Those transactions were brutal.

So, what do we do? How do we get out of the confidence, or lack thereof, trap? A few things I've learned ...

-You need a tribe. You need people who will have confidence in you when you don't have it in yourself. People who will help to lift you up.

-You need to remember who you are, and what you bring to the table. And what you bring is far more than the ability to just "open a door". It's so easy to forget, especially when it seems like much of the world is poised and waiting to point out your every misstep. It's hard to have confidence in what you do right, when all of the focus is on what you've done wrong.

-You need a specialty, and you need to know it well. Relatively early on in my career I became a listing specialist, and not only did I practice that skill a lot (by myself and with colleagues) but I also went on a lot of appointments. Many, many, many appointments. There were seasons where I would go on 2-3 per day, weeks that I would have 5+ per week. There were many years when I would average carrying 20-30 listings at a time, by myself. It was a pace that I enjoyed and thrived in. I became a master at my listing presentation, running comps, identifying pricing, and the listing paperwork. Having this specialty, knowing this aspect of my job so well, gave me tremendous confidence, and that confidence brought even more success.

Confidence is a tricky thing. It ebbs and flows through the seasons of our lives ... and in the various parts of who we are. I've had seasons where I was super confident in my work, but at the same time lacking confidence in my most important role of mom, or as a wife, or as a daughter caring for my dad. And vice versa.

One of my favorite books is, "You Are a Badass" by Jen Sincero. It's a good one. One of few that has earned a permanent spot on my bookshelf and has been read again and again. Confidence is a major theme, and I hope you will check it out if you haven't already.

March 7, 2023

You know how much I love Disney, right? When we were there in January nearly every night we saw the fireworks either from inside the park, or from our resort. The theme of the show and the song ended with "you are the magic". The idea behind it being that the experience there is wonderful, but that it is you, the guest, that really makes the magic.

Without the guests, the performers would have no one to perform for. Without the guests, the fun rides would have no reason to run. You get the idea.

I was having a conversation yesterday with a friend who was worried and nervous about a new experience with some new folks. Not sure she would fit in. She felt out of her league, out of her element. But the truth, is that she is the magic, and they were lucky to have the time spent with her.

The same goes for you. You are the magic. Don't you forget it.

March 16, 2023

Things don't always go the way you want. This week has been a lot of that.

There was a momentary glimmer of hope for a correction/reduction on my IRS audit and the amount I owe (it is a staggering number), but that got shot down by the powers that be.

I've had a super sore spot along one of my incision lines to develop this week, which turned out to be a suture trying to work its way out in the wrong place. So, my doctor had to cut open an incision to get it out (yep, it hurts) and I'm back on antibiotics and bandaging weeping wounds.

We found a beautiful pup that we thought would be the perfect addition to our family, but we weren't selected. She had visual impairment, and the family selected had specific experience in that area.

Two kids with disappointments this week and things that didn't go as planned (including losing a beloved fish).

And it's only Thursday.

There has also been a lot of good stuff this week. A fun adventure with my girl Vicky Noufal, meeting and lunch with my team, celebrating Jackie Fields-Gleadall's birthday, meeting/conversations with several agents on and off our team, a fabulous podcast interview with friends, growing our PG Network at

Real, an unexpected YouTube interview, spending some time with my oldest boy after his game, lunch with a friend and watching my middle play tonight. Being honored with an appointment to the board nominating committee for Embark.

And it's only Thursday. It's all in how you look at it.

March 17, 2023
Happy St. Patrick's Day! I have a little Irish Blessing for you today. My very favorite telling of it comes at the end of Brian Buffini's podcast (now called "It's a Good Life") and is read by his mother. I smile every time I hear it.

May the road rise to meet you.
May the wind be always at your back.
May the sun shine warm upon your face.
And rains fall soft upon your fields.
And, until we meet again, may God hold you in the hollow of His hand.

April 13, 2023
Earlier this week I was listening to a podcast episode that shared the simplest of formulas …

Connections, lead to …

Conversations, which lead to …

Conversions, which lead to sales!

We talked about this several times at our team's first quarter review on Monday. As our top producers for the quarter described where their business came from, connection was the name of the game.

Real estate doesn't happen from your couch. I wish it did! The more connections you make, the more conversations you will have, and in time those conversations will convert into sales. So simple, right?

But how to make those connections? You could cold call and door knock, and hope that the day you are connecting with that person is the day that they have a real estate need (which is why this type of lead generation needs such a high volume of contacts in order to result in even just one sale), or you could connect authentically with people that you know. People in your community. People that you have worked with before. Nurture them. Make sure that they know (and are reminded again and again) what you do, and that you are here to serve, and when they (or their friends or family) have a real estate need, they'll come to you.

It's the long game my friends, which is why consistency is your best friend. When you start and stop your business does too.

April 25, 2023

One of my first "real" jobs when I finished school was working as a teller at the local bank. I LOVED it. Counting the money, making sure my drawer reconciled each day, processing the transactions and serving our customers as quickly and efficiently as possible.

My favorite was working the drive thru on Friday afternoons. It was usually super busy as customers came to cash or deposit their paychecks (this was 30 years ago, long before you could deposit checks on your phone!). I loved bouncing between customers in both lanes, the quick pace. The friendly faces that we saw week after week, and the not so friendly (you got to know quickly who was who, lol).

It was a small local bank in my hometown, maybe just 5-6 total employees. Everyone was kind and friendly, except for 1. The mean girl. She was the "head teller" and would be nice enough to my face but always catty and talking about others behind their (and my) back.

The bank had a dress code, which I don't specifically remember anymore, but had something to do with the length of skirts/dresses and pantyhose. At the time I was the tall, thin beauty queen, just 20 years old … and she was not. This woman seemed to make it her mission to take exception to what I wore. I was never one for miniskirts, but apparently some of mine were too short for bank standards and she loved to make an issue of it.

Only instead of letting me know, she would report it to the manager (who I had known my entire life). I would walk in the door and head to my station, she would slide down off her stool while giving me the side eye with a smirk on her face. I remember the clicking sound of the half door opening and closing as she walked out of the teller area and the swishing noise her hosiery made as she stalked over to the branch managers office, going inside and closing the door.

A minute or two later the manager would kindly speak to me, usually in the kitchen. I think a ruler may have even been involved once or twice to "verify" the length (hemline needed to be a certain distance above the knee when sitting, I believe). I remember being sent home once to change. This little show happened on a weekly basis.

The funny thing is, while I'm sure it was frustrating and maybe even embarrassing at the time, I have no memories of that (the frustration and embarrassment). I can only remember the mean girl (who, last I heard, 30 years later still works at a neighboring bank in a similar role), and the smug expression on her face. The lesson was less about the length of my skirt and had everything to do with who I wanted to be more like as I advanced in my career and life, and who I didn't (I'll let you guess which is which).

Recently when having lunch with a friend who is also in the business she asked about the "haters". It seems that the more success her team has, the more these people come out of the woodwork to point out where they may have gone wrong, to "report" them for supposedly egregious things (vs asking a question or having a direct conversation), and just blatantly being disrespectful and gossipy.

I get it, I really do. These people, sometimes masquerading as your friends, are everywhere. There is an invisible line of how much success you are "allowed" to have before it starts to become uncomfortable for them. Some fall prey to the false narratives and gossip spread by others. It's easier and certainly more fun to consider and share a salacious story than it is to ask a direct question or to view an alternative side.

Some will see what you do, what you've accomplished, and cheer, for they know it speaks to what is possible for them. Others will begin to make excuses for why you have what you have. How it's not fair, not right, it was somehow achieved unjustly.

The good news is this ... while the mean girls (and mean boys) exist everywhere, they are far outnumbered by the rest of us who genuinely want to see you succeed and win. And while it may hurt in the moment, let it be the fuel for your fire, not what extinguishes it. For in years to come, when you look back, the memories you have of the mean-spirited ones will be more like pity for their mindset or humor at their foolishness.

May 16, 2023

Let's chat this morning about dreams, shall we? On Friday I had the opportunity to watch Empowering Women in Real Estate® community member Marie Lee speak on stage at a brand building conference.

EMPOWERING WOMEN IN REAL ESTATE

If you don't already know Marie, she has been building her real estate career for just 2 ½ years now and has closed over $10M in sales volume FROM INSTAGRAM! While I loved listening to what Marie shared and her experience, I loved her post about it even more.

More than 3 years ago she journaled about her future, casting her vision ... and in what she wrote she saw herself on a stage leading others. Her experience on Friday very much mirrored that vision.

When is the last time you dared to dream? Wrote out a vision for your life? Took the time to visualize where you want to go and who you want to be?

Nearly 10 years ago, I did. Because Vicky Noufal made me at our first team retreat, before we were even an official team.

My team members know about my famous "purple notebook". It was a gift from my friend Shaila Millman more than 10 years ago. I took it with me on that first retreat and have carried it to every one since. Inside is a history and account of goals made and achieved by me, my friends, and my team in our real estate businesses and personal lives for every year since. It's falling apart at the seams (literally).

On the last page of that purple notebook is my letter, written to my grandmother (because Vicky really wanted to make all of us cry during that exercise ... she also insisted on having the fireplace on and some sort of crazy music playing, so we were simultaneously melting not just from the tears but the perspiration too). My first, dearest and longest time friends in real estate were in that room.

When I wrote that letter my boys were in elementary school and preschool.

When I wrote that letter, I was a managing broker who had willingly put my own goals and dreams aside.

When I wrote that letter my mom was still in remission, and still here. So was my dad, Vicky's Mom and her beloved husband. Both of my breasts were still my own, I didn't know what it meant to have a foreign body inside my body, and I had far fewer scars and no radiation perma tan.

When I wrote that letter there was literally no way that I could have envisioned what that next year would bring ... much less the next 10, but there were intentions made that have slowly come to be.

I've always wanted to "design my life". Make decisions based on growth and abundance (not fear). Spend my time and focus on and with those that matter most to me ... my family, my friends, my team — who have become my friends and family.

I wanted to empower other women to see what was possible for their life. To find joy in connection with others, to feel inspired and motivated. To learn to extract all the goodness and possibility from this career and industry that is also so, so hard.

When I wrote that letter, Empowering Women in Real Estate® was just a few months old. We were probably well less than 500 members at that time. Now we are over 33,000. Now many hundreds of us get together monthly for our meet ups. We gather annually for our conference. Not only do I still get to write to you each morning on the regular, but I get to talk to you in podcast form. It is a gift. Thank you for being here.

Marie, thank you for sharing your vision, your goal, your knowledge. You never know who you will inspire when you share openly and freely.

Time for me to write a new letter.

May 25, 2023
When is the last time you took a "real" vacation?

One where you weren't glued to your laptop or cell phone the entire time?

I learned my lesson big time on this my very first month in real estate. We had a long planned (even before I knew real estate was on the horizon for me and before I started my class!) vacation with extended family which took place a few weeks after I started.

Essentially, I allowed that vacation to be ruined because I didn't know how to manage my business, my clients or my time. We left a couple days late so I could handle some showings, then came back a couple days early for more showing to the same person (who literally never bought anything ... I checked the tax records for years), and the few days we were there I was on the phone or my laptop most of the time.

Lesson learned.

For literally 20 years since I have been perfecting my system for vacationing in real estate which allowed me to take a largely unplugged honeymoon, 3 maternity leaves, multiple surgery recoveries, and vacations every year.

I've shared that system in many ways over the years. You can listen to a very old episode of the podcast (it's episode 24, we are now on episode 250!) and there is even a mini course I did on it that is now available for free!
Check out this screenshot of a post from one of our members, Rebecca Huff, posted in our Inner Circle group last night. It works!

EWRE Inner Circle
Rebecca Huff · 10h

I took my first REAL vacation last week. 100% unavailable. No internet, no text, no phone calls. I never thought this would have been possible without learning from Karen Wenner Cooper about how to take a real vacation in real estate. My files were in order, my clients had a point of contact, I had a great agent who backed me up while I was gone, and my closing the day after I got back was ready to go! If you haven't listened to the podcast on how to take a vacation you should run and listen to it now! It's a game changer! Thanks, Karen, for such great tools that help us enjoy our lives!

PS...don't get me wrong, I'm playing catch up this week, but I'm doing it with memories of the Caribbean fresh on my mind 🌴🍹😎

June 4, 2023

Today is my FIFTIETH birthday! That seems a little surreal to say. Didn't I just turn 30? or 40?

I'm not usually one to put a lot of emphasis on a milestone birthday, but this one feels different. Big. Important.

Fifty feels like it comes with a mindset shift. A life shift. I no longer have time for, interest in or patience for silly games. Gossip. Bullshit. High school level drama. Take that trash somewhere else, I have important things to do. Goals to accomplish. Dreams to actualize. Time no longer feels never-ending.

I am a grown woman. I have created a career that spans decades and grown businesses that I am proud of. My children are rapidly becoming their own people. Time and possibility span out in front of me like never before.

I have the gift of knowledge. Experience. Hard fought wisdom. I know clearly what I don't want and what I won't tolerate.

I'm still envisioning what I want. It grows and evolves as time marches on. I notice bits and pieces of former dreams that have come to life, but the rest of the pieces don't seem so applicable anymore, and so the possibilities continue to unfold.

My 40s were an absolute shit show. Some of the most beautiful experiences and biggest successes in my life happened during that decade, and so also did a lifetime worth of trauma and loss.

What will my 50s bring? There will be more loss and trauma, that is life I have learned. There will still be stress and hard times but maybe now I will be more prepared. More understanding. The naïveté of youth is long gone. Each wrinkle and gray hair are like a badge of honor. Every scar proof that I am a survivor, an overcomer, capable of things my young self couldn't even comprehend.

And so, I will step into this decade and declare it to be the most successful of my life, because it is MY life, and I will live it and design it as I damn well please.

June 6, 2023

You've heard the stories about my new dog, right? Princess Leia the German Shepherd who joined our family on May the 4th (iykyk).

Everyday Leia and I go out for at least 1 walk, most often 2, covering 1-3 miles each day.

While out on our walk the other morning I had a realization …

For years and years and years the story I've told myself is that I didn't have time to exercise in the morning anymore.

Morning exercise was always something I did as a young person. Working out to the early morning shows before school (Who remembers Gilad and Denise Austin?), going to the gym across the street from my office before work and walking on my lunch break. There was even a period of time when my oldest was small and I was pregnant with my second that I would go to the gym early then shower at my real estate office … truth be told primarily because it was easier to do that and spend 20 minutes on the treadmill than to try to get myself ready at home with an 18-month-old. Other than during COVID when my kids were home and I had a strong morning yoga routine, I've consistently said I didn't have time.

Until Leia came along.

For the last month we've walked together in the morning every day ... and nothing else has changed about my schedule.

I still get up at roughly the same time. I still do my morning chores and my morning routine. I still get myself ready for the workday and take my youngest to his education center.

What has changed is me. What has changed is what I prioritize.

Instead of scrolling social media for a while longer I'm getting up and taking her for a walk. Instead of diving headfirst into my email long before anyone would expect a response so early in the day I'm going outside to move.

Your schedule or to do list isn't the problem, what you choose to prioritize is.

Don't have time to exercise or move each day?

Can't seem to find time to write those notes or make your calls?

Is working on your business (vs in it) at the bottom of your to do list and so it never gets done?

It's not that you don't have time for these things, you do, you just aren't putting the big rocks in the jar of your day first. When you start with and focus on the small (but often still important, I get it) things ... the pebbles and the sand, your day fills and of course there is no room left for the big, important things that we try to fit last. Or not at all.

Put the big rocks in first. The rest will flow around it. You'll be amazed at how it all works.

June 8, 2023

Today is the last official day of school in my county, but all my kids have been done for a few days.

My oldest came home from college a couple weeks ago.
My middle has been practicing for his senior year (next year) and barely gone the past week as "nothing was happening".
My youngest finished a week ago.

And so begins another summer of working and working from home while the kids are home. Anyone else losing their mind yet too?

Luckily, they (all teenage boys) sleep essentially until afternoon, so I do have a good block of time to work in the morning largely uninterrupted.

But once they are up ...

It's a steady flow in and out of my office ... "what's up mom", "how's your day going", "how's your work going", "can I go ...", "I need to buy ...", plus a variety of teenage nonsense questions that I don't understand.

Truth be told, I love this, but it also repeatedly stirs up the anxious new dog. I've largely got her "trained" now to rest on the couch in my office while I work, but anytime I get up or the boys come in she is up and ready to go.

Every year, every season, every summer looks different. Right now, most nights around 11-11:30 pm I get a text from the older two saying they are going to get food following their workout. Keep in mind, a) I'm asleep and usually have no idea until I see the message in the morning, and b) we live in the country so there is no door dash (what the oldest had grown accustomed to at college). Last night they went to Sheetz for subs at 11:20 pm. Do anyone else's kids do this??

A few days in and I am already feeling a little guilty for constantly ignoring my 13-year-old, the only one that still seems eager and happy to spend time with dear old mom.

We've created a summer bucket list, which he and I will be tackling bit by bit each week. I have learned for sure that if you don't plan it and make time for it, the time is going to pass you by.

June 12, 2023

Today marks our 4-year anniversary of the Empowering Women in Real Estate® Inner Circle! I remember exactly the day this idea came to be. For years we had been trying to figure out a way to provide a higher level of service and benefit to our EWRE® community.

We also had many agents outside of our area who wanted to join our real estate team, but didn't live close enough (or even in the same state!). We wanted to offer parts of our Client & Community Care Program, plus training and direction to anyone, anywhere ... but how?

Enter, the Inner Circle!

Only we didn't start out as the Inner Circle. When the program first launched, it was called Empower Coaching, and I remember sitting in my favorite chair by the window with my morning coffee watching the program registrations come in on the product page I'd cobbled together the day before. It was thrilling!

Oh, how far we've come.

Here's a glimpse into the Inner Circle, by the numbers!

In the past 4 years we have …
-Served 357 women, and a few brave men!
-Sent 208 Plan of the Week emails.
-Conducted 96 Group Coaching Sessions.
-Shared 208 Weekly Quick Lesson videos.
-Provided 148 social media graphics.
-Offered 90 postcard templates.

Our members have …
-Written 1040+ personal notes.
-Posted 624+ business social media posts.
-Sent 48+ email newsletters.

Plus, hundreds of contacts added to databases, reviews given and requested, events hosted, coffees and lunches enjoyed, and SO. MUCH. MORE.

We have a robust Referral Network which has resulted in many tens of thousands of dollars in commissions for our members.

When we started, we didn't even have a fully functioning website, just a half-baked one that I started creating on Wix from a hotel room in Roanoke, Virginia where Vicky and I were attending the Virginia Association of Realtors conference. Initially our program ran entirely out of a Facebook group. Can you imagine??

Since then, we've re-vamped and revised our website twice over, and now have a fully standalone educational portal for our members where they can find all of their content organized in tabs with explanation videos. You can find every piece of content and training from the past 4 years with just a few clicks.

Our membership has been bigger, and it has been smaller.

It's been pricier and it's been less expensive.

When quarantines started, we suspended all billing for our members while we all got our bearings. What was supposed to be 1 month for our members turned into 6 months of free delivery of the program to anyone who wanted to participate.

From day one we've stood by our mantra of cancel anytime with no hard feelings, and we mean it. We've had members with us for just a month or two, others that have left and come back, and some that have been with us every single month without fail for 4 years!

I'm so proud of what we've built here. If I can be vulnerable with you, it is one of the things I love the most, but often ends up lowest on the list. We've got the system and the program down, what I want for all of us is more connection, collaboration and engagement (and I mean by me) and we are taking all the right steps in the right direction there.

Thank you for 4 years of learning and growth, here's to many more!

June 13, 2023

Yesterday on my Instagram stories I shared this funny cat video that I came across. In the video the cat is walking by a pool and its back leg slips over the edge into the water. It was a minor slip, but the cat FREAKED OUT. And in its freak out ended up fully submerging itself multiple times in the pool, jumping and pawing wildly until it got out.

The caption to the video said, "when your anxiety level makes the situation 10x worse than it is."

Who can relate to this? I sure can.

I'm sure I've always been this way, though I don't necessarily remember it as much when I was younger. The older I've gotten the worse it has become, in part I think because I've experienced some pretty rotten things, so being naive to thinking they won't happen isn't an option anymore.

Last year at our 2nd Annual Empowering Women in Real Estate® Conference, "Mastering the Juggle", we had a guest expert speak about health and taking care of our bodies and our minds. This is a practitioner that I myself and many other local Realtors® I know have personally seen, and one of the things in common that we all have is super high cortisol levels, the stress hormone.

I'm pretty sure I don't need to tell you all that. The stress levels from our work in this industry is often off the charts.

This morning during my real estate team's meeting we are covering unique and challenging situations that have happened recently, what we learned and how to handle them in the future.

Not just one or two, but there have been FOUR different situations to share, and there could have been a fifth, but that team member is away this week and won't be present to share her story.

Each of these situations turned the transactions upside down, brought out the worst in everyone involved, and caused extreme levels of stress. With the exception of 1, all of these situations happened in just the PAST 7 DAYS. It's a wild world out there right now in our industry. You can read many posts here in our group or in others to see example after example.

I don't have a perfect solution. I know for myself that going through the challenging situations and markets throughout my past 21 years in this industry have made me a better agent, a better business owner, a better team leader, and a better friend.

It's rare that I think back on the many wonderful transactions that went smoothly. When I'm counseling my team members or helping them through challenging situations, I'm referencing back to the difficult ones that I've had, either the same as what they are dealing with or similar.

Now more than ever before, it is the people you align yourself with that will make the difference in just surviving or thriving ... and how happily you do it.

June 15, 2023

I am so excited to announce the theme of our 3rd Annual Empowering Women in Real Estate® Conference ... Align 2023!

It has been my experience of over 2 decades in the real estate industry, through up markets and down markets and everything in between, that distraction is one of the biggest reasons that we struggle and sometimes fail. When we ALIGN our businesses with our authentic selves, that is when the magic starts to happen.

At Align 2023 you will hear from incredible speakers and panelists who enact this principle in their own businesses to see massive success. You'll leave not only inspired, but with tactical actions and strategies to put to work in your own business right away.

June 22, 2023

This ... "Decide what kind of life you really want. Then, say no to everything that isn't that." I feel like this is the season of life that I have fully entered.

It's how I've wanted to operate for a long time but was never quite there. The past couple months this has been something I have written down in my PowerSheets Goal Planner each time when planning my month. Listing out the things that I want under the "things I'm saying yes to" column, and writing "anything that isn't that" under things I'm saying no to.

Last night we watched the first episode of "Arnold", a docuseries on Netflix about Arnold Schwarzenegger. The first episode was about his dream, goal, vision ... and subsequent career as an athlete. He spoke about the power of visualization and how he became obsessed with his dreams and doing what it took to make them come to life (and they did).

What really struck me though was a theme he returned to more than once about community. How he knew that in order to reach his goal that he needed to be surrounded by, and train with, the best in the world in his field. He said that he learned how to build a supportive community and that he brought that skill with him and built a community everywhere he went in his life.

I love that so much. When I think back, I've always known the power of community, though I maybe didn't always call it that. As a kid, as a young person, in every career, every hobby, every everything I assembled a group of people. Mentors, partners, friends. People I wanted to be associated with. People I wanted to grow with. People I shared a vision with.

A community.

I'm a little obsessed with building that right now. I know the power and the benefit that it can bring. And I'm saying no to everything that isn't that.

July 10, 2023

Good Morning Monday! How is everyone feeling this morning?

No, seriously, how are YOU?

On Friday I received the most beautiful message from my friend Sherrie Vaughan. She talked about how as leaders we spend so much time and effort taking care of others, and how so rarely others (especially those we take care of) truly see us. It's rare for someone to ask, "how are you", and really mean it … or expect to get a true answer.

Here's the thing. We are ALL leaders in one way or another (sometimes in multiple ways).

We are leaders in our home.
Leaders in our families.
Leaders in our business.
Leaders in our community.
Leaders for our clients.

You might be a team leader. A brokerage owner or manager. You may have leadership responsibilities with employees or team members.

When is the last time anyone in any of those areas that you lead asked you, "how are you", and meant it? Waited for an answer beyond "good", "fine", "okay"?

This morning, I am asking you … HOW ARE YOU?

I genuinely want to know.

July 11, 2023

Today is a big day in our world, it's the day of my team's Mid-Year Review & State of the Union Meeting.

There is a book that *my* first team leader 21 years ago (Sherry Wilson) had us all read called, "The Four Agreements" by Don Miguel Ruiz. One of those agreements is to "be impeccable with your word."

Every year at this time not only are we as a team going back and reviewing how our business has been … what worked and what didn't … YTD and year over year, but also as Team Leaders Vicky Noufal and I are reviewing how we've done.

What did we offer?
What did we promise?
What enhancements were/are we working on?
What do our team members want, what are they feeling, what are they finding beneficial and not from our offerings? (We gather this from our annual mid-year survey.)

Basically, if we said we were going to do it, offer it, provide it, we find a way.

Mid-Year is a major evaluation point in our business, and what we learn, the feedback we receive, the data that presents itself are all used to set the course for our business for the next 12-18 months.

It's a lot of work, but it's also a lot of fun.

Today we will announce the theme, location and more about our Annual Business Planning & Goal Setting Retreat that happens this fall.

We will unveil the VIP Experience that our 2023 top producers will earn at the end of the year.

We'll provide updates on new things we've been working on, and what's on the horizon.

It's going to be a very good day indeed.

July 17, 2023
Good Morning Monday! The past couple weeks I have completely fallen out of my Sunday prep routine, deciding instead to do it on Monday morning.

Well, last Monday I was so slammed and overwhelmed with meetings and getting ready for our team's Mid-Year Review Meeting the next day that I didn't do my prep for the week. Then after the big meeting, by the time I got home and did my follow up it was dinner time, and I didn't do my prep. Then Wednesday came, and well, you know where this is going.

Even though my Wednesday schedule was largely open, I was spinning my wheels … starting one thing, bouncing to something else, moving back to the other thing, on and on. At one point I found myself in tears for no good reason, feeling so overwhelmed, and then I realized I still hadn't done my prep.

So, I shut off my email, turned on do not disturb on my phone and finally around 3:30 pm on Wednesday afternoon I did my prep for the week. I timed it, curious to see how long it took since I had been putting it off … and it took 15 minutes.

And let me tell you, once I completed those fifteen minutes, I felt 1000 times better … and I got more done in the next few hours of that day than I had all week. Because I had a clear plan and focus.

So, what is this magical Sunday prep? It has evolved over the years, and changes with my season of life. No lie … there was a time in my life when my husband was on shift work, I had 3 very young kids and was selling 50-60 homes in a year with little to no assistance. I was either in hair on fire mode or half dead on the couch. There was literally no in between. During that season I actually had Sunday checklists pre-made with my prep (that routine took about an hour) which included things like "refill bathrooms with toilet paper" because I am the only female (except for my dogs #solidarity) in a house of males (husband, 3 sons, 3 cats) and no one else seems to think of these things. When I had little kids and someone usually in potty training mode and running around like a crazy person, we always ran out of toilet paper at a critical moment. Doing this every Sunday saved me time (and some sanity) during the week. I wish I could remember the other things on that list, they clearly illustrated how type-A and un-fun I really am, lol.

Back to now … nowadays my Sunday prep is focused on my to do list and action plan for the week. It takes at most 20-30 minutes.

First, I write out my appointments for the week in my planner (I use the weekly edition of The Simplified Planner by Emily Ley). My calendar lives in iCal, but I've found over the years that taking a few minutes to write out my schedule helps to cement it into my brain and I feel more connected to what is going on. As the week goes on, if appointments are changed or added I'll update them in my planner as well.

Next, I write in my recurring tasks. To help me stay focused each of my days have a "theme" which includes certain recurring tasks. For example, Monday is always my prospecting day and the majority of my proactive work on Mondays centers around my personal real estate sales business.

Then I'll write out any tasks that are specific to the week and/or are related to my appointments that week (or for the following week) and preparation I need to do. For example, looking ahead to next week I am doing a training for my team (which will later be shared with the EWRE® Inner Circle on "My Simple CMA Formula ... and How to Price the Most Challenging Properties". This week I'll begin work on that presentation.

Lastly, I'll look at the previous week and note any tasks that didn't get completed (I always highlight them at the end of the day so they don't get lost) and will move them ahead.

When my brain is extra full of things going on I'll start this entire process with a brain dump ... writing out every single thing on my mind, which helps to clear the mental clutter, and then I will also include those tasks as needed.

Last week was a perfect example of how this relatively quick process helps to keep me centered and grounded. It is first up on my list this morning.

August 3, 2023

Yesterday I attended my brokerage's Monthly Meeting. Before all of the announcements and recognitions and numbers that accompany the typical brokerage meeting, the president of our company did a mini training. This was definitely not typical.

I took so many notes and was even "spam texting" our team's chat line with some of my favorite quotes and lessons for those who weren't able to join the meeting live.

Here was one of my favorites ...

"When you don't know your options, you don't have any."

I was thinking about a potential contractual issue I've talked to one of my team members about a couple times this week.

Or the potential situation with another team member and a new listing.

Or the agent referral I received that may need an adjustment.

We ALWAYS have options.

In every situation there are options, but sometimes we or our clients don't know what they are, and that feels like there aren't any and that never feels good.

Here's the thing about options ... sometimes we don't like our options, and we'd rather ignore them and pretend we don't have any than to pick one, take action and move on.

I get it. I've done this so many times. In my business, with my clients, at various stages of my career, in my personal life, and even in my various treatment plans.

We are so afraid to make a mistake, to pick the wrong one, or they all feel hard, so we do nothing. I've done this too. When I think back over the million decisions and options in my life, only 1 comes to mind that I truly regret (which was related to a treatment plan). Every other time the option I chose worked itself out.

When you do nothing, you get nothing.

When you sow (risk) nothing, you reap nothing.

Having options, even when you don't like what they are, is ALWAYS better than no options.

October 3, 2023

The typical online lead conversion = 1%, which equates to 1 out of 100.

Of course, when the average conversion rate is 1%, you DO need hundreds of leads in order to have a consistent, sustainable real estate business.

But there's a better way ...

These are the ACTUAL numbers for leads generated by Vicky Noufal and I for our team for the first three quarters of 2023.

Q1 - 106 leads, 12 closed

Q2 - 38 leads, 16 closed
Q3 - 29 leads, 14 closed

100% of these opportunities came from our sphere, repeat clients, referrals, geographic farming and social media.

These are "bonus" deals on top of what our team members are already producing on their own by implementing our systems. We've already served over 200 families with their real estate needs YTD in 2023.

The real estate market is … unusual. Virtually everywhere. Fewer transactions overall mean fewer opportunities (you see that in our numbers above).

Right now, more than ever, every.single.opportunity counts.

Which would you rather have … more "leads" with a 1 in 100 close rate, or more closings from a smaller number of actual opportunities that don't require you to chase, cold call, or beg? I know what I would choose.

October 5, 2023
It's Align Day!!

We had the most fun last night! First, we welcomed our speakers/panelists, Inner Circle Members and out of town conference attendees with a casual Happy Hour. Then we had a lovely dinner with our speakers and panelists.

Between those in the room today and our livestream attendees, we are just shy of 200 women (and a few good men) coming together to learn and grow.

Thank you to our sponsors, our Empowering Women in Real Estate® team, our speakers, panelists and those coming from near and far (and at home!) to be a part of this event.

October 6, 2023
Well. Yesterday was amazing. Align 2023 was our 3rd Annual Empowering Women in Real Estate® Conference … and I have to say that not only did we have our largest audience to date (160+ in the room, 30+ on livestream), but it was also our most engaged and enthusiastic crowd ever … and that energy made all the difference.

We had more women than ever before traveling to see us. Virginia, Maryland, Washington DC, West Virginia, Tennessee, Florida, Colorado, New Jersey,

Pennsylvania, North Carolina. I'm sure there are a few more I missed. To have you spend your time, energy, and financial resources to be with us is truly an honor bestowed. To the women who committed their day to be with us on livestream from Texas, Idaho, Indiana, California and many more, we appreciate your commitment.

It is a very special thing to have so many dynamic, focused, powerful women (and a few brave men!) in one room.

The content shared was second to none. Our keynote speakers and panelists all freely gave and shared so much knowledge, wisdom and practical how tos.

I'm so proud of what we have built with our Empowering Women in Real Estate® community. Next year will be our 10-year anniversary, and we are truly just getting started.

A huge thank you to our sponsors, and most especially to our Empowering Women in Real Estate® and Platinum Group Real Estate support team for making the most monumental of tasks look like a walk in the park. I appreciate you more than you know.

Here's to next year's event ... we know already that it will be bigger and better than ever before.

October 10, 2023

This is Leia. She is a 60+ pound German Shepherd and she jumps the highest of fences, and just about everything else, with ease.

Except this little stretchy piece of netting in my car.

She loves riding in the car with me, and would rather sit up front, which I don't feel is safe for her or me. Even with her harness/seatbelt in the back she would still constantly push up between the seats, standing on the center console.

Until I bought this little $10 netting on Amazon.

I wasn't sure it would actually work, since she could easy push through it, but she doesn't even try.

This, of course, I found to be a perfect metaphor.

What is holding you back from the next level in your business?

Lack of training?
Bad (or no) systems and processes?
No focus?
Spending too much time with butter knife people? (You know what I'm talking about.)
Netflix? (Yes, I said it.)
Your mindset? (Ouch.)

Or maybe it's just not knowing what to do to grow your business authentically (I can help with that part).

All of these things are like that little stretchy piece of netting to Leia. If you only push against it, try something new, you'd find that the only thing that is really holding you back ... is you.

Just don't tell Leia. I really need her to stay in the back seat.

October 11, 2023

Chances are you've heard the phrase, "iron sharpens iron" before.

Back in the day, I was a Franklin Covey planner devotee. Remember when they had 1 and 2 day in-person workshops? I remember getting permission from my employer to go, I was SO EXCITED. One of the workshops included the planner. I can't remember the name of it exactly, but it came with this brown binder thing to keep your extra pages in, and there was a snap in "bookmark" to mark your page in the binder that you could write on. Your daily compass maybe? One of the things to complete each week was "sharpen the saw". Am I the only one who remembers this???

Anyway. Back to why we are here.

Spending time sharpening your saw is always time well spent. What does that mean? Investing in your craft. Improving your skills. Learning, training, education. It is critical to our careers and the health of our businesses. I get it, this takes time. I'm ashamed to admit that there was a time in the first handful of years of my career where I thought that because I knew how to execute, could write a killer offer for my clients, and won more listing appointments than I lost that I knew all the things. That I didn't need to go to classes or workshops or conferences or training anymore.

And that was the moment my career began to stall. Until I remembered that iron sharpens iron.

Training, classes, workshops, conferences ... all of these things will help you to improve, if only you apply what you learned. And let's face it, many of us come home or turn off the webinar ON FIRE with pages of notes, excited and enthusiastic. Then your client calls, or the appraisal comes back low, and now you are back to putting out fires instead and nothing gets implemented.

You want to know the life hack for this? The ONE THING (wait, was that what that planner system was called?) that has helped my career in real estate to grow as it has?

It's the people I surround myself with. My day to day. My tribe. My circle.

That's it. That's the punchline. It's like learning through osmosis. Nothing will raise your vibe (and your bank balance) or increase your pipeline faster.

You know those texts threads you are on? Your friend group, the colleagues you gel with. When those conversations are a nonstop loop of talking about others in our industry who are actually making things happen and working to improve their lives and businesses, or a gripe fest about how bad the market is ... those are butter knife people. How do you think those conversations are going to help your business? Are you being elevated in any way? Or is your energy and mindset being dragged down?

Conversely, when those group chats are focused on growth, that is where the magic happens. Sharing podcast episodes on strategies to grow your business or wins others have experienced with the how so you can do it too. Conversations around buying investment properties, building portfolios, being better Realtors®, community members, moms and leaders.

THAT is iron sharpening iron, and you can't help but be pulled forward.

You know that saying, you are the sum of the 5 people you spend the most time with. Take a long, hard look at those people.

Are there elements of their life that look like yours, or where you aspire to be? Do you want more of the same or incremental improvements taking you where you want to go?

Beware of the butter knife. It may look like it's getting the job done, until you realize that where you want to go is getting further and further away from where you are ... still sitting at the table trying to saw through the same old piece of stale dry bread.

October 12, 2023

Today is my 21st wedding anniversary! And yes, I've been in real estate for 21 years too. Here's the story ...

Back in the early spring of 2002 I found out that I was getting laid off (again) from my job working at a pharmaceutical company (I was a project manager for the patient registry of a diabetic insulin delivery device).

I had two choices, stay in the industry and take a job in Princeton, New Jersey for another company that I had been consulting with or find something else.

That something else turned out to be real estate, and I started working on my licensing courses online right away. I passed my test about a week before my official last day of work and started my real estate career the following week (early July 2002) ... after a quickie marriage by a justice of the peace, lol.

My husband and I had been engaged for about 6 months at that point, and already had a beautiful wedding planned for October 12th of that year. When we realized that my health benefits were going to run out, and I would be without insurance for about 4 months, we decided to make things official sooner. And thus, the running joke that I just married my husband for the health benefits. It is really good insurance though, lol.

We call June 28th our "special day" and typically just exchange cards. We only told our closest family members and friends. His mom was the only person there (he's an only child, I wasn't going to win that fight), and I wore a red dress. I think he wore shorts. And maybe a fire department t-shirt.

Our wedding continued as planned on October 12th, and that is the day we celebrate ... sometimes with our kids at Disney, and sometimes away for a night or two on our own as we are right now.

It's been a long, and sometimes bumpy ride. Both the marriage and the real estate career. Nothing is a straight, smooth line (how I wish it were). I'm blessed to say that the bumpiness has had everything to do with the trials and tribulations of life, and not the partner I chose. Having the right partner makes all the difference.

There were many years of my career (especially in the beginning) that he resented my work. As someone with a more "typical" job (though being in the fire service isn't exactly typical) that comes with a mostly set schedule and regular paycheck, he didn't understand this crazy new career of mine that had me on the phone all hours of the day and night and running out to appointments constantly.

In time we both figured it out (me, boundaries, him, how it worked), and he's my biggest cheerleader. Family/friend/partner/spouse relationships and real estate are often a complicated mix. Not everyone understands (or even tries to) and it can make a challenging career even more so.

I know that I am beyond blessed to be where I am now. We worked hard, sacrificed and risked to do so. We still do every day. Many days we are still just figuring it out as we go along, and I wouldn't have it any other way.

October 19, 2023

I feel like everywhere you look right now there is sadness. There are unspeakable horrors happening in the world.

Many in our industry are struggling to make ends meet, taking second jobs, or leaving all together. I see post after post about it. And I'm tired of it.

Yes, our industry is changing. This should be news to no one. It is constantly changing.

Yes, interest rates are high and coupled with other factors there are many people who don't want to move right now (or can't afford to) ... but that doesn't mean no one is moving.

Yes, the overall number of transactions are down across the board across the country. I get it, there are more of us and less to go around.

What you look at or look for is what you will see.

There are tiny wins happening all around us ... probably in your own business ... that we are disregarding right now. The way you approach that is going to bring you more of the same. Either more disappointment and lack, or more inspiration and energy to continue to do the work.

Which one do you want?

Lots of you message me or text me with your wins, and I love it, and now I want others to celebrate you too. Here's the thing ... your win isn't just YOUR win; it is also proof to everyone else of what is possible right now. I hope you will share them.

October 23, 2023

I suddenly found myself down for the count on Friday with a nasty cold. We were supposed to be in Delaware all weekend for my middle son's lacrosse tournament, but a MCL sprain playing the weekend before took him out. My husband spent the day yesterday watching our oldest play in a college tournament at Frostburg, and I spent the better part of the weekend in bed.

And it was just what I needed.

Yesterday afternoon I finally turned a corner, and while still not 100% I'm definitely on the way there. I was thinking this morning what a privilege sleep and rest is, and yet how it is often truly the cure to what ails us. I stayed in bed (working, of course) all of Friday afternoon. Saturday, I felt truly awful and again stayed in bed all day. The magic though was that Saturday night I was finally able to sleep (Have you ever tried Breathe Right nose strips when you are congested? I feel like it was a game changer!), and I slept a solid 14+ hours.

Also, being able to sleep and rest shouldn't feel like it is a privilege, should it? It is one of the most basic human needs, and yet one that we often deny ourselves … on purpose. I'm grateful for the chance to sleep and rest this weekend. Now let's dive into the week, shall we?

Today is all about Real and real estate. I'm meeting on Zoom with a fabulous agent in Kansas to share the "behind the scenes" of our technology, marketing and transaction management as she decides what makes the most sense for her in the next phase of her business. I also have a call with a local to me agent to discuss the "Legacy Agent" tier available within our team. It's Platinum Group-lite, providing the most needed benefits, services and training for those who are dual career agents or moving into a new phase of their business planning to do just a few deals per year and/or starting to look forward to retirement. There is definitely a need for this in our industry right now. I'll also be going with my middle son to his first physical therapy appointment for that MCL sprain.

Tuesday is a full-on pumpkin carving day!! Our team is having a pumpkin carving party, a first for us, which will be so fun. That will be followed up by me hosting pumpkin carving at my youngest's educational center. I'll just be loading up those carving supplies and taking them from one spot to another!

Wednesday is my dedicated working at my computer day. A lot is happening right now to prepare for our team retreat next month, 2023 review and 2024 goal setting with my team and the Empowering Women in Real Estate® Inner Circle, 2024 Marketing Debut and more. I need to make an even bigger dent on this.

Thursday through the weekend we will be at my happy place, Disney World! We are going for the full-on fall experience and Halloween party, my favorite. This was a last-minute trip (booked less than 6 weeks ago), and just the injection of happy that my people and I need. This is the first time going without my oldest who isn't able to break away from class and fall lacrosse.

Also happening this week is my Real Brokerage's RISE Conference in San Diego, CA. Many of my friends and colleagues are there, and I am looking forward to following along with the news, stories and educational opportunities that will be flowing back this way. I know without a doubt that Vicky Noufal will be texting me things non-stop. It's already started, lol.

November 7, 2023

Distraction is the #1 threat to Realtors® ... and we do it to ourselves.

I believe it was my friend Martha Mason who shared this photo about consistency a while ago, and it is one of the best representations I've ever seen. You know we talk around here a lot about being consistent.

Consistently following up with your clients.
Consistently showing up on social media.
Consistently staying top of mind.

Consistently. Consistently. Consistently.

Listen, it's what I know works. If you want consistent closings and consistent income, you have to be consistent with your activities. Period. But being consistent doesn't mean being perfect. It means showing up week after week, day after day, some doing more than others, but repeatedly showing up and doing the work.

When I re-launched my real estate career in 2015 after stepping away to be a managing broker I had to start over, and I did that with my Daily Business Builders™. It's my kindler, gentler form of prospecting, a series of activities that I did every day, every week ... and have for the last 8 years. Those specific activities have shifted a bit over the years both in type and in numbers, but they have never gone away.

They are also never done perfectly. Yes, many weeks I check off all the things, but many weeks I don't. Yet every week I take at least a little bit of action, and that action creates a compound effect which is the most powerful thing that can happen in your business. What does that look like in real life?

It means that YTD in 2023, I have ...
-Written 483 notes (my goal for the year was 260)
-Made 122 calls/texts (my goal for the year was 104)
-Delivered 221 pop bys (my goal for the year was 180)
-Given 178 referrals (my goal for the year was 156)
-Added 101 people to my database (my goal for the year was 52)

I've also sent 11 email newsletters (I do these monthly), mailed 27,500 postcards (yes, I said 27,500!), invited 25 of my A+ clients to a client event, sponsored multiple community related activities, and posted more social media posts than I can count.

I should also add that I have taken 5 weeks off on vacations this year, plus 2 weeks to recover from surgery, and nearly 3 weeks helping my family/grieving from a personal tragedy.

Here's the thing, I haven't met my goal every week ... but taking action and staying focused weekly, even when it is just the tiniest thing (1 note, 1 text), means that a lot of weeks I get momentum, and I end up doing a lot more.

Want to know the results? YTD in 2023, I have ...
-Received 49 referrals
-Generated 91 other leads (geographic farming, social media primarily)

By the end of 2023 I will have personally generated well over $15M in closed sales volume that has been passed to my team members and out of state referral partners.

I've been out of personal production for 4 years now, and yet I still regularly produce close to the same amount of business that I generated when I was ... and that is without the benefit of the multiplied additional business that comes from each transaction (when referring out like this, you often miss out on additional referrals or repeat transactions).

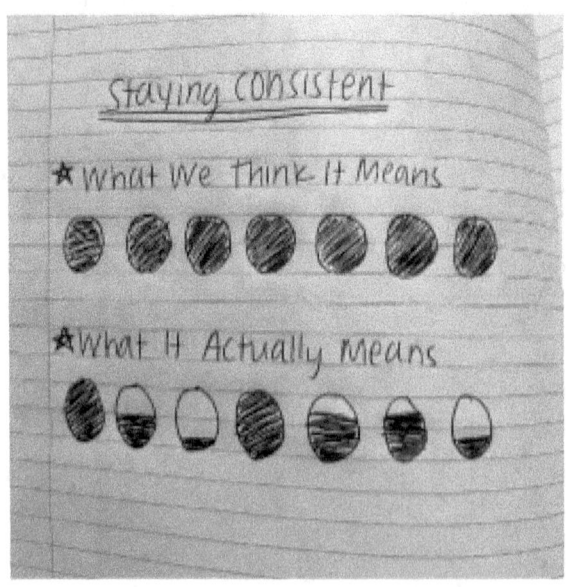

November 9, 2023

Yesterday Vicky Noufal and I had a meeting with someone that was fascinating and eye opening in many ways. During that conversation this person talked about "attention management" vs "time management" … and you know that got my attention (pun intended).

I'm all about managing my time, efficiency is practically my middle name. Anything I can do to shave a few minutes here and there and I'm all over it.

For the wrong reasons.

I'm all over it because I am trying to open up time so I can complete more of what is on my to do list.

And a lot of what is on my to do list is the wrong stuff.

I'm trying to make more time and move faster … to do the wrong things. Not just to do the wrong things, but to do more of the wrong things. While the right things get pushed further and further down the line.

Somewhere along the line I was conditioned to work on stuff that didn't really matter (I started working with a new therapist yesterday, I'm sure we'll get to this, and you know I'll tell you the story when I figure it out).

The big things, the important things, the ones that will ACTUALLY move the needle forward not only for my business but for my team members as well consistently get pushed to the back burner. And if I'm telling the truth, they have for years.

Why?

Partly because they are uncomfortable. It's uncomfortable to do big things, new things, not part of the status quo things. It's easier to just keep doing what I've always done. Don't rock the boat.

Partly because I have been worried about the opinions of others … both the perceived opinions and the ones that are shared either directly with me or to me through someone else. It's easier to let the opinions … and fears … of others keep you small. Just keep rowing, even when you're doing it in circles.

The result? My stress level has grown in equal proportion to the amount of time I manage and save to add more and more of the wrong things to my plate. My plate has broken under the weight of the expectations, fears (of others and my own), and mound of busy work that never should have been on my plate to begin with.

It's time to get a new plate.

Not just going to rock the boat, going to flip the whole thing over.

And we will all be better for it.

> The magic you are looking for is in the work you are avoiding.
>
> @KAREN.W.COOPER
> EMPOWERINGWOMENINREALESTATE.COM

11-14-2023

Many years ago, I read a book called, "UnMarketing" by Scott Stratten after hearing him speak at Brian Buffini's Success Tour in Richmond, Virginia. Something he said there has stuck with me all these years ... that we market for business one way but behave as consumers in a completely different way.

No wonder so many of us struggle. Here are my examples ...

I don't mind getting postcards or mailers from businesses I support, but I don't want to get them every week. (I send a monthly postcard mailer to my database and geographic farm)

I don't mind getting an email newsletter from my favorite people and businesses, but it better be short, have something in it I love (the first two quotes from James Clear and Emily Ley's seasonal wallpaper!), and I definitely don't want to get it every day, probably not even every week unless it's really, really good. (I send a monthly email newsletter with a giveaway inside to my entire database)

I LOVE when people send me cards and handwritten notes. Those get opened first every single time and go on the shelf in my kitchen for at least a few days. (I send hundreds upon hundreds of handwritten notes every year to clients, vendors, colleagues and more)

I'm not a big socializer, happy hour or events person. If it was something involving my kids when they were younger, then it was something I might do. Otherwise, no way. A casual "open house style" pop in and pop out something I don't mind. (I do a Thanksgiving reverse pop by event every year, where our clients stop in to get their pie, in the past our other best events have been kid-centric like the movies or breakfast with Santa)

I'm always tickled when someone mails or drops off a little gift. I'm very likely to take a picture and tag them on social media. (I mail and/or have delivered 30-50 pop by mailers and/or pop bys every month)

I really enjoy connecting with my favorite people (not companies or brands) on social media. My favorites I have "saved" and am most likely to check in with their accounts each day vs get lost in a scroll. I don't think I follow any "brands" or companies on Instagram ... for example, I follow Emily Ley the founder of Simplified, but I don't follow Simplified the company ... and while I do often like or follow brands/businesses on Facebook I almost always mute them, so they don't show up in my feed. (I strive to put out some engaging "business-related" content on my business accounts each week, but the overwhelming majority of my content, followers and engagement comes from my personal accounts)

Don't knock on my door. I'm not going to answer, and I'm probably going to be pissed because the dogs start acting like maniacs and it takes forever to calm them down so I can get back to work or whatever I was doing. (I don't door knock)

Don't cold call me. I don't usually answer my phone if I don't recognize the phone number or am not expecting a call. 99% of the time when that happens it is spam. When I think back to the 150+ referrals and leads I have generated this year, nearly every single one initiated contact with me either through email, text or social media. (I don't cold call)

Doing business in a way that feels authentic and in alignment with who you are and how you interact will always be more effective. What is that old adage, "do unto others as you would have them do unto you"?

Are you a reluctant spammer, as Seth Godin says? No one wants to be dripped on. There is a better way.

November 17, 2023

It's been a wonderful retreat with my team! This is our 9th year. Every year is different, every group is different, the focus is always different. Every day of the trip this year the sunrise was so different.

Our theme this year was "Dare to Dream", and a big focus for us was vision ... identifying the vision for our life, and how our business is the vehicle to get to that vision.

We also had a huge emphasis on Daily Business Builders™. Each team member declared their goal for 2024, shared their pillars and then we went through together and identified their 3-5 things that they would do every day/week/month in those pillars to get to their goal.

It was so powerful. Often, we put all the focus on the goal ... what we want to achieve, but don't actually take the time to think about or focus on the actions that we need to take to get there.

Yes, keeping your goal front and certain is important ... but I would argue that keeping your action steps front and center is even more important.

I promise you ... if you identified those 3-5 things and spend your energy on doing those things day after day, week after week and month after month, this time next year you will have a completely different business.

November 20, 2023
Good Morning Monday!

This is a short work week in my world, but a chaotic one.

While I was away at our team retreat last week …
-My dog got kicked out of daycare
-My youngest had an issue with a fellow member at his education center and can't return until he has a "restorative circle" meeting
-Our HVAC company came for our winter service, and now the heat has stopped working in half of our house

Today we have 3 contractors scheduled to be at our house … one for an improvement and 2 for repairs.

At the same time, I have a personal doctor's appointment, then I'll be taking my son for his meeting, and taking my leadership meeting for my team from my car in the parking lot. I'm not sure if I will be coming or going today.

Tuesday, we have our team's annual reverse pop by pie event. While I'm there I have 2 groups coming in for meetings/conversations because there just isn't time elsewhere.

The rest of this week will be primarily devoted to family. My oldest will be home from college at some point on Tuesday, and Wednesday will be my only "proactive" workday, for at least part of the day. Thursday we will celebrate Thanksgiving. We host, and like the past several years, this one will look painfully different as we miss another loved one. This will be our smallest gathering yet.

Friday is one of my favorite days of the year as I'll spend the day (and part of the weekend) putting up Christmas decorations. I have too many ornaments and too many trees, but they make me happy, so I lean hard into that.

On the way home from the retreat last week, Vicky Noufal and I took advantage of our several uninterrupted hours together in the car to work on OUR goals … something we don't get to do very often.

Her schedule has been out of control too, so we talked through it and worked out a plan that feels so simple and so clear. There are always exceptions in our business and things that come up, but what we developed for her will work a solid 80+% of the time (with discipline), and that's huge.

Now I need to work on mine.

November 21, 2023
This right here, is a hill I'm willing to die on.

The small things you do everyday matter more than the big things you do occasionally. It's the truth. I know it. I think you probably know it, but we get so, so distracted.

One of the exercises we do as part of our annual goal setting process for my real estate team and for our Empowering Women in Real Estate® Inner Circle is to identify our Daily Business Builders™ (yep, trademark pending!).

Your Daily Business Builders™ are a series of activities, 3-5 is a good number, that you complete every day (or week) in your business.

My Daily Business Builders™ are ...
-Calls/Texts/Messages (3)
-Notes (5)
-Pop Bys (1)
-Add to Database (1)
-Give Referrals (3)

I've done some version of these Daily Business Builders™ for 21 years. Literally.

I've been tracking them consistently for more than 8 years now. I know for sure that my tracking and focus on these activities was instrumental when I restarted my business from zero back in 2015 (after letting it go dormant for 2 ½ years while I worked as a managing broker).

The actual number of things that I do varies by the season I'm in. What you see above is my goal for each week, and I strive to complete them all on Mondays. When I was restarting my business, the numbers you see above are what I did DAILY. Sometimes I wouldn't quite get it all done, but my commitment to myself was that I wouldn't "wrap up" my proactive workweek on Fridays until I had checked all the boxes.

As a result of this, our team's Client & Community Care Program (which includes postcards, email newsletters, social media and events), and a lot of getting out there and taking full advantage of every single opportunity, I went from 0 to $20M in less than two years.

Some years I've adjusted what you see here and my Daily Business Builders™ have included things like coffees or social media posts. Sometimes, when going through a particularly brutal life season, my Daily Business Builders™ consisted of one thing ... write 1 note per week. When I couldn't muster anything else, committing to doing this one thing per week felt doable, and kept me moving in a forward direction.

There are two things I've learned about committing to this process ...
1) You don't need to do it perfectly. 80% of the time should be the goal.
2) It's okay to have lower, "achievable", numbers here because you build momentum and will end up doing much more.

Want to know my results YTD?
-Calls/Texts/Messages 128 (Annual Goal 141)
-Notes 495 (Annual Goal 235)
-Pop Bys 223 (Annual Goal 47)
-Add to Database 101 (Annual Goal 47)
-Referrals Given 229 (Annual Goal 141)

These are my activity results. These activities resulted in 51 referrals received, 125 other leads received, and over $15M in sales volume closed by my team and referral partners.

Ages and ages ago I did an episode of Empowering Women in Real Estate® - The Podcast on my Daily Business Builders™ ... way back on episode 51. You can find it on your favorite podcast app. I'm working on an updated version of it for early 2024.

What you do for your Daily Business Builders™ doesn't need to look just like mine. Your activities should reflect your business pillars. When doing this exercise with my team at our retreat last week, we heard many different options. One team member committed to 1 open house per week (among other things). Another committed to 8 connections per day (among other things). Others committed to mailing a certain number of CMAs, posting in their community group, and many other things.

Stop looking for the shiny thing, the new thing that will transform your business. **You, working consistently on focused activities is what will transform your business.** I promise you that if you identify YOUR specific and unique Daily Business Builders™ that support the pillars in your business and commit fully to doing them in 2024 that this time next year your business will look completely different ... in a good way.

December 14, 2023

Yesterday Vicky Noufal and I were having a conversation about people we want to work with. We always want to work with all the people. Sometimes who we are and how we operate as a team and a network is clear.

Other times it isn't. Sometimes simply because of perception. Maybe sometimes we don't explain it very well. It's clear in our hearts and our minds but it doesn't come out clearly in our words.

I'm not sure exactly what she said yesterday to prompt it, but my response was something to the effect of we need to be less of who we aren't and more of who we are.

Being more of who we are …

Professionals who are super driven and focused on our careers, clients, education and growth.

Moms who love our children (3 sons each!) with our whole hearts and would do anything to make sure they are happy, healthy and well.

Friends who give (sometimes until it hurts) generously of time, knowledge, energy and more, understanding the power of proximity and collaboration.

Being more of who we are means that we will attract more people who are like us into our world.

Leaning hard into that will change your life.

Not everyone will like you, no matter what you do.

Not everyone will choose you, no matter how hard you work.

Not everyone is for you … but many are. And the more time you spend being more authentically you, the faster you will find them.

December 22, 2023

This is not a post about Christmas. Keep reading and you'll see what I mean.

I have 3 teenage boys. They are at varying stages of self-absorption. (Boy moms know what I'm talking about.)

There have been a lot of conversations in my house the past few weeks amongst each other surrounding Christmas. "What do you want for Christmas?", etc. Occasionally they ask dear old mom, lol. Most especially in the last week as they are all last-minute shoppers.

My typical response (which they generally also hear on Mother's Day and my birthday) is that I like a nice candle, gift cards for books or new slippers. Blah, blah, and blah. (But true!)

Then last week, a mic drop from my middle (he's always the one) when I gave my usual answer. "Mom, I think you're so busy worrying about what everyone else wants that you don't think about what you really want."

Subtext: You're so busy making it happen for everyone else, you don't do it for yourself. See, it's not about Christmas.

I spend 99% of my day, every day, making sure everyone else has what they need. Yes, my kids and my family, but also my clients, my team members, our support team, our Empowering Women in Real Estate® community (members, Local Leaders, the Inner Circle, those that purchase our courses and attend our events) and our national team.

I'm always actively looking for opportunities for everyone, trying to make their job easier, keeping the focus (and the peace), making sure everyone feels appreciated and seen. Pouring out, pouring out, pouring out.

By the time I get to that 1% of time in my day (if it happens at all), I'm so worn out, my creativity is zero, and my brain is mush.

It's hard to even consider or visualize what I really want. I mean, I set the goals and achieve them on the regular, but they often feel like "surface" goals. Not soul-filling ones.

I know I'm not alone in this.

Your turn.

What do YOU really want for your life and your business?

Not what your clients want, or your broker wants or your team leader wants. Not what your kids want or your partner or your friends want.

What do YOU want?

It feels like a really hard question to answer. Which is why we end up saying things like a nice candle, a gift card for books or new slippers.

2024

Milestones
6-12-2024 – 5-year anniversary of the Inner Circle group coaching program
7-29-2024 – 10-year anniversary of Empowering Women in Real Estate®

January 9, 2024
"If you are persistent, you will get it. If you are consistent, you will keep it."

When I saw that quote from Elena Cardone, it stopped me in my tracks.

It so perfectly describes my 22-year real estate career, what has led to my success, and how I've gotten here.

I've spent more than 15 years total actively selling homes, personally averaging 50-60 transactions per year.

I've been a team owner for almost 9 years now, and our team has closed over $1.2 Billion in sales volume.

I continue to prospect in my personal real estate sales business every day and every week, producing $15-20M in sales volume every year that is closed by my team members and referral agent partners.

What I do isn't necessarily hard, but it definitely isn't easy.

Most people don't have the patience ... or the confidence in what they are doing.

If you want a long-term successful career in real estate ...

-It takes persistence. Pushing back against objections, trying again when you fail, putting yourself out there again and again.

-It takes consistency. Doing the same or similar things over and over and over again. Seriously, it's one of my superpowers.

Your business isn't here to entertain you. Can it feel "boring" and repetitive? Sure can! Does it work? Absolutely!

Want to succeed in real estate? You need a plan, and you need to execute on it consistently. That's it.

You can do it too, I promise. Not sure how? I can show you.

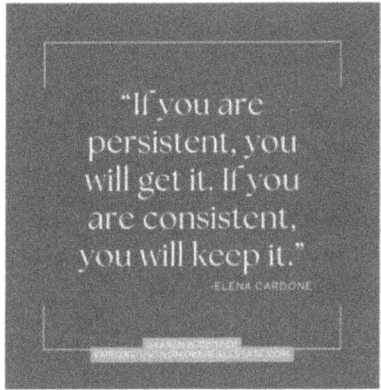

January 10, 2024

Chances are you've heard me use the term, "Daily Business Builders™" at least a time or two ... and on today's episode of Empowering Women in Real Estate® - The Podcast I'm diving deep into what it all means ...

WHAT they are ...
WHY they are important to your business ...
And HOW to utilize them to revolutionize your business in 2024!

You can listen in on your favorite podcast app. Be sure to check out last week's episode on Business Pillars (episode 282), it is the perfect counterpart.

January 18, 2024

Yesterday was a fantastic day ... and such a demonstration of growth, and example of the legacy Vicky Noufal and I want to leave in this world and in our real estate community.

A couple months ago our team member Robin Gebhardt came to us with a desire to give back. She wanted to tell her story as she really felt that there were other agents out there, right now especially, that need to hear it.

And what a story it is.

When Robin joined our team 5 years ago, she was at rock-bottom. Deep in debt, owing six figures to the IRS, and in the midst of a transaction drought. She went more than 235 days without a commission. Can you imagine?

Through a lot of hard work, perseverance, aligning herself with the right people, getting in the right rooms and applying our systems, she is now a completely different Robin living a completely different life.

Not only has she paid off the debt, but she has quadrupled her real estate sales business, and even bought a beach condo for her family to enjoy.

What I love so much about her story is having climbed the mountain she is now turning around and pulling others up with her by sharing her story, and even establishing a local accountability group for agents in our area.

Robin, you made, and make, us all so proud ... and not just yesterday with your successful event. There was a passage from my morning reading that made me think of you ... you chose to make the change that changed it all.

January 19, 2024

Life isn't slowing down. Not today. Not tomorrow. Not ever.

Your business isn't going to magically improve.

The debt isn't going to just go away.

That beach house isn't going to buy itself. The fully funded retirement account or college funds aren't going to fund themselves. That European vacation isn't going to pay for itself. Your house isn't going to pay itself off.

Insert whatever big goal or dream you have here.

It's not happening on its own. Not today. Not tomorrow. Not ever.

There is going to come a moment where you have to make the choice to make the change that will change it all.

You could do it tomorrow and continue to delay what you want and where you are going.

You could do it never, and just continue wishing, hoping, wanting and living in a cycle where no amount of business, sales volume, clients or transactions will ever be enough.

Or you could do it today.

22 years ago, I made the choice to get my real estate license and joined a team that not only taught me what to do but helped me to build the foundation of the business I have today. That choice changed it all.

15 years ago, I made the choice to leave that team and join a brokerage where I kept more of my commissions, was able to make a name for myself as a solo agent, and eventually became their managing broker. That choice changed it all.

10 years ago, I made the choice to start Empowering Women in Real Estate®, this community literally lifted me through my lowest moments and has grown into more than I ever could have dreamed. That choice changed it all.

9 years ago, I made the choice to partner with Vicky Noufal and build the Platinum Group Real Estate Team at a different brokerage that allowed us to keep even more of our commissions and begin teaching our team members to

do what we have done in our businesses to be so successful. That choice changed it all.

5 years ago, we made the choice that I would step out of personal sales production to focus on building our team, building up our team members, focusing on lead generation, operations and systems which allowed for the space to create our Empowering Women in Real Estate® Inner Circle. That choice changed it all.

15 months ago, we made the choice to move our team to Real Brokerage. For the first time in my career I have a retirement fund that is growing at a pace faster than I have ever been able to do on my own, we are keeping more of our commissions with lower overhead costs and I am learning more about the industry and the business than I have since those first few years of my career when literally everything was brand new …

And that choice is truly the one that has changed it all. The culmination of 2+ decades of career decisions that is changing the trajectory of my business, my life, my family and my team member's lives forever.

I've said many times that I have never regretted a choice that I have made in my business, except that I would have made some of them a lot sooner. This choice is the epitome of that.

Is today the day that you will make the choice that changes it all?

What are the choices leading up to today in your business that changed it all for you?

January 29, 2024
Good Morning Monday!

I've been up since 3:24 am. I finally gave up and got out of bed just after 5 am. A combination of perimenopausal fun (burning up hot and freezing cold, alternate every 5 minutes) and just a very, very busy brain.

I'm not the only one up … our team chat line is already going this morning. We ratified 8 contracts over the past week with several more out in negotiations.

Today I get to celebrate my best girl, Vicky Noufal, on her birthday.

I have a pretty reasonable mix of calls, meetings and "work time" this week. Tomorrow marks 2 years since my dad passed away, and what would have been my nephew's 15th birthday. I'm not sure if I'll be able to acknowledge all of that tomorrow, so I'm tossing it out there now.

Lately I've been obsessed with figuring out new ways of working together. Think part Inner Circle and mentorship, part team benefits and collaboration, coupled with solo agent "independence" and very, very attractive splits. With some new options our brokerage is rolling out, plus better understanding on our part of what we can do, it's pretty exciting.

For years and years and years, long before my team was really a team, I've longed for ways to help and serve more women in the real estate industry (hence the launching of this group almost 10 years ago). For the first time ever, I no longer have the restraints of space and geography, and we are so close to putting all the pieces together without massive (or any) increases to overhead costs.

A culmination of years of work and puzzle pieces that finally fit together. It's super exciting, and that makes it hard to sleep.

February 14, 2024

Today's episode of Empowering Women in Real Estate® - The Podcast is something that we have never done before … it is an interview with my husband!

I've been in business for 22 years and we've been married for 22 years, so he has been there literally since the beginning … and it hasn't always been smooth. What we do is so different, the non-stop nature is so unique, that not everyone in our lives understand, especially if that partner comes from a more traditional career. You can listen in on your favorite podcast app.

Episode 288: Love & Real Estate - An Interview with MY HUSBAND!

February 20, 2024

Looking for success and growth in your real estate business?

Here's the secret ... consistency.

Be honest, when is the last time you ...
-Posted anything about real estate?
-Logged into your CRM?
-Sent a mailer or email to your database?
-Added someone to your database?

How is anyone supposed to remember who you are and what you do if you don't show up or tell them?

In the past 22 years I have been personally responsible for or played a part in over $1.7 BILLION in real estate sales volume.

Here are a few of the consistent habits that have led to this success ...
-A rock-solid morning routine that goes with me everywhere.
-Logging into my CRM every.single.day.
-Adding at least 1 new contact to my database every week.
-Monthly postcard mailers.
-Monthly emails to my database.
-Showing up on social media at least 3-5 times per week.
-Quarterly pop bys or pop by mailers. Sometimes both.
-Reading personal or business development every day.

There's more, but neither you nor I have all day.

It's not fancy, it's not sexy, it's not shiny and new ... but it is wildly effective.

Everything I do I teach step-by-step with the templates and text to back it up in our Empowering Women in Real Estate® Inner Circle. You can learn more on our website, EmpoweringWomenInRealEstate.com

April 8, 2024

I've never been a big sports fan, but I did really get into the NCAA Women's Basketball Final 4. Did you watch the championship game yesterday between Iowa and South Carolina?

What drew me in was all the talk of Caitlin Clark, an unbelievably talented player for Iowa, who is expected to be the #1 draft pick for the WNBA later this month. She is without a doubt a dynamic player, and I loved watching her play. Not only is she more than capable of scoring on her own (she scored 30 points in the national championship game!) but she is a prolific passer credited with many assists.

But what got me hooked was the coaching. I am fascinated by powerful female leaders and how they use their talents and experience to empower others to be successful.

Most specifically, Dawn Staley, the head coach for South Carolina. Their team was not only undefeated for the season, but they won the championship game as well. In all of the interviews with her, the players, the information shared about the team and her coaching style what came up again and again was their "unselfish" team culture. It wasn't about any one individual player or star, but a true collaborative team effort.

A few things I learned that I found impressive ...
-At the end of last season, they lost all 5 of their starting players when they graduated and/or went to the WNBA and basically re-built their roster.

-Part of their recruiting strategy to the team is telling players that if they want 25 individual points per game, they should probably go somewhere else, but if they want a national championship, they should play for them.

-SC rotates 9 players per game (in contrast, Iowa primarily played the same 5).

-None of the players played more than 28 minutes in a single game all season.

Am I the only one who finds this stuff fascinating? Clearly their strategy is one that works, and teamwork is truly, as they say, what makes the dream work!

April 11, 2024
Today's post has exactly nothing to do with real estate.

Well, that's not exactly true. This statement has to do with real estate ... how often do you take time out for fun? For joy? For hobbies?

Our business can run us ragged. There's typically too much to do and not enough time to do it in. We spend so much time trying to please everyone else, trying to take care of everyone else, taking on more and more constantly trying to prove our value.

But what do you do for you? I'm not talking about the things we do to take care of ourselves ... the walks, the workouts, the journaling, reading personal development.

I mean, what do you do for you, for fun?

My friend Vicky Chrisner bowls in a league on Thursday mornings. That's for fun.

My friend Jodi Hooper regularly fosters puppies and kittens (if you're local to me, she has puppies right now!). That's for fun (and for a good cause).

My friend Jeni Harmon is a prolific creator. Crocheting washcloths, making cards. It fills her up and makes the recipients of her gifts feel good too.

I used to bowl in a league too. I also used to volunteer at the animal shelter on my lunch hour (pre-real estate) and I've done a couple stints fostering puppies. I also used to create all the time. Making wreaths and ornaments that I sold at craft fairs. Sewing pillows, doing cross stitch, making floral arrangements out of silks (I even made the altar flowers and bouquets for my wedding). I used to play golf on Fridays with my dad.

Notice "used to".

Over the weekend I read this article on Cup of Jo about not just finding time for joy in our lives but making time for it. Doing things simply for the purpose of the fun of it. You can read it here ...
https://cupofjo.com/2024/03/12/singing-as-adult/

So, my question this morning is ...

What do you do just for fun, just for you?

May 21, 2024

I was walking through the garden section at Walmart a week or so ago and saw this little beauty. Only she wasn't so beautiful then.

-Her soil was dry.
-The entire plant was leaning over sideways in the pot.
-Her leaves were droopy and a sickly shade of green.
-Most of the flowers were past their peak with their heads hanging down.

But there was this one flower that was open and blooming in the most beautiful shade of purple-y pink and so into my cart she went.

The potential was there, she just needed someone to believe in her, to nurture her.

I took her home and ...
-Planted her in a bigger pot.
-Added fresh, nutrient-rich soil.
-Watered her consistently.
-Put her in a spot where the sun would shine on her most of the day, but still with the protective shade of the porch.

Six days later and she's unrecognizable in the best way possible.

Tell me again how your environment doesn't matter.

If you are feeling less than your best in your life and your business right now, chances are you aren't the problem, your environment is.

Being surrounded by the right people, being poured into by women who are where you want to be or heading in the same direction truly makes all the difference.

It's one of the reasons I started this group almost 10 years ago, and has been my passion, my mission for the majority of my career.

May 23, 2024

As a realtor and a mom, here's what I'm most proud of ... and it's probably not what you think.

My real estate business is older than my children.

The list of accolades and accomplishments are long ...
-22 Years in Business
-9 Years as a Team Leader
-Over $1.7 BILLION in real estate sales volume
-Many, many (many) hundreds of homes sold personally

Top producer this, top producer that. #1 here, #1 there. You know the drill.

Add to that this *little* community I created 10 years ago called Empowering Women in Real Estate® with over 37,000 women in the real estate industry, a podcast of the same name with hundreds of thousands of downloads, Monthly Meet Ups in cities across the country, the Inner Circle monthly membership group coaching program and a registered trademark from the US Patent and Trademark Office.

It all pales in comparison to being there for my family.

-Raising 3 sons from helpless newborns to crazy teens to responsible young men.
-Prioritizing showing up to volunteer in their classrooms, chaperone the field trips and cheer them on at their games.
-Playing a leading role in caring for aging family members on both sides, not just for a season, but for YEARS at a time.
-Figuring out and giving myself what I need, so I can give them what they need. (Actively working on this one.)

I've done NONE of this perfectly, but I have shown up consistently where it matters most to me, nd I'm really freaking proud of that.

You can do both. You can kick ass in all the ways that are most important to you, at home and while you are selling homes.

If you are surrounded by people that respect the hustle and the vanity metrics more than your priorities and devotion to your family, then you're in the wrong place.

I said what I said.

May 27, 2024

Good Morning Monday! It's still morning, right? It's been a lovely few days over here and I have truly lost track of the time and day.

The last few days I've been feeling so peaceful, purposeful, intentional and creative. I was trying to figure out why, what's different and here's what I came up with …

My weekend started with some "social" time that filled my cup. If you are a fellow introvert, you will know exactly what I am talking about. A lot of social things drain me (I'm learning the difference and giving myself permission to say no), and the vision story that I have written for myself and read every morning literally references social things that fill my cup, and Friday I had two of those.

Vicky Noufal and I had the opportunity to sit down for a beautiful lunch and conversation with our friend Andrea Boeye and her husband. They are also team leaders and serve the Quad Cities of Iowa/Illinois. They happened to be in Northern Virginia this weekend and it was so good to spend time together. We could have talked the entire day. After they had to leave, Vicky and I spent a couple hours with a leisurely walk and lots of meaningful conversation … something that has always been a big part of our friendship and business partnership but has been put aside so much the past few years as we have prioritized "doing the work" over solidifying the dream.

Every morning for the past 2+ weeks I've been starting my day with the Growth Day app and the "daily fire" mindset message/teaching from Brendan Bruchard. I listen as I am getting ready or tidying up around the house. When you pour good stuff in, you get good stuff out. I've known this and done some version of it for years … though there is so much "stuff" out there it can be hard to find what is really good for you. Right now, this is working for me. You can learn at https://www.growthday.com/?via=ewre

I've resumed journaling in the morning. I stopped after my nephew passed away last August. My last entry (I was doing a gratitude practice each morning) was about him the day after he died, and I haven't opened it up since. Right now, I am using the "Be Her Now" journal from Kim Fitzpatrick and it is working for me. You can learn more at LegacyByKim.com Another favorite journal I've used in the past is the "Start Today" journal from Rachel Hollis, which I see is now back in stock.

These are just a few examples. How do I know that all of this is working for me? Two things …

First, on Friday evening a team member called me in tears. She was dealing with a horrible client situation, and the way she was being treated and threatened was not only completely uncalled for but also essentially extortion. I worked through it with her and our broker calmly, as always. Normally when dealing with a situation like this I would be calm on the outside but completely fall apart on the inside and would feel a ripple effect for DAYS (even when it was something happening to a friend/team member and not me directly). This time felt different. My resolve isn't just on the outside, I feel it on the inside too.

Second, it feels like my brain is firing on all cylinders, which means my creativity is way, way up. On Sunday morning instead of sitting with my coffee and scrolling or reading blogs as usual, I was inspired by another team member and our conversations and created my "5 Simple Steps to Jumpstart Your Business". She has been seeing great results with what we talked through, and it felt so good and exciting to systematize and package it to share more widely (for free!). You can get it on my Instagram (@karen.w.cooper), just comment on any post with the word ACTION.

So, short story long, which is typically how we roll around here ... but when things are working for me, you know I like to share them.

I also can't close out today's message without acknowledging that today is Memorial Day here in the US. A day that we honor and mourn those who died while serving our country. Men and women throughout our history have given their lives to protect our freedoms ... there is no greater reason to live our lives to the fullest and to lean into our purpose more than in honor of those who cannot.

May 30, 2024

I'm excited to share that on June 1st we will be kicking off my birthday month GIVEAWAYS!! Not only is June my birthday month, but it also marks the 5 year anniversary of the Empowering Women in Real Estate® Inner Circle! Instead of doing my usual coffee giveaway I wanted to do something different.

In my 22-year career I've been a part of over $1.7 BILLION in real estate sales volume. The majority of this business has been generated by social media, geographic farming, or referrals from my sphere or database.

I've been teaching, coaching and mentoring women in the real estate industry for what feels like forever, but most specifically in a formal capacity for the past 10 years. During that time, I've built up quite a body of work ...

hundreds of hours and pieces of content, resources, presentations, events. So many things that I am proud to have created ... and I've decided that this is the perfect chance to give it all away.

Every day this month I'll be sharing something for FREE ... a course, a template that I've personally used, a conference replay. Pop by tags, postcards, pdfs for buyers or sellers, invitations. All the things!

The freebies I'm giving away are all just a SMALL part of the value and benefits our Inner Circle members receive all year long!

(Author's Note: All giveaways now have a permanent spot on my Instagram profile, @karen.w.cooper, under a highlight called, "Giveaways".)

June 12, 2024
5 years ago today I did something I've always wanted to do ...

It was June 12, 2019.

At that point I had been in the real estate industry for 17 years. Nearly since the beginning women had been coming to me, no matter which brokerage I was with, asking for help.

You know those coffees, the ones where someone wants to "pick your brain"? I was going on those at least once or twice a week. Plus, two times that in the number of phone calls or messages asking for advice.

I loved it.

I've always been a leader, a teacher, a mentor at heart. In every role I've ever taken on in every single facet of my life … Captain of the cheerleading team at junior college, Chief of the rescue squad in my 20s, marketing department tech support (which is truly laughable that there would be a time in my life when I would know enough tech-y stuff that colleagues would come to be before putting in a support ticket for the actual tech support) and first aid instructor at the pharmaceutical company I worked for (my actual job was market research and project management).

Five years earlier I launched a Facebook community called Empowering Women in Real Estate®, which had grown rapidly. Every single day, 5-7 days per week, I would show up in that group to share, start a discussion, give a tip, start the day with some sort of inspiration. I still do that, ten years later.

The question that had been on my mind for years was how to take that to the next level. How to create a business from this community that could reach and serve even more women by offering powerful, cost-effective tools that they could use to grow their business exponentially. I wanted to share the exact strategies and systems that I used personally to grow my own business and to support my family. We shared those things with our real estate team, but at that time our team was limited by how many women we could serve and by geography. I wanted to make a bigger, wider, broader impact.

On June 12, 2019, the Empowering Women in Real Estate® Inner Circle was born. Once the idea and the structure finally came to me, I literally implemented it within less than 48 hours. I created an online product with a way to take recurring payments and launched it in the early hours of that morning. By the end of the day, we had 50 plus members. The original price was $59 per month (just as it is right now), and our "launch name" was Empower Coaching. For those first couple years I operated it 100% out of a Facebook Group and using MailChimp to email plans to our members each week and each month. It took about 2 years to have our first real (meaning I didn't make it myself) website built, and maybe another year after that to complete our rebrand to the Inner Circle and to build out our education portal.

When quarantines started in the spring of 2020 and everyone in our industry became fearful that we wouldn't be able to work (and in many places across the country realtors couldn't work), I decided to suspend payments for our existing members for a month. That ended up being 6 months of the program being delivered for free, and I offered it to anyone who wanted to take part. We had over a thousand women participating with us during that time.

Five years in and we still have quite a few members with us right now that joined on that very first day. I get messages from women all the time about how the program has been a blessing to them. That the strategies that they learn, and implement has changed their businesses for the better. That their businesses have grown (many have doubled!) and become more consistent when they follow the plan.

I started an album in my camera roll called "proof", because sometimes when you pour so much out of yourself there will be moments of resistance either from the outside or the inside that will cause you to question why you do it. When I receive those messages from members I remember why, helping women to grow their real estate business without sacrificing their quality of life has been the mission from day 1.

And I'm so, so grateful to have had this opportunity.

June 18, 2024

It's a big day in our family ... high school graduation day for this guy, my middle son Ryan!

It is so true what they say, the days are long, but the years are short.

Lessons learned from Ryan ...

It's okay to change your mind, listen to your gut and follow your heart.

Not everyone will understand, and that's okay.

No one else gets to live your life.

One of my very favorite memories from when he was little ...

It was 2008, he was a little more than 2 years old. We were walking down from our hotel to the beach, my husband and I carrying twelve tons of things. Chairs, umbrellas, coolers, toys. You know how it goes, especially when you have little kids.

His big brother (who was 4 at the time) was keeping up with us, probably leading the way, I think even carrying things, but Ryan was lagging behind. I kept hearing this thumping, scraping noise and I look to see him just strolling along, dragging his bucket. Hat all sideways up on his head, not in a rush or with a care in the world, just looking around, taking it all in.

Some 16 years later, he is still taking it all in, moving at his pace on his terms, and we couldn't be more proud.

Your light shines brightly my sweet boy, and so is your future.

July 2, 2024

I've spent 22 years in the real estate industry and sold thousands of homes and here's what I know for sure ...

There is always more than enough to go around.

Her success doesn't mean there will be less for you and vice versa.

Let's say it louder for the people in the back.

To be clear though, just because there is enough to go around doesn't mean you can just sit back and wait (and hope) for it to come to you.

If you want to succeed as a realtor, you must be working at your craft every day. Previewing properties, showing homes to buyers, listing appointments with sellers, running CMAs, marketing, connecting and putting yourself out there.

The work is worth the reward, and it's there for you when you are ready to claim it.

Recently I helped a team member to get moving in her business. She started implementing a few simple steps I shared with her, and now she is going on appointments nearly every day, is building her database, has opportunities flowing to her, and is making some money in the process while she plants seeds that will produce an even bigger payoff in the future.

This work isn't necessarily "hard", but the consistency required to make it happen is far from easy. What activities do you do each day to stay engaged with your business?

July 4, 2024

Independence. It's one of the reasons that many of us became realtors in the first place.

The freedom to choose when and how we work and with whom. The opportunity to brand ourselves and to market in a way that aligns with our authentic selves.

And then the reality of the business sets in.

It's lonely. Being a solo agent means just that ... solo. Alone. Your colleagues are your competitors. It's hard to be vulnerable and ask questions or to run a scenario by someone when you need advice when next week you could be going up against them on a listing appointment.

This is one of the biggest reasons so many agents turn to teams ... only to lose their independence, and to be disappointed when they realize that the entire model is built to ensure the team leader's production success, not theirs.

It doesn't have to be that way.

In fact, it isn't always that way.

I'm consistently surprised by the stories I hear from agents about their team experiences. I totally get why they feel apprehensive. I mean, aren't all teams the same?

They aren't. Just like all brokerages aren't the same and all agents aren't the same.

Our Platinum Group Real Estate Team is special.

Our motto is be in business for yourself, not by yourself. Our mission is to help women grow their real estate business without sacrificing their quality of life.

We do this by sharing, teaching and helping you to implement our time-tested marketing and lead generation systems. We open our playbook and don't just tell you how to build a stronger, more efficient business and a better life, but we demonstrate it through leadership that actually walks the walk and doesn't just talk the talk.

Our agent partners have complete flexibility and independence with their branding; they can use ours or create their own. We have the confidence in what we do to offer the choice because after 9 years together as a team and over $1.7 BILLION closed in real estate sales volume we know what others are afraid to tell you ... people work with you because you are you, not because of the logo on your sign or the colors on your business card.

When you work with us you always do business in your own name. We invest significant time and resources in YOUR growth as an agent and as a person, and when you join our tribe of powerhouse women you have a built-in support system where no question is too small, and they are never used against you.

High splits, low caps, no monthly or quarterly fees, and zero geographic limitations ... plus the opportunity to develop additional revenue streams if you want them. It's a powerful combination.

Message me if you would like to learn more. We're enlarging our circle, and we'd love to include you.

July 6, 2024

Summer 2024 Bucket List for Realtors:
-Sellers that take your advice over their third cousin twice removed.
-Taking a vacation without being glued to your phone.
-Buyers who understand that they will actually get a better deal when they don't try to cut you out of it.
-Builders that pay more than a flat fee.
-The MLS honoring your sellers wishes over their bureaucratic rules (and they stop trying to fine you for it).
-Agents that show up for their scheduled showings on your listings ... or cancel in advance.

Tapping "cancel showing" in the app > not showing up ... am I right?

What would you add to the list?

Happy Summer!

July 9, 2024

I was chatting with an agent yesterday and I asked her what she was looking for, what she felt she needed in her business. She hesitated to express it ... saying that she thought it might be unrealistic.

This is not the first time I have heard this from an agent this year. Feeling uneasy, like they've outgrown where they are ... but almost feeling bad about wanting more, thinking it isn't possible or reasonable.

It is.

Early this morning I got a text from a friend sharing a video from the leadership at our brokerage talking about agents building their investment portfolio. She was so happy to see this. For decades she's talked about this, encouraged this, taught this, wanted this for others in our industry ... but when you aren't around people who want this too, encourage this too it can feel defeating, like it isn't okay to want something different.

It is.

For close to a decade, I've been teaching, training and mentoring women in real estate. Hosting events and Facebook lives, selling courses and programs. Offering far more content for free. I've always done this from a position of AND ... I am a producing realtor AND someone who is paid to coach, train and mentor others in the industry.

And for years I've felt bad about this. Like it was a part of me that I had to hide, or not talk about too loudly or too much, that it wasn't "right" or reasonable to have goals in this area. Like I am supposed to be this one set of things (realtor, team leader) and so it doesn't make sense, or I shouldn't also be these other things (a coach and mentor that is paid for her time, knowledge and experience).

Then I had an environment change, and I started being around different people. I started working with a coach who not only does what I do and have wanted to do (generate real estate sales AND coach others) but teaches others how to do the same. During the first meeting we had it was like the clouds parted and I could see the sun.

I no longer felt strange or out of place. My goals and dreams no longer felt unrealistic. I didn't feel bad for wanting the things I do ... in fact within this group it is celebrated and is what others are striving for as well.

What you want for your life and business ... whatever that is ... it isn't unrealistic. If you are feeling that it is, that it isn't possible, that is not a reflection of you, it is a reflection of where you are and who you are surrounded by. They aren't bad or wrong and neither are you, you just want different things.

We live in a big, huge world. There are infinite ways of doing things and accomplishing our goals in our business.

You can grow your real estate business without sacrificing your quality of life.

You can be in business for yourself, but not by yourself.

You can go on vacation or take a break and turn your phone off.

You can generate business and partner with someone else to serve those clients.

You can produce at a very high level without burning yourself out.

You can have a consistent business without buying leads.

I could go on and on. What you want isn't unrealistic, it just might be for where you are. Change your perspective, your mindset, your environment, and you might just find that what once seemed so unreasonable and impossible actually is both reasonable and possible for you.

Because it is.

July 11, 2024

Earlier this week I had the opportunity to speak to some agents that were in a similar season of life and business that I am.

They were in their 50s and 60s, strong, vibrant, and have been building successful real estate businesses and teams for 20-30 years. A massive accomplishment to do so much for such a long period of time.

They aren't done yet either. They have a vision for the future of their business, and they have a lot to offer, but they have evolved. The things they want and where they want to focus their time, effort and energy now is different than what it was at the beginning of their career, near the middle, or even 5 years ago.

But they are fatigued. It feels hard to create something new when you are still weary from the last battle with the market and your P&L.

As we were discussing what's next, one of them said, "I don't want to, but when the time comes, I guess I'll just quit."

Imagine that ... building something so successful for so long, and just walking away. Much of our industry teaches us that is the only way, but it isn't.

When you are successful in real estate, especially for so long, it becomes a part of your identity.

I view it like a knit sweater that you wear.

When the seasons change and you are ready to wear something else, you could take it off and throw it away, but that seems like a terrible waste.

You could try to sell it to someone, there are lots of websites and consignment places now where you can do that, but what is the market willing to pay for something that is heavily worn, thread-bare in a few places, maybe a hole or two? Not much, if anything.

Instead, I view it as a slow unraveling. Picture pulling one of those loose threads at the bottom and tugging on it gently. You can unravel it more quickly, but I envision unraveling it slowly over a period of many years.

A little less of this here, a little more of that there. Adjusting what you do and how and with whom. Continuing to be compensated for your work, knowledge and experience all along the way. Coming alongside others who are eager to learn from you and have the energy and enthusiasm to do the parts of the job that are no longer for you. Truly a win-win.

And when you're done unraveling, then comes the best part. A pile of yarn that you can use to knit something completely different, but equally as beautiful.

July 23, 2024

I feel like this is a message a lot of us can use right now. This work has always been hard, and throughout my 22-year career there have been many moments, conversations and people I would encounter who didn't appreciate the work that I did. Those that thought it wasn't necessary, that I was overpaid, that I was "just a slimy salesperson" who "only cared about the commission".

For the most part those people and interactions were a very small number each year in comparison to the many clients I served who saw the value and were appreciative of my work. I know, without a shadow of a doubt, I made a difference in the lives of those families.

Since the announcement of the NAR settlement, our "worthiness" seems to be on debate on a much larger scale.

Sellers who once found great value in paying a commission that included a coop, suddenly believe it is no longer necessary, and believe the media hype that they have overpaid all these years.

Buyers who oftentimes struggle as it is coming up with their down payment and closing costs trying to figure out how they can pay for the representation they need when housing costs are sky high.

Other agents, "coaches" even, saying publicly that sellers will never contribute to buyer's agent compensation again and that they plan to gobble up all the listings come 8/17 when they don't offer it anymore. What?

Yesterday I watched Brian Buffini's Bold Predictions Mid-Year Update (you can watch the replay on his website), and he is always a voice of calm. Something he said was for years we haven't done ourselves any favors when we would essentially tell the buyers our services were "free" to them because the seller paid them ... in some way indicating/sending the message that we worked for free/had no value in what we did.

I can see that. I've said that. In my state (Virginia) we've always had to sign a buyer agency agreement, so that isn't new, and so many times when explaining it to buyers and they would express concerns about having to pay me if the seller didn't, I would say some version of that or write in that I was paid only through the seller or per the MLS listing. It's a message a lot of us have shared for a long time.

Right now, feels hard and unclear. Deadlines are looming with the date buyer's agent compensation disclosures come out of the MLS (less than 30 days), and yet in my area our contract forms were changed to reflect that as of 7/1, so we already have to act as if. Which means lots of confusion. Our MLS posts about hefty fines and fear of litigation if we reference anywhere the compensation our seller wishes to offer. So where do we put it? I've seen Facebook groups pop up to share it (pretty sure those aren't okay) and I'm sure some enterprising realtor somewhere is working on a website that they will charge a fee to share your listings and offers of compensation.

We know the "new rules", but how we will actually work within them is still a bit of a mystery. I'm grateful that we are getting consistent direction from our brokerage, but even then, things will flux a bit here and there as we learn how to go about being who we are and what we do.

I have no hard and fast solutions for you today, but I do have a bit of advice … it's time to let go of "how we used to do it". Instead of waiting for the powers that be to dictate what and how you can do what and where, get clear on how YOU will work. What do you charge for the services you provide? Who do you work with, how, when and where? The more clear you are about those things, the easier it will be to explain your value … and when not to bother. Not every client and every scenario will be right for you and your business. That was true 5, 10 and 15 years ago, and will remain true tomorrow, next month, next year and beyond.

Don't hang the future of your career and your livelihood on the scraps of what someone is willing to toss your way. You are a business owner, time to start acting like it.

July 29, 2024

Today we are celebrating 10 YEARS of Empowering Women in Real Estate® … and announcing our 4th Annual Conference!

It was ten years ago today that I hit publish on this little Facebook community called Empowering Women in Real Estate®, with no intention other than to bring women in the real estate industry together.

Now with over 38,000 members, literally thousands of posts written by me (5-7 days per week for TEN YEARS), our Inner Circle monthly membership program that just celebrated its 5 year anniversary, over 300 podcast episodes, hundreds of Monthly Meet Ups in cities across the country, hundreds of hours of coaching and teaching through Facebook lives and webinars, soon to be our 4th major conference and a registered trademark later … and this has been one of the biggest surprises and delights of my life.

What started as a passion project became a full-fledged business. What's that saying, when you do what you love you'll never work a day in your life? It's that. Every single morning for 10 years, whether I am home or on vacation, no matter how early, no matter what is happening that day, the first thing I do after sitting down with my coffee is open my iPad, check in with the group and start writing. To be able to share so openly with others who support, understand and can relate is a blessing.

Our community members are truly the best around. They don't tolerate spam, scammy posts, cold messaging or hatefulness in the group. We are over 38,000 grown women, professionals who can debate and have differing opinions without tearing others apart or down. Our group is about as drama free as it gets, something that has been noted more than once when we have been written up in industry publications.

Empowering Women in Real Estate® went from just a glimmer in my eye, one of those shower ideas, to an actual fully functioning group within just a day or two. When you are hit so strongly with an idea, you can't wait to take action. Even though I initially had no plans for this group other than an online community, the day God granted me this idea I also bought the domain name. I think deep down there was always a part of me that knew it could be, would be so much more. That URL sat unused for years before I created my own shoddy website on Wix (a website developer I am not), with encouragement from Vicky Noufal, Jackie Fields-Gleadall and Edyta Simmons. I remember Vicky and I were sitting in our room at The Hotel Roanoke, on break from attending sessions of the Virginia Association of Realtors conference when I finally started the site.

I'm grateful to Madi Harmon, our first official full-time employee, our Empowering Women in Real Estate® Program Manager who for the last 2 ½ years has served our members, podcast listeners and programs with top notch customer service and a million other details behind the scenes.

It's been a long and winding road to get here, and there is no end in sight.

Today is the perfect day to announce our 4th Annual Empowering Women in Real Estate® Conference, Reinvention Roadmap, which will take place on November 12, 2024 in Ashburn, Virginia.

The real estate industry has undergone a massive amount of changes, especially in the past six months, and we are on the verge of one of the biggest changes in how we do business that I have seen in my 2+ decades in the industry.

If you want your business to not only survive, but to thrive, you can no longer sit back and hang on to how it "used to be". It's time to grow and evolve in our businesses, just as we always have in life.

At this year's conference we have dynamic speakers who will teach lead generation strategies and how to build trust in your business. We will have panels of top producing realtors who have already made shifts in their businesses in a variety of different ways and are thriving.

If you've read this far, thank you!

Thank you for being here, for your support and for being part of our Empowering Women in Real Estate® community!

WHAT'S NEXT

The collection of stories in this book may end on July 29, 2024, the 10th anniversary of Empowering Women in Real Estate®, but the mission and community continues on.

Every morning for the past 10+ years, no matter the day of the week, whether I am on vacation or at home, the first thing I do when I sit down with my cup of coffee is to open the Facebook app on my iPad and navigate over to our Empowering Women in Real Estate® group.

I write or post in this group more days than I don't, and it still brings me joy and fills my cup. From the professional side of my life, nothing else has ever brought this level of fulfillment or purpose. To share a story from my heart, and then have other women comment or message me privately to say it resonated with them, or that they thought they were the only one that felt that way … the feeling is indescribable.

Isn't that all any of us ever really want? To feel seen. To BE seen. To feel like we aren't alone, no matter what we are going through. Whether it is a difficult client, a personal health crisis or parenting struggles … we are all just figuring it out as we go along. When you can be around others that understand, that care more than they judge, that are open to sharing their experiences, it is truly priceless.

So, what's next? My vision is that our Empowering Women in Real Estate® community will continue to grow. I want to positively impact as many women as possible through our group and through my Platinum Group Real Estate team.

I want to be a role model for women in the real estate industry. For those who think or have been told that the only way to be successful and to grow their real estate business is to sacrifice their family and their quality of life.

I want to help as many women as possible to have the power of choice.

The choice to generate business in the way that is authentic to them.

The choice to design their life in the way that brings them joy.

The choice to spend their precious time in the way that fills their cup.

I want to model and provide OPTIONS for women in how to build their real estate business, how to serve their clients, and how to create multiple streams of income.

What you want is attainable. It's possible. You are worthy of your dreams.

Thank you for being a part of our Empowering Women in Real Estate® community. Thank you for reading these stories. In doing so you have helped me to realize a dream. I'd love to help you to do the same.

ABOUT THE AUTHOR

Karen Wenner Cooper is a wife, mom to 3 sons, and owner of the Platinum Group Real Estate team at Real Brokerage along with her business partner Vicky Noufal. The Platinum Group is a team of 50+ phenomenal women and moms based in Northern Virginia and serving clients with agents located throughout the US. Licensed since 2002, Karen personally served well over 700 clients during her sales career, and many thousands more through her team that has closed over $1.5 BILLION in sales volume since its inception in 2015.

A nationally recognized expert, she has been featured on local, regional and global podcasts, and has been a speaker at women's real estate and business conferences. Passionate about helping women in the real estate industry, she is the Founder and CEO of Empowering Women in Real Estate®, with over 38,000 members nationwide, host of Empowering Women in Real Estate® - The Podcast, and the principle behind the EWRE® Inner Circle monthly membership coaching program for women in the real estate industry. An avid real estate investor, she is actively building her personal portfolio and loves helping other women to do the same.